Struts 2
for Beginners

Struts 2
for Beginners

Third Edition

Sharanam Shah
Vaishali Shah

Published in the USA by:

SHROFF PUBLISHERS & DISTRIBUTORS PVT. LTD.
Mumbai   Bangalore   Kolkata   New Delhi

Struts 2 for Beginners Third Edition
by Sharanam Shah and Vaishali Shah

Copyright © 2009, 2013 Sharanam Shah and Vaishali Shah. All rights reserved.
ISBN 13: 978-93-5110-104-3
Originally printed in India.

Published by Shroff Publishers & Distributors Pvt. Ltd. C-103, T.T.C. Industrial Area, M.I.D.C., Pawane, Navi Mumbai - 400 703 Tel.: (91-22) 4158 4158 Fax: (91-22) 4158 4141
E-mail: spdorders@shroffpublishers.com. Web: www.shroffpublishers.com
CIN: U22200MH1992PTC067760

Series Editor: Ivan Bayross

Printing History:
    First Edition: May 2013

Reprinted in the USA by Arizona Business Alliance.
Under license from Shroff Publishers & Distributors Pvt. Ltd., India.

First USA Reprint: July 2014
ISBN 13: 978-1-61903-004-6

All rights reserved. No part of this work may be reproduced or transmitted in any form or by any means, electronic or mechanical, including photocopying, recording, or by any information storage or retrieval system, without the prior written permission of the copyright owner or the Publishers.

Published by **Arizona Business Alliance LLC** 7169 W. Ashby Drive, Peoria AZ 85383
Tel: 623 297 4448, Fax: 623 687 9524 e-mail: aba.us@hotmail.com

Preface

Welcome to the *Third* edition of Struts 2 for Beginners!

Thank you for picking up this book.

This book is dedicated to **Janya**, our little princess. Thank you for coming to this world as our daughter. You are the most precious daughter we could ever ask for. We love you more than our life.

This book would not exist if it were not for a dedicated group of individuals who came together to create the Struts 2 application framework itself.

Our purpose in writing this book is to help you come up to speed as quickly as possible with using Struts 2 framework.

I need to make a few basic assumptions about you as the reader:

- You are a Java developer working with Web applications quite familiar with JSP
- You may have worked with Struts 1 framework in the past or some similar framework
- You have heard about Struts 2

Whichever path has led you here, you are definitely on the right path!

If you have never heard of Struts 2, this book covers the basics in enough depth.

If you know what Struts 2 does, but want a deeper and practical understanding of how it does it, this book provides that too.

This book takes an application-centric approach. This means the development of an application drives Struts 2 coverage not the other way around. This approach has proven to be the best approach for beginners.

This book aims serving the beginners as well as intermediate developers. The application being built in this book is very simple and easy to follow, so anyone with a basic understanding of **JavaServer Pages** and **Servlets** should be able to very quickly follow along.

The organization of this book aims to walk you through Struts 2 in a sequence of increasing complexity.

We start with a couple of preliminary chapters enclosed in a section called **All About The Struts 2 Framework** that introduce the technological and fundamental context of the framework and give a high-level overview of the architecture and the framework components.

After this brief introduction, we begin by **Setting Up The Development Environment**. Here, NetBeans IDE is used as the development platform. This section then moves on to the installation of Struts 2 framework.

We then set off into a series of chapters [held within **Getting Started With Struts 2**] that cover the CORE concepts and components of Struts 2 framework one by one in depth. This section uses the application-centric approach and thus aims at building a simple Web application called **GuestBook**.

GuestBook application is built chapter by chapter as follows:

In *Chapter 7: Working With Actions*
A Bean class and an Action class [which is one of Struts 2 components also known as the Model layer of the application] are created.

In *Chapter 8: Building Views*
JavaServer Pages are created that form the view layer of the application. These JSP are then mapped to the Action class created in Chapter 7.

In *Chapter 9: Building Interceptors*
An Interceptor class [again another important component of Struts 2 framework] is created.

In *Chapter 10: OGNL And The Value Stack*
Here, an in-depth understanding of how these components perform their roles is given.

In *Chapter 11: Validation Framework*
Server/Client side validations are added to the application using the built-in Validators that Struts 2 framework comes bundled with.

That's it. These chapters build GuestBook application.

In *Chapter 12: Using Data Store*
This application is enhanced to interact with the MySQL database.

In Chapter 13: Integrating with Hibernate

This application is integrated with Hibernate, a popular, powerful and a free, open source Object Relational Mapping library for the Java programming language. This makes the application portable to all the SQL databases supported by Hibernate.

All the learning done so far is strongly reinforced using two completely well-documented projects called **BookShop** and **Customer**.

The last section of this book, demonstrates building Customer application. This application is build using **Struts 2.x.x** and **Hibernate 4**.

The complete, well-documented code spec for both these projects is included on the books accompanying CD-ROM.

This book's accompanying CD-ROM holds downloaded executables for the following:
- Java Development Kit [JDK] 7 Update 6
- NetBeans IDE 7.2
- Struts 2.3.4.1
- Display Tag
- Hibernate 4.1.6.FINAL
- MySQL Community Server 5.5.27
- MySQL Connector/J 5.1.21
- SLF4J 1.6.4

Writing this book has been one of the most challenging endeavors we've taken on and it would not have been possible without the help and support from several people.

Our sincere thanks go to:
- Our publisher Mr. Aziz Shroff for bringing up the **X-Team** concept that has brought enormous changes in our lives
- Our family for their patience, support and love
- The many programmers who read this book. We welcome both your brickbats and bouquets
- All those who helped through their comments, feedback and suggestions

If you have any questions, comments or just feel like communicating, please contact us at **enquiries@sharanamshah.com**.

We are now also available on Facebook [http://facebook.sharanamshah.com]. You can Sign up to connect with both of us.

We hope that you will enjoy reading and working through the project in this book as much as we enjoyed documenting and developing it.

For additional information on this book visit:

- http://www.sharanamshah.com
- http://www.vaishalishahonline.com

Sharanam & Vaishali Shah

Table Of Contents

SECTION I: ALL ABOUT STRUTS FRAMEWORK

1. FUNDAMENTALS OF STRUTS AND STRUTS 2 1
   - STANDARD APPLICATION FLOW 1
     - Framework 2
     - Why Struts? 3
       - MVC 3
   - APPLICATION FLOW IN MVC 4
   - WHAT IS STRUTS? 5
   - WHAT IS STRUTS 2? 5
   - STRUTS 1 AND STRUTS 2 5
   - WHY STRUTS 2? 6
   - HISTORY OF STRUTS 8

2. ARCHITECTURE OF STRUTS 2 9
   - WHAT IS MVC? 9
     - Model 10
     - View 10
     - Controller 11
   - THE REQUEST RESPONSE PARADIGM IN STRUTS 2 12
   - STRUTS 2 FRAMEWORK ARCHITECTURE 14
     - Request Initiation [HttpServletRequest] 15
     - Struts 2 Servlet Filter [StrutsPrepareAndExecuteFilter] 15
     - Action Mapper 15
     - Action Proxy 15
     - Action Invocation 16
   - SUMMARY 16

3. STRUTS 2 FRAMEWORK CORE COMPONENTS 17
   - StrutsPrepareAndExecuteFilter 18
     - StrutsPrepareAndExecuteFilter In The Execution Flow 18
   - ACTIONS 19
     - Actions In The Execution Flow 19
     - Role Of Action 19
       - Performs As A Model 19
       - Serves As A Data Carrier 20
       - Helps Determine Results 21
     - Single Or Multiple Results 21
   - INTERCEPTORS 22
     - Why Interceptors? 23
     - Interceptor Configuration 24
     - Interceptor Stack 24
     - Interceptors In The Execution Flow 25

VALUE STACK / OGNL 25
   Value Stack 25
      Value Stack In The Execution Flow 26
      Temporary Objects 26
      Model Object 26
      Action Object 26
      Named Objects 26
   Accessing Value Stack 27
   OGNL [Object-Graph Navigation Language] 27
   OGNL Examples 28
   OGNL In The Execution Flow 29
   Role Of OGNL 29
RESULTS AND RESULT TYPES [VIEW TECHNOLOGIES] 30
   Results 30
   View Technologies 31
   Result Types 31

SECTION II: SETTING UP THE DEVELOPMENT ENVIRONMENT

4. INSTALLING AND SETTING UP NETBEANS IDE 33
WHAT IS NETBEANS? 34
   NetBeans Development Platform 34
INSTALLING JAVA DEVELOPMENT KIT 35
DOWNLOAD NETBEANS 35
INSTALLING NETBEANS IDE 36

5. INSTALLING AND SETTING UP STRUTS 2 41
CREATING THE FIRST WEB APPLICATION 41
DOWNLOAD STRUTS 2 LIBRARIES 45
ADDING STRUTS 2 LIBRARIES 45
CREATING STANDARD DEPLOYMENT DESCRIPTOR [web.xml] 46
ADDING STRUTS 2 FILTER IN web.xml 48
CREATING STRUTS ACTION JAVA CLASS 50
MAP THE ACTION JAVA CLASS TO A RESULT PAGE 51
RUN THE WEB APPLICATION PROJECT 55

SECTION III: GETTING STARTED WITH STRUTS 2

6. GETTING STARTED 57
APPLICATION REQUIREMENTS 58
APPLICATION DEVELOPMENT 59
CREATING A WEB APPLICATION 60
ADDING STRUTS 2 LIBRARIES 61

CREATING STANDARD DEPLOYMENT DESCRIPTOR [web.xml]..................................... 62
ADDING STRUTS 2 FILTER IN web.xml 62
CREATING STRUTS 2 CONFIGURATION FILE [struts.xml]..................................... 62

7. WORKING WITH ACTIONS 65
ROLE OF ACTION 66
Actions Provide Encapsulation 66
Actions Help Carry Data.. 67
Data Entry Form And Action... 68
Actions Return Control String 69
Helper Interfaces... 70
Action Interface 70
ActionSupport Class 71
Role Of Struts 2 Filter... 72
struts.xml 73
<struts> 73
<package>... 73
The name Attribute [name="myApp"]... 74
The namespace Attribute [namespace="/"] 74
The extends Attribute [extends="struts-default"] 74
The abstract Attribute [abstract="true"] 75
<action>.. 75
The name Attribute [name="simpleApp"] 75
The class Attribute [class="com.book.myApp.simpleApp"].................. 75
The method Attribute [method="execute"].. 76
<result>... 76
The name Attribute [name="success"]... 76
The type Attribute [type="dispatcher"].. 76
<include> 76
The file Attribute [file="guestbook-config.xml"] 76
GETTING STARTED WITH ACTIONS 77
Application Requirements 77
A Bean Class... 78
Package... 79
Variables... 80
Setter/Getter Methods 80
Action Class.. 80
Imports.. 82
com.opensymphony.xwork2.ActionSupport... 82
java.text.DateFormat... 83
java.text.SimpleDateFormat 83
java.util.ArrayList 83
java.util.Date... 83
Date Format 83
static Modifier.. 83
execute() 84

8. BUILDING VIEW 85
HOW DOES VIEW COME INTO PICTURE? 85
Result Types And The Result 86
dispatcher 86
location 87
parse 87
####### Embedding OGNL 88
redirect 88
location 89
parse 89
####### Embedding OGNL 89
redirectAction 89
actionName 90
namespace 90
####### Embedding OGNL 90
TAG LIBRARIES 91
TagLib 91
KIND OF TAGS 92
Generic Tags 92
Data Tags 92
The action Tag 92
The property Tag 93
The bean Tag 94
The set Tag 96
The include Tag 97
The url Tag 98
The text Tag 99
The i18n Tag 99
The param Tag 100
Control Tags 101
The iterator Tag 101
The if, elseIf And else Tags 103
UI Tags 104
Form UI Tags 105
The head Tag 106
The form Tag 107
The hidden Tag 108
The label Tag 109
The textfield Tag 110
The textarea Tag 110
The password Tag 111
The file Tag 112
The checkbox Tag 112
The select Tag 113
The checkboxlist Tag 114

Table Of Contents   xiii

  The radio Tag 115
  The submit Tag 116
  The reset Tag 117
 Non Form UI Tags 117
  The div Tag 117
  The tabbedPanel Tag 119
  The tree Tag 120
CONTINUING WITH THE APPLICATION 121
 guestBookEntry.jsp 122
  Struts 2 Taglib 124
  <s:head> 124
  <s:form> 125
 guestBookView.jsp 125
 index.jsp 127
 Configuration - struts.xml 127
  GuestBook Action 128
  GuestBookSuccess Action 128
 Process Flow Diagram 129
RUNNING GUESTBOOK APPLICATION 129

9. BUILDING INTERCEPTORS 133
 Request And Interceptor 134
BUILT-IN INTERCEPTORS 134
 Alias Interceptor [alias] 134
 Chaining Interceptor [chaining] 135
 Checkbox Interceptor [checkbox] 135
 Conversion Error Interceptor [conversionError] 135
 Create Session Interceptor [createSession] 135
 Debugging Interceptor [debugging] 135
 Execute And Wait Interceptor [execAndWait] 135
 Exception Interceptor [exception] 136
 File Upload Interceptor [fileUpload] 136
 Internationalization Interceptor [i18n] 136
 Logging Interceptor [logger] 136
 Message Store Interceptor [store] 136
 Model Driven Interceptor [modelDriven] 136
 Scoped Model Driven Interceptor [scopedModelDriven] 136
 Parameters Interceptor [params] 137
 Prepare Interceptor [prepare] 137
 Profiling Interceptor [profile] 137
 Scope Interceptor [scope] 137
 Servlet Configuration Interceptor [servletConfig] 137
 Static Parameters Interceptor [staticParams] 137
 Roles Interceptor [roles] 137
 Timer Interceptor [timer] 137
 Token Interceptor [token] 138

    Token Session Interceptor [tokenSession] 138
    Validation Interceptor [validation] 138
    Workflow Interceptor [workflow] 138
  PRE-CONFIGURED STACKS OF BUILT-IN INTERCEPTORS 138
    basicStack 139
    validationWorkflowStack 139
    fileUploadStack 139
    modelDrivenStack 139
    chainStack 139
    i18nStack 140
    paramPrepareParamsStack 140
    defaultStack 140
    executeAndWaitStack 141
  ROLE OF THE INTERCEPTOR IN THE EXECUTION CYCLE 141
  DECLARING INTERCEPTORS AND STACKS 142
  MAPPING INTERCEPTORS TO ACTIONS 143
    Parameterize Interceptors 145
  BUILDING A CUSTOM INTERCEPTOR 145
    Interceptor Interface 145
  CONTINUING WITH THE APPLICATION 146
    ActionTimer.java 146
      Imports 147
        com.opensymphony.xwork2.ActionInvocation 147
        com.opensymphony.xwork2.interceptor.Interceptor 147
      Implements... 147
      Variables 147
      intercept() 147
      init() And destroy() 148
    Declaring Interceptor 148
    Process Flow Diagram 150
  RUNNING GUESTBOOK APPLICATION 150

10. OGNL AND THE VALUE STACK.. 153

  VALUE STACK 154
  DATA TRANSFER AND TYPE CONVERSION 154
  OGNL 155
    Expression Language 156
    Type Converters 156
      Built-in Converters 157
    OGNL's Role In Data Transfer And Type Conversion 157
      Accessing Action Context Properties Using # 158
    Form and OGNL 158
      How Is An OGNL Expression Resolved 159
    Accessing Object Properties 160
    Accessing Object Properties From The Context Map 160

11. VALIDATIONS 161
KINDS OF VALIDATIONS 162
DECLARATIVE - DOMAIN OBJECT LEVEL VALIDATION 163
Validators Scope 164
Validators Precedence 165
Short Circuiting Validations 165
VALIDATOR TYPES 165
required 166
fieldName 166
requiredstring 166
fieldName 166
trim 166
stringlength 167
fieldName 167
maxLength 167
minLength 167
trim 167
int 168
fieldName 168
max 168
min 168
double 169
fieldName 169
maxInclusive 169
minInclusive 169
maxExclusive 169
minExclusive 169
date 170
fieldName 170
max 170
min 170
expression 171
expression 171
fieldExpression 171
fieldName 171
expression 172
email 172
fieldName 172
url 173
fieldName 173
conversion 173
fieldName 173
regex 173
fieldName 174
expression 174

- caseSensitive ... 174
- trim ... 174
- visitor ... 174
  - fieldName ... 175
  - context ... 175
  - appendPrefix ... 175
- CONTINUING WITH THE APPLICATION ... 175
  - struts.xml Modifications ... 180
  - Process Flow Diagram ... 181
- CLIENT SIDE VALIDATION ... 182
  - JavaScript Code Spec Inclusion ... 182
- RUNNING GUESTBOOK APPLICATION ... 184

12. USING THE DATA STORE ... 187

- APPLICATION REQUIREMENTS ... 188
  - Table Structure ... 188
- CONTINUING WITH THE APPLICATION ... 188
  - Database Creation ... 188
  - Table Creation ... 188
  - Add MySQL Driver ... 189
  - Action Class Modifications ... 190
    - java.sql Package ... 191
    - Objects And Variables Declaration ... 192
    - Removing static Keyword From ArrayList Declaration ... 192
    - Establishing A Connection With The MySQL Database Engine ... 192
    - Adding The Captured Data To The Database Table ... 193
    - Retrieving The Stored Data From The Database Table ... 193
    - Adding The Retrieved Data To The ArrayList ... 193
- RUNNING GUESTBOOK APPLICATION ... 193

13. INTEGRATING HIBERNATE WITH STRUTS 2 ... 195

- ABOUT HIBERNATE ... 196
- CONTINUING WITH THE APPLICATION ... 197
  - Downloading Hibernate ... 198
  - Adding Hibernate Library Files ... 198
  - Creating Session Factory ... 199
    - Imports ... 200
      - org.hibernate.HibernateException ... 200
      - org.hibernate.Session ... 200
      - org.hibernate.SessionFactory ... 200
      - org.hibernate.cfg.Configuration ... 200
      - org.hibernate.service.ServiceRegistry ... 200
      - org.hibernate.service.ServiceRegistryBuilder ... 200
    - Objects Declaration ... 200
  - configureSessionFactory() ... 201
  - getSession() ... 201

- Creating Struts 2 Dispatcher 201
  - Imports 202
    - java.servlet.FilterConfig 202
    - java.servlet.ServletException 202
    - org.apache.struts2.dispatcher.ng.filter.StrutsPrepareAndExecuteFilter 202
    - org.hibernate.HibernateException 203
  - init() 203
  - Activating Struts 2 Dispatcher 203
  - Creating Hibernate Configuration File 204
  - Modifying GuestBook.java 208
    - java.persistence.* Package 209
    - @Entity 210
    - @Table 210
    - java.io.Serializable 210
    - @Id 210
    - @GeneratedValue 210
    - @Column 210
  - Adding A Mapping Class 210
  - Creating Data Access Object 211
    - GuestBookDAO.java 211
    - GuestBookDAOImpl.java 212
      - Imports 213
        - java.util.List 213
        - org.hibernate.Session 213
        - org.hibernate.Transaction 213
      - Objects Declaration 213
      - listGuestBook() 214
      - saveGuestBook() 214
  - Modifying GuestBookAction 214
    - Implements ModelDriven 217
    - Objects And Variables Declarations 217
    - getModel() 217
    - execute() 218
    - Getter/Setter Methods 218
- RUNNING THE APPLICATION 218

SECTION IV: APPLICATION DEVELOPMENT USING STRUTS 2

14. DEFINING THE PROJECT AND ITS REQUIREMENTS 221
- BUSINESS MODEL 221
  - Workflow 222
- APPLICATION REQUIREMENTS 222
  - Intended Users 223
- OPERATING ENVIRONMENT 224
  - Operating System 224

External Software Applications 224
Framework 224
USER INTERFACE AND DATA ENTRY FORM REQUIREMENTS 224
User Login 224
Steps 225
Alternate Steps 225
Search Books 225
Steps 226
Alternate Steps 226
Manage Books 226
View Books 227
Steps 227
Add Books 228
Steps 229
Alternate Steps 229
Edit Books 230
Steps 231
Alternate Steps 231
Delete Books 232
Steps 232
PROPOSED ACTIONS 233
LoginAction 233
InsertBookAction 233
EditBookAction 233
UpdateBookAction 234
DeleteBookAction 234
ManageSearchBooksAction 234
SearchBooksAction 234
LogoffAction 234

15. PROJECT SPECIFICATIONS 235

JAVA SERVER PAGES 235
ACTIONS 236
INTERCEPTORS 236
CSS 236
BEANS 236
CONFIGURATION [struts.xml] 236
PROCESS FLOW DIAGRAMS 239
VALIDATIONS 246
loginAction-validation.xml 246
searchBookAction-validation.xml 247
insertBookAction-validation.xml 247
updateBookAction-validation.xml 247
LIBRARIES 247
TABLE STRUCTURE 248
Database Name 248

Table Definitions 248
　　　SystemUsers 248
　　　Books 249

16. THE ADMINISTRATION HOME PAGE [INDEX.JSP] 251
　　Code Spec 251
　　Login Form [login.jsp] 252
　　　Form Specifications 252
　　　Data Fields 252
　　　Data Controls 252
　　　Micro-Help For Form Fields 252
　　　Code Spec 253
　　　Process Flow 254
　　doLogin [loginAction.java] 254
　　　Code Spec 254
　　Validations [loginAction-validation.xml] 257
　　　Code Spec 258

17. SEARCH BOOKS [SEARCHBOOKS.JSP] 259
　FORM SPECIFICATIONS 260
　DATA FIELDS 260
　DATA CONTROLS 261
　MICRO-HELP FOR FORM FIELDS 261
　CODE SPEC 261
　　Process Flow 263
　doSearchBooks [searchBooksAction.java] 263
　　Code Spec 264
　VALIDATIONS [searchBooksAction-validation.xml] 267
　　Code Spec 267

18. MANAGE BOOKS [MANAGEBOOKS.JSP] 269
　ADD BOOKS [addBooks.jsp] 270
　　Form Specifications 271
　　Data Fields 271
　　Data Controls 272
　　Micro-Help For Form Fields 272
　　Code Spec 272
　　Process Flow 275
　　doInsertBooks [insertBookAction.java] 276
　　　Code Spec 276
　　　Process Flow 279
　　　Validations [insertBooksAction-validation.xml] 280
　　　　Code Spec 280
　SEARCH RESULTS [manageBooks.jsp] 283
　　Code Spec 284
　　Process Flow 286

Struts 2 For Beginners

    doManageSearchBooks [manageSearchBooksAction.java] 287
        Code Spec 287
        Process Flow 288
  UPDATE BOOKS FORM [updateBooks.jsp] 290
    Form Specifications 292
    Data Fields 292
    Data Controls 293
    Micro-Help For Form Fields 293
    Code Spec 293
    Process Flow 296
    showEditBooks [editBookAction.java] 297
        Code Spec 297
        Process Flow 300
    doUpdateBooks [updateBookAction.java] 301
        Code Spec 302
        Process Flow 305
        Validations [insertBooksAction-validation.xml] 306
            Code Spec 306
  DELETE BOOKS [manageBooks.jsp] 309
    Process Flow 309
    doDeleteBooks [deleteBookAction.java] 309
        Code Spec 310
        Process Flow 310

19. LOGOUT 313

  PROCESS FLOW 313
    doLogout [logOffAction.java] 314
        Code Spec 314
        Process Flow 314

20. BEANS AND INTERCEPTORS 317

  BOOK BEAN CLASS 317
    Class Specifications 317
    Code Spec 318
  dbConnection 321
    Class Specifications 321
    Code Spec 322
  AuthenticationInterceptor 322
    Class Specifications 323
    Code Spec 323
    Process Flow 324
        intercept() 325

21. RUNNING THE APPLICATION 327

  LOGIN 328
  SEARCH BOOKS 330

| MANAGE BOOKS 332
        Add Books 332
        Edit Books 334
        Delete Books 337
     LOGOUT 338

SECTION V: APPLICATION DEVELOPMENT USING STRUTS 2.X.X AND HIBERNATE 4

22. DEFINING THE PROJECT AND ITS REQUIREMENTS 339
   DATABASE TABLES 340
     Entity Relationship Diagram 340
     Table Specifications 340
        City 340
        State 340
        Country 341
        Customer 341
   DATA ENTRY FORM 341

23. BUILDING THE APPLICATION 343

24. ADDING THE LIBRARY FILES TO THE PROJECT 349
   DOWNLOADING THE REQUIRED LIBRARY FILES 349
     Hibernate 349
     MySQL JDBC Driver 350
     Display Tag 350
     Simple Logging Facade for Java [SLF4J] 350
     Struts 2.x.x 350
     A Dedicated Library Directory 351
     Adding Library Files To The Application 351
        Hibernate 351
        Struts 351
        MySQL Connector/J 352
        Display Tags 352
        SLF4J 352

25. HIBERNATE AND STRUTS CONFIGURATION 353
   com.sharanamvaishali.development.utility Package 354
     Hibernate Utility Class 354
     Development Support Class 356
     Struts 2 Dispatcher Class 357

26. POJOS AND DAOS 359
   com.sharanamvaishali.development.domain Package 360
     City 360
        @ManyToOne 361

@JoinColumn	361
State	361
@OneToMany	363
Country	363
Customer	364
com.sharanamvaishali.development.dao Package	367
City	367
CityDAO	367
CityDAOImpl	367
listCity()	368
listCityByState()	368
State	368
StateDAO	368
StateDAOImpl	369
listState()	369
listStateByCountry()	369
Country	370
CountryDAO	370
CountryDAOImpl	370
listCountry()	371
Customer	371
CustomerDAO	371
CustomerDAOImpl	371
saveCustomer()	372
deleteCustomer()	373
listCustomer()	373
listCustomerByCustomerNo()	373
MAPPING POJOS IN HIBERNATE CONFIGURATION	373

27. ACTION CLASSES 375

AjaxAction	375
getStateList()	377
getCityList()	377
CustomerIndexAction	378
CustomerAction	379
execute()	382
edit()	383
delete()	383

28. JSP, JAVASCRIPT AND CSS 385

JSP	385
customer.jsp [/jsp]	385
footer.jsp [/jsp]	389
ajax.jsp [/jsp]	390
JAVASCRIPT	390
customer [/javaScript]	390

    jquery2 [/javaScript] 391
    CSS 392
    IMAGES 392
    INDEX PAGE 392

29. CONFIGURATION 395

    DISPLAY TAG PROPERTIES 395
    STRUTS XML CONFIGURATION FILES 396
    web.xml 398

30. RUNNING THE APPLICATION 399

    PROCESS FLOW 400

SECTION I: ALL ABOUT THE STRUTS 2 FRAMEWORK

Fundamentals Of Struts And Struts 2

The Java world is very vast. Web application development in this vast world has come a long way with several Integrated Development Environments such as NetBeans, Eclipse and so on which has made creating standard Java based web applications quite easy.

The main Java based technologies that one commonly uses to develop web applications are **Servlet** and Java Server Pages [JSP].

Standard Application Flow

In a standard Java EE Web application:

1. Using Web based data entry form information is submitted to the server
2. Such information is handed over to a **Java Servlet** or a **Java Server Page** for processing
3. Java Servlet or JSP:
   ❑ Interacts with the database

- Produces an HTML response

As an application grows in complexity, it becomes more and more difficult to manage the relationship between the JSP pages, the **backend business logic** and the **forms** and **validations**. Developers start finding it increasingly difficult to maintain and add additional functionality to the applications.

Both the technologies [Java Servlets and JSP] mix the **application** and the **business logic** with the **presentation** layer and thus make maintenance very difficult. This is not suitable for large enterprise applications. This means there's something still missing in these technologies which create a gap.

In such scenarios, most experienced developers, split various pieces of an application's functionality into small manageable pieces of code spec. These small pieces of code spec hold single piece of functionality and when taken together as a whole, forms the basis for an application development framework.

Framework

A framework is a collection of services that provide developers with common set of functionality, which can be reused and leveraged across multiple applications.

A framework usually comes into existence by:
- Making generalizations about the common tasks and workflow of a specific domain
- Providing a platform upon which applications of that domain can be more quickly built

A framework helps automate all the tedious tasks of the domain and provides an elegant architectural solution to the common workflow of the domain.

A framework allows developers to focus on coding the **business logic** and the **presentation layer** of the application and not the overhead jobs such as heavy code spec to capture user input or to generate drop down list boxes.

Nowadays with several frameworks available, application development projects no longer begin with the question:

Should we use a framework?

Instead, they begin with:

Which framework should we use?

Why Struts?

Struts, a Java based **framework,** allows a clean separation between the application logic that interacts with a database from the HTML pages that form the response.

It cuts time, out of the development process and makes developers more productive by giving them prebuilt components to assemble Web applications from.

Struts is not a technology, it's a framework that can be used along with Java based technologies.

Struts makes the development of enterprise Web application development easier by providing a flexible and extensible application architecture, custom tags and a technique to configure common workflows within an application.

Struts framework is a strong implementation of the widely recognized Model View Controller **design pattern**. The key focus of MVC pattern is separation which is what is desired.

MVC

MVC design pattern is amongst the well developed and mature design patterns in use today and is an excellent fit for Web application development

By using MVC design pattern, processing is broken into three **distinct** sections:
- Model
- View
- Controller

Each component of the MVC pattern:
- Has a unique responsibility
- Is independent of the other component

Changes in one component has no or less impact on other component.

The **advantage** that the MVC pattern brings in is:
- The business or the model specific logic is not written within the view component
- The presentation logic is not written within the model and business layers

This thus allows reusing the component and changing one layer's code spec with minimal effect on the other layers. This is a key point and one of the main benefits of **Struts**.

Application Flow In MVC

In MVC design pattern, the application flow is mediated by a **Controller**.

The Controller delegates **HTTP requests** to an appropriate **handler**.

A **handler** is nothing more than the set of logic that is used to process the request. In Struts framework, the handlers are called **Actions**.

The handlers are tied to a **Model** and each handler acts as an adapter or bridge, between the **Request** and the **Model**. A handler or action may use one or more JavaBeans or EJBs to perform the actual business logic.

The Action gets any information out of the request necessary to perform the desired business logic and then passes it to the JavaBean or EJB.

Technically:
- Using Web based data entry form information is submitted to the server
- The controller receives such requests and to serve them calls the appropriate handler i.e. Action
- Action processes the request by interacting with the application specific model code
- **Model** returns a result to inform the **Controller** which output page to be sent as a response

Information is passed between Model and View in the form of special **JavaBeans**.

A powerful **Tag Library** allows reading and writing the content of these beans from the presentation layer without the need for any embedded Java code spec.

From the development point of view, Struts:
- Provides a **Controller**
- Facilitates writing **templates** to form the **View** i.e. the presentation layer [JSP]
- Facilitates writing the **Model** code spec

A central configuration file called **struts.xml** binds all these [Model, View and Controller] together.

What Is Struts?

Struts is an application **Framework** for building Web based applications in Java using the Java Enterprise Edition platform.

Struts [formerly located under **Apache Jakarta Project**] was originally developed by **Craig McClanahan** and donated to the Apache Foundation in May, 2000. It was formerly known as **Jakarta Struts**. Struts is maintained as a part of Apache Jakarta project.

Struts comes with an Open Source license which means it has no cost and its users have free access to all its internal source code.

Today, Apache Struts Project offers the two major versions of Struts framework:
- **Struts 1** which was recognized as the most popular Web application framework for Java
- **Struts 2** originally known as **WebWork 2** is now the best choice which provides elegant solutions to complex problems

What Is Struts 2?

Struts 2 is a brand new framework. It is a completely **new release** of the older Struts 1 Framework. Struts 2 is very simple as compared to Struts 1.

It is the second generation web application framework based on **OpenSymphony WebWork framework** that implements MVC [Model View Controller] design pattern. In other words, Struts 2 is the rebranding of WebWork under Apache Struts make.

Struts 2:
- Uses JavaBeans instead of Action Forms
- Is more powerful and can use Ajax and JSF
- Can easily integrate with other frameworks such as Webwork and Spring

Struts 2 provides a cleaner implementation of MVC and introduces several new architectural features that make the framework cleaner and more flexible.

Struts 1 And Struts 2

Both versions of Struts provide the following three key components:
- A **request** handler that maps Java classes to Web application URIs

- A **response** handler that maps logical names to server pages or other Web resources
- A **tag library** that helps creating rich, responsive, form-based applications

In Struts 2, all three components have been redesigned and enhanced. Struts 2 is designed to be simpler to use and closer to how Struts was always meant to be.

For those who have used Struts 1, the following section indicates how Struts 2 is different from Struts 1:

- Struts 1 used a Servlet controller such as the **ActionServlet** class.

  Struts 2 uses a **Filter** to perform the same task.

- In Struts 1, an HTML form is mapped to an **ActionForm** instance.

  In Struts 2, there are no Action forms which make maintenance easier as there are fewer classes. Here, an HTML form maps directly to a POJO, which does not need a separate data transfer object to be created.

  In Struts 2, user inputs can be programmatically validated by simply writing the validation logic in the action class.

- Struts 1 provided several tag libraries such as HTML, Bean and Logic that allow using custom tags in JSP.

  Struts 2 provides a single tag library that covers all.

- Java 5 and Servlet 2.4 are the prerequisites for Struts 2. Java 5 is mandatory because annotations, added to Java 5, play an important role in Struts 2.

- Struts 1 action classes had to extend org.apache.struts.action.Action.

  In Struts 2 any POJO can be an action class.

- In Struts 1, JSTL and the Expression Language [Servlet 2.4] were used to replace the **Bean** and **Logic** tag libraries.

  In Struts 2, instead of the JSP Expression Language and JSTL, OGNL is used to display object models in JSP.

- Tiles that was available as a subcomponent of Struts 1, has matured to an independent Apache project. It is still available in Struts 2 as a plug-in.

Why Struts 2?

The following are a few reasons why Struts 2 is recommended for Web application development:

- **Action** based framework
- **Interceptors** for layering cross-cutting concerns away from action logic

Fundamentals Of Struts And Struts 2

- **Annotation** based configuration to reduce or eliminate XML configuration
- Object Graph Navigation Language [OGNL]: A powerful expression language that transverses the entire framework
- Simplified **Actions** which are simple POJOs. Any Java class with execute() can be used as an Action class
- Spring, SiteMesh and Tiles integration
- MVC based **tag API** that supports modifiable and reusable UI components
- Multiple view options [JSP, Freemarker, Velocity and XSLT]
- Plugins to extend and modify framework features
- Classes are based on interfaces
- Most configuration elements have a default value that can be set and forgotten
- Style sheet driven markup which allow creating consistent pages with less code spec
- Struts 2 **checkboxes** [Stateful checkboxes] do not require special handling for false values. These checkboxes have the capability to determine if the toggling took place
- **Cancel** button can be made to do a different action. For example, Cancel button can be used to stop the current action
- **Quick start feature** i.e. many changes can be made on the fly without restarting a Web container
- Manual testing time is saved as built-in **debugging** tools are provided for reporting problems
- Themes based tag libraries and Ajax tags
- Struts 2 supports **AJAX** with features such as:
  1. AJAX based client side validation
  2. Remote form submission support [works with the submit tag as well]
  3. An advanced DIV template that provides dynamic reloading of partial HTML
  4. An advanced template that provides the ability to load and evaluate JavaScript remotely
  5. An AJAX only tabbed Panel implementation
  6. A rich pub-sub event model
  7. Interactive auto complete tag

History Of Struts

Struts was originally created by **Craig R. McClanahan**. It was then donated to Jakarta project of Apache Software Foundation [ASF] in 2000.

In June of 2001, Struts 1.0 was released. Since then, many people have contributed both source code and documentation to the project and Struts has flourished

When Craig McClanahan donated Struts to Apache Jakarta project, it became an open source software. This means that developers can download the source for Struts and modify that code spec as desired for use in their application. The standard code spec provided by ASF remains unaltered.

However, with the growing demand of Web applications, Struts did not stand firm and needed to be changed with demand. So, the team of Apache Struts and another J2EE framework, WebWork of OpenSymphony joined hands together to develop an advanced framework with all possible developing features that will make it developer and user friendly.

The Struts communities and the WebWork team brought together several special features in WebWork 2 to make it more advance in the Open Source world. Later WebWork 2 was renamed to Struts 2 which is more developer friendly with features like Ajax, rapid development and extensibility.

Struts 2 has now reached a point where it is stable and mature enough for production applications. A lot of Web applications all over the world are running production applications based on the Struts 2 framework.

Chapter 2

SECTION I: ALL ABOUT THE STRUTS 2 FRAMEWORK

Architecture Of Struts 2

Before plunging into application development using Struts 2, it's essential to understand the **architecture** of **Struts 2**.

Struts 2 framework is based on **MVC** [Model-View-Controller] architecture.

What Is MVC?

A lot of beginners misunderstand MVC to be a Java library or an API. But that is not true.

MVC is a **Design Pattern**.

Design Patterns help define the coding pattern / style.

The MVC architecture separates an **application** into **three** different parts:

1. The object **Model** of the application

2. The **View** through which the user interacts with the application
3. The **Controller** that controls all the processing done by the application

Model

In an MVC application, the **Model** is considered the largest and most important part.

The Model represents the enterprise information / data of the application. Anything that an application **persists** becomes a part of Model.

The Model also defines the manner of accessing such data and the business logic for data manipulation.

It is unaware of the way the data will be displayed by the application. It simply serves the data and allows modifying it.

In **Struts 2**, the Model is implemented by the **Action** component.

Struts 2 does not provide any constraints for developing the Model layer of the application.

Even though **Struts 2** is designed for building MVC applications, it **does not dictate** how the Model should be built.

Struts 2 gives the application the flexibility to use any desired approach or technology for building the Model code spec. It can be Enterprise Java Beans [EJB], Java Data Objects [JDO], or the Data Access Objects [DAO] pattern. Struts will simply have room for them.

View

The **View** represents the application's presentation. The View queries the Model for its content and renders it.

The View defines the manner in which the Model i.e. the data / information will be rendered.

The view is independent of the data or the Application Logic changes. It remains the same even if the Business Logic undergoes modification.

A single model can have multiple views for different purposes. For example, an application could have a **Web** interface and a **Wireless** interface. Each interface is separate but both of them use the same **Model**.

The primary purpose of having a View object is to maintain consistency in data presentation with constant Model changes.

A View does not contain:
- **Business Logic** such as calculating rate of interest or deleting items from a shopping cart and so on
- Code for persisting data to or retrieving data from a data source

Struts 2 provides an out-of-the-box support for using most common view layer technologies as **Results**.

A **View** in **Struts 2** can be:
- HTML/JSP
- XML/XSLT
- Velocity
- Swing

and many more.

Since HTML / JSP is the most common and typical **View** technology used for Java based Web applications, this book uses it.

Controller

All the user interaction between the View and the Model is managed by the Controller. All user requests to an MVC application flow through the Controller. The Controller **intercepts** such requests from View and passes it to the Model for appropriate action.

Based on the result of the action on data, the Controller directs the user to the subsequent view.

The controller does not include any business logic.

It **strictly** exposes only those methods that are included in the Model to the user through the View.

In **Struts 2**, the role of the **Controller** is played by the **Filter Dispatcher**. This is a **Servlet filter** that examines each incoming request to determine the **Action** that will handle the request.

In practical scenario,

A **Model** is the business object that has <u>no user interface</u>

A **View** either:
- Determines the updates by <u>querying</u> the **Model** for changes
- Expects the **Controller** to update the **View** when the view needs to be re-rendered

Keeping the **Model** and **View** separate from one another allows an application's interface to change **independent** of the **Model** layer and vice versa.

The Request Response Paradigm In Struts 2

To understand how the requests and responses are handled in Struts 2, let's take a practical example.

A user desires to view a list of books available to buy using the online Shopping Cart.

Example

The user achieves this by reaching:
www.sharanamshah.com/bookshop/showBooks.action

Doing so, retrieves the data from the **Model** [A database that holds book information] and displays the same as a list in a Web browser.

Technically, this happens as follows:

1. A user using a Web browser requests for showBooks.action
2. **Filter Dispatcher [Controller]** of Struts 2 framework consults the application configuration and determines the appropriate Action

   In this case, the action is **showBooks**
3. After the **Action** is determined, the **Interceptors** are applied

   Interceptors help applying common functionality to the request such as workflow, validation, file upload handling and so on
4. After the **Interceptors** are applied, the action method is executed

   In this case, the action method when executed retrieves the data i.e. a list of books from the database [**Model**]

5. Finally, the **Result [View]** renders the output to the Web browser that requested it in the form of book list

The above defined process is diagrammatically represented, as shown in diagram 2.1.

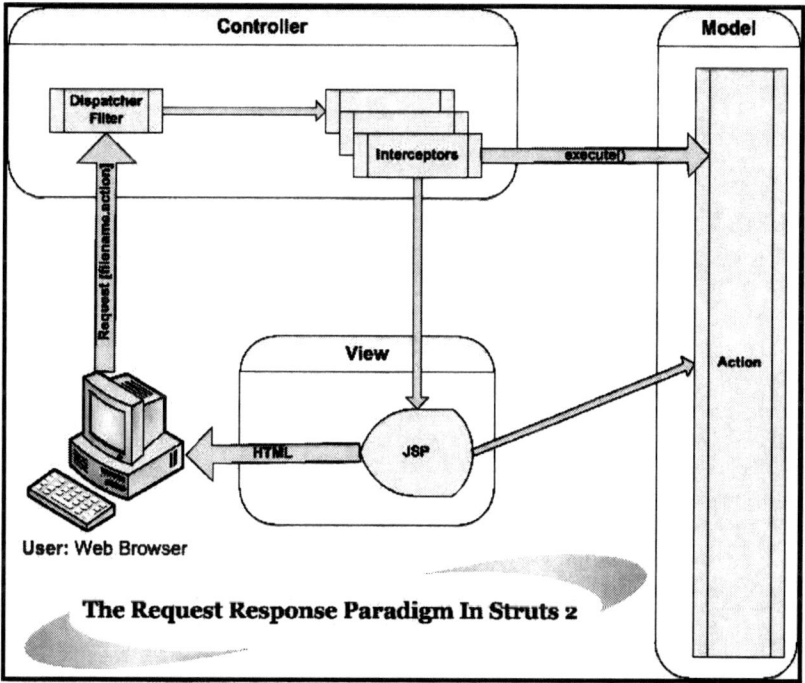

Diagram 2.1: The Request Response Paradigm In Struts 2

Model-View-Controller in **Struts 2** is recognized using with the following **CORE** components:
1. Filter Dispatcher
2. Actions
3. Interceptors
4. Value stack / OGNL
5. Results and Result types [View technologies]

In **Struts 2**, the **Controller** is implemented by a dispatch **Servlet Filter** and **Interceptors**, the **Model** is implemented by **Actions** and the **View** as a combination of **Result Types** and **Results**.

14   Struts 2 For Beginners

The **Value Stack** and **OGNL** provide common thread, linking and enable integration between the other components.

Struts 2 Framework Architecture

Diagram 2.2 shows the core components that participate in the Request Response paradigm.

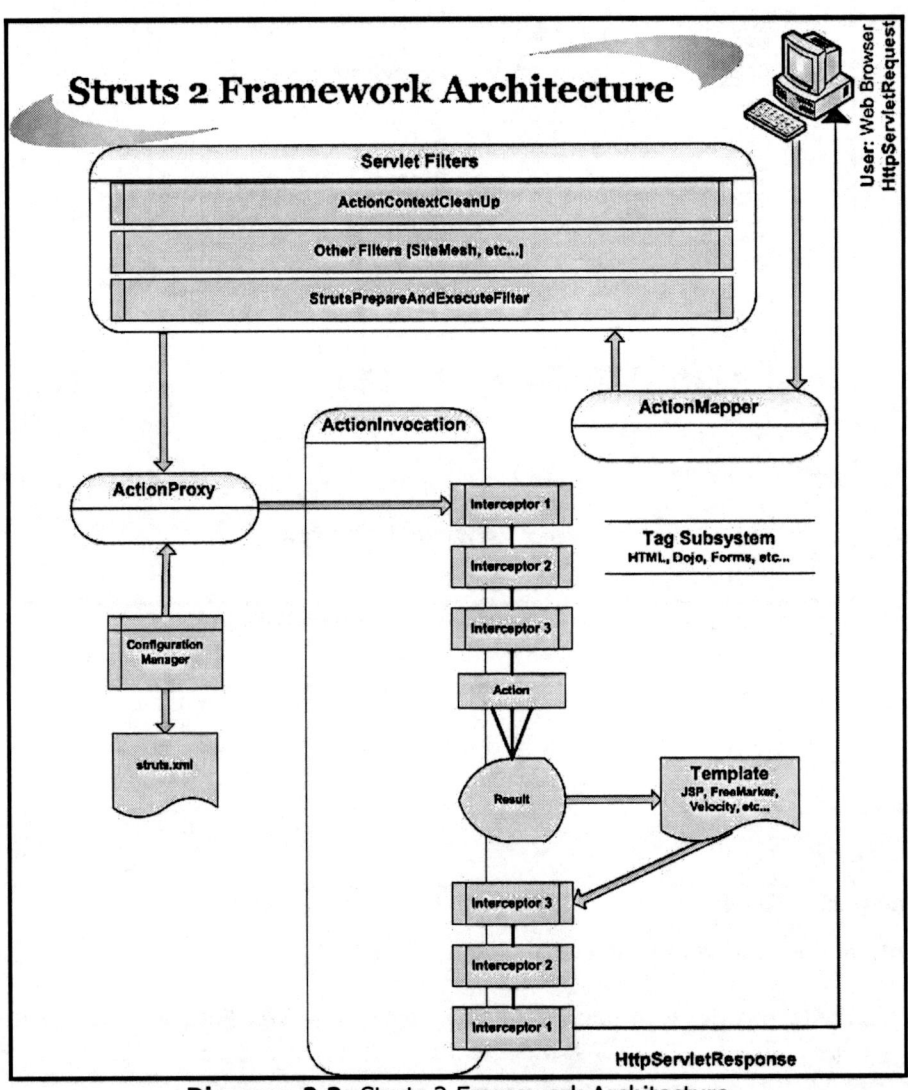

Diagram 2.2: Struts 2 Framework Architecture

Diagram 2.2 depicts the following:

Request Initiation [HttpServletRequest]

A request begins from and ends in a user's Web browser. A request is in form of a URL that represents an **Action**.

A user request is passed through a standard filter chain which makes the actual decision by invoking the required **StrutsPrepareAndExecuteFilter**.

Struts 2 Servlet Filter [StrutsPrepareAndExecuteFilter]

REMINDER

FilterDispatcher which was used instead of **StrutsPrepareAndExecuteFilter** has been deprecated, since Struts version 2.1.3.

StrutsPrepareAndExecuteFilter plays the role of the **Controller** in Struts 2. This filter handles both the preparation and execution phases of the Struts dispatching process. It is advisable to use this filter when there is no other filter that needs access to the action context information.

This filter when called consults the **ActionMapper** to determine if the request should invoke an **Action**.

The framework handles all of the controller work. The framework only needs to be informed about which request URL maps to which action. This information is passed to the framework using an XML configuration file [struts.xml].

Action Mapper

If **ActionMapper** determines that an Action should be invoked, StrutsPrepareAndExecuteFilter delegates control to **ActionProxy**.

Action Proxy

ActionProxy consults the framework **Configuration Manager** [struts.xml] and holds the **configuration** and **context** information to process the request and the **execution** results after the request has been processed.

Action Invocation

ActionProxy creates an **ActionInvocation**, which is responsible for the command pattern implementation.

ActionInvocation does the following:

1. Consults the configuration being used and then creates an <u>instance</u> of the **Action**
2. Invokes the **Interceptors** [if configured] and then invokes the **Action**
3. Once the Action returns, ActionInvocation looks for a result that is associated with the Action result code spec mapped in struts.xml
4. Executes the result, which involves rendering of JSP or templates

HINT

> In Struts 2, a new action object instance is created for each and every request that is received.

REMINDER

> Interceptors provide a simple way to add processing logic around the method being called on the action.
>
> The prime purpose of having Interceptors is to add cross-functional features in a convenient and consistent manner thus avoiding the need for adding code spec to each and every action.

Interceptors that are set to be called after the action is invoked are executed again in reverse order.

Finally the response returns [if one is generated] back to the user, which completes the current <u>request processing cycle</u>.

Summary

This chapter has revealed how Struts 2 implements **MVC** with a strong understanding of the **Request-Response paradigm** that Struts 2 follows and brief induction to **Struts 2 Framework Architecture** taking care of all the important players in the processing of HTTP requests.

This book now moves towards the **CORE components** of the Struts 2 framework.

Chapter 3

SECTION I: ALL ABOUT THE STRUTS 2 FRAMEWORK

Struts 2 Framework Core Components

After understanding the fundamentals and the architecture of Struts 2, it's time to learn about the CORE components of Struts 2.

This chapter takes a complete and a comprehensive look at each CORE component of the Struts 2 architecture along with an in-depth explanation of the roles these components play in the framework.

These components make up the functionality of the application as well as the framework itself.

In **Struts 2** the **Model-View-Controller** design pattern is recognized with the following CORE components:

- **MODEL** - Actions
- **VIEW** - Results and Result Types [View Technologies]
- **CONTROLLER** - StrutsPrepareAndExecuteFilter

18   Struts 2 For Beginners

- Interceptors
- Value Stack / OGNL

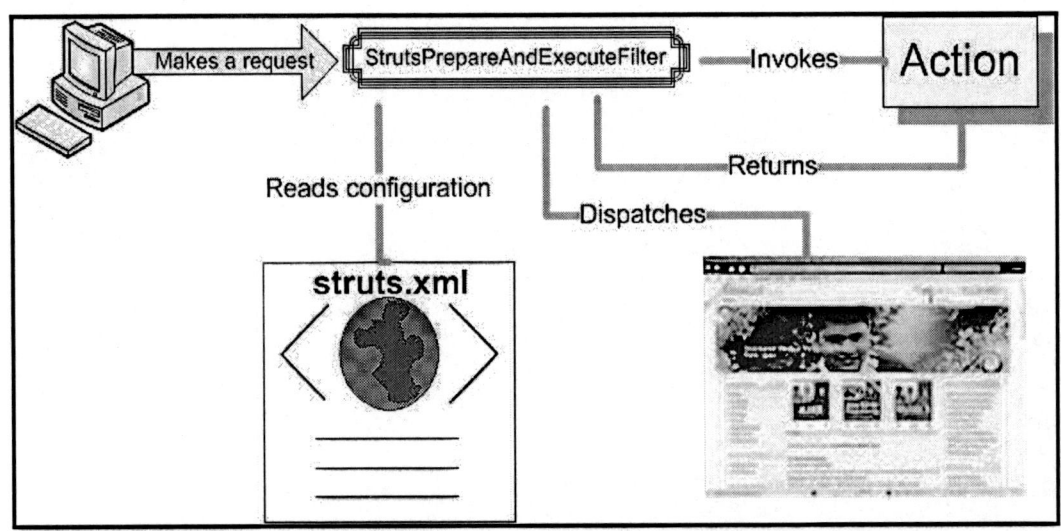

Diagram 3.1: MVC Components in Struts 2 interacting with each other

Diagram 3.1 indicates how the MVC components in Struts 2 interact with each other.

Let's begin with the **Controller**.

StrutsPrepareAndExecuteFilter

The controller is the first component that takes charge when processing a request. In Struts 2 StrutsPrepareAndExecuteFilter plays the role of the Controller.

StrutsPrepareAndExecuteFilter maps requests to actions.

StrutsPrepareAndExecuteFilter In The Execution Flow

1. A Web browser submits a HTTP request for one of the application resources. A request is nothing but a set of commands that the user issues to the application
2. One of the fundamental tasks of a Web application is routing these requests to the appropriate set of actions that should be taken within the application itself
3. **StrutsPrepareAndExecuteFilter** inspects each incoming request to determine which Action should handle the request. This is determined using the **configuration file**

4. The framework executes the action to process the request

Struts 2 allows an application to **map** an <u>action handler</u> to the actual <u>action class</u> using a configuration file named **struts.xml**. This mapping is quite simple, it simply defines which request URLs map to which of action classes.

Actions

Action [the Action class] is <u>heart and soul</u> of the Struts 2 framework. It processes input and interacts with other layers of the application.

It is associated with a **HTTP request** received from the user. Each HTTP request [in form of a URL] is mapped to a specific Action. This Action class holds the code spec that helps serve the user request.

Actions are used to:
- Encapsulate the actual work to be done for a given request
- Serve as a data carrier from the request to the view
- Assist the framework in choosing the response that has to be sent to the user i.e. view

Actions In The Execution Flow

1. A Web browser submits a request for one of these resources
2. The framework selects an appropriate Action class based on the **mappings** available in **struts.xml**
3. The input values from the request are transferred to properties on an Action class
4. The framework calls a default method on the Action to invoke the business logic associated with the request

The **default entry method** to the action class is defined by the Action **interface**. All actions may implement this interface, which exposes **execute()**.

Role Of Action

Performs As A Model

Action performs as a **Model** by encapsulating the actual work to be done for a given request based on the input parameters [if any].

20   Struts 2 For Beginners

Encapsulation is done using **execute()**. The code spec inside this method should only hold the business logic to serve a Request.

Example

Solution:
```
public String execute() {
   setWelcomeMessage(MESSAGE + getUserName());
   return "SUCCESS";
}
```

Explanation:

Here, a welcome message is shown to the user along with the name using String concatenation.

Serves As A Data Carrier

Action serves as a **data carrier** from the Request to the View.

Action being the **Model** component of the framework carries the data around. The data that it requires is held locally which makes it easy to access using JavaBeans properties during the actual execution of the business logic.

execute() simply references the data using the JavaBeans properties.

Example

Solution:
```
private String username;

public String getUserName() {
   return username;
}
public void setUserName(String uname) {
   this.username = uname;
}

private String msg;

public String getWelcomeMessage() {
   return msg;
}
public void setWelcomeMessage(String message) {
```

```
    this.msg = message;
}
```

Explanation:

Here, Action implements **JavaBeans** properties for all the data being carried.

The framework automatically maps the **FORM Request parameters** to the JavaBeans properties that have matching names.

Helps Determine Results

Action determines the Result that will render the **View** that will be returned in the request's response. This is achieved by returning a control string that selects the result that should be rendered.

The value of the return string must be identical to the result name as configured.

Example

Solution:
```
public String execute() {
    setWelcomeMessage(MESSAGE + getUserName());
    return "SUCCESS";
}
```

Explanation:

Here, Action returns the string **SUCCESS**.

The XML [struts.xml] configuration holds the following code spec:
```
<action name="MyFirstStruts2App" class="book.MyFirstStruts2App">
    <result name="SUCCESS">/apps/WelcomeToStruts.jsp</result>
</action>
```

Explanation:

Here, **SUCCESS** is the name of the one of the result components that is identical to the return string.

Single Or Multiple Results

The most basic action performs the required task and always returns a single result.

In such a scenario, the action code spec will be:

```
class TheAction {
    public void String execute() throws Exception {
        setWelcomeMessage(MESSAGE + getUserName());
        return "SUCCESS";
    }
}
```

An action can also return different results depending on the complexity of the business logic.

In such a scenario, the action code spec will be:

```
class TheAction {
    public void String execute() throws Exception {
        if(thisIsTrue()) {
            setWelcomeMessage(MESSAGE + getUserName());
            return "SUCCESS";
        } else {
            return "ERROR";
        }
    }
}
```

Explanation:

In this case, there are two different results that can be returned depending upon the business logic flow.

Since Action returns more than one kind of results, appropriate configuration is required to handle the result rendering to the user.

Action returns a **String** which matches an action configuration in struts.xml.

The XML [struts.xml] configuration will therefore look like:

```xml
<action name="MyFirstStruts2App" class="book.MyFirstStruts2App">
    <result name="SUCCESS">/apps/WelcomeToStruts.jsp</result>
    <result name="ERROR">/apps/SorryNoEntry.jsp</result>
</action>
```

Interceptors

Interceptors allow developing code spec that can be run before and/or after the execution of an action.

A request is usually processed as follows:

- A user requests a resource that maps to an Action

- Struts 2 framework invokes the appropriate Action to serve the request

If interceptors are written, available and configured, then:
- <u>Before the Action is executed</u>, the invocation could be intercepted by another object
- <u>After the Action executes</u>, the invocation could be intercepted again by another object

Such objects who intercept the invocation are called **Interceptors**.

Conceptually, Interceptors are very similar to **Servlet Filters** or the JDKs **Proxy class**.

HINT

> A useful example where writing an Interceptor can be considered is **logging** all the application activities that the user performs.
>
> After an action is executed, this interceptor can be configured to execute which will help log user activates in a data store for reporting and auditing purposes.

Why Interceptors?

Interceptors are one of the best aspects of Struts 2 framework. Interceptors are mainly used to encapsulate **common functionality** in a <u>re-usable</u> form that can be applied to one or more Actions in the application.

Developers can define code spec that can be executed before and/or after the execution of an action. This thus means that Intercepting can be done:
- Before the action
- After the action

REMINDER

> Multiple interceptors can be applied to an action request.

The following are a few common requirements where Interceptors can be used:
- Checking security and bottleneck
- Tracing the logging
- Validating User Input
- Uploading file
- Preventing double page submissions

❏   Populating drop-down list boxes and other such controls prior page loads

An interceptor can be written to achieve such common requirements. Interceptors not only have access to the Action being executed but also to the environmental variables and execution properties.

In Struts 2, a lot of the CORE functionality such as exception handling, double-submit guards, type conversion, object population, validation, file upload, page preparation and so on is implemented as pluggable **Interceptors**.

Since these are pluggable **Interceptors** the developer can choose the required ones for the **Action** being developed.

Interceptor Configuration

Interceptors configured in struts.xml appear as:

```xml
<interceptors>
    <interceptor name="timer" class="..."/>
    <interceptor name="logger" class="..."/>
</interceptors>

<action name="MyFirstStruts2App" class="book.MyFirstStruts2App">
    <interceptor-ref name="timer"/>
    <interceptor-ref name="logger"/>
        <result name="SUCCESS">/apps/WelcomeToStruts.jsp</result>
        <result name="ERROR">/apps/SorryNoEntry.jsp</result>
</action>
```

Explanation:

Here, two interceptors named **timer** and **logger** are defined. Both of these are then mapped to the Action named **MyFirstStruts2App**.

Interceptor Stack

Interceptors can be bundled together using an Interceptor **Stack** which can be referenced together. This helps applying the same set of Interceptors over and over again rather than reiterating the same list of Interceptors. Hence, instead of configuring a number of interceptors every time, an interceptor stack can be configured with all the required interceptors held within.

Stacked Interceptors configured in struts.xml appear as:

```xml
<interceptors>
    <interceptor name="timer" class="..."/>
```

```
    <interceptor name="logger" class="...."/>

    <interceptor-stack name="theStack">
       <interceptor-ref name="timer"/>
       <interceptor-ref name="logger"/>
    </interceptor-stack>
</interceptors>

<action name="MyFirstStruts2App" class="book.MyFirstStruts2App">
    <interceptor-ref name="theStack"/>
       <result name="SUCCESS">/apps/WelcomeToStruts.jsp</result>
       <result name="ERROR">/apps/SorryNoEntry.jsp</result>
</action>
```

Explanation:

Here, two interceptors named **timer** and **logger** are defined and a stack named **theStack** bundles them both.

The stack holding both these interceptors is then mapped to the Action named **MyFirstStruts2App**.

Interceptors In The Execution Flow

Interceptors are executed as follows:

1. The framework receives a **request** and decides on the **Action** the URL maps to
2. The framework consults the application's configuration file, to discover which interceptors should fire and in what sequence
3. The framework starts the invocation process by executing the first **Interceptor** in the **Stack**
4. After all the interceptors are invoked, the framework causes the Action itself to be **executed**

Value Stack / OGNL

Now that the Action and Interceptor components are covered, let's move on to the next component in Struts 2 framework.

Value Stack

Value Stack is exactly what the name suggests **a stack of objects**.

The Value Stack is a storage area that holds all of the data associated with the processing of a Request.

Value Stack In The Execution Flow

1. The framework receives a **request** and decides on the **Action** the URL maps to
2. The framework moves the data to the Value Stack whilst preparing for request processing
3. The framework manipulates the data as required during the action execution
4. The framework reads the data from there and renders the results i.e. response page

Struts 2 maintains a stack of the following objects in the **Value Stack:**

Temporary Objects

Are objects that are spawned and placed in the **Value Stack** during execution. These objects provide temporary storage and are usually spawned whilst processing a request.

For example, the **current iteration value** for a collection being looped over in a JSP tag.

Model Object

If the application uses Model objects, the current model object is placed in the **Value Stack** before the Action executes.

Action Object

Is the Action that is currently being executed.

Named Objects

In Struts 2, any object can be assigned an identifier thus making it a **Named Object**.

These objects can either be created by the developer of pre-defined such as #application, #session, #request, #attr and #parameters and refer to the corresponding Servlet scopes.

HINT

All of these objects held in the Value Stack have properties. The Value Stack exposes properties of all these objects as properties of the Value Stack itself.

Accessing Value Stack

The **Value Stack** can be accessed by simply using the tags provided for JSP.

When the Value Stack is queried for an **attribute value**, each stack element, in the provided order, is asked whether it holds the queried property.

If it holds the queried property, then the value is returned.

If it does not hold the queried property, then the next element down is queried.

This continues until the **last element** in the stack is scanned. This is very useful as the developer need not know where the attribute value currently is. Is it available in:
- The **Action**
- The **Model**
- The **HTTP Request**

The developer simply needs to know that such a value exists somewhere and Struts 2 returns it!

WARNING

If duplicate properties exist i.e. if two objects in the Value Stack have a name property, then the property of the **highest object** in the Value Stack will be the one exposed on the Virtual Object represented by the Value Stack.

OGNL [Object-Graph Navigation Language]

OGNL [Object-Graph Navigation Language] is a fully featured expression language [the default expression language] for **Retrieving** and **Setting** properties of the Java objects. It helps **data transfer** and **type conversion**.

In the **Value Stack**, **searching** or **evaluating**, a particular **expression**, can be done using OGNL. OGNL provides a mechanism to navigate object graphs using a **dot notation** and **evaluate** expressions, including calling methods on the objects being retrieved.

HINT

In **Dot Notation**, each property name is separated by a period to provide navigation within an object graph.

OGNL supports:
- Type conversion
- Calling methods
- Collection manipulation
- Generation
- Projection across collections
- Expression evaluation
- Lambda expressions

OGNL Examples

The following are a few examples where OGNL is used:

- **employee.name**

    Returns the value that is actually returned when **getEmployee().getName()** is invoked

- **employee.toString()**

    Returns the value that is actually returned when **getEmployee().toString()** is invoked

- **@book.author.name@firstName()**

    Returns the value that is actual returned when the static method named **firstName()** is invoked on the class **name**

- **firstName in {"Sharanam", "Vaishali"}**

    Invokes **getfirstName()** and determines if the value returned is either Sharanam or Vaishali. If it is, then returns **True**

- **author.{firstName}**

    Returns a collection obtained by invoking **getfirstName()** on each of the elements available in the **author** collection. Technically, this is called Projection

- **top**

    Returns the object on the top of the Value Stack

- **item.books[0]**

    Returns the **first** element of **books** object

- **#session['cart']**

    Returns the object named **cart** that is available in the **HTTP session**

OGNL In The Execution Flow

1. A user enters the data in the data entry form and submits the form
2. The Request enters Struts 2 framework and is made available to the Java language as an **HttpServletRequest** object
3. The request parameters are stored as name/value pairs where the names are the **Names** of the data entry form's **text** fields and the **Values** are the Values entered by the user when the form is submitted

   Till now all the values are in form of pure Strings.
4. Now the OGNL comes into picture, to handle the **transfer** and **type conversion** of the **data** from these request parameters
5. Using the OGNL expression, the **Value Stack** is scanned to locate the destination property where the data has to be moved
6. On locating the correct property in the Value Stack, the data is moved to the property by invoking the property's **SETTER** method with the appropriate value. The **Value Stack** acts as a place holder for viewing the data model throughout the execution
7. Whilst moving such data, OGNL consults its set of available type converters to determine if any of them can handle this particular conversion, if a conversion is required. The value is converted and set on the object's property. This makes the data available when **Action** begins its job, immediately after the available **Interceptors** have fired
8. After Action completes its job successfully, a **Result** fires that renders the result view to the user
9. Results have access to the **Value Stack**, via the OGNL expression language with the help of tags. These tags retrieve data from the **Value Stack** by referencing specific values using OGNL expressions
10. Whilst rendering the view, once again, the value that is accessed from the Value Stack is converted from the Java type to a String that is written on the HTML page

Role Of OGNL

The journey begins when the user submits a request and ends with the response that comes back to the user.

In this journey, OGNL plays an important role of binding and converting the data as it moves across the journey.

30   Struts 2 For Beginners

To understand the role of OGNL, let's assume that a data entry form accepts a few inputs of different kind [String, Number]. The data entry form when submitted does some processing and returns the processed values as HTML.

OGNL helps:
- Bind form fields such as text fields, check boxes and so on to the model objects
- Convert values from one type to another

By:
- Moving data from the request parameters into the action's JavaBeans properties
- Moving data from the action's JavaBeans properties out into rendering HTML pages

Now that what OGNL is and what it does is clear, let's move on the Result and Result Types.

Results And Result Types [View Technologies]

After the Action completes its job, the resulting information needs to be sent back to the user as a **Response**.

In Struts 2, this task is split into the **Result Type** and the **Result** itself.

Results

Result and Result Types come into picture only after the processing of the Action is complete.

Results define what happens next after the Action has been executed.

For example, Results can help determine, if the control is shifted to a success view, an error view or back to the data entry input view.

The method of the Action class that processes the Request returns a String as the result. The value of the String is used to select a Result element. This return value is mapped via the configuration file to an implementation of the Result interface.

The XML [struts.xml] configuration:

```xml
<action name="MyFirstStruts2App" class="book.MyFirstStruts2App">
    <result name="SUCCESS">/apps/WelcomeToStruts.jsp</result>
    <result name="ERROR">/apps/SorryNoEntry.jsp</result>
</action>
```

View Technologies

The most common way of rendering **Results** [View Technology] is Java Server Pages [JSP]. However, JSP is not the only view technology. There are a few others that can replace JSP in a **Struts 2** application:

- **Velocity** Templates
- **Freemarker** Templates
- **XSLT** Transformations

Freemarker and Velocity are very similar to JSP. In terms of configuration, the name of the JSP template is simply replaced with the name of either the Velocity or Freemarker template in the actions configuration file.

For example, the XML [struts.xml] configuration for Freemarker template would be:

```xml
<action name="MyFirstStruts2App" class="book.MyFirstStruts2App">
    <result type="freemarker" name="SUCCESS">/apps/WelcomeToStruts.ftl</result>
    <result type="freemarker" name="ERROR">/apps/SorryNoEntry.ftl</result>
</action>
```

The XSLT result is a little different. Instead of replacing the template name with the style sheet name, additional parameters are used.

REMINDER

This book focuses on JSP as the **View Technology**.

Result Types

The response that the Result interface generates can vary between different concrete class implementations which are nothing but Result Types.

The Result Type provides the implementation details for the type of information that is returned to the user.

For example, a response could modify the HTTP response codes, generate a byte array for an image or render a JSP and so on.

This completes a comprehensive look at the Core Components. Let's setup the required development environment to start off.

Chapter 4

SECTION II: SETTING UP THE DEVELOPMENT ENVIORNMENT
Installing And Setting Up NetBeans IDE

Before getting started with Struts 2 development, the development environment needs to be set up first. There are several ways in which a complete development environment for Java EE with Struts 2 can be setup.

To develop a Web application using Struts 2 framework, the following is what is required:
- Java Development Kit
- A Web Server
- Struts 2 libraries for NetBeans

To make the setting up of the development environment easy, this book uses an IDE called NetBeans.

What Is NetBeans?

NetBeans refers to both a platform for the development of Java applications and an IDE developed using the NetBeans Platform.

NetBeans IDE is open source and is written in the Java programming language. It provides the services common to creating desktop applications such as window and menu management, settings storage and fully supports JDK 7.0 features.

NetBeans platform and IDE are free for commercial and noncommercial use and they are supported by Sun Microsystems.

The two base products are NetBeans IDE and NetBeans Platform. Both products are free for commercial and non-commercial use. The source code to both is available to anyone to reuse as they see fit within the terms of use.

NetBeans Development Platform

NetBeans development platform comes bundled with the following based on the download option that is chosen:

- **Technologies**
    - NetBeans Platform SDK
    - Java SE
    - Java FX
    - Java EE
    - Java ME
    - Java Card™ 3 Connected
    - C/C++
    - Groovy
    - PHP
- **Web Servers**
    - GlassFish Server Open Source Edition 3.1.2.2
    - Apache Tomcat 7.0.27

Installing Java Development Kit

Prior installing the IDE, the **Java SE Development Kit** [JDK] 6 Update 7 or newer [including JDK 7] **must be installed** on the system.

If JDK is not available on the machine, NetBeans cannot be installed.

Visit **http://www.oracle.com/technetwork/java/javase/downloads/index.html** to download the latest version of the Java SE Development Kit. At the time of writing this book, the latest version was JDK 7 Update 6 [available in this Book's accompanying CDROM].

Download the latest version and install it.

> **HINT**
>
> Sometimes com.oracle.com may provide a link to a **bundled version** of the JDK and NetBeans, which if available, can be used to install both at the same time.
>
> Otherwise install the JDK and then download and install NetBeans, which can be downloaded from www.netbeans.org.
>
> This book uses an independent JDK with a bundled download of NetBeans.

To ensure that Java is already installed or to determine the Java version, issue the following command at the command prompt:

```
<System Prompt>java -version
```

If running this command does not show an appropriate output, **JDK needs to be installed** on the machine prior installing NetBeans.

Download NetBeans

Download and install the latest version of NetBeans IDE from http://www.netbeans.org/downloads/, as shown in diagram 4.1.

On the NetBeans IDE 7.2 Download page, one of several installers can be downloaded, each of which contains the base IDE and additional tools.

At the time of writing this book, the latest version that was available is **NetBeans IDE 7.2** and the kind of download that was chosen is **All** [available in this Book's accompanying CDROM].

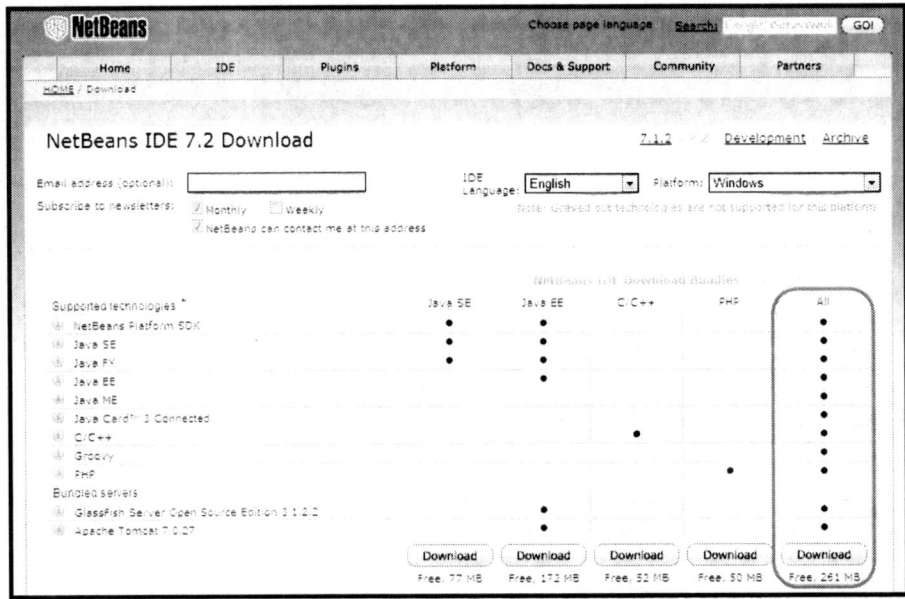

Diagram 4.1: Download link for NetBeans IDE 7.2

In the upper right area of the page, select the platform from the drop down list box, click **Download** for the desired download option and save the setup file to the machine.

After the download completes, run the setup file.

Installing NetBeans IDE

To install NetBeans on a **Windows** based operating system simply initiate the installer by double clicking the setup file named **netbeans-7.2-ml-windows.exe**.

REMINDER

If the complete NetBeans installer i.e. **All** is downloaded, choose exactly what tools and runtimes to install. Click **Customize** at the Welcome page and select the desired features.

HINT

Apache Tomcat 7.0.27 is included in the **Java** and **All** download options but it is not installed by default from either of these options. To install Apache Tomcat from the **Java** or **All** download, launch the installer and select **Apache Tomcat 7.0.27** in the **Customize** Installation dialog box.

Installing And Setting Up NetBeans IDE   37

After the setup file is executed, the screen as shown in diagram 4.2 appears.

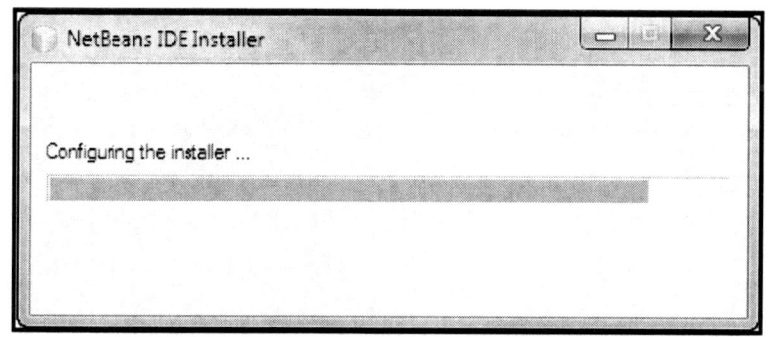

Diagram 4.2: NetBeans IDE Installer

Just after the **configuration** is complete, **Welcome page** of the installation wizard appears, as shown in diagram 4.3. Click **Customize** to select the tools and runtimes to be installed.

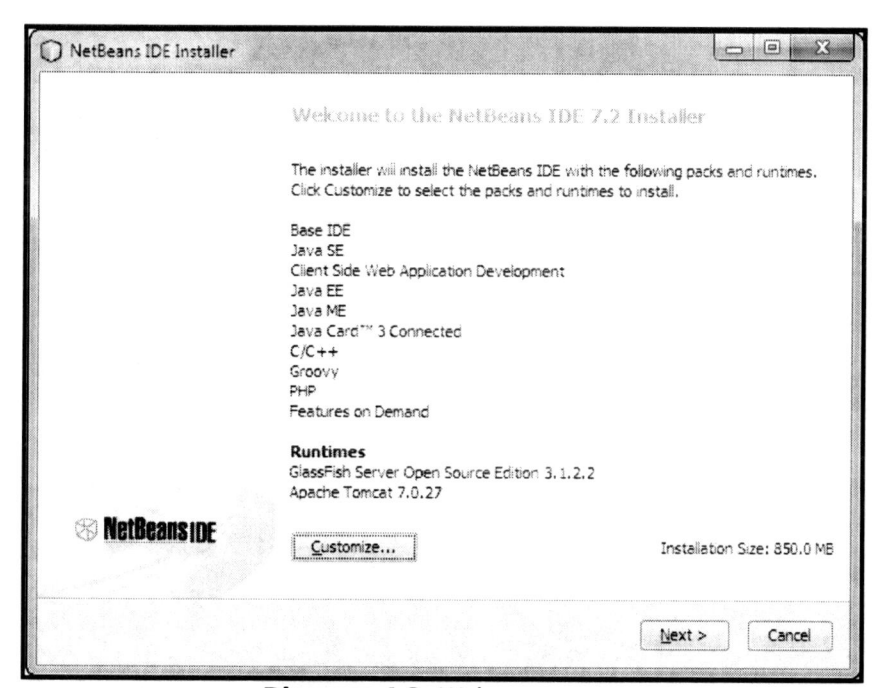

Diagram 4.3: Welcome screen

Customize Installation dialog box appears, as shown in diagram 4.4.

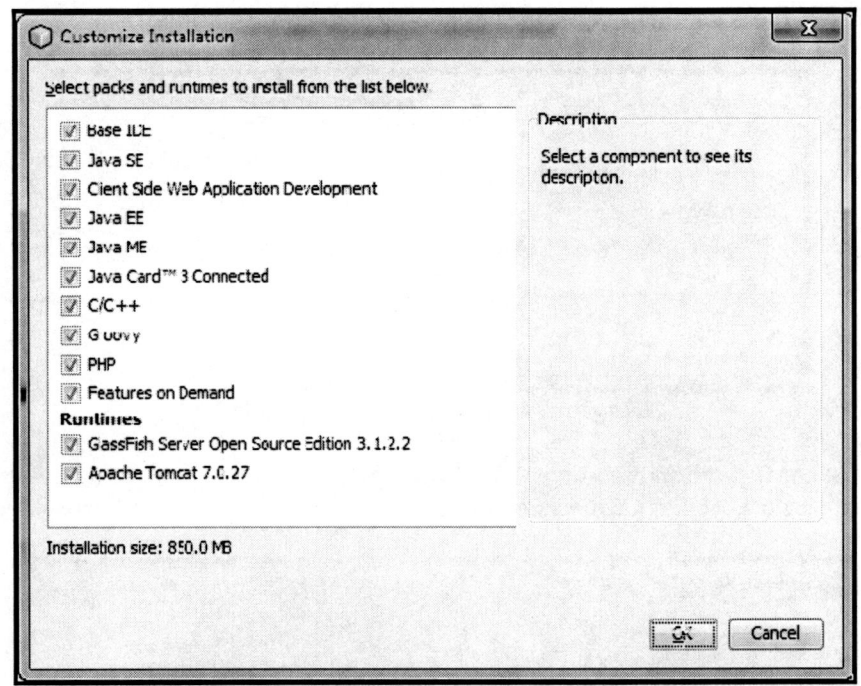

Diagram 4.4: Customize Installation dialog box

Select the desired packs and runtimes to install from the list. Click **OK**.

Proceed with the installation.

After the installation completes, the installer displays **Setup Complete** screen, as shown in diagram 4.5.

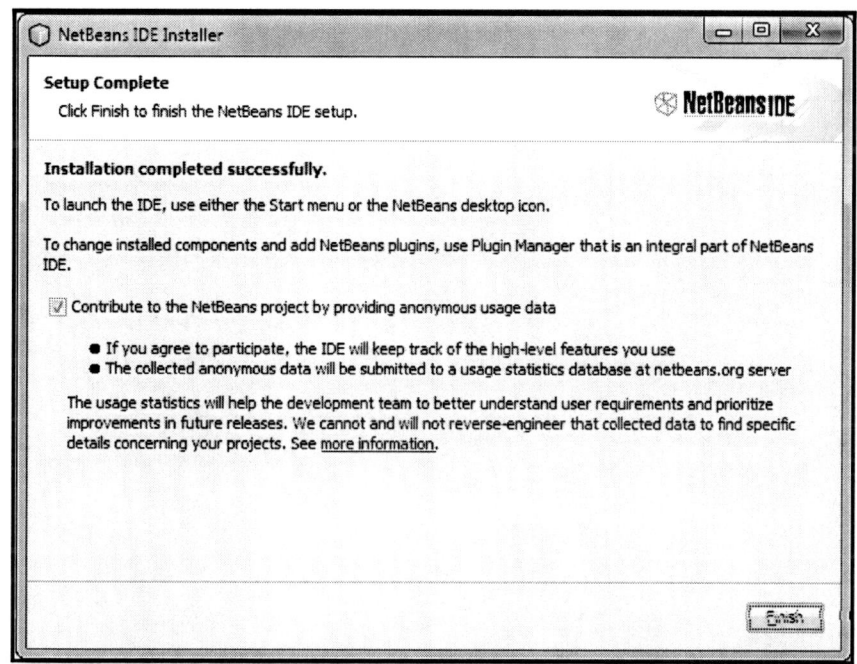

Diagram 4.5: Setup Complete screen

Click **Finish** to exit the installation wizard.

Chapter 5

SECTION II: SETTING UP THE DEVELOPMENT ENVIRONMENT

Installing And Setting Up Struts 2

Since NetBeans is the development platform of choice, Struts 2 libraries need to be made available to NetBeans platform in order to begin the development.

Creating The First Web Application

Now that NetBeans IDE is installed, let's create the first web application.

Run the NetBeans IDE and select **File → New Project**.

New Project dialog box appears, as shown in diagram 5.1.1.

Struts 2 For Beginners

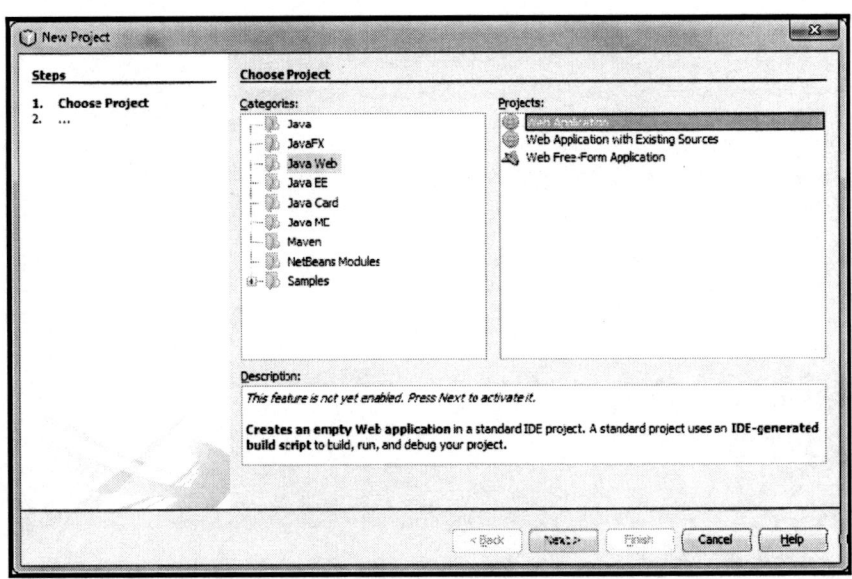

Diagram 5.1.1: New Project dialog box

Select **Java Web** available under the **Categories** section and **Web Application** available under the **Projects** section, as shown in diagram 5.1.1.

Click **Next >**. **New Web Application** dialog box appears, as shown in diagram 5.1.2.

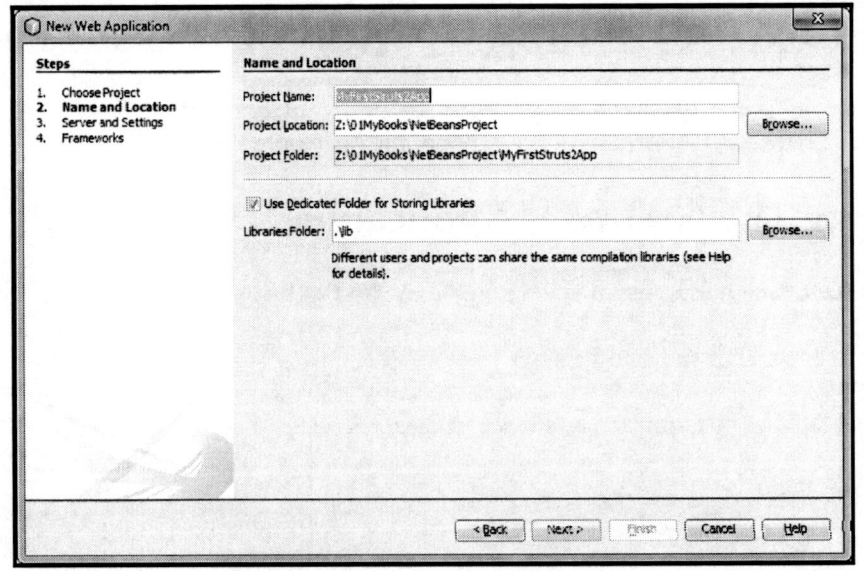

Diagram 5.1.2: Name and Location

Enter the Project Name as **MyFirstStruts2App** and select the option **Use Dedicated Folder for Storing Libraries**, as shown in diagram 5.1.2.

Click [Next >]. **Server and Settings** section of **New Web Application** dialog box appears, as shown in diagram 5.1.3.

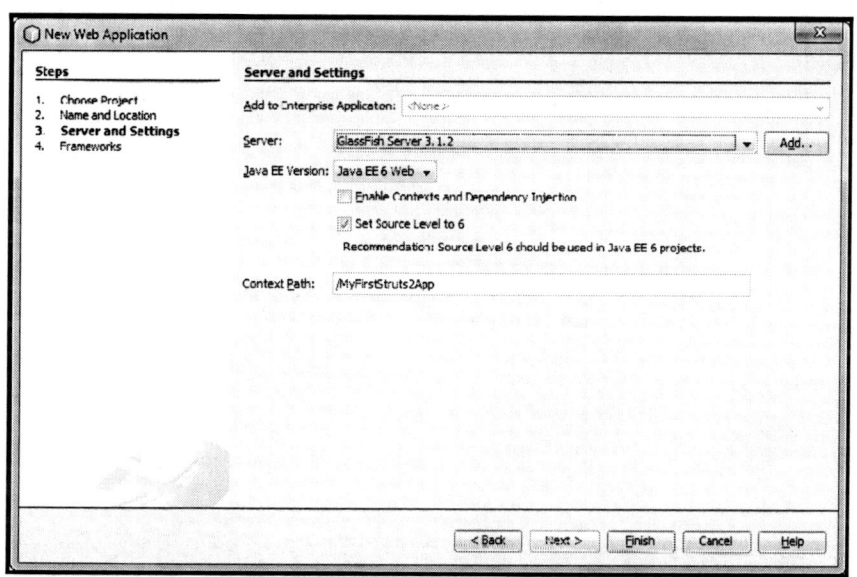

Diagram 5.1.3: Server and Settings

Keep the defaults, as shown in diagram 5.1.3.

Click [Next >]. **Frameworks** section of **New Web Application** dialog box appears, as shown in diagram 5.1.4.

Diagram 5.1.4: Frameworks

Do not select any framework.

Click Finish . This brings up the project **MyFirstStruts2App** in the NetBeans IDE, as shown in diagram 5.1.5.

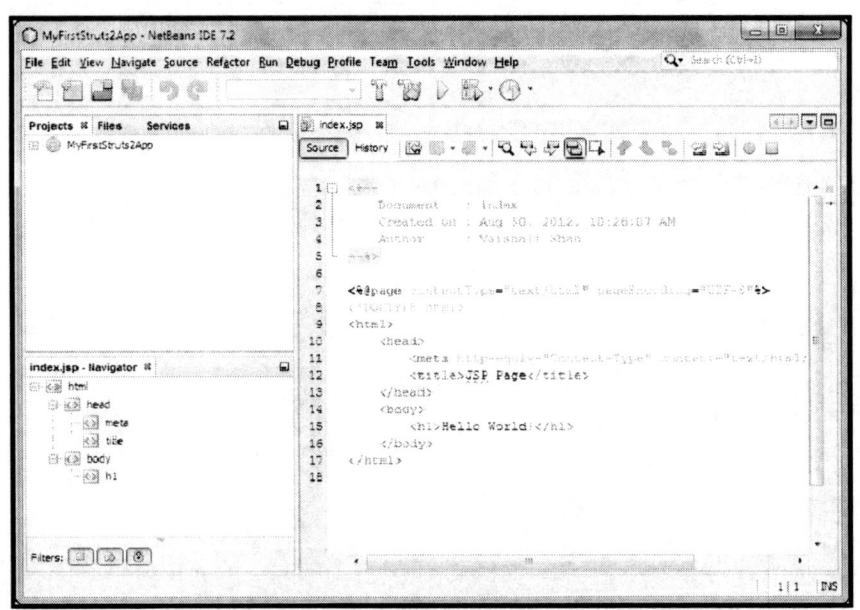

Diagram 5.1.5: MyFirstStruts2App in NetBeans IDE

Next step is to integrate Struts 2 with NetBeans, download the libraries of Struts 2 framework.

Download Struts 2 Libraries

Struts 2 is available for download from **http://struts.apache.org/download.cgi**. Download the full distribution.

At the time of writing this book the latest version that was available for download is **2.3.4.1** [available in this Book's accompanying CDROM].

Extract the contents in a directory.

The extracted directory contains two important sub directories:
- **apps:** Contains .war files that hold examples of Struts 2 applications
- **lib:** Contains all Struts 2 .jar files. These .jar files are required for Struts 2 based web applications. The .jar files contain Struts 2 API in the form of interfaces, classes and some default configuration files

Adding Struts 2 Libraries

Once NetBeans IDE brings up the web application project, add Struts 2 library files to the Web application.

The following library files from the **<Drive:>\struts-X.X.X\lib** directory needs to be added to **MyFirstStruts2App** application:
- commons-fileupload
- commons-lang
- commons-logging
- freemarker
- javassist
- ognl
- struts2-core
- xwork-core

Expand the Web application project structure in the **Project** pane, if not already expanded.

Right-click **Libraries** folder and select **Add JAR/Folder...**, as shown in diagram 5.2.1.

46   Struts 2 For Beginners

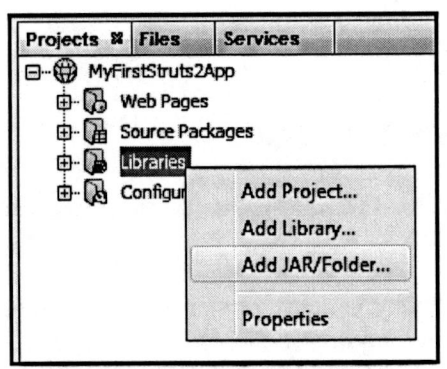

Diagram 5.2.1: Add Jar/Folder

Add JAR/Folder dialog box appears, as shown in diagram 5.2.2. Browse to the <Drive:>\struts-X.X.X\lib directory and select the desired JAR files to add to the project. Hold down the Ctrl key to select multiple files.

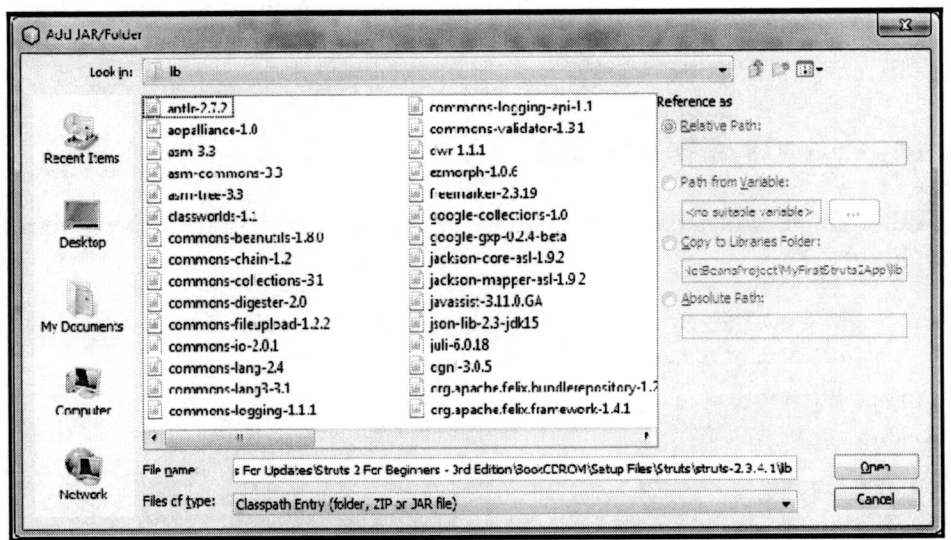

Diagram 5.2.2: Add Jar/Folder dialog box

However, additional JAR files can be added as per the requirement.

Creating Standard Deployment Descriptor [web.xml]

To create web.xml, right-click **MyFirstStrust2App** project and select New → Other..., as shown in diagram 5.3.1.

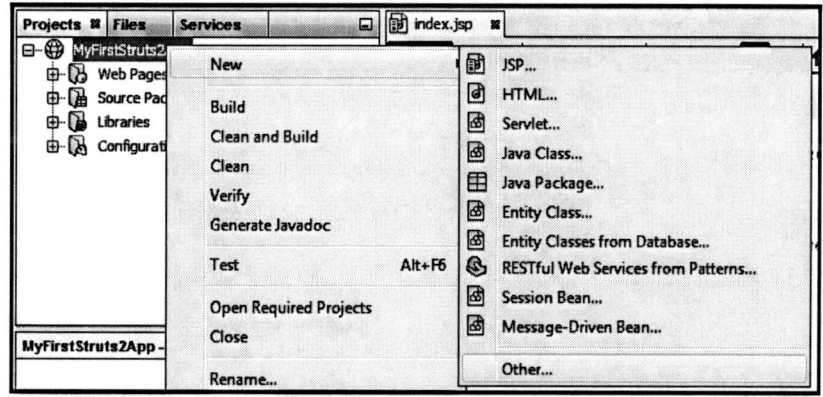

Diagram 5.3.1: Selecting Other...

New File dialog box appears, as shown in diagram 5.3.2.

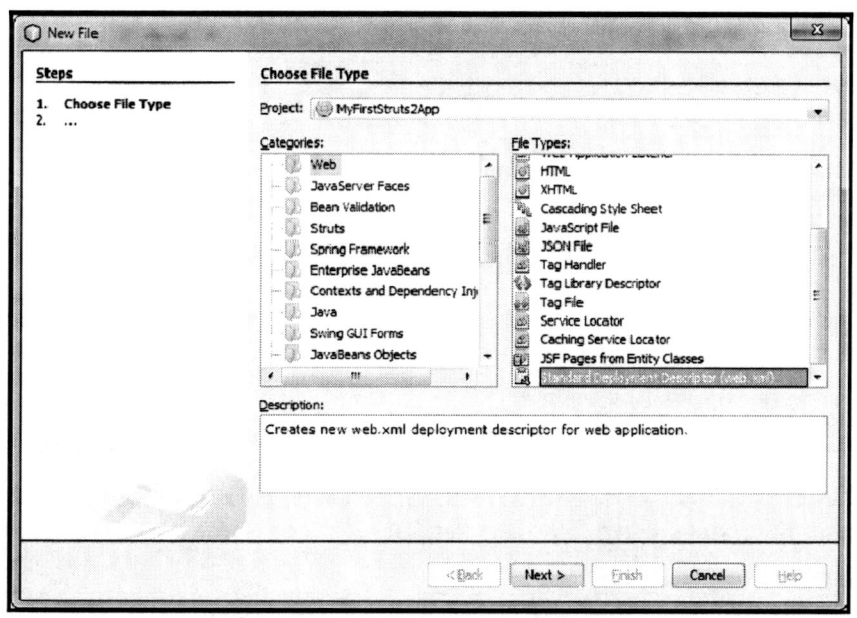

Diagram 5.3.2: New File dialog box

Select **Web** available under the **Categories** list and **Standard Deployment Descriptor (web.xml)** available under the **File Type** list, as shown in diagram 5.3.2.

Click **Next**. The details of web.xml are shown in the dialog box, as shown in diagram 5.3.3, which is not editable.

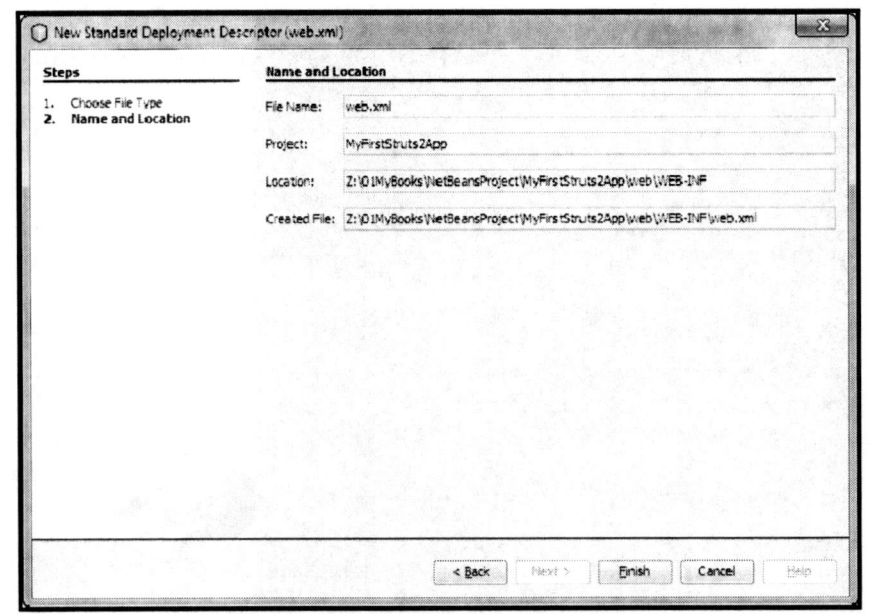

Diagram 5.3.3: Name and Location

Click **Finish**. web.xml is created under the folder /WEB-INF in NetBeans IDE.

Adding Struts 2 Filter In web.xml

Add a filter element to **web.xml** deployment descriptor to enable Struts 2 handle all the requests for the Web application.

To do so, open **web.xml** and select the **Filters** tab.

Click [Add Filter Element...]. This displays the **Add Servlet Filter** form, as shown in diagram 5.4.1. Populate the form with the following details:

Filter Name	Struts2Filter
Filter Class	org.apache.struts2.dispatcher.ng.filter.StrutsPrepareAndExecuteFilter

Installing And Setting Up Struts 2   49

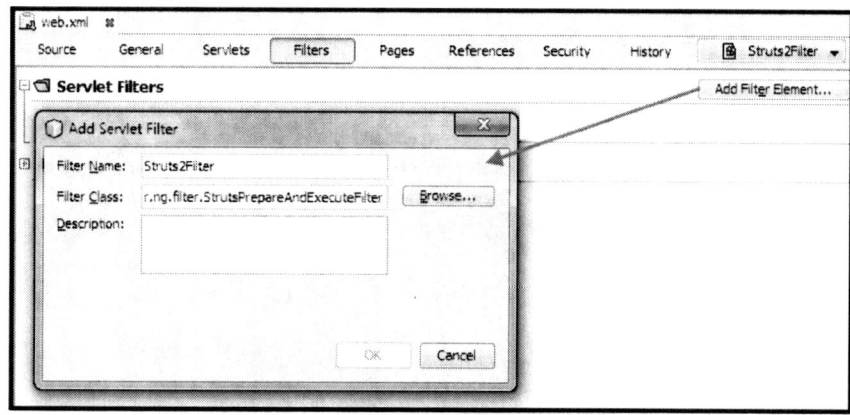

Diagram 5.4.1: Add Servlet Filter

Click [OK] when done.

Click [Add...] under the **Filter Mappings** section to add a Filter mapping. This brings up the **Add Filter Mapping** form, as shown in diagram 5.4.2. Populate the form with the following details:

Filter Name	Struts2Filter
URL Pattern	/*

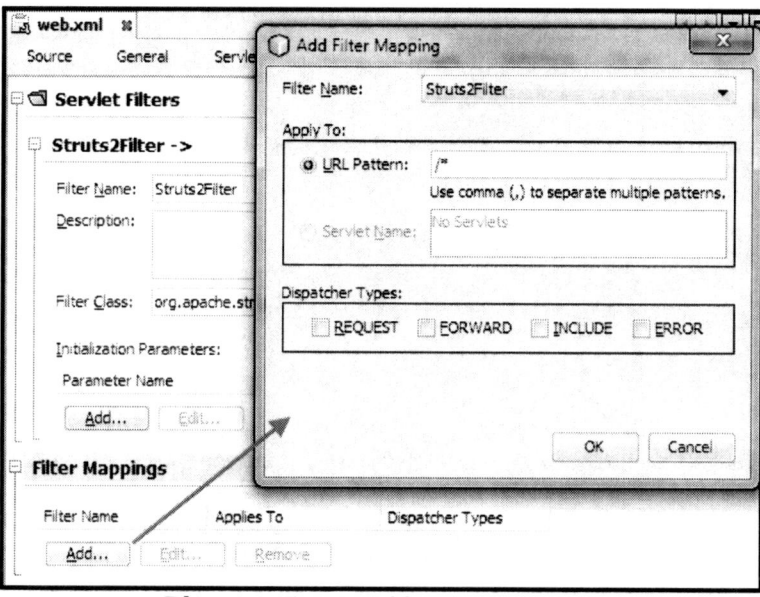

Diagram 5.4.2: Add Servlet Mapping

Creating Struts Action Java Class

Right click **MyFirstStruts2App** project, select **New → Java Class...**, as shown in diagram 5.5.1.

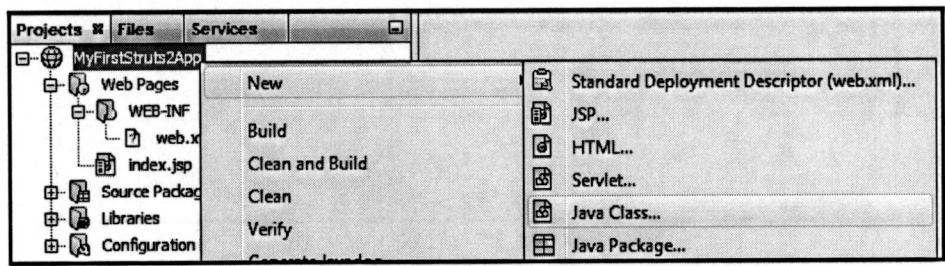

Diagram 5.5.1: Creating Java Class file

New Java Class dialog box appears, as shown in diagram 5.5.2.

Enter **Class Name** as **HelloStruts2World** and **Package** as **com.sharanamvaishali**, as shown in diagram 5.5.2 and click **Finish**.

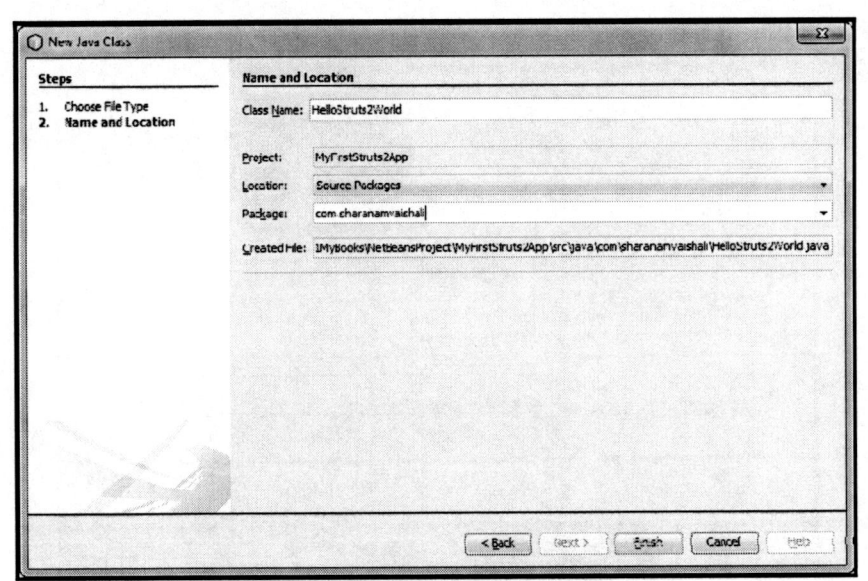

Diagram 5.5.2: New Java Class dialog box

Key in the following code spec in HelloStruts2World.java:

```
1  package com.sharanamvaishali;
2
```

```
 3  import com.opensymphony.xwork2.ActionSupport;
 4
 5  public class HelloStruts2World extends ActionSupport {
 6      private String userName;
 7      private String message;
 8
 9      public String getUserName() {
10          return userName;
11      }
12      public void setUserName(String userName) {
13          this.userName = userName;
14      }
15
16      public String getMessage() {
17          return message;
18      }
19
20      @Override
21      public String execute() {
22          message = "Hello, " + userName;
23          return SUCCESS;
24      }
25  }
```

Map The Action Java Class To A Result Page

Now the Java class created in the above step needs to be configured as a Struts 2 Action and mapped to a result page.

To do so, create Struts 2 configuration file **struts.xml**.

To do so, right-click **MyFirstStruts2App** project and select New → Other..., as shown in diagram 5.6.1.

Diagram 5.6.1: Creating struts.xml

52   Struts 2 For Beginners

New File dialog appears, as shown in diagram 5.6.2. Select **XML** from the **Categories** list and select **XML Document** from the **File Types**, as shown in diagram 5.6.2.

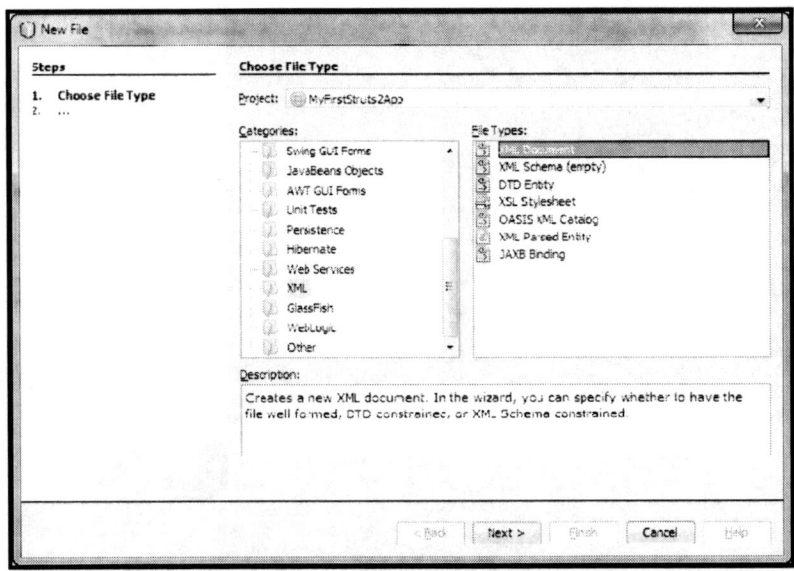

Diagram 5.6.2: New File dialog box

Click **Next >**. **New XML Document** dialog box appears, as shown in diagram 5.6.3. Enter **struts** as File Name and select **Folder** as **src\java**, as shown in diagram 5.6.3.

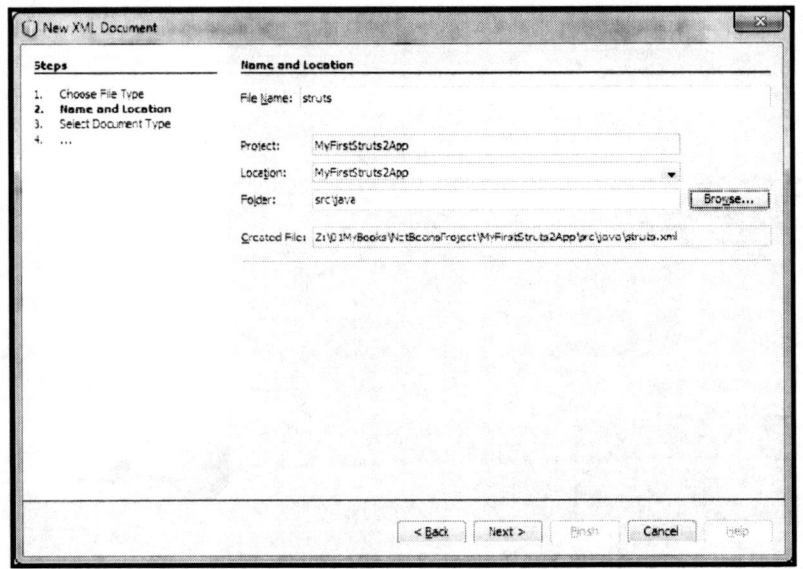

Diagram 5.6.3: Name and Location section

Click **Next >**. **Select document Type** section of **New File** dialog box appears, as shown in diagram 5.6.4.

Select the option **DTD-Constrained Document**, as shown in diagram 5.6.4.

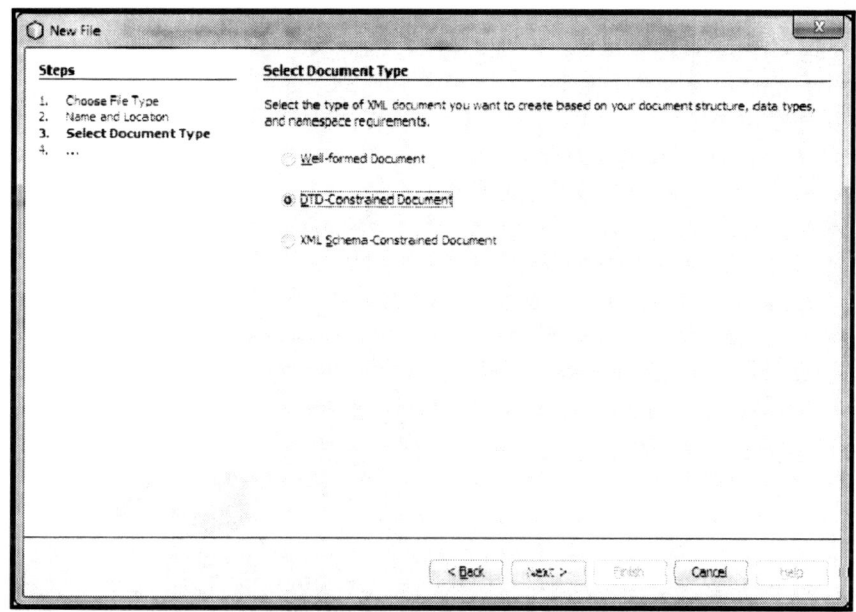

Diagram 5.6.4: Select Document Type section

Click **Next >**. **DTD Options** section of **New File** dialog box appears, as shown in diagram 5.6.5.

Specify the following **DTD Options** values for the XML document type, as shown in diagram 5.6.5:

DTD Public ID [Default Value]	-//Apache Software Foundation//DTD Commons Validator Rules Configuration 2.3//EN
DTD System ID	http://struts.apache.org/dtds/struts-2.3.dtd
Document Root	struts

54   Struts 2 For Beginners

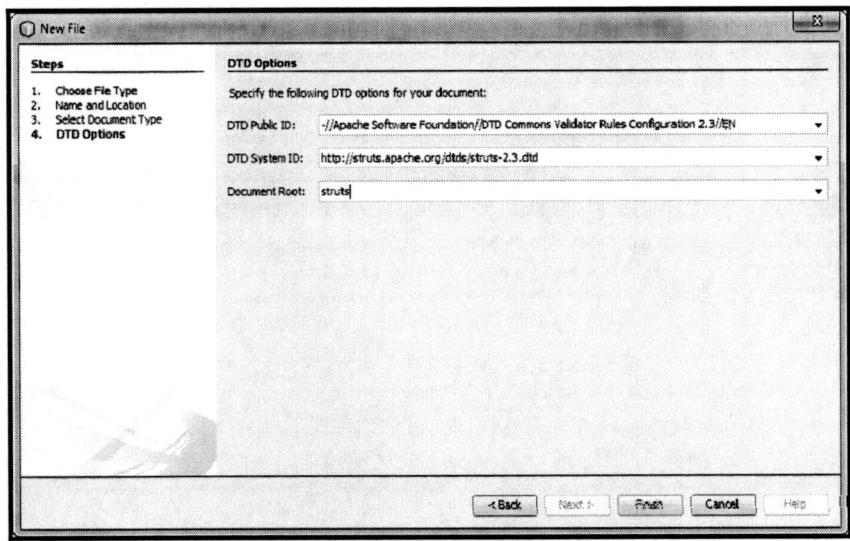

Diagram 5.6.5: DTD options section

Click **Finish**.

Key in the following code spec in struts.xml:

```
1  <?xml version="1.0" encoding="UTF-8"?>
2  <!DOCTYPE struts PUBLIC '-//Apache Software Foundation//DTD Commons Validator
   Rules Configuration 2.3//EN' 'http://struts.apache.org/dtds/struts-2.3.dtd'>
3  <struts>
4    <package name="/" extends="struts-default">
5      <action name="HelloStruts2World"
          class="com.sharanamvaishali.HelloStruts2World">
6        <result name="success">/index.jsp</result>
7      </action>
8    </package>
9  </struts>
```

This maps the requests sent to the **/HelloStruts2World.action** URL to **HelloStruts2World.java** Struts 2 action and after the successful execution of the request, it gets directed to **index.jsp** result page.

Let's access the **message** property set by **HelloStruts2World** action and display it in **index.jsp**, which was created by default when the web application was created.

Key in the following code spec in **index.jsp**:

```
1  <%@page contentType="text/html" pageEncoding="UTF-8"%>
2  <%@taglib prefix="s" uri="/struts-tags" %>
3  <!DOCTYPE html>
```

```
 4  <html>
 5    <head>
 6      <meta http-equiv="Content-Type" content="text/html; charset=UTF-8">
 7      <title>Hello Struts 2 World Result Page</title>
 8    </head>
 9    <body bgcolor="pink">
10      <h2><s:property value="message" default="Guest" /></h2>
11      <s:form method="GET" action="HelloStruts2World">
12        <table border="0" cellpadding="0" cellspacing="2">
13          <tr>
14            <td align="right">Enter your name:</td>
15            <td align="left"><s:textfield theme="simple" name="userName"
                /></td>
16          </tr>
17          <tr>
18            <td align="center" colspan="2"><s:submit value="Submit"
                theme="simple" /></td>
19          </tr>
20        </table>
21      </s:form>
22    </body>
23  </html>
```

Run The Web Application Project

MyFirstStruts2App Web application project structure, with relevant folders expanded, should look like the one shown in diagram 5.7.1.

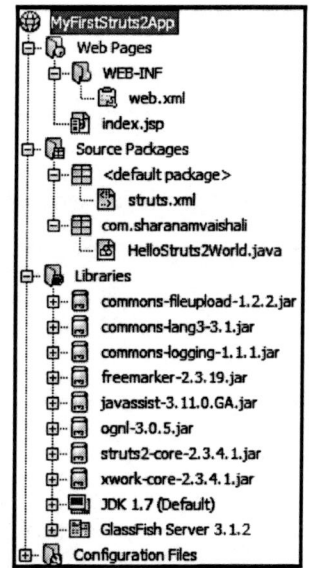

Diagram 5.7.1: Directory Structure

Run the Web application by right-clicking **MyFirstStruts2App** project and selecting **Run**.

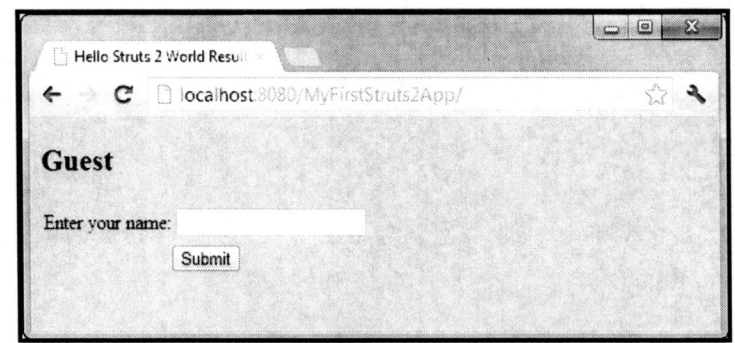

Diagram 5.7.2: Running the application

By default, the word **Guest** appears, as shown in diagram 5.7.2.

Enter the name as shown in diagram 5.7.3.

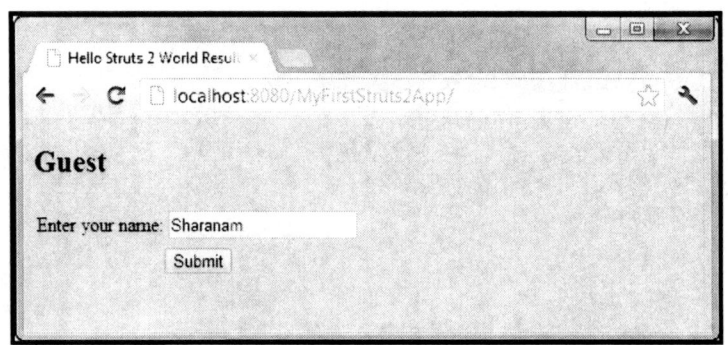

Diagram 5.7.3: Entering the name

Click Submit. The word **Guest** changes to **Hello, Sharanam**, as shown in diagram 5.7.4.

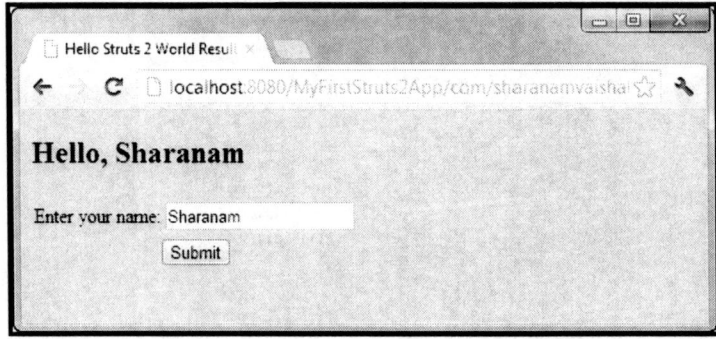

Diagram 5.7.4: Displaying the message

Chapter 6

SECTION III: GETTING STARTED WITH STRUTS 2

Getting Started

Beginning to work with a new technology or framework can be frightening.

Often developers come up with questions such as:

- What to start with? Actions, Interceptors, Views, ...
- What classes to implement?
- How to configure?

and many more...

The simplest way to start is to follow an example that covers answers to all such questions.

This section covers everything that is needed to get started with Struts 2 and begin developing Web applications using Struts 2:

- Creating Actions
- Interceptors

- Validators
- Views
- OGNL and Value Stack

The goal of this section is to provide the information on how to develop a Web application using Struts 2 in a practical and hands-on manner. The learning approach taken here is that a single example called **GuestBook** is built in an incremental manner, chapter-by-chapter.

Building the GuestBook application in an incremental manner helps understanding the role of each component in Struts 2 framework and how the different parts of a basic Struts 2 application interact.

Each chapter in this section works towards exploring each of the components, providing more and more information until a complete Web application emerges.

This chapter begins by describing the application requirements for the GuestBook example.

Application Requirements

The application to be built is called GuestBook. This application should be capable of accepting and displaying visitor's comments.

To achieve this, it should provide a user interface that accepts visitor's name and message/comments.

Diagram 6.1: GuestBook data entry form

Whilst submitting such information to the server, the application should ensure that the visitor has filled in all the required information. Hence the application needs to perform some kind of client-side validation. In case of an error, the application should display an appropriate error message, as shown in diagram 6.2.

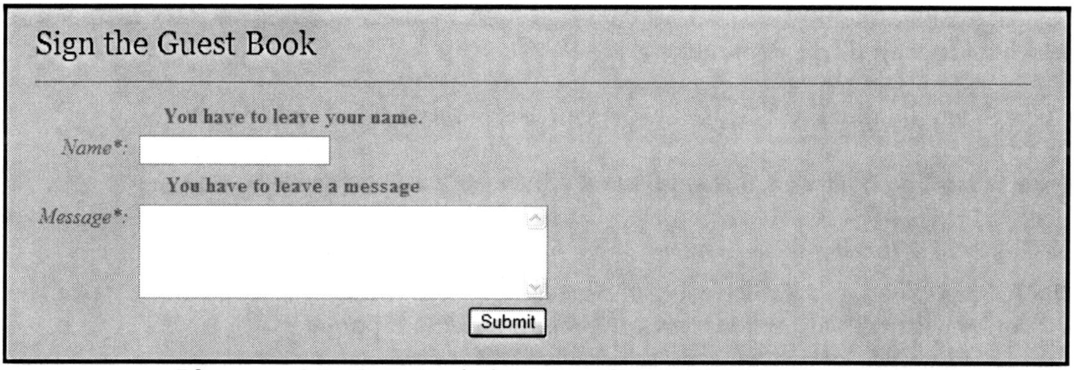

Getting Started

Diagram 6.2: GuestBook data entry form with error messages

After such information is captured, validated and stored, other visitors to the application should be able to view all the available comments, as shown in diagram 6.3.

This user interface displays the visitor's name along with the message and the date when the message was keyed in. It should also provide a link to sign the GuestBook which when clicked should display the GuestBook data entry form, as shown in diagram 6.1.

Diagram 6.3: View GuestBook

Every time, the application is invoked, the time taken to invoke the application should be logged and outputted to the system console.

The data that is captured will be stored in an ArrayList for simplicity purpose. No permanent data store [database] is required.

Application Development

Based on the requirements, it is quite clear that there are two user interfaces involved.

- Guest Book data entry form to capture entries
- View Guest Book page to view the captured entries

No database is involved instead an ArrayList will be used to store the data temporarily which will persist till the application is alive.

Client Side validations will be used to perform **not empty** kind of validations.

From Struts 2 point of view this application will be built as follows:

In Chapter 7: Working With Actions
- A **Bean** class i.e. GuestBook.java and an **Action** class [**Model**] i.e. GuestBookAction.java will be created. This Action class will process the data captured

In Chapter 8: Building Views
- Two Java Server Pages [**View**] i.e. guestBookEntry.jsp that will accept the visitor's name and comments and guestBookView.jsp that will display the visitor's comments will be created
- The **relationship between the View and the Model** [View/Results → Action mappings] will be documented in the configuration file i.e. struts.xml

In Chapter 9: Building Interceptors
- An **Interceptor** class i.e. ActionTimer.java will be created. This class will be invoked before and/or after the execution of the action to log and output the execution time
- The <u>Interceptor → Action mappings</u> will be documented in the configuration file i.e. struts.xml

In Chapter 10: OGNL And The Value Stack
Just read through this chapter to understand how these components perform their roles.

In Chapter 11: Validation Framework
- A **Validator** file i.e. GuestBookAction-validation.xml will be created. This file will document the validations to be carried out

That's it, this should be enough to bring up the application as per the requirements.

Creating A Web Application

Since NetBeans is the IDE of choice throughout this book. Use it to create a new Web Application Project called **GuestBook**.

Run NetBeans IDE and select **File → New Project**.

New Project dialog box appears.

Click **Next**. Name this Web application as **GuestBook**.

Click **Next**. **Server and Settings** section of **New Web Application** dialog box appears.

Keep the default as it is.

Do not choose a framework in the Frameworks dialog box. Let's build this application using the manual method.

Click **Finish**.

GuestBook application is created in NetBeans IDE.

Adding Struts 2 Libraries

Once the NetBeans IDE brings up the GuestBook application, the next step is to add the Struts 2 library files to the GuestBook application.

Now add the following libraries in the NetBeans IDE from the **<Drive:>/struts-X.X.X/lib** directory:

- commons-fileupload
- commons-lang
- commons-logging
- commons-io
- freemarker
- javassist
- ognl
- struts2-core
- xwork-core

Expand the Web application project structure in the **Project** pane, if not already expanded.

Right-click **Libraries** folder and select **Add JAR/Folder...**.

Add JAR/Folder dialog box appears. Browse to the **<Drive:>\struts-X.X.X\lib** directory and select the desired JAR files to add to the project.

Creating Standard Deployment Descriptor [web.xml]

Once the libraries are added, the next step is to create a standard deployment descriptor i.e. web.xml for the Web application.

To create web.xml, right-click **GuestBook** project and select **New → Other...**

New File dialog box appears.

Select **Web** available under the **Categories** list and **Standard Deployment Descriptor (web.xml)** available under the **File Type** list.

Click **Next**. The details of web.xml are shown in the dialog box, which is not editable.

Click **Finish**. web.xml is created under the folder /WEB-INF in NetBeans IDE.

Adding Struts 2 Filter In web.xml

Once the libraries are added, the next step is to add a filter element to **web.xml** to enable Struts 2 handle all the requests for the Web application.

To do so, open **web.xml** and select the **Filters** tab.

Click [Add Filter Element...]. This displays the **Add Servlet Filter** form. Populate the form with the following details:

Filter Name	Struts2Filter
Filter Class	org.apache.struts2.dispatcher.ng.filter.StrutsPrepareAndExecuteFilter

Click [OK] when done. Click [Add...] under the **Filter Mappings** section to add a Filter mapping. This brings up the **Add Filter Mapping** form. Populate the form with the following details:

Filter Name	Struts2Filter
URL Pattern	/*

Creating Struts 2 Configuration File [struts.xml]

Once the libraries and the filters are added, the next step is to create Struts configuration file **struts.xml**.

Getting Started 63

To do so, right-click **GuestBook** project and select **New → Other…**.

New File dialog appears. Select **XML** from the **Categories** list and select **XML Document** from the **File Types**.

Click **Next**. **New XML Document** dialog box appears. Enter **struts** as **File Name** and select **Folder** as **src\java**.

Click **Next**. **Select document Type** section of **New File** dialog box appears.

Select the option **DTD-Constrained Document**.

Click **Next**. **DTD Options** section of **New File** dialog box appears.

Specify the following **DTD Options** values for the XML document type:

DTD Public ID [Default Value]	-//Apache Software Foundation//DTD Commons Validator Rules Configuration 2.3//EN
DTD System ID	http://struts.apache.org/dtds/struts-2.3.dtd
Document Root	struts

Click **Finish**.

That's it, save this project. The chapters that follow will use the same project to create required classes and files.

Let's get started!

Chapter 7

SECTION III: GETTING STARTED WITH STRUTS 2

Working With Actions

Struts 2 has a single controller that handles all the user requests by invoking appropriate classes containing the required business logic. These classes are known as **Action classes**.

All the heavy lifting in the Web application is done by Actions. Actions interact with database and business rule engines, thus help transform the HTML into a rich, dynamic Web experience. After doing its job, an Action returns a control result string to indicate what the framework should do next.

Often, the next step is to render the result or display an error. In either case, the Action does not worry about generating the response. It only decides which logical result to present next.

Actions are simple Java objects. Actions are instantiated **one object per request**.

Struts 2 filter based on the request URI decides which action to instantiate. After the action to be instantiated is chosen, an instance of that action is created and execute() is invoked.

Role Of Action

Actions Provide Encapsulation

One of the prime responsibilities of this role is to hold the business logic. Actions use **execute()** for this purpose. The code spec inside **execute()** should only hold the logic of the work associated with the request.

HINT

> By convention, Actions are invoked by calling execute(). However, any other method that returns a String value can be used instead, simply by adding the appropriate configuration in struts.xml.

Example

Solution:
```
package myApp;

public class simpleApp {
   public String execute() {
      setMessage("Hi " + getName());
      return "SUCCESS";
   }
}
```

Explanation:

Here, the Action class is named **simpleApp**. The method that is invoked when this action is processed is **execute()** that encapsulates the business logic which in this case is a simple concatenation of two strings.

The action class does not need to:

- **Extend** another class
- **Implement** any interfaces

Struts 2 Actions classes are simple objects very similar to a POJO [Plain Old Java Object].

REMINDER

> POJOs are ordinary Java objects which do not implement any interface or extend any other Java class and hence, does not depend on other APIs.

Working With Actions

The importance of POJO as action is that there is no need to use extra objects in Struts 2 framework. It is faster, simpler and easier to develop. It also shows how to organize and encapsulate the domain logic, access the database, manage transactions and handle the database concurrency.

The action class has one method named [by convention] execute(). This method need not be named execute, it can be called anything as desired, **provided** that method returns a String. The only change needed would be in the configuration file [struts.xml]. If needed, the method **may** throw an **exception**.

execute() does not accept any parameters, but it does returns a String object. Different return types can be used, by using the helper interfaces available in Struts 2 framework.

Helper interface provides common results such as SUCCESS, NONE, ERROR, INPUT and LOGIN.

These are string constants that can be utilized to return values to the framework that in turn help the framework decide the appropriate **View**.

From the MVC point of view, the **Action Class acts as a Model**. It executes particular business logic depending on the **Request** object and the **input parameters** it receives.

Actions Help Carry Data

Actions also carry the data around. The data is held local to the Action which makes it available during the execution of the business logic. The data can be set and retrieved using a bunch of **JavaBeans properties**. execute() references the data using these properties.

```
1  package com.sharanamvaishali;
2
3  public class simpleApp {
4      private String name;
5      public String getName() {
6          return name;
7      }
8      public void setName(String name) {
9          this.name = name;
10     }
11
12     private String message;
13     public String getMessage() {
14         return message;
15     }
16     public void setMessage(String message) {
17         this.message = message;
18     }
19
```

JavaBeans properties Getter/Setter methods

```
20      @Override
21      public String execute() {
22          setMessage("Hi " + getName());
23          return SUCCESS;
24      }
25  }
```

Explanation:

The above code spec justifies the following:
   The data can be set and retrieved using a bunch of **JavaBeans properties**.

Here, for the data i.e. Name and the Message, the action class uses JavaBeans properties.

Data Entry Form And Action

In most standard Web applications, there are usually a set of data entry forms with a few form fields that allow data capture. Actions require such data for further processing as per the application's business logic, which is available in the request string or the Form data.

Struts 2 framework follows the **JavaBean paradigm**. This means to access a form field's data, a **GETTER / SETTER** method is required.

Struts 2 framework, automatically, moves the Request parameters from the **Form** to the JavaBeans properties that have matching names. In this case, the **name** parameter from the Form is automatically assigned to the **name** JavaBeans property in the Action class.

In **Struts 2** providing access to the request string and form values is not very different. Here, each request string or form value is a simple **NAME-VALUE** pair. The **action class** should hold a **setter** method to assign the **VALUE** for a particular **NAME** and a **getter** method to retrieve the **VALUE** of a particular **NAME**.

In case of a call to a JSP page:
www.myserver.com/guestbook.action?**page**=1&**msg**=Hi

In this case, the Action would need the following SETTER methods:

- setPage(String page)
- setMsg(String msg)

Similarly when accessing such values in view mode, the following GETTER methods will be required:

- getPage()
- getMsg()

REMINDER

> The setter does not always need to be a String value. Struts 2 is capable of converting a String to the required data type.

HINT

> JavaBeans properties in the Action class also help expose the data received [from the Form] to the View/Result. For example, in the above code spec, using **setMessage()**, the message is assigned to the **msg** JavaBeans property. This, thus, exposes it to the View/Result.

Actions Return Control String

After the job is done, the action returns a control string. This string helps **Struts 2 Filter** to decide the result/view that should be rendered.

Actions must return a string that map to one of the result components available for rendering the view for that action. These **mappings** are placed in the configuration file called struts.xml.

```
1  <?xml version="1.0" encoding="UTF-8"?>
2  <!DOCTYPE struts PUBLIC '-//Apache Software Foundation//DTD Commons Validator
   Rules Configuration 2.3//EN' 'http://struts.apache.org/dtds/struts-2.3.dtd'>
3  <struts>
4    <package name="myApp" namespace="/" extends="struts-default"
     method="execute">
5      <action name="simpleApp"
       class="com.sharanamvaishali.book.myApp.simpleApp">
6        <result name="success">/simpleView.jsp</result>
7        <result name="error">/simpleError.jsp</result>
8      </action>
9    </package>
10 </struts>
```

```
21  public String execute() {
22     setMessage("Hi " + getName());
23     return SUCCESS;
24  }
```

Explanation:

The value that is returned as the control string must match the name of the desired result in the configuration file i.e. struts.xml.

In the action class code spec, the action returns the string SUCCESS. In struts.xml, **success** is the name of the one of the result components that point to a JSP page that will be rendered as the view.

Helper Interfaces

Although, the action class does not need to:

- **Extend** another class
- **Implement** any interfaces

Sometimes it makes sense to extend helper classes or implement interfaces provided by Struts 2 framework.

Struts 2 provides two such helpers that can be used. The first being the **Action** interface which can be used to create action classes.

Action Interface

Action interface is a helper interface which exposes execute() to the action class implementing it.

Code Spec:
```
1  public interface Action {
2      public static final String SUCCESS = "success";
3      public static final String NONE = "none";
4      public static final String ERROR = "error";
5      public static final String INPUT = "input";
6      public static final String LOGIN = "login";
7
8      public String execute() throws Exception;
9  }
```

This interface:

- Provides the common string based return values as CONSTANTS
- Enforces that implementing classes provide the default execute()

The following table lists the CONSTANTS i.e. common results that can be returned by execute():

Results	Description
SUCCESS	The action execution was successful.
NONE	The action execution was successful but do not show a view.

Results	Description
ERROR	The action execution was a failure.
INPUT	The action execution requires more input in order to succeed.
LOGIN	The action could not be executed as the user was not logged in.

These constants can conveniently be used as the control string values returned by execute(). The true benefit is that these constants are also used internally by the framework. This means that using these predefined control strings allows tapping into even more intelligent default behavior.

ActionSupport Class

ActionSupport class is fairly simple. It adds a few useful utilities to the class that **extends** it.

ActionSupport class implements Action interface and some more useful interfaces.

Since ActionSupport implements Action interface, static fields such as ERROR, INPUT, LOGIN, NONE and SUCCESS can be used in the class that extends it. There is already an implementation of execute(), inherited from Action, that simply returns Action.SUCCESS.

If a class implements Action interface directly instead of extending ActionSupport, an implementation of execute() needs to be provided. Hence, it's more convenient to extend ActionSupport than to implement Action interface.

In addition to Action interface, ActionSupport also implements other interfaces:

- **Validateable** and **ValidationAware** interfaces that provide programmatic, annotation-based and declarative XML-based validation
- **TextProvider** and **LocaleProvide** interfaces that provide support for localization and internationalization
- **Serializable** interface used to create classes which enable the transfer of any binary object over a communication channel by transferring all the data of the object in a byte by byte manner

Code Spec:
```
public class ActionSupport implements Action, Validateable, ValidationAware,
TextProvider, LocaleProvider, Serializable {
   . . .
   public String execute() throws Execption {
      return SUCCESS;
   }
}
```

ActionSupport provides default implementations of several useful interfaces. If the actions extend this class, they automatically gain the use of these implementations.

Since ActionSupport class provides default definitions of methods of all interfaces implemented by it, action class can be created by just **extending** this class and using its methods.

Example

simpleApp class shown earlier, if it extends ActionSupport class looks like:

```
1   package com.sharanamvaishali;
2
3   import com.opensymphony.xwork2.ActionSupport;
4
5   public class simpleApp extends ActionSupport {
6       private String name;
7       public String getName() {
8           return name;
9       }
10      public void setName(String name) {
11          this.name = name;
12      }
13
14      private String message;
15      public String getMessage() {
16          return message;
17      }
18      public void setMessage(String message) {
19          this.message = message;
20      }
21
22      @Override
23      public String execute() {
24          setMessage("Hi " + getName());
25          return SUCCESS;
26      }
27  }
```

- Line 5: Extending the ActionSupport class
- Line 22-23: execute() overridden
- Line 25: CONSTANT

Role Of Struts 2 Filter

Struts 2 filter:

- Instantiates the Action
- Executes the method that is specified in the configuration
- Reads the control string i.e. the return value and chooses the View/Result to present

Struts 2 filter whilst handling an Action:

- Looks for a method called **execute**, if no method is specified in the configuration
- Generates the default view, if the return value is **success**

struts.xml

struts.xml holds the configuration information that is added/modified as actions are developed. This is the place where Struts 2 filter looks for configurations.

Example

Solution:
```
1  <?xml version="1.0" encoding="UTF-8"?>
2  <!DOCTYPE struts PUBLIC '-//Apache Software Foundation//DTD Commons Validator
   Rules Configuration 2.3//EN' 'http://struts.apache.org/dtds/struts-2.3.dtd'>
3  <struts>
4     <package name="myApp" namespace="/" extends="struts-default"
      method="execute">
5        <action name="simpleApp"
         class="com.sharanamvaishali.book.myApp.simpleApp">
6           <result name="success">/simpleView.jsp</result>
7           <result name="error">/simpleError.jsp</result>
8        </action>
9     </package>
10 </struts>
```

Being an XML file, the first element is the XML versioning and encoding information.

This is followed by **Document Type Definition** i.e. DTD for the XML. DTD provides structural information that the elements in the file should have and is used by XML parsers and editor.

<struts>

This is the **outermost tag** that contains Struts 2 specific configuration. All other tags are held within this tag.

<package>

struts.xml is broken down into logical units called **packages**.

<package> is used to group together configurations that share common attributes such as interceptor stacks or URL namespaces.

Packages are meant to help group the application's components based on commonality of function or domain.

Packages group the following into a logical configuration unit:
- Actions
- Result types
- Interceptors
- Interceptor stacks

REMINDER

Every action configured within a package inherits that package's configuration.

The name Attribute [name="myApp"]

Indicates the name of the package.

The namespace Attribute [namespace="/"]

The **namespace** attribute helps in separating different package into different namespace and hence, help in avoiding action mapping confliction.

The **namespace** attribute indicates the location where the action is placed. It is used to generate the URL namespace to which the actions of these packages are mapped.

In this case, the namespace specified is /. Hence to reach the **simpleApp** action, the Web browser will need to request **/simpleApp.action** within the Web application's context.

This means, if the web-app is called my-app and it is running on a server called www.myserver.com, the URL to access the action will be:
http://www.myserver.com/my-app/simpleApp.action

The extends Attribute [extends="struts-default"]

The **extends** attribute indicates the name of the parent package to inherit from. This attribute holds a package name whose components will be inherited by the current package that is being defined. This is very similar to the **extends** keyword in Java.

Working With Actions 75

> **HINT**
>
> The **struts-default** package declares a huge set of commonly needed Struts 2 components ranging from complete interceptor stacks to all the common result types. These can be inherited by simply extending it.

Extending the struts-default package helps a developer avoid a lot of manual labor. This is because extending this package brings a lot of components along with it. One such component is the default Interceptor Stack.

> **REMINDER**
>
> struts-default.xml [available in the distribution's main JAR file i.e. struts2-core.2.x.x.x.jar] holds the declarations of all the interceptors that the struts-default package brings in.

The abstract Attribute [abstract="true"]

The **abstract** attribute, if set to true, indicates that this package will only be used to define inheritable components, not actions.

In short, the abstract attribute is used to create a base package that can omit the action configuration.

<action>

The action maps an identifier to handle an action class. The action's name and framework use the mapping to determine how to process the request, when a request is matched.

The name Attribute [name="simpleApp"]

The action's **name** attribute indicates the name of the action within the Web application.

The action's name is concatenated with the package's namespace to come up with the URL of the request:
http://www.myserver.com/my-app/simpleApp.action

The class Attribute [class="com.book.myApp.simpleApp"]

The **class** attribute indicates which Java class will be instantiated for the Request.

The method Attribute [method="execute"]

This is an optional attribute. This indicates the method to be invoked on a Request.

REMINDER

> If this is un-specified, the filter assumes **execute()**.

\<result\>

Each action element can have **one or more** result elements.

Each result is a possible view that the action can launch.

The name Attribute [name="success"]

This is an optional attribute, which indicates the result name.

REMINDER

> If this is un-specified, the filter assumes **success** as the name.

The type Attribute [type="dispatcher"]

This is an optional attribute, which indicates the kind of result.

REMINDER

> If this is un-specified, the filter assumes dispatcher which forwards the Web browser to the View [JSP] specified.

\<include\>

\<include\> can be used to modularize a Struts 2 application. This tag allows including other configuration files. It is always a child to **\<struts\>**.

The file Attribute [file="guestbook-config.xml"]

This is the only attribute of \<include\>. It allows specifying the name of the file to be included. The file being included should have a structure identical to **struts.xml**.

Example

Solution:
```xml
<?xml version="1.0" encoding="UTF-8"?>
<!DOCTYPE struts PUBLIC '-//Apache Software Foundation//DTD Commons Validator Rules Configuration 2.3//EN' 'http://struts.apache.org/dtds/struts-2.3.dtd'>
<struts>
   <include file="guestbook-config.xml" />
   <include file="bookMaster-config.xml" />
   . . .
</struts>
```

Explanation:

Here, configurations for the guestbook as well as the bookMaster are defined using two different configuration files.

Getting Started With Actions

Now it's time to begin developing an Action. To understand Actions better, let's build a simple application [source code available on the Book's accompanying CDROM].

Application Requirements

Create a Guest Book application that provides an interface to accept visitor comments, as shown in diagram 7.1. These comments should be viewable by other Web site visitors.

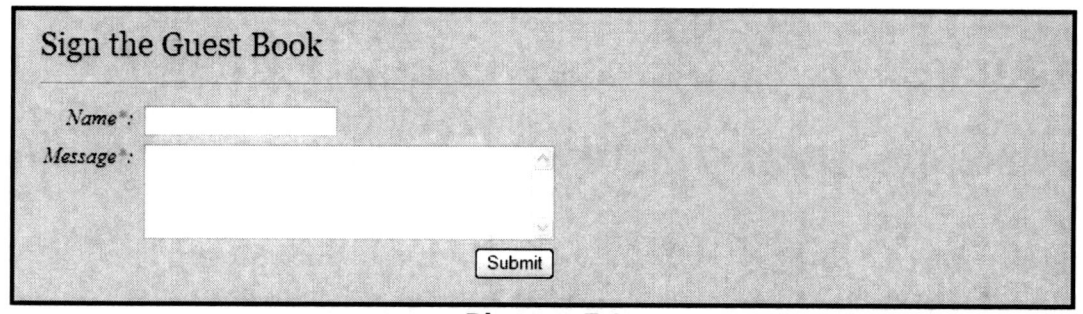

Diagram 7.1

Since this chapter focuses on the **Model** i.e. the Action class, let's build the action class to support guestbook application. In the chapters that follow, the other components that make up the entire guestbook application will be built.

After all the components are in place, the visitors should be able to view the existing guestbook entries and from the view using a link add new entries to the guestbook, as shown in diagram 7.2.

```
View the Guest Book                              Click here to sign the guestbook.

On 12/1/08,
Sharanam Shah: This is the first message.

On 12/1/08,
Mahesh: Testing this book.
```

Diagram 7.2

After the visitor adds an entry in the guestbook, the entry will be added to the guestbook and the visitor will be taken back to the page where such entries can be viewed.

Based on the above requirements, **Action class** will therefore be responsible for the following:
- Displaying existing entries that are available in the guestbook
- Accepting new entries to the guestbook

Technically, the following two kinds of files will be created to achieve this:
- A Bean class i.e. GuestBook.java
- An Action class i.e. GuestBookAction.java

A Bean Class

To hold the captured data in a structured manner a bean class is required.

The primary purpose of having such a class is to hold individual guestbook entry as and when they are captured.

Open GuestBook application in the NetBeans IDE that was created earlier in *Chapter 06: Getting Started*.

Let's create a Bean class i.e. GuestBook.java using NetBeans IDE.

Right click **GuestBook** project, select New → **Java Class...**.

New Java Class dialog box appears.

Enter **Class Name** as **GuestBook** and **Package** as **com.sharanamvaishali.myApp.domain** and click **Finish**.

Now the bean class named GuestBook.java is created in the **com.sharanamvaishali.myApp.domain** package.

Key in the following code spec in **GuestBook.java**:

```
1   package com.sharanamvaishali.myApp.domain;
2
3   public class GuestBook {
4       private String guest;
5       private String message;
6       private String when;
7
8       public String getGuest() {
9           return guest;
10      }
11      public void setGuest(String guest) {
12          this.guest = guest;
13      }
14
15      public String getMessage() {
16          return message;
17      }
18      public void setMessage(String message) {
19          this.message = message;
20      }
21
22      public String getWhen() {
23          return when;
24      }
25      public void setWhen(String when) {
26          this.when = when;
27      }
28  }
```

Explanation:

GuestBook is a simple bean class that holds individual records.

Package

A package named **com.sharanamvaishali.myApp.domain** is declared. This creates directory **com\sharanamvaishali\myApp\domain** under the <Web Application>\build\web\WEB-INF\classes\ and **GuestBook.class** is placed in the **domain** directory when deployed.

Variables

The following variables are declared to collect data from the JSP file [where the user enters data]:

Property Name	To Store
guest	Visitor's Name.
message	Message that the visitor enters.
when	The date/time on which the message was entered.

Setter/Getter Methods

Variables in a JavaBean normally have two methods associated with each variable i.e. a **get** method and a **set** method.

The **get method or getter** retrieves the value stored in the variable. The **set method or setter** sets the value for the variable. Both the set and the get methods are **public**.

While developing beans for processing form data, follow a common design pattern by matching the names of the bean properties with the names of the form input fields. Also the corresponding getter or setter method needs to be defined for each property within the bean.

For example, within GuestBook.java, the property guest, the accessor methods getGuest() and setGuest() correspond to the form input element named guest in guestBookEntry.jsp:

1. **GuestBook.java:**

```java
private String guest;
public String getGuest() {
   return guest;
}
public void setGuest(String guest) {
   this.guest = guest;
}
```

2. **guestBookEntry.jsp:**

```
<s:textfield required="true" key="Your Name" name="guest" />
```

Action Class

The visitor adds an entry using the data entry form.

Action class will do the following:

1. **Spawn** an object of the bean class

Working With Actions

2. Pass the captured values to the spawned object of the bean class
3. Store the data in a **Static ArrayList** by adding the populated object of the bean class in that ArrayList

Using NetBeans create one more class called GuestBookAction.java using the same steps as shown earlier.

Key in the following code spec in **GuestBookAction.java**:

```
1  package com.sharanamvaishali.myApp.action;
2
3  import com.opensymphony.xwork2.ActionSupport;
4  import com.sharanamvaishali.myApp.domain.GuestBook;
5  import java.text.DateFormat;
6  import java.text.SimpleDateFormat;
7  import java.util.ArrayList;
8  import java.util.Date;
9
10 public class GuestBookAction extends ActionSupport {
11     private static final long serialVersionUID = -8577843349235520003L;
12     DateFormat dateFormat = new SimpleDateFormat("yyyy/MM/dd");
13     Date date = new Date();
14     private String guest;
15     private String message;
16     private String when = (dateFormat.format(date)).toString();
17     private static ArrayList<GuestBook> messages = new ArrayList<GuestBook>();
18
19     @Override
20     public String execute() {
21        GuestBook guestBookMsgs = new GuestBook();
22        guestBookMsgs.setGuest(guest);
23        guestBookMsgs.setMessage(message);
24        guestBookMsgs.setWhen(when);
25        messages.add(guestBookMsgs);
26        return SUCCESS;
27     }
28
29     public String getGuest() {
30        return guest;
31     }
32     public void setGuest(String guest) {
33        this.guest = guest;
34     }
35
36     public String getMessage() {
37        return message;
38     }
39     public void setMessage(String message) {
40        this.message = message;
41     }
42
```

Struts 2 For Beginners

```
43    public String getWhen() {
44        return when;
45    }
46    public void setWhen(String when) {
47        this.when = when;
48    }
49
50    public ArrayList<GuestBook> getMessages() {
51        return messages;
52    }
53    public void setMessages(ArrayList<GuestBook> messages) {
54        GuestBookAction.messages = messages;
55    }
56 }
```

Explanation:

GuestBookAction is still a POJO, which extends ActionSupport class.

GuestBookAction uses basic Java techniques that allow tracking the messages as they come in. GuestBookAction is the business object. It can accept, store [in memory] and retrieve messages.

An object of GuestBook is created in the action class to hold an individual record. These individual records are then added to the messages ArrayList which is used to display these messages on demand.

Imports

The following interfaces/classes are included using the import statement:

com.opensymphony.xwork2.ActionSupport

ActionSupport is a convenience class that provides default implementations of Action interface and several other useful interfaces and helps add a few useful constants such as SUCCESS, INPUT, LOGIN and ERROR. These are string constants that can be utilized to return values to the framework to decide the view as:

return SUCCESS;

HINT

☺ The framework does not make it mandatory to use this class, but it is a good idea to use it at least when learning the framework.

Working With Actions

java.text.DateFormat

DateFormat is an abstract class for date/time formatting subclasses which formats and parses dates or time in a language-independent manner.

java.text.SimpleDateFormat

SimpleDateFormat is a concrete class for formatting and parsing dates in a locale-sensitive manner. It allows for formatting [date → text], parsing [text → date] and normalization.

java.util.ArrayList

ArrayList is a resizable-array implementation of **List** interface. ArrayList implements all optional list operations and permits all elements including null.

In addition to implementing List interface, this class provides methods to manipulate the size of the array that is used internally to store the list.

HINT

ArrayList is roughly equivalent to Vector [is deprecated], except that it is unsynchronized.

java.util.Date

Date is a wrapper for a date. This class allows manipulating dates in a system independent way.

Date Format

The current date is formatted according to yyyy/MM/dd, which is later converted to String data type.

static Modifier

Java's **static** modifier creates a class-level variable, so that no matter how many GuestBooks are instantiated, there will be only one **messages**, which is shared amongst all the instantiated GuestBooks. Even when there are no instantiated GuestBooks, **messages** will remain intact.

execute()

@Override indicates that a method declaration is intended to override a method declaration in a superclass. If a method is annotated with '@' annotation type but does not override a superclass method, then compilers are required to generate an error message.

execute() is declared, which implements the logic of the action.

Inside execute() the name of the guest, its message and the date of capture is added to ArrayList messages by calling ArrayList's add().

Actions must return a string that map to one of the result components available for rendering the view for that action.

The value that is returned as the control string must match the name of the desired result in the configuration file i.e. struts.xml.

In the action class code spec, the action returns the string **SUCCESS**. In struts.xml, **SUCCESS** is the name of the one of the result components.

This completes the Action component for Guestbook application. As indicated earlier, the other components will be created in the chapters that follow.

Let's move on to the View layer and start exploring the rich options that the framework offers for rendering result pages. The next chapter heads towards the **Result** component of the framework and describes how data is pulled from the **Model** [using Struts 2 tag libraries] and rendered in the **View**.

Chapter 8

SECTION III: GETTING STARTED WITH STRUTS 2

Building View

The last chapter took care of building **Actions** that hold the business logic. This chapter focuses on building the View layer. The most common technologies for the View layer are JSP, Velocity and FreeMarker. This book focuses on using JSP as the view technology of choice.

How Does View Come Into Picture?

The method of the action class that processes the request returns a **string** as the outcome. This string is then mapped to an implementation of Result interface.

Result interface either creates output or dispatches to another resource, like a server side page, to create the output based on the result type.

Each action can have one or more results, mapped to whatever result types are needed.

HINT

Regardless of the type of result being generated, the action only needs to return a string. The action does not need to know how the response is being handled.

Result Types And The Result

View is the resulting information that is sent back to the user after an action has been processed.

To build a view, Struts 2 provides the result type and the result itself.

Result Type provides the implementation details for the type of information that is returned to the user. Result types are usually preconfigured in Struts 2 with the default result type as **dispatcher** which uses a JSP to render the response to the user.

Struts 2 provides several Result types however the following are the most common ones:
- dispatcher
- redirect
- redirectAction

After a **result type** is defined, it can be used many times by different action results.

dispatcher

This is the most common and the **default** result type. It is used to render a JSP page as the result of the action.

This means a request is received, action processes the request and hands over to a Result that writes the response back to the user.

In most of the examples in this book, dispatcher will be used as the result type.

Technically, a dispatcher allows one Servlet to hand **processing** over to another resource of the same Web application. This means that all the data from the first resource is available to the second resource via both the Servlet API and the Struts 2 ActionContext.

Example

Solution:
```
<action name="ShowMail" class="myApp.ShowMail">
   <result type="dispatcher">/myWebApp/showApp.jsp</result>
</action>
```
OR
```
<action name="ShowMail" class="myApp.ShowMail">
   <result>/myWebApp/showApp.jsp</result>
</action>
```

The default result type being dispatcher, it need not be specified as the result **type**.

It is also possible to parameterize the dispatcher result type, but this is rarely used.

dispatcher accepts the following **two** parameters:

location

This is the first parameter which indicates the actual location of the Servlet resource to which the dispatch is being done.

parse

This is the second parameter which determines whether the location string will be parsed for OGNL expressions. The parse parameter is set to **true** by default.

Example

The earlier code spec, if re-written with parameters will look like:

```
<action name="ShowMail" class="myApp.ShowMail">
   <result type="dispatcher">
      <param name="location">/myWebApp/showApp.jsp</param>
      <param name="parse">true</param>
   </result>
</action>
```

The location parameter is the default parameter of <result> which can be passed as the text content to <result>.

Embedding OGNL

If the **parse** parameter is set to **true** [which by default is], an OGNL expression can be used in the **location** parameter value in order to pass some data forward to the second resource.

Example

The following code spec shows how a value is pulled from the Value Stack, at the runtime, and passed as a query string parameter to the URL:

```
<action name="ShowMail" class="myApp.ShowMail">
   <result>/myWebApp/showApp.jsp?userName=${username}</result>
</action>
```

redirect

A redirect allows handing over **control** to another resource. It considers the current request finished and issues an HTTP redirect response that informs the Web browser to point to a new location.

This results in the form of a new request.

HINT

☺ If it is required to carry data over to the second resource, use dispatcher.

A redirect is useful when it is required to change the URL that is shown in the Web browser. When a redirect is issued, the Web browser handles the response by making a new request to the URL given in the redirect.

Example

Solution:

```
<action name="ShowMail" class="myApp.ShowMail">
   <result type='redirect'>http://www.hotmail.com</result>
</action>
```

To redirect to another resource in the Web application, specify a full or relative URL.

redirect also can be **parameterized**, using the same **two** parameters i.e. **location** and **parse**.

These are the same parameters that are supported by **dispatcher**.

Building View

Redirect accepts the following **two** parameters:

location

This is the first parameter which indicates the actual location of the Servlet resource to which the dispatch is being done.

parse

This is the second parameter which determines whether the location string will be parsed for OGNL expressions. The parse parameter is set to **true** by default.

Embedding OGNL

If the **parse** parameter is set to **true** [which by default is], an OGNL expression can be used in the **location** parameter value in order to pass some data forward to the second resource.

Example

The following code spec shows how a value is pulled from the Value Stack, at the runtime and passed as a query string parameter to the URL:

```
<action name="ShowMail" class="myApp.ShowMail">
   <result type='redirect'>
      http://www.myserver.com/myWebApp/showApp.jsp?userName=${username}
   </result>
</action>
```

redirectAction

redirectAction does the same thing as redirect, with one important difference.

redirectAction accepts logical action names that are defined in the configuration. This means a URL is not required instead the action name along with namespaces can be specified.

Example

Solution:
```
<action name="Login" class="myApp.Login">
   <result type="redirectAction">
      <param name="actionName">LoginAction</param>
      <param name="namespace">/myApp/app</param>
   </result>
</action>
```

The same if written using redirect would look like:

```
<action name="Login" class="myApp.Login">
   <result type="redirect">/myApp/app/Login.action</result>
</action>
```

redirectAction accepts the following **two** parameters:

actionName

This is the default parameter which provides the name of the action class, to which the URL is redirected.

namespace

This is the second parameter which provides the namespace in which the action class to which the URL directed is present.

Additional parameters can also be passed using <param>.

Example

Solution:

```
<action name="Login" class="myApp.Login">
   <result type="redirectAction">
      <param name="actionName">LoginAction</param>
      <param name="namespace">/myApp/app</param>
      <param name="mode">backend</param>
      <param name="showPerPage">10</param>
   </result>
</action>
```

<param> can be passed by giving it a **name** and **value** as desired. These arbitrary name-value pairs are appended as query string parameters to the generated URL.

Embedding OGNL

An OGNL expression can also be used in the parameter value in order to pass some data forward to the second resource.

Building View

Example

The following code spec shows how a value is pulled from the Value Stack, at the runtime, and passed as a query string parameter to the URL:

```
<action name="Login" class="myApp.Login">
   <result type="redirectAction">
      <param name="actionName">LoginAction</param>
      <param name="namespace">/myApp/app</param>
      <param name="mode">backend</param>
      <param name="showPerPage">=${perpagevalue}</param>
   </result>
</action>
```

Tag Libraries

To build the View Layer using JSP, **Tag Libraries** are used. In Struts 2, tag libraries are generally used to define a feature exclusive to JSP that provide reusability.

Tag libraries allow picking up dynamic information from the Actions to be rendered to display at runtime. These tags render dynamic content into HTML so that it can be presented by a standard Web browser.

A typical Request workflow would be:

1. A Web browser makes a request
2. The framework looks at the request and determines the appropriate Action
3. The framework automatically applies common functionality to the request such as property population, validation, authorization, file uploading and so on
4. The Action method executes and does what its suppose to [usually storing and/or retrieving information from a database]
5. The Result either renders the output [images, PDF, JSON] or dispatches to another resource, such as JavaServer Page, to complete the response
6. JSP utilizes the Tags to output dynamic data to the Web browser

This is where the tag library comes into picture.

TagLib

To make the tags available to a JSP file import the tag library as:

```
<%@ taglib prefix="s" uri="/struts-tags" %>
```

The **taglib** directive <u>identifies the URI defined</u> and <u>states that all tags should be prefixed with the string [s]</u>.

Kind Of Tags

Struts 2 Tags can be divided as follows:
- Generic Tags
- UI Tags

Generic Tags

Generic tags are used to control the execution flow when the pages are rendered.

Generic tags are also used for data extraction.

Data Tags

Data tags are used for data manipulation or creation such as bean, push and i18n.

Data tags allow retrieving data out of the Value Stack or place variables and objects onto the Value Stack.

Following are the types of Data tags:

The action Tag

The **action tag** allows invoking another action from the view layer [JSP page]. This is achieved by specifying the action name and an optional namespace in the action tag.

This tag is useful for creating simple reusable components without having to add scriptlets to the JSP pages.

The following table provides the attributes of the action tag:

Attributes	Description
id	It is used for referencing element.
name	It is the name of the action to be executed.
executeResult	Is the most important attribute. It is the used to state whether the result of the action should be executed or rendered.
namespace	It is the namespace for action to call.

Building View

Attributes	Description
flush	It is used to state whether the writer should be flushed upon end of the action component tag.
var	It is the reference name of the action bean for use later in the page.
ignoreContextParams	It is used to indicate whether the request parameters are to be included when an action is invoked.

Example

Solution:

```
<h3>The following books were deleted:</h3>
<s:action name="deleteBookAction" executeResult="true" />
```

Explanation:

The Action named **deleteBookAction** is invoked directly. The Action will execute and return the result for inclusion in the current page.

The property Tag

The property tag allows writing a property value into the rendering HTML tags.

The properties retrieved are usually stored in Value Stack or in some other object in ActionContext.

Since these properties could be of any Java data type, they will be converted to strings prior rendering in the result page. This conversion is handled by the framework's type converters.

The following table provides the attributes of the property tag:

Attributes	Description
id	It is used for referencing element.
value	It is the value to be displayed on the page.
default	It is the value which will be displayed if the value attribute is not stated.
escape	It is used to indicate whether the HTML will be escaped.

Example

Solution:

```
Welcome, <s:property value="user.username"/>!
```

Output:

```
Welcome, Sharanam!
```

Explanation:

Here, the **username** property holds **Sharanam**. When the property tag pulls the property out to render, it is converted to a string based with the help of built-in type converters. Even though, this property is a Java String, it must be formally converted to a text string in order for it to render.

Example

Solution:
Welcome, <s:property value="user.username" default="Guest" />!

Output:

```
Welcome, Guest!
```

Explanation:

Here, if the **username** property does not hold a value, the default value is used.

The bean Tag

The **bean** tag is used to instantiate a class that confirms to the JavaBeans specification which means it should have a zero-argument constructor and JavaBeans properties for instance fields that need to be initialized using the **param** tags.

With the help of the bean tag, an instance of an object can be created. Then the instance of an object can be:

❑ Either pushed onto the Value Stack

OR

❑ A top level reference can be set to the object in ActionContext

By default, the instance of the object [or the bean] will be on the Value Stack for the execution of all the tags that occur in between the opening and closing tags of the bean tag.

The following table provides the attributes of the bean tag:

Attributes	Description
id	It is used for referencing element.
name	It is the class name of the bean to be instantiated.

Building View

Attributes	Description
var	It is the variable name used if the bean outside the scope of the closing bean tag needs to be referenced.

Example

Solution:
```
<s:bean name="myApp.book.deleteBookAction" id="deleteBook">
   <s:param name="BookNo" value="1" />
   The book <s:property value="getBookName()" /> is deleted.
</s:bean>
```

Explanation:

The bean tag's **name** attribute points to the class that should be instantiated. The **id** attribute specifies the reference name i.e. **deleteBook**. A bean called **deleteBookAction** is instantiated and passed **BookNo** as the **parameter** which indicates the book to be deleted. This parameter is automatically received by the bean as long as the bean implements a JavaBeans property that matches the name of the parameter.

The deleteBookAction bean is pushed onto the Value Stack. This means that its accessor method can be called with the property tag and retrieve their values.

Since the bean object is placed on the Value Stack, its properties and methods can be referred **directly**. This makes the code spec concise.

The bean is automatically popped from the Value Stack at the close tag.

The book <s:property value="getBookName()" /> is deleted.

Here, an **OGNL** method invocation syntax, is used to retrieve the book name that was deleted using **getBookName()**.

Example

Solution:
```
<s:bean name="myApp.book.deleteBookAction" var="deleteBook">
   <s:param name="BookNo" value="1" />
</s:bean>
<h3>The book <s:property value="#deleteBook.getBookName()" /> is deleted.</h3>
```

Explanation:

The **var** attribute specifies the reference name under which the bean will be stored in ActionContext.

In this case, it is called deleteBook which is referred in the property tag using appropriate OGNL.

Since the bean is in ActionContext, rather than on the Value Stack, the # operator needs to be used, resulting in the OGNL expression **#deleteBook**.

The set Tag

The **set** tag allows evaluating an expression in the value stack and assigning a value to a variable in a specified scope.

The following are the scopes, which can be specified in the set tag:
- application
- session
- request
- page
- action [the default value]

The set tag is useful when a variable is assigned to a complex expression. The same variable is referenced each time whenever the complex expression is needed. This is useful:
- When a complex expression takes time [performance improvement]

OR
- Is difficult to read [code readability improvement]

The following table provides the attributes of the set tag:

Attributes	Description
id	It is used for referencing element.
name	It is the reference name of the new variable set in the specified scope.
value	It is the expression of the value to be set.
scope	It is the scope in which to assign the variable.

Building View

Example

Solution:
```
<s:set name="firstName" value="user.firstName"/>
   Welcome, <s:property value="#firstName" />!.
```

Explanation:

The set tag sets the value from the user.firstName expression to the new reference specified by the name attribute.

Since the scope is not specified, the new firstName reference exists in the default **action** scope.

Example

Solution:
```
<s:set name="firstName" scope="application" value="user.firstName"/>
   Welcome, <s:property value="#application['firstName']" />!.
```

Explanation:

Here, the data persist across the lifetime of the application by changing to application scope.

The include Tag

The **include** tag is used to include the Servlet or JSP page's result to the current page. It also allows passing the request parameters to the included resource.

This means the output of another Web resource can be included in the currently rendering page using this tag.

The following table provides the attributes of the include tag:

Attributes	Description
value	It is the name of the page, action, servlet or other Web resources.

Example

Solution:
```
<s:include value="showUpdatedBooks.jsp"/>
```

The url Tag

When building Web application, URL management plays a crucial part.

This tag:

- Renders relative or absolute URLs
- Handles parameters
- Encodes the URL so that it can be used with Web browsers that do not have cookies enabled

The following table provides the attributes of the url tag:

Attributes	Description
id	It is used for referencing element.
value	It is the base URL.
action	It is the action name as configured in the declarative architecture.
anchor	It is the anchor for the URL.
var	It is used to not write the URL but save the URL in the action context for future use.
encode	It is used to add the session ID if cookies are not enabled.
includeParams	It has the values **none**, **get** [default value] and **all**.
includeContext	It is used to state whether the actual context should be included in the URL.
method	It is the method of the Action to be used.
namespace	It is the namespace to be used.
scheme	It allows specifying the protocol [Default is the current scheme i.e. HTTP or HTTPS].

Example

Solution:
```
<s:url action="Login.action" var="loginURL">
    <s:param name="mode" value="backend"/>
</s:url>
<a href='<s:property value="#loginURL" />'>Login to Backend</a>
```

Explanation:

The url tag is used along with its param tags to embed the URL in the anchor tag.

The **param** tag specifies the query string parameters to be added to the generated URL.

`<s:param name="mode" value="backend"/>`

Building View

The anchor tag thus converts to:

```
<a href='/myApp/Login.action?mode=backend'>Login to Backend</a>
```

The URL is pulled from ActionContext with a property tag and some OGNL.

```
<s:property value="#loginURL" />
```

This is very useful when the same URL is required in more than one place on the same page.

The text Tag

Many Web applications need to use multiple languages which is possible using internationalization or **i18n**.

The **text** tag allows rendering an i18n [short for **Internationalization**, as there are 18 letters the I and N in the word] text message. It allows displaying language specific text such as English or France based on a key lookup into a set of text resources.

This tag retrieves a message value from ResourceBundles exposed through the framework's own internationalization mechanisms. It takes a name attribute that specifies the key under which the message retrieval should occur. The framework's default Locale determination will determine the Locale under which the key will be resolved.

The message must be in a resource bundle with the same name as the action that it is associated with. In practice this means that a properties file should be created in the same package as the Java class with the same name as the class, but with **.properties extension**.

If the named message is not found, then the body of the tag will be used as the default message. If no body is used, then the name of the message will be used.

The following table provides the attributes of the text tag:

Attributes	Description
id	It is used for referencing element.
name	It is the name of the resource property to fetch.
var	It is used to state whether to store the text in the action context under this name.

The i18n Tag

The **i18n** tag retrieves a resource bundle and places it on the value stack.

This allows the text tag to access messages from any bundle and not just the bundle associated with the current action.

The following table provides the attributes of the i18n tag:

Attributes	Description
id	It is used for referencing element.
name	It is the name of the resource bundle.

Example

Solution:
```
<s:i18n name="myApp.myResourceBundle_french">
    <s:text name="Welcome" var="translatedWord"/>
</s:i18n>
<s:property value="#translatedWord"/>, <s:property value="user.username"/>!
```

Explanation:
The i18n tag simply specifies the resource bundle to be used. The bundle is only used during the body of the tag.

var="translatedWord"

This allows persisting the value from the bundle and set the same to **ActionContext** as a named reference.

`<s:text name="Welcome" var="translatedWord"/>`

The text tag stores the message associated with the key Welcome under the reference name translatedWord.

Output:
```
Bienvenue, Sharanam!
```

The param Tag

The **param** tag is already used throughout this chapter. It allows parameterizing other tags.

The following table provides the attributes of the param tag:

Attributes	Description
id	It is used for referencing element.
name	It is the name parameter to be set.
value	It is the value expression of the parameter set.

When the param tag is declared, the value can be defined in either a <u>value attribute</u> or <u>as text between the start and end tag</u>.

Building View

> *Example*

Solution:

`<s:param name="color">Red</s:param>`

Explanation:

The value is evaluated to the stack as a String object.

Alternatively, the above code spec can be written as:

`<s:param name="color" name="Red" />`

Explanation:

The value is evaluated to the stack as an Object object.

Control Tags

A lot of Web pages today are dynamic. They are built on the fly. To have such dynamism, it is important to learn manipulating, navigating over and displaying data using a set of Control Tags that make it easy to control the flow of page execution.

Control Tags are used for controlling the page execution flow using if, else and iterator.

The iterator Tag

The **iterator** tag is used to iterate over a value. In other words, the iterator tag allows looping over collections of objects.

The iterator tag can iterate over any:

- Collections
- Maps
- Enumerations
- Iterators
- Arrays

The following table provides the attributes of the iterator tag:

Attributes	Description
id	It is used for referencing element.
value	It is the object to be iterated.

Attributes	Description
status	It is used to state whether an instance of IteratorStatus needs to be pushed into the stack on each iteration.

Example

Solution:

```
<s:iterator status="num" value="{1,2,3,4,5}" >
   <s:property value="#num.index" />
   <s:property value="top" />
</s:iterator>
```

Explanation:

In the above code spec, the iterator tag loops five times. Property **#num.index** grabs the index i.e. starts loop from 0. Property **top** grabs the top of the stack which is the current iteration value i.e. 0, 1, . . . ,5.

Example

Solution:

```
<s:iterator value="messages" status="stats">
   <tr>
     <td>
        <s:property value="#stats.count" />.<br />
        On <s:property value="when"/>,<br />
        <b><s:property value="guest"/></b>
        <s:property value="message"/>
        <br /><br />
     </td>
   </tr>
</s:iterator>
```

Explanation:

In the above code spec, the action object exposes a set of messages and the iterator tag iterates over those messages available in the collection object called **messages**.

Using the property tag the values when, guest and message are referenced and displayed with appropriate HTML formatting.

The iterator also declares an IteratorStatus object by specifying the status attribute.

Whatever name is given to this attribute will be the key for retrieving the iterator status object from ActionContext, with an OGNL expression such as #stats.

In this case, the iterator status's **count** property is used to fetch a sequential list of messages.

REMINDER

The **status** attribute provides **status information** about the current iteration such as the size, current index and whether the current object is in the even or odd index in the list.

Output:
1.
On 03rd December 2008,
Sharanam: Hi, This is my first message in this guestbook!

2.
On 04th December 2008,
Vaishali: Hi, This is my also first message in this guestbook!

3.
On 05th December 2008,
Sharanam: Hi, This is my second message in this guestbook!

The if, elseIf And else Tags

These tags allows performing basic condition flow. The if tag is used to check the condition and execute some code spec defined in its body, when the condition is tested to be true.

The if tag body is executed when the test expression returns true. Sometimes, some other logic needs to be executed when the test expression given in the if tag returns false. In such situation, if-else construct is used i.e. the if tag and the else tag.

The if tag is used to check a single condition. Sometimes a number of possible conditions needs to be tested. In such situation, if-elseif-else construct is used i.e. the if tag, the elseif tag and the else tag

The flow of the **if, elseIf and else tags** are:

- If the condition in the if tag evaluates to **true**, then only this tag is evaluated and others are discarded
- If the condition in the if tag evaluates to **false** and the elseif tag evaluates to **true**, then the body of the elseif tag is processed
- If the condition in the if tag and the elseif tags evaluates to **false**, then only the else tag is processed

The following table provides the attributes of the if, elseIf and else tags:

Attributes	Description
id	It is used for referencing element.
test	It is the expression to determine if the body of tag is to be displayed.

Example

Solution:
```
<s:set name="userName" value="%{'admin'}"/>
<s:if test="%{#userName=='admin'}">
   <div>Welcome, <s:property value="%{#userName}" />!</div>
</s:if>
<s:elseif test="%{#userName=='sharanam'}">
   <div>Hello, <s:property value="%{#userName}" /></div>
</s:elseif>
<s:else>
   <div>The username is invalid.</div>
</s:else>
```

Explanation:

Here, using this tag, a check is made to determine if the username holds the value **admin** or **sharanam**. If it holds, an appropriate Welcome message is displayed, otherwise an error message is displayed.

UI Tags

UI tags are mainly designed to use the data from the Action/Value Stack or from Data tags. In short, the UI tags are used to display the data in the rich and reusable HTML.

Tags, templates and **themes** work together to provide feature-rich, flexible, extensible UI components.

Struts 2 UI tags are backed with templates that do the actual rendering of HTML.

Template is a chunk of code that is used in HTML pages.

Templates group together to form the themes. The following are the themes used in UI tags:

- **simple:** Renders basic HTML element
- **xhtml:** Renders the UI tags using a table to provide a layout. It is the default theme
- **css_xhtml:** Renders the UI tags using pure CSS to provide a layout
- **ajax:** Provides rich AJAX components. It is used to build AJAX based Web applications

Form UI Tags

The form UI tags are used to display the data in a simple and reusable format.

The form UI tags are used to create a basic HTML form such as the login form or the registration form.

Each UI tag generates the actual HTML markup. This markup defines the corresponding HTML element and frequently some additional layout markup.

For example, Struts 2 textfield UI tag creates an HTML text input element.

Example

A UI Tag:

```
1  <s:form action="GuestBookSuccess">
2      <s:textfield label="Name" name="guest" />
3      <s:textarea rows="4" cols="36" label="Message" name="message" />
4      <s:submit />
5  </s:form>
```

Generates the following HTML markups:

```
1  <form id="GuestBookSuccess" name="GuestBookSuccess">
2      <table class="wwFormTable">
3          <tr>
4              <td class="tdLabel">
5                  <label for="GuestBookSuccess_guest" class="label">Name:</label>
6              </td>
7              <td>
8                  <input type="text" name="guest" value="" id="GuestBookSuccess_guest"/>
9              </td>
10         </tr>
11
12         <tr>
13             <td class="tdLabel">
14                 <label for="GuestBookSuccess_message" class="label">Message:</label>
15             </td>
16             <td>
17                 <textarea name="message" cols="36" rows="4" id="GuestBookSuccess_message"></textarea>
18             </td>
19         </tr>
20
21         <tr>
22             <td colspan="2">
23                 <div align="right">
24                     <input type="submit" id="GuestBookSuccess_0" value="Submit"/>
25                 </div>
26             </td>
27         </tr>
28     </table>
29 </form>
```

The **TABLE** markup is produced by the **XHTML** theme, which is one of the themes that can be chosen to determine the layout style used when rendering the UI component.

In the above code spec, the textfield UI tag produced:

- A label tag
- An input tag

It uses an **id** attribute and sets its value by concatenating the enclosing form's name with the input field's name. It also adds some pre-defined class attributes for CSS control.

Once the HTML elements are in place, these form input fields are bound to the properties on the Value Stack. The name of a UI component is what binds the component to a Value Stack property.

During rendering, a UI tag pulls the value from the Value Stack, if it exists, to pre-populate the form. On submission, that same name is used to locate the target of the framework's automatic data transfer.

Now that the basics of UI tags are in place, let's begin exploring the different kinds of UI tags.

The following are the Form UI tags:

The head Tag

The head tag renders parts of the HEAD section of the HTML file. It generates links to CSS style sheets and JavaScript library files.

The head tag must be placed within the HTML head element.

The following table provides the attributes of the head tag:

Attributes	Description
theme	It is used to set the theme for rendering the elements.

Example

Solution:
```
1  <html>
2      <head>
3          <meta http-equiv="Content-Type" content="text/html; charset=ISO-8859-1">
4          <title>Guest Book</title>
5          <s:head theme="ajax" />
6      </head>
```

Generates the following HTML markups:
```
1  <!DOCTYPE html PUBLIC "-//W3C//DTD HTML 4.01 Transitional//EN" "http://www.w3.org/TR/html4/loose.dtd">
2
3  <html>
4      <head>
5          <meta http-equiv="Content-Type" content="text/html; charset=ISO-8859-1">
6          <title>Guest Book</title>
7          <link rel="stylesheet" href="/GuestBook/struts/xhtml/styles.css" type="text/css"/>
8          <script type="text/javascript">
9              // Dojo configuration
10             djConfig = {
11                 baseRelativePath: "/GuestBook/struts/dojo",
12                 isDebug: false,
13                 bindEncoding: "UTF-8",
```

Building View

```
14              debugAtAllCosts: true // not needed, but allows the Venkman debugger to work with the includes
15          };
16     </script>
17     <script type="text/javascript"
18             src="/GuestBook/struts/dojo/dojo.js"></script>
19     <script type="text/javascript"
20             src="/GuestBook/struts/simple/dojoRequire.js"></script><script type="text/javascript"
21             src="/GuestBook/struts/ajax/dojoRequire.js"></script>
22     <script type="text/javascript"
23             src="/GuestBook/struts/CommonFunctions.js"></script>
24
25  </head>
```

Explanation:

Here, HTML link elements that can reference CSS stylesheets, as well as script elements that can define JavaScript functions or reference files of such functions are placed. Since many of the UI tags come with rich functionality, the head tag links to commonly used JavaScript libraries that help implement that functionality.

The form Tag

The form tag acts as a container for all other Form UI tags and is the most important of all the other tags as it targets Struts 2 actions.

The form tag allows the form to be submitted without the page being refreshed. The results from the form can be inserted into any HTML element on the page.

The following table provides the attributes of the form tag:

Attributes	Description
action	It is the name of the action [without the *.action* extension] to which the current page is to be submitted.
enctype	It is the HTML Form element's ENCTYPE attribute.
method	It is the HTML Form element's METHOD attribute. The default method is post.
name	It is the name for the element.
namespace	It is the namespace of the action.
target	It is the HTML Form element's TARGET attribute.
validate	It is used to define the client side validation. It also works with Validation Framework.
windowState	It is used to define the state of window in which the page after form submission is displayed.

Example

Solution:

```
1  <s:form action="GuestBookSuccess">
2      <s:textfield label="Name" name="guest" />
3      <s:textarea rows="4" cols="36" label="Message" name="message" />
```

Struts 2 For Beginners

```
4       <s:submit />
5   </s:form>
```

Generates the following HTML markups:

```
48  <form namespace="/" id="GuestBookSuccess" name="GuestBookSuccess" onsubmit="return validateForm_GuestBookSuccess();"
        action="/GuestBook/GuestBookSuccess.action" method="post">
49      <table class="wwFormTable">
50          <tr>
51              <td class="tdLabel">
52                  <label for="GuestBookSuccess_guest" class="label">Name:</label>
53              </td>
54              <td>
55                  <input type="text" name="guest" value="" id="GuestBookSuccess_guest"/>
56              </td>
57          </tr>
58
59          <tr>
60              <td class="tdLabel">
61                  <label for="GuestBookSuccess_message" class="label">Message:</label>
62              </td>
63              <td>
64                  <textarea name="message" cols="16" rows="4" id="GuestBookSuccess_message"></textarea>
65              </td>
66          </tr>
67          <tr>
68              <td colspan="2">
69                  <div align="right">
70                      <input type="submit" id="GuestBookSuccess_0" value="Submit"/>
71                  </div>
72              </td>
73          </tr>
74      </table>
75  </form>
```

Explanation:

The action attribute holds the action name which is the logical name given to the action in struts.xml.

The form tag also creates values for several other attributes such as id and method attributes. The ID is unique and built on the name of the action itself.

The hidden Tag

Quite often, embedding hidden request parameters into a form without showing them is required. These values could either be set from the server or using some JavaScript functionality for holding intermediate calculations.

The hidden tag creates an INPUT field, which is hidden from the user.

The following table provides the attributes of the hidden tag:

Attributes	Description
id	It is used for referencing element.
name	It is the name for the element.
value	It is the value of the input element.

Example

Solution:

```
1   <s:form action="GuestBookSuccess" validate="true">
```

Building View

```
2      <s:hidden name="hidBookNo" id="hidBookNo" value="1"/>
3      <s:hidden name="hidSelDel" id="hidSelDel"/>
4      ...
5      <s:submit />
6  </s:form>
```

Generates the following HTML markups:

```
52 <form namespace="/" id="GuestBookSuccess" name="GuestBookSuccess" onsubmit="return validateForm_GuestBookSuccess();"
       action="/GuestBook/GuestBookSuccess.action" method="post">
53     <table class="wwFormTable">
54         <input type="hidden" name="hidBookNo" value="1" id="hidBookNo"/>
55         <input type="hidden" name="hidSelDel" value="" id="hidSelDel"/>
56         ...
57         <tr>
58             <td colspan="2">
59                 <div align="right">
60                     <input type="submit" id="GuestBookSuccess_0" value="Submit"/>
61                 </div>
62             </td>
63         </tr>
64     </table>
65 </form>
```

The label Tag

The label tag is used to display read-only data on a page.

The following table provides the attributes of the label tag:

Attributes	Description
id	It is used for referencing element.
name	It is the name for the element.
for	It is the HTML FOR attribute.

Example

Solution:

```
1  <s:form id="frmSearch" name="frmSearch" method="post">
2      <table border="0" cellpadding="0" cellspacing="0" width="100%">
3          <tr>
4              <td align="right" valign="middle" class="Arial13GrayB">
5                  <s:label theme="simple" id="ISBN" name="ISBN">ISBN: </s:label>
6              </td>
7          </tr>
8      </table>
9  </s:form>
```

Generates the following HTML markups:

```
1  <form id="frmSearch" name="frmSearch" onsubmit="return true;"
       action="/BookShop/manageBooks.jsp;jsessionid=53828F4C62FB1EA6D608CCAF24BJ1066" method="post">
2      <table border="0" cellpadding="0" cellspacing="0" width="100%">
3          <tr>
4              <td align="right" valign="middle" class="Arial13GrayB">
5                  ISBN: <label id="ISBN"></label>
6              </td>
7          </tr>
8      </table>
9  </form>
```

The textfield Tag

The textfield tag renders an HTML INPUT textbox field.

The following table provides the attributes of the textfield tag:

Attributes	Description
id	It is used for referencing element.
label	It is the string to be displayed as label with the element.
maxlength	It is the maximum length of the data entered by the user.
readonly	It is used to state whether the field is uneditable.
size	It is the size of the field.
name	It is the name of the element.
value	It is used to preset the value of the input element.

Example

Solution:
```
1  <s:form id="frmSearch" name="frmSearch" method="post">
2      <table border="0" cellpadding="0" cellspacing="0" width="100%">
3          <tr>
4              <td align="right" valign="middle" class="Arial13GrayB">
5                  <s:label theme="simple" id="ISBN" name="ISBN">ISBN: </s:label>
6              </td>
7              <td align="left" valign="top">
8                  <s:textfield theme="simple" id="ISBN" title="Enter the ISBN" size="20" value="" />
9              </td>
10         </tr>
11     </table>
12 </s:form>
```

Generates the following HTML markups:
```
1  <form id="frmSearch" name="frmSearch" onsubmit="return true;"
   action="/BookShop/manageBooks.jsp;jsessionid=53828F4C62FB1EA6D608CCAF24B31066" method="post">
2      <table border="0" cellpadding="0" cellspacing="0" width="100%">
3          <tr>
4              <td align="right" valign="middle" class="Arial13GrayB">
5                  ISBN: <label id="ISBN"></label>
6              </td>
7              <td align="left" valign="top">
8                  <input type="text" name="" size="20" value="" id="ISBN" title="Enter the ISBN"/>
9              </td>
10         </tr>
11     </table>
12 </form>
```

The textarea Tag

The textarea tag renders an HTML TEXTAREA field, which supports multiple lines.

The following table provides the attributes of the textarea tag:

Attributes	Description
id	It is used for referencing element.
label	It is the string to be displayed as label with the element.

Building View

Attributes	Description
readonly	It is used to state whether the field is uneditable.
name	It is the name of the element.
value	It is used to preset the value of the input element.
cols	It is the number of columns.
rows	It is the number of rows.
wrap	It is used to specify whether the text written in the textarea is to be wrapped.

Example

Solution:
```
1  <s:form action="insertBooks" method="post" name="frmBooks" >
2     <s:textarea id="BookSynopsis" theme="simple" name="BookSynopsis" title="Enter the synopsis"
       cols="80" rows="5"></s:textarea>
3  </s:form>
```

Generates the following HTML markups:
```
1  <form id="insertBooks" name="frmBooks" onsubmit="return true;"
   action="/BookShop/bookShop/insertBooks.action" method="post">
2     <textarea name="BookSynopsis" cols="80" rows="5" id="BookSynopsis" title="Enter the
       synopsis"></textarea>
3  </form>
```

The password Tag

The password tag renders an HTML INPUT textbox's password field.

The user when entering data cannot view the characters keyed in as the data in the form of * [asterix].

The following table provides the attributes of the password tag:

Attributes	Description
id	It is used for referencing element.
label	It is the string to be displayed as label with the element.
maxlength	It is the maximum length of the data entered by the user.
readonly	It is used to state whether the field is uneditable.
name	It is the name of the element.
value	It is used to preset the value of the input element.
size	It is the size of the field.
showPassword	It is used to state whether to show the value in the field.

Example

Solution:

```
1  <s:form id="frmLogin" name="frmLogin" method="post" action="loginAction">
2      <s:password maxLength="8" name="password" title="Enter Password" theme="simple" />
3  </s:form>
```

Generates the following HTML markups:

```
1  <form id="frmLogin" name="frmLogin" onsubmit="return true;" action="/BookShop/loginAction.action" method="post">
2      <input type="password" name="password" maxlength="8" id="frmLogin_password" title="Enter Password"/>
3  </form>
```

The file Tag

The file tag renders an HTML INPUT file field. The user can upload any file such as the JPEG, GIF, PDF, TEXT and so on. This tag prompts the user to choose any file location.

The following table provides the attributes of the file tag:

Attributes	Description
id	It is used for referencing element.
accept	It is the HTML ACCEPT attribute, which indicates the accepted file mime types.
name	It is the name of the element.
value	It is used to preset the value of the input element.
size	It is the size of the field.

Example

Solution:

```
1  <s:form action="insertBooks" method="post" name="frmBooks" >
2      <s:file accept="gif|jpg" theme="simple" id="CoverPage" name="CoverPage" title="Upload the cover page of the book"/>
3  </s:form>
```

Generates the following HTML markups:

```
1  <form id="insertBooks" name="frmBooks" onsubmit="return true;" action="/BookShop/bookShop/insertBooks.action" method="post">
2      <input type="file" name="CoverPage" value="" accept="gif|jpg" id="CoverPage" title="Upload the cover page of the book"/>
3  </form>
```

The checkbox Tag

The checkbox tag renders a checkbox field on the page. The checkbox tag is not similar to the HTML INPUT field of type checkbox, but is specialized for Boolean values only.

Building View 113

The following table provides the attributes of the checkbox tag:

Attributes	Description
id	It is used for referencing element.
fieldvalue	It is the actual HTML VALUE attribute on rendered html element.
name	It is the name of the element.
value	It is used to preset the value of the input element.

Example

Solution:

```
1  <s:form id="frmLogin" name="frmLogin" method="post" action="loginAction">
2    <s:checkbox theme="simple" cssClass="logInCheck" name="RememberMe" value="1" />Remember Password
3  </s:form>
```

Generates the following HTML markups:

```
1  <form id="frmLogin" name="frmLogin" onsubmit="return true;" action="/BookShop/loginAction.action" method="post">
2    <input type="checkbox" name="RememberMe" value="true" checked="checked" id="frmLogin_RememberMe" class="logInCheck"/><input type="hidden" name="__checkbox_RememberMe" value="true" />Remember Password
3  </form>
```

The select Tag

The select tag creates a list of options to select from. It renders the HTML INPUT field of type select.

The following table provides the attributes of the select tag:

Attributes	Description
id	It is used for referencing element.
name	It is the name of the element.
headerKey	It is the key for first item in the list.
headerValue	It is the value expression for the first item in the list.
multiple	It allows users to select more than one value.
emptyOption	It is used to state whether or not to add an empty option after the header option.
size	It is the size of the select box.
list	It is used to set an Iterable source to populate from.
listValue	It is the property of list objects to retrieve the field content from.
listKey	It is the property of list objects to retrieve the field value from.

Struts 2 For Beginners

> *Example*

Solution:

```
1  <s:form id="frmHome" name="frmHome">
2    <s:select label="Select the author name(s)" name="authorName" emptyOption="true" list="{'Sharanam Shah', 'Vaishali Shah', 'Stuti Shah'}"/>
3  </s:form>
```

Generates the following HTML markups:

```
1  <form id="frmHome" name="frmHome" onsubmit="return true;"
      action="/;jsessionid=71F369396CC004DFEFBA82E10E281F79" method="post">
2    <table class="wwFormTable">
3      <tr>
4        <td class="tdLabel">
5          <label for="frmHome_authorName" class="label">Select the author name(s):</label>
6        </td>
7        <td>
8          <select name="authorName" id="frmHome_authorName">
9            <option value=""></option>
10           <option value="Sharanam Shah">Sharanam Shah</option>
11           <option value="Vaishali Shah">Vaishali Shah</option>
12           <option value="Stuti Shah">Stuti Shah</option>
13         </select>
14       </td>
15     </tr>
16   </table>
17 </form>
```

The checkboxlist Tag

The checkboxlist tag creates a series of checkboxes from a list. It is same as the select tag. The only difference being that instead of displaying the list of options, the checkboxlist tag renders a series of checkboxes to select and deselect.

The following table provides the attributes of the checkboxlist tag:

Attributes	Description
id	It is used for referencing element.
name	It is the name of the element.
list	It is used to set an Iterable source to populate from.
listValue	It is the property of list objects to retrieve the field content from.
listKey	It is the property of list objects to retrieve the field value from.

> *Example*

Solution:

```
1  <s:form id="frmHome" name="frmHome">
2    <s:checkboxlist title="Select the author name(s)" name="authorName" list="{'Sharanam Shah', 'Vaishali Shah', 'Stuti Shah'}"/>
3  </s:form>
```

Generates the following HTML markups:

```
1  <form id="frmHome" name="frmHome" onsubmit="return true;"
      action="/;jsessionid=71F369396CC004DFEFBA82E10E281F79" method="post">
2    <table class="wwFormTable">
3      <tr>
```

Building View

```
 4            <td class="tdLabel"></td>
 5            <td>
 6                <input type="checkbox" name="authorName" value="Sharanam Shah" id="authorName-1"
                   title="Select the author name(s)"/>
 7                <label for="authorName-1" class="checkboxLabel">Sharanam Shah</label>
 8
 9                <input type="checkbox" name="authorName" value="Vaishali Shah" id="authorName-2"
                   title="Select the author name(s)"/>
10                <label for="authorName-2" class="checkboxLabel">Vaishali Shah</label>
11
12                <input type="checkbox" name="authorName" value="Stuti Shah" id="authorName-3"
                   title="Select the author name(s)"/>
13                <label for="authorName-3" class="checkboxLabel">Stuti Shah</label>
14            </td>
15        </tr>
16    </table>
17 </form>
```

The radio Tag

The radio tag renders HTML radio button input field. It allows users to select an option of choice from the list of options provided in the form of radio options.

The following table provides the attributes of the select tag:

Attributes	Description
id	It is used for referencing element.
name	It is the name of the element.
list	It is used to set an Iterable source to populate from.
listValue	It is the property of list objects to retrieve the field content from.
listKey	It is the property of list objects to retrieve the field value from.

Example

Solution:

```
1 <s:form id="frmHome" name="frmHome">
2     <s:radio label="Author Name(s)" name="authorName" list="{'Sharanam Shah', 'Vaishali Shah', 'Stuti Shah'}"/>
3 </s:form>
```

Generates the following HTML markups:

```
 1 <form id="frmHome" name="frmHome" onsubmit="return true;"
    action="/;jsessionid=71F369396CC004DFEFBA82E10E281F79" method="post">
 2     <table class="wwFormTable">
 3         <tr>
 4             <td class="tdLabel">
 5                 <label for="frmHome_authorName" class="label">Author Name(s):</label>
 6             </td>
 7             <td>
 8                 <input type="radio" name="authorName" id="frmHome_authorNameSharanam Shah"
                    value="Sharanam Shah"/>
 9                 <label for="frmHome_authorNameSharanam Shah">Sharanam Shah</label>
10
11                 <input type="radio" name="authorName" id="frmHome_authorNameVaishali Shah"
                    value="Vaishali Shah"/>
12                 <label for="frmHome_authorNameVaishali Shah">Vaishali Shah</label>
13
14                 <input type="radio" name="authorName" id="frmHome_authorNameStuti Shah" value="Stuti Shah"/>
15                 <label for="frmHome_authorNameStuti Shah">Stuti Shah</label>
16             </td>
17         </tr>
18     </table>
19 </form>
```

The submit Tag

The submit tag renders the submit button. It is used together with the form tag to provide asynchronous form submissions.

The following table provides the attributes of the select tag:

Attributes	Description
action	It is used to set the action attribute.
name	It is the name of the element.
errorText	It is the text to be displayed in case there is an error while fetching the content.
executeScripts	It is used to decide if the JavaScript code spec in the fetched content will be executed.
formFilter	It is the function name used to filter the fields of the form.
formId	It is the form ID whose fields will be serialized and passed as parameters.
handler	It is the JavaScript function name that will make the request.
href	It is the URL to call to obtain the content.
id	It is used for referencing the element.
indicator	It sets the indicator.
listenTopics	It is the topic that will trigger the remote call.
loadingText	It is the text to be shown while content is being fetched.
method	It sets the method attribute.
notifyTopics	It is the topics that will be published when the remote call completes.
showErrorTransportText	It sets whether errors will be shown.
src	It supplies an image source for image type submit button.
type	It is the type of submit to use. Valid values are input, button and image.
value	It preset the value of input element.

Example

Solution:

```
1  <s:form action="insertBooks" method="post" name="frmBooks" >
2     <s:submit theme="simple" cssStyle="backgroud:url(../images/submit_bg.gif) no-repeat 45px 0px;
       margin:8px 0px 0px 15px;" cssClass="buttonText" name="btnSubmit" id="btnSubmit" value="Submit" />
3  </s:form>
```

Generates the following HTML markups:

```
1  <form id="insertBooks" name="frmBooks" onsubmit="return true;"
       action="/BookShop/bookShop_insertBooks.action" method="post">
2     <input type="submit" id="btnSubmit" name="btnSubmit" value="Submit" class="buttonText"
       style="backgroud:url(../images/submit_bg.gif) no-repeat 45px 0px; margin:8px 0px 0px 15px;"/>
3  </form>
```

Building View 117

The reset Tag

The reset tag renders a reset button. It is used together with the form tag to provide form resetting.

The following table provides the attributes of the select tag:

Attributes	Description
id	It is used for referencing element.
name	It is the name of the element.
action	It sets action attribute.
method	It sets method attribute.
type	It is the type of submit to use. Valid values are input, button and image.
value	It presets the value of input element.

Example

Solution:

```
1  <s:form action="insertBooks" method="post" name="frmBooks" >
2      <s:reset theme="simple" cssStyle="backgroud:url(../images/more_bg.gif) no-repeat 45px 0px;
           margin:8px 0px 0px 15px;" cssClass="buttonText" name="btnReset" id="btnReset" value="Reset"/>
3  </s:form>
```

Generates the following HTML markups:

```
1  <form id="insertBooks" name="frmBooks" onsubmit="return true;"
       action="/BookShop/bookShop/insertBooks.action" method="post">
2      <input type="reset" name="btnReset" value="Reset" class="buttonText"
           style="backgroud:url(../images/more_bg.gif) no-repeat 45px 0px; margin:8px 0px 0px 15px;"/>
3  </form>
```

Non Form UI Tags

The non-form UI tags are used for other than designing form components.

These tags are used to:
- Display the output text such as the error messages
- Create components such as tabs, div and so on

The div Tag

The div tag is used when the <u>theme of the template is set to **ajax**</u>. It provides a remote call from the current page to update a section of content without having to refresh the entire page.

118   Struts 2 For Beginners

The div tag creates a HTML DIV element, which obtains its content via a remote XMLHttpRequest call via the DOJO framework.

The following table provides the attributes of the select tag:

Attributes	Description
autoStart	It starts timer automatically.
name	It is the name of the element.
delay	It states how long to wait before fetching the content [in milliseconds]
errorText	It is the text to be displayed in case there is an error while fetching the content.
executeScripts	It is used to decide if the JavaScript code spec in the fetched content will be executed.
formFilter	It is the function name used to filter the fields of the form.
formId	It is the form ID whose fields will be serialized and passed as parameters.
handler	It is the JavaScript function name that will make the request.
href	It is the URL to call to obtain the content.
id	It is used for referencing the element.
indicator	It sets the indicator.
listenTopics	It is the topic that will trigger the remote call.
loadingText	It is the text to be shown while content is being fetched.
openTemplate	It sets the template to use for opening the rendered html.
notifyTopics	It is the topics that will be published when the remote call completes.
refreshOnShow	The contents will be loaded when div becomes visible. It is used only inside the tabbedPanel.
showErrorTransportText	It sets whether errors will be shown.
startTimerListenTopic	It is the topics that will start the timer [for auto update].
stopTimerListenTopic	It is the topics that will stop the timer [for auto update].
updateFreq	It states how often to reload the content [in milliseconds].
value	It preset the value of input element.

Example

Solution:
```
1   <s:form id="frmHome" name="frmHome">
2       <s:div theme="ajax" id="ajaxLoader" href="../images/ajax-loader.gif">
3           Wait for the data to be loaded . . .
4       </s:div>
5   </s:form>
```

Building View 119

Generates the following HTML markups:

```
1  <form id="frmHome" name="frmHome" onsubmit="return true;"
       action="/;jsessionid=71F369396CC004DFEFBA82E1OE281F79" method="post">
2      <table class="wwFormTable">
3          <div dojoType="struts:BindDiv" id="ajaxLoader" href="../images/ajax-loader.gif"
              showError="true">
4              Wait for the data to be loaded . . .
5          </div>
6      </table>
7  </form>
```

The tabbedPanel Tag

The tabbedPanel tag widget is an AJAX component, where each tab can either be local content or remote content [refreshed each time the user selects that tab].

The following table provides the attributes of the select tag:

Attributes	Description
closeButton	It states where the close button will be placed. Valid values are tab and pane.
name	It is the name of the element.
doLayout	It is a Boolean value. If the value is false, the tab container's height equals the height of the currently selected tab.
openTemplate	It sets the template to use for opening the rendered html.
selectedTab	It is set with the id of the tab that will be selected by default.
value	It preset the value of input element.

Example

Solution:

```
1  <s:form id="frmHome" name="frmHome">
2      <s:tabbedPanel id="firstTabbedPanel">
3          <s:div theme="ajax" id="ajaxLoader" href="../images/ajax-loader.gif">
4              Wait for the data to be loaded . . .
5          </s:div>
6      </s:tabbedPanel>
7  </s:form>
```

Generates the following HTML markups:

```
1  <form id="frmHome" name="frmHome" onsubmit="return true;"
       action="/;jsessionid=71F369396CC004DFEFBA82E1OE281F79" method="post">
2      <table class="wwFormTable">
3          <script type="text/javascript">
4              dojo.require("dojo.widget.TabContainer");
5              dojo.require("dojo.widget.LinkPane");
6              dojo.require("dojo.widget.ContentPane");
7          </script>
8          <div dojoType="TabContainer" id="firstTabbedPanel" doLayout="false">
9              <div dojoType="struts:BindDiv" id="ajaxLoader" href="../images/ajax-loader.gif"
                  showError="true">
10                 Wait for the data to be loaded . . .
11             </div>
12         </div>
13     </table>
14 </form>
```

120   Struts 2 For Beginners

The tree Tag

The tree tag renders a tree widget with AJAX support. It renders a tree-like structure where nodes can be clicked to expand and collapse.

The following table provides the attributes of the select tag:

Attributes	Description
blankIconSrc	It is the blank icon image source.
name	It is the name of the element.
childCollectionProperty	It is the childCollectionProperty property.
expandIconSrcMinus	It is the expand icon image source.
expandIconSrcPlus	It is the expand icon image source.
gridIconSrcC	It is the image source for under child item child icons.
gridIconSrcL	It is the image source for last child grid.
gridIconSrcP	It is the image source for under parent item child icons.
gridIconSrcV	It is the image source for vertical line.
gridIconSrcX	It is the image source for grid for sole root item.
gridIconSrcY	It is the image source for grid for last root item.
iconHeight	It is the icon height.
iconWidth	It is the icon width.
nodeIdProperty	It is the nodeIdProperty property.
nodeTitleProperty	It is the nodeTitleProperty property.
openTemplate	It sets the template to use for opening the rendered html.
rootNode	It is the rootNode property.
showGrid	It shows grid.
showRootGrid	It is the showRootGrid property.
toggle	It is the toggle property.
toggleDuration	It is the toggle duration [in milliseconds].
treeCollapsedTopic	It is the treeCollapsedTopic property.
treeExpandedTopic	It is the treeExpandedTopic property.
value	It preset the value of input element.

Example

Solution:

```
1  <s:form id="frmHome" name="frmHome">
2      <s:tree theme="ajax" rootNode="%{rootNode}" nodeIdProperty="id" childCollectionProperty="children"
         nodeTitleProperty="name"></s:tree>
3  </s:form>
```

Building View

Generates the following HTML markups:

```
1  <form id="frmHome" name="frmHome" onsubmit="return true;"
       action="/;jsessionid=71F369396CC004DFEFBA82E10E281F79" method="post">
2      <table class="wwFormTable">
3          <script type="text/javascript">
4          <!--
5              dojo.require("dojo.lang.*");
6              dojo.require("dojo.widget.*");
7              dojo.require("dojo.widget.Tree");
8              // dojo.hostenv.writeIncludes();
9          -->
10         </script>
11         <div dojoType="Tree" id="frmHome_" toggle="fade"></div>
12     </table>
13 </form>
```

Now that the tag library is learned, let's apply the learning to Guestbook application.

Continuing With The Application

To continue further with Guestbook application and make it usable, let's build the view layer.

Based on the application requirements documented in *Chapter 06: Getting Started*, the view layer will consist of two distinct JSP pages. One that will be a data entry form to accept guest book entries and another to view the entries.

Before creating the JSP page, first let's create a directory to hold the JSP pages.

To create the directory, right click **Web Pages** directory and select **New → Folder...**, as shown in diagram 8.1.

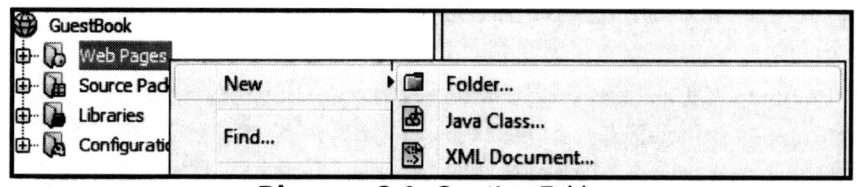

Diagram 8.1: Creating Folder

Enter the name **jsp** in the **Folder Name** textbox, as shown in diagram 8.2.

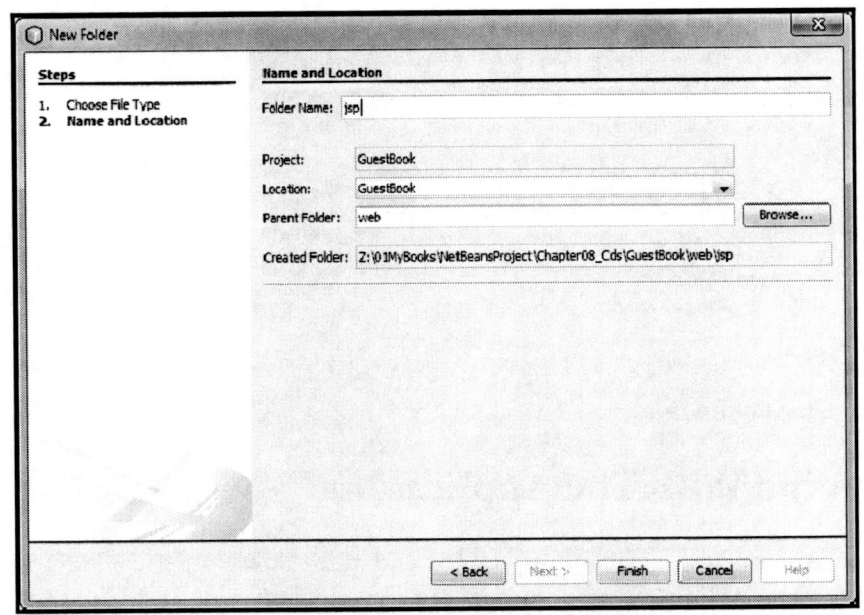

Diagram 8.2: Naming the folder

Click **Finish**. The directory named **jsp** is created in the Web Pages.

guestBookEntry.jsp

To create guestBookEntry.jsp, right click **jsp** directory, select **New → JSP...**, as shown in diagram 8.3.

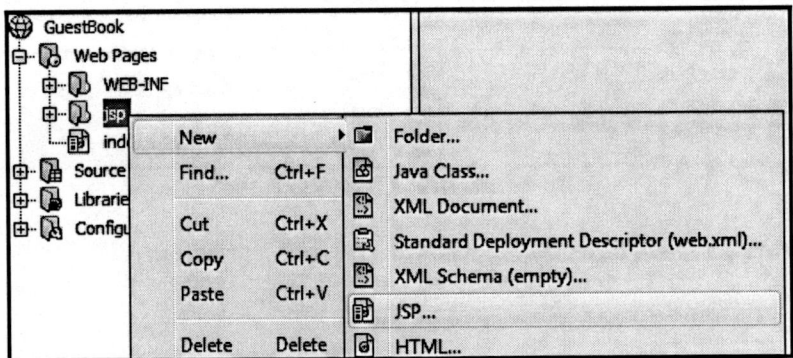

Diagram 8.3: Creating JSP file

Enter the name **guestBookEntry** in the **JSP File Name** textbox, as shown in diagram 8.4.

Building View   123

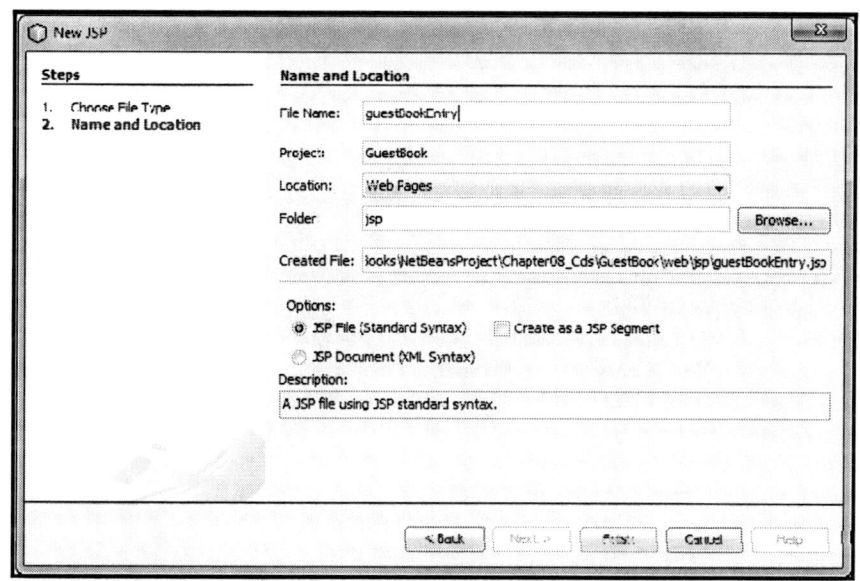

Diagram 8.4: Naming the JSP file

Click **Finish**. The JSP page named **guestBookEntry.jsp** is created in the jsp folder.

Key in the following code spec in **guestBookEntry.jsp**:

```
1   <%@ page language="java" contentType="text/html; charset=ISO-8859-1"
     pageEncoding="ISO-8859-1"%>
2   <%@ taglib prefix="s" uri="/struts-tags"%>
3   <!DOCTYPE html>
4   <html>
5     <head>
6       <meta http-equiv="Content-Type" content="text/html;charset=ISO-8859-1">
7       <title>Guest Book</title>
8       <s:head />
9     </head>
10    <body bgcolor="pink">
11      <table border="0" cellpadding="0" cellspacing="0" align="center" width="760">
12        <tr>
13          <td>
14            <table border="0" cellpadding="0" cellspacing="0" width="100%">
15              <tr>
16                <td valign="top" align="left" style="padding-right:0px;
                    padding-left:0px; padding-bottom:0px; font:24px/30px Georgia;
                    width:228px; color:#786e4e; padding-top:0px; height:37px;">
17                  Sign the Guest Book
18                </td>
19              </tr>
20            </table>
21          </td>
22        </tr>
```

```
23              <tr align="left" valign="top">
24                <td height="20">
25                  <hr />
26                </td>
27              </tr>
28              <tr>
29                <td>
30                  <s:form action="GuestBookSuccess" validate="true">
31                    <s:textfield required="true" label="Name" name="guest" />
32                    <s:textarea required="true" rows="4" cols="36" label="Message"
                         name="message" />
33                    <s:submit />
34                  </s:form>
35                </td>
36              </tr>
37            </table>
38          </body>
39        </html>
```

Explanation:

This JSP page is built using **Struts 2 tags**.

Struts 2 Taglib

To use the taglib:

```
2   <%@ taglib prefix="s" uri="/struts-tags"%>
```

struts2-core-2.x.xx.x.jar file must be included as library in the NetBeans IDE.

<s:head>

The **Head** section of the **HTML** code spec holds **<s:head>**. This tag adds the appropriate JavaScript code spec which ensures smooth running especially where some **Struts 2** functionality that is in use requires JavaScript.

<s:head> allows specifying the theme for the JSP page.

To build the data entry form the following tags are placed:

- <s:form>
- <s:textfield>
- <s:textarea>
- <s:submit>

<s:form>

<s:form> allows specifying the **action** and the **namespace**. Based on the attribute values, this tag creates a URL and the necessary markup, which ensures proper data transfer to the action specified on form submission.

<s:textfield> and <s:textarea> generate input form fields.

HINT

> The most important attributes when creating form fields using tags are **key** and **name**. The **key** attribute assigns a label to the attribute. The **name** attribute is similar to the HTML name attribute for a form field which is the name of the parameter passed during form submission.

REMINDER

> The tag name **must match** a **setter** method in the action class.

Struts 2 framework:

- Converts all the form fields to the appropriate data types
- Invokes the matching setters methods

This is done just before the specified action method is invoked.

required="true" generates a small red asterisk which visually indicates that the form field is mandatory, however, it does not enforce the validation. Validations will be added to this application later in *Chapter 11: Validations*.

guestBookView.jsp

Using NetBeans create one more JSP page called guestBookView.jsp using the same steps as shown earlier.

Key in the following code spec to **guestBookView.jsp**:

```
1  <%@ page language="java" contentType="text/html; charset=ISO-8859-1"
   pageEncoding="ISO-8859-1"%>
2  <%@ taglib prefix="s" uri="/struts-tags"%>
3  <!DOCTYPE html>
4  <html>
5    <head>
6      <meta http-equiv="Content-Type" content="text/html;charset=ISO-8859-1">
7      <title>Guest Book</title>
```

```
8            <s:head />
9         </head>
10        <body bgcolor="pink">
11           <table border="0" cellpadding="0" cellspacing="0" align="center" width="760">
12              <tr>
13                 <td>
14                    <table border="0" cellpadding="0" cellspacing="0" width="100%">
15                       <tr>
16                          <td width="60%" valign="top" align="left"
                               style="padding-right:0px; padding-left:0px; padding-bottom:0px;
                               font:24px/30px Georgia; width:228px; color:#786e4e;
                               padding-top:0px; height:37px;">
17                             View the Guest Book
18                          </td>
19                          <td valign="bottom" align="right" style="font:12px/16px Georgia,
                               serif; color:#786e4e;">
20                             <b>Click <a href="<s:url action="GuestBook" />"> here</a>
                               to sign the guestbook.</b>
21                          </td>
22                       </tr>
23                    </table>
24                 </td>
25              </tr>
26              <tr align="left" valign="top">
27                 <td height="20">
28                    <hr />
29                 </td>
30              </tr>
31              <tr>
32                 <td>
33                    <table border="0" cellpadding="0" cellspacing="0" align="center"
                         width="100%">
34                       <s:iterator value="messages">
35                          <tr>
36                             <td style="font:12px/16px Georgia; color:#786e4e;">
37                                On <s:property value="when"/>,<br />
38                                <b><s:property value="guest"/>:</b>
39                                <s:property value="message"/>
40                                <br /><br />
41                             </td>
42                          </tr>
43                       </s:iterator>
44                    </table>
45                 </td>
46              </tr>
47           </table>
48        </body>
49     </html>
```

Explanation:

This JSP accesses data from the messages **ArrayList** available in the Action class.

<s:iterator> accepts an object that implements java.util.ArrayList interface.

The **value** attribute is set to **messages**. The tag looks into the **Value Stack** for such an object and accesses its value using the ArrayList's method in this case **add()**.

Since the action is on the stack, each of the objects in the List is also available in the Value Stack. The value from the getter methods can be retrieved using **<s:property>**.

This completes the view layer for the Guestbook application. Now all that is left is the entry point and the configuration bit.

index.jsp

After the JSP files are defined, edit index.jsp [which already exist] and key in the following code spec:

```
1  <% response.sendRedirect("GuestBook.action"); %>
```

Now when this application is invoked, index.jsp [being the default file] is served. This file holds a redirect command which serves GuestBook application.

Configuration - struts.xml

To configure the results for the actions, open struts.xml and key in the following code spec:

```
1  <?xml version="1.0" encoding="UTF-8"?>
2  <!DOCTYPE struts PUBLIC '-//Apache Software Foundation//DTD Commons Validator
   Rules Configuration 2.3//EN' 'http://struts.apache.org/dtds/struts-2.3.dtd'>
3  <struts>
4    <package name="guestbook" extends="struts-default">
5      <action name="GuestBook">
6        <result>jsp/guestBookEntry.jsp</result>
7      </action>
8      <action name="GuestBookSuccess"
         class="com.sharanamvaishali.myApp.action.GuestBookAction">
9        <result name="success">jsp/guestBookView.jsp</result>
10     </action>
11   </package>
12 </struts>
```

Explanation:

A package called **guestbook** is created that holds the configuration for actions.

Here, two actions are defined and mapped to appropriate results.

GuestBook Action

GuestBook action is the one that takes charge when the user invokes the application.

When the user invokes the application i.e. index.jsp, a redirect command requests for GuestBook.action.

The framework on receiving such request looks into the configuration and finds the following:

```
<action name="GuestBook">
    <result>jsp/guestBookEntry.jsp</result>
</action>
```

This indicates rendering the result using guestBookEntry.jsp which is the data entry form.

GuestBookSuccess Action

When the user populates the message in the data entry form i.e. guestBookEntry.jsp and clicks Submit, GuestBookAction takes charge.

This action saves the data i.e. the guestbook entry and returns success. The framework on receiving success, looks into the configuration and finds the following:

```
<action name="GuestBookSuccess"
class="com.sharanamvaishali.myApp.action.GuestBookAction">
    <result name="success">jsp/guestBookView.jsp</result>
</action>
```

This indicates to render the response using guestBookView.jsp.

Process Flow Diagram

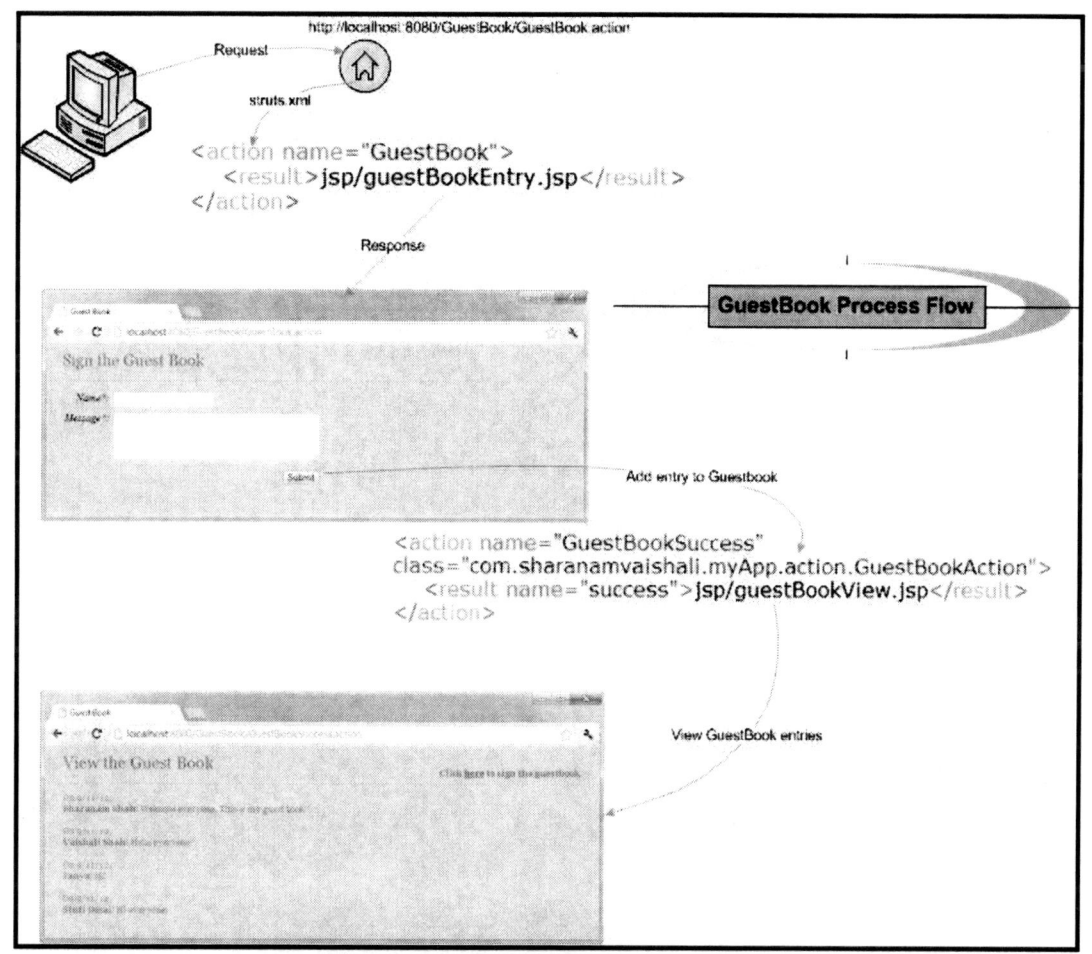

Diagram 8.5: GuestBook Process Flow

Running GuestBook Application

Now that the action and the view [Result and Result Types] is in place. Let's run this application [source code available on the Book's accompanying CDROM].

Begin by building the project using NetBeans IDE.

To do so, right click **GuestBook** project and select **Build**, as shown in diagram 8.6.

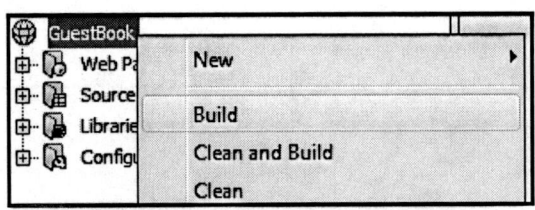

Diagram 8.6: Building the project

Then run the application by right clicking **GuestBook** project and selecting **Run**, as shown in diagram 8.7.

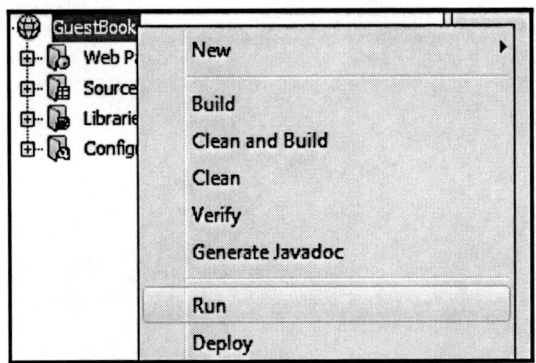

Diagram 8.7: Running the project

index.jsp is served in the Web browser, which automatically invokes **GuestBook.action**, as shown in diagram 8.8.

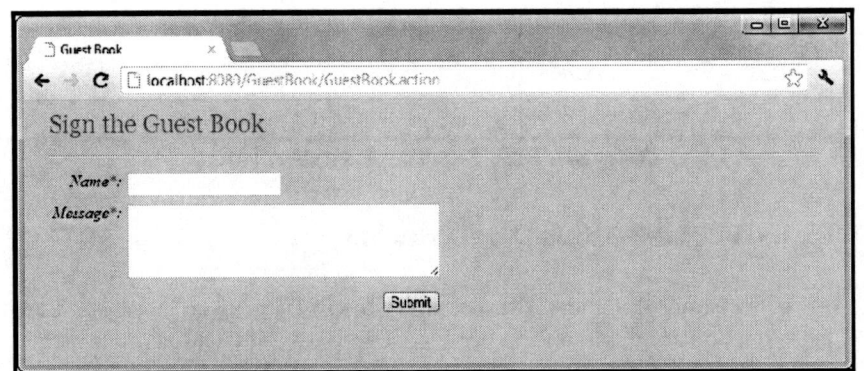

Diagram 8.8: The application run in the Web browser

Enter the name and the comments in the Name and Message fields, as shown in diagram 8.9.

Building View 131

Diagram 8.9: Entering data

Click [Submit]. This displays the already existing messages [entered by others who visited the site before] along with the newly added message.

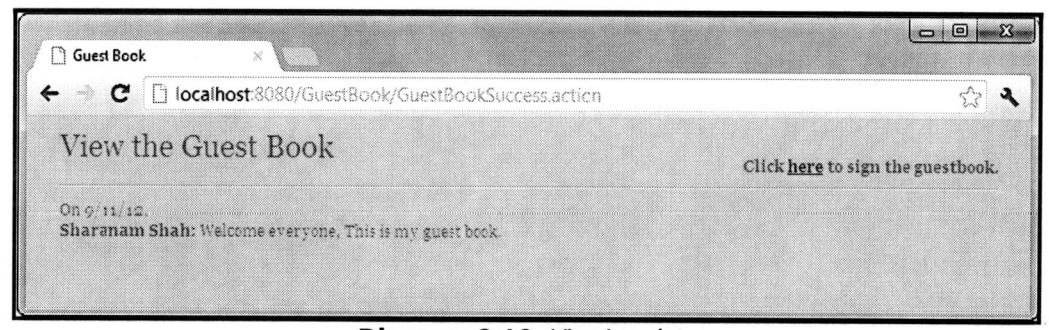

Diagram 8.10: Viewing data

Click here link available on the top right corner of the page to go back to the Guest Book data entry form.

Chapter 9

SECTION III: GETTING STARTED WITH STRUTS 2

Building Interceptors

Most of the software engineers look towards ways of software reuse as it helps save time, money and maintainability. Struts 2 framework helps achieving this by:

- Isolating the logic [code spec] to be reused in a clean separated unit i.e. an Interceptor
- Dropping the isolated logic i.e. wrap/apply it around the desired actions

The moment a developer begins using Struts 2 as the framework of choice, the software/code spec reuse benefits are automatically gained. This means, if a Struts 2 application inherits the **defaultStack** by extending the **struts-default** package, code spec is already being reused. For example, the defaultStack interceptor allows reusing the data transfer code spec which is already written by the Struts 2 development team.

This chapter focuses on wrapping the action with a stack of the appropriate **Interceptors** which work silently in the background.

Interceptors help inject custom logic into the request processing pipeline. They provide a mechanism to supply pre-processing and post-processing around the action. They are conceptually very similar to Servlet filters. This is how Interceptors help avoid the need for adding additional code spec to each and every Action that over time would create additional maintenance overhead.

In Struts 2 framework, the built-in interceptors [declared in the **struts-default** package's **defaultStack**] perform most of the processing. Activities such as data transfer and property population, data validation, exception handling, file uploading, lifecycle callbacks, authorization and many more are carried out by Interceptors, which can fire before and after the Action executes.

Struts 2 framework has a rich set of the built-in interceptors due to which, most of the times, the need to custom develop an interceptor does not arise. However, if the need arises, a customer interceptor can be built and wrapped around the desired actions.

Request And Interceptor

Every request that the framework receives passes through each Interceptor.

The Interceptor can:
- Ignore the request
- Act on the request data
- Short-circuit the request and prevent the Action class method from firing

Since interceptors deal with actions, they have access to the action being executed, as well as all environmental variables and execution properties.

Built-In Interceptors

Struts 2 framework automates most of the routine tasks with the help of built-in interceptors.

The following are the built-in interceptors available in Struts 2 framework. Each of these built-in interceptors provides a distinct feature to the action.

Alias Interceptor [alias]

This interceptor allows parameters to have different name aliases across requests. This is particularly useful when chaining actions with different names for the same information.

Chaining Interceptor [chaining]

This interceptor is used to copy all objects in the value stack of currently executing action class to the value stack of the next action class to be executed in action chaining.

This interceptor thus allows the previously executed action's properties to be available to the current action. This interceptor is usually used with the result type **chain**.

Checkbox Interceptor [checkbox]

This interceptor helps managing check boxes. It looks for the hidden identification fields, which are used to specify the original value of the checkbox.

It adds a parameter value [false] for check boxes that are not checked. This means, if the checkbox is left unchecked, the value added in the parameters for the current checkbox is false.

Conversion Error Interceptor [conversionError]

This interceptor places error information from converting strings to parameter types into the action's field errors.

Create Session Interceptor [createSession]

This interceptor automatically creates an HTTP session if one does not already exist.

Debugging Interceptor [debugging]

This interceptor provides several different debugging options to the developer by giving an inner look of the data behind the page.

Execute And Wait Interceptor [execAndWait]

This interceptor displays an intermediary waiting page whilst the action executes in the background.

Often while running a long action, the user gets impatient, in case of a long delay in response. To avoid this, this interceptor is used, which runs a long running action in the background and displays the page with a progress bar to the user.

This interceptor also prevents the HTTP request from timing out.

Exception Interceptor [exception]

This interceptor maps exceptions that are thrown by the action to a result, allowing automatic exception handling via redirection.

File Upload Interceptor [fileUpload]

This interceptor allows easy file uploading. It transforms the files and metadata from multipart requests into regular request parameters so that they can be set on the action just like normal parameters.

Internationalization Interceptor [i18n]

This interceptor helps keep track of the selected locale during a user's session.

Logging Interceptor [logger]

This interceptor provides simple logging. It logs the start and end point of the execution of action or the execution of whole stack defined for the action including all interceptors and actions itself with details of date and time in the log file.

Message Store Interceptor [store]

This interceptor stores and retrieves the messages, field errors and action errors in the session for actions.

Model Driven Interceptor [modelDriven]

This interceptor places the model object onto the value stack for actions implementing ModelDriven interface.

Scoped Model Driven Interceptor [scopedModelDriven]

This interceptor stores and retrieves the model object from a configured scope for actions implementing ScopedModelDriven interface.

Parameters Interceptor [params]

This interceptor sets the request parameters on the action.

Prepare Interceptor [prepare]

Sometimes there is a need to ensure some processing before execute() is invoked. In such a scenario, this interceptor helps by invoking prepare() of the action class containing logic such as initializing null objects, loading an object from database and so on.

Profiling Interceptor [profile]

This interceptor allows simple profiling information to be logged for actions.

Scope Interceptor [scope]

This interceptor stores and retrieves the action's state in the session or application scope.

Servlet Configuration Interceptor [servletConfig]

This interceptor provides the action with access to Servlet based information.

Static Parameters Interceptor [staticParams]

This interceptor sets statically defined param tags values on the action.

Roles Interceptor [roles]

This interceptor allows the action to be executed only if the user is one of the configured roles.

Timer Interceptor [timer]

This interceptor records the duration of an execution and provides simple profiling information in the form of how long the action takes to execute.

Token Interceptor [token]

Often time users double click the Submit button. This can cause issues on the execution of the action class.

This interceptor ensures that there are no issues created by such careless users. This interceptor achieves this by allowing the processing of one request per token.

Token Session Interceptor [tokenSession]

This interceptor is the same as the token interceptor, but for invalid tokens, the submitted data is stored in the session.

Validation Interceptor [validation]

This interceptor provides validation support for actions.

This interceptor checks the action against all validation rules declared in Validation framework configuration files. The interceptor adds field-level and action-level error messages into the action context.

In other words, this interceptor enables the execution of action class through the standard validation framework.

Workflow Interceptor [workflow]

This interceptor redirects to an INPUT view without executing the action when validation fails.

This interceptor provides basic validation workflow before the rest of the interceptor chain is allowed to continue. This interceptor ensures a specific flow of execution. The execution in the workflow is dependent on the interface implemented by the action class to be executed.

Pre-Configured Stacks Of Built-In Interceptors

In a real world web application, most of the time more than one interceptor is applied. In such a scenario, instead of configuring each and every required interceptor for each action, Struts 2 framework allows creating a stack of required interceptors which can then be referenced by actions.

Building Interceptors

Struts 2 framework comes with a set of preconfigured stacks. When interceptors are placed in a stack, each interceptor is invoked in the order of their placement.

defaultStack is one of the common stack which most of the applications would inherit by extending the **struts-default** package.

The following are the **preconfigured stacks** that Struts 2 framework provides:

basicStack

- exception
- servletConfig
- checkbox
- params
- conversionError

validationWorkflowStack

- basicStack
- validation
- workflow

fileUploadStack

- fileUpload
- basicStack

modelDrivenStack

- modelDriven
- basicStack

chainStack

- chain
- basicStack

i18nStack

- i18n
- basicStack

paramPrepareParamsStack

- exception
- alias
- params
- servletConfig
- prepare
- i18n
- chain
- modelDriven
- fileUpload
- checkbox
- staticParams
- params
- conversionError
- validation
- workflow

defaultStack

- exception
- alias
- servletConfig
- prepare
- i18n
- chain
- debugging
- profiling
- scopedModelDriven

- modelDriven
- fileUpload
- checkbox
- staticParams
- params
- conversionError
- validation
- workflow

executeAndWaitStack

- execAndWait
- defaultStack

Role Of The Interceptor In The Execution Cycle

To understand what an interceptor does and how, let's go through the execution cycle.

1. When the framework receives a user request, it decides which action the URL maps. An instance of this action is added to a newly created instance of ActionInvocation
2. The framework then consults the configuration to discover which **Interceptors** should fire and in what **sequence**
3. References to these interceptors are added to **ActionInvocation**
4. After ActionInvocation has been created and populated with all the objects and information it needs, the invocation begins
5. ActionInvocation exposes **invoke()**, which is called by the framework to start the execution of the action
6. When the framework calls this method, ActionInvocation starts the invocation process by executing the **first Interceptor** in the stack

HINT

invoke() **does not** always map to the first interceptor.

7. ActionInvocation keeps track of what stage the invocation process has reached and passes the control to the appropriate interceptor in the stack. It does this by calling that interceptor's **intercept()**

8. Each time invoke() is called, ActionInvocation consults its state and executes whichever **Interceptor** comes next

   An **Interceptor** when invoked does the following:
   - Pre-Processing [For example recording the start time of the process]
   - Passes the control on to the successive interceptors and ultimately the action, by calling invoke() or divert execution by itself returning a control string
   - Post-Processing [For example recording the end time of the process]

9. In this manner, the invocation process tunnels down through all of the **interceptors** until, finally, there are <u>no more interceptors in the stack</u>

10. When all of the interceptors have been invoked, invoke() <u>causes the action itself to be executed</u>

Declaring Interceptors And Stacks

To create, work with and use the built-in interceptors, it is important to learn **declaring** and then **mapping** Interceptors to Actions.

Interceptors are declared and configured in struts.xml. In this file, interceptors can be declared using <interceptor> by specifying a unique name and the interceptor implementation class name.

Example

Solution:

```
<interceptor name="myInterceptor" class="myBook.myFirstInterceptor" />
```

This is a single interceptor that is declared.

A stack of multiple interceptors can also be declared as:

```
<package name="myPg" extends="struts-default" abstract="false" namespace="/" >
   . . .
   <interceptors>
      <interceptor name="myInterceptor" class="myBook.myFirstInterceptor" />
      <interceptor-stack name="myStack">
         <interceptor-ref name="defaultStack" />
         <interceptor-ref name="myInterceptor" />
      </interceptor-stack>
   </interceptors>

   <default-interceptor-ref name="myStack" />
```

```
. . .
</package>
```

Explanation:

When declaring interceptors, keep in mind the following:

- **<interceptors>** can hold **multiple** <interceptor> and <interceptor-stack> tags
- The **name** attribute must hold a **unique** value across both the <interceptor> and <interceptor-stack> tags
- The value for the name attribute of the **<interceptor-ref>** and **<default-interceptor-ref>** tags can represent either an **interceptor** or **interceptor stack**
- **<interceptor-stack>** is a convenient way of referencing a sequenced chunk of interceptors by name and can contain **multiple <interceptor-ref>** tags
- **<default-interceptor-ref>** allows setting either an **interceptor** or **interceptor stack** as the **default**. This sets the indicated **interceptor** or **interceptor stack** as the default interceptor for all the actions in the package
- **<default-interceptor-ref>** applies to all the actions being executed in the current package that is defined
- Each interceptor is invoked **in the order/sequence** in which it is configured

All the built-in Interceptors that the framework provides are defined in **struts-default.xml** which is available in struts2-core-2.x.x.x.jar library. This file also holds the definitions of the built-in Interceptor stacks.

These built-in Interceptors and Interceptor stacks definitions can be extended to the Web application from struts-default.xml.

To use these built-in Interceptors bundled with the framework, all that needs to be done is, use the **extends** attribute of the package element and set it to struts-default package.

Mapping Interceptors To Actions

After the interceptors are declared, they need to be mapped to the actions for which they have been declared.

An interceptor can be mapped to an action using **<interceptor-ref>**.

Struts 2 For Beginners

Example

Solution:

```xml
<package name="myPg" extends="struts-default" abstract="false" namespace="/" >
. . .
   <interceptors>
      <interceptor name="myInterceptor" class="myBook.myFirstInterceptor" />

      <interceptor-stack name="myStack">
         <interceptor-ref name="defaultStack" />
         <interceptor-ref name="myInterceptor" />
      </interceptor-stack>
   </interceptors>

   <default-interceptor-ref name="myStack" />

   <action name="myAction" class="myBook.myAction">
      <interceptor-ref name="timer"/>
      <interceptor-ref name="logger"/>
      <interceptor-ref name="myStack"/>

      <result>SuccessView.jsp</result>
   </action>
</package>
```

Explanation:

Here, two interceptors named **timer** and **logger** and one interceptor stack named **myStack** [declared earlier] are mapped to the action named **myAction**.

These interceptors fire in the order in which they are listed.

Since this package extends **struts-default**, the interceptors named **timer** and **logger** are already declared in struts-default package.

HINT

☺ Actions that **do not define** any interceptors using <interceptor-refs> **inherit** the default interceptors.

Actions that **define** interceptors using <interceptor-refs> **lose** the automatic default inheritance and therefore **must explicitly** name the **defaultStack** in order to use it.

Parameterize Interceptors

Interceptors that accept parameters can be passed parameters from within <interceptor-ref> using <param>.

Example

Solution:
```
<interceptor-ref name="workflow">
   <param name="excludeMethods">input,back,cancel,browse</param>
</interceptor-ref>
```

Explanation:

Here, the interceptor named **workflow** in the defaultStack is passed a parameter named **excludeMethods**. This parameter holds the value **input, back, cancel, browse**. This indicates that the workflow interceptor will ignore requests to action methods named input, back, cancel and browse.

Building A Custom Interceptor

To build a custom interceptor, create a Java class that implements **com.opensymphony.xwork2.interceptor.Interceptor** interface.

Interceptor Interface

Example

Solution:
```
1  package com.opensymphony.xwork2.interceptor;
2
3  import com.opensymphony.xwork2.ActionInvocation;
4  import java.io.Serializable;
5
6  public interface Interceptor extends Serializable {
7     void destroy();
8     void init();
9     String intercept(ActionInvocation invocation) throws Exception;
10 }
```

Interceptor interface defines three methods. destroy() and the init() methods are **lifecycle methods** that facilitate **initialization** and **clean up** of resources if desired.

intercept() holds the actual business code spec and is invoked by the recursive ActionInvocation.invoke().

When the Interceptor is first instantiated, **init()** is invoked. Any resources the Interceptor needs can be allocated in init().

intercept() is invoked for every request that passes through the Interceptor. Just like the Action's execute(), intercept() also returns a result code.

Conceptually, Interceptor methods have a **before** and **after** part, either of which is optional. The dividing line between before and after is a call to **invocation.invoke()**.

All Interceptors must include the code spec that invokes invocation.invoke() and return the result code on an outcome.

Continuing With The Application

Let's continue with the same Guestbook application. Create an interceptor that calculates the actual time taken by the application to add and then display the guest book entries.

Basically, the interceptor will have to capture the current time before as well as after invoking the actions and calculate the difference between the two times.

ActionTimer.java

Using NetBeans, create one more class called **ActionTimer** using the same steps as shown in *Chapter 07: Working With Actions*.

Key in the following code spec in **ActionTimer.java**:

```
1   package com.sharanamvaishali.myApp.interceptor;
2
3   import com.opensymphony.xwork2.ActionInvocation;
4   import com.opensymphony.xwork2.interceptor.Interceptor;
5
6   public class ActionTimer implements Interceptor {
7       private long startTime;
8       private long endTime;
9
10      @Override
11      public String intercept(ActionInvocation invocation) throws Exception {
12          startTime = System.currentTimeMillis();
13          invocation.invoke();
14          endTime = System.currentTimeMillis();
```

```
15        System.out.println("Action " + invocation.getAction().getClass().getName() + "
          took " + (endTime - startTime) + " millisecs");
16        return "SUCCESS";
17     }
18
19     @Override
20     public void init() {
21     }
22
23     @Override
24     public void destroy() {
25     }
26 }
```

Explanation:

Imports

The following interfaces/classes are included using the import statement:

com.opensymphony.xwork2.ActionInvocation

ActionInvocation represents the execution state of an Action. ActionInvocation interface holds the Interceptors and the Action instance.

com.opensymphony.xwork2.interceptor.Interceptor

Interceptor is a stateless class that follows the interceptor pattern, as found in Filter.

Implements

ActionTimer [as required] implements **Interceptor**.

Variables

Two private variables are declared to mark the start time and the end time of the execution of the actions.

intercept()

The most interesting section in this code spec is **intercept()**.

This interceptor is invoked for every action that is executed in this application. It begins by capturing the current time as the **start time** using System.currentTimeMillis().

After it does this, the interceptor uses **ActionInvocation** object [in this case **next**] to invoke() the actual action.

After the action completes its job, the framework shifts the control back to this interceptor. The interceptor captures the current time as the end time using System.currentTimeMillis().

Finally, using System.out.println() the difference between the two times i.e. the start and end time is displayed on the console.

init() And destroy()

destroy() and init() are **lifecycle methods** that facilitate **initialization** and **clean up** of resources, **if desired**.

When the Interceptor is first instantiated, **init()** is invoked. Any resources the Interceptor needs can be allocated in init().

Declaring Interceptor

Edit struts.xml and add the following additional code spec to deal with the interceptor:

```xml
 1  <?xml version="1.0" encoding="UTF-8"?>
 2  <!DOCTYPE struts PUBLIC '-//Apache Software Foundation//DTD Commons Validator
    Rules Configuration 2.3//EN' 'http://struts.apache.org/dtds/struts-2.3.dtd'>
 3  <struts>
 4      <package name="guestbook" namespace="/" extends="struts-default">
 5          <interceptors>
 6              <interceptor name="actiontimer"
                   class="com.sharanamvaishali.myApp.interceptor.ActionTimer" />
 7              <interceptor-stack name="myStack">
 8                  <interceptor-ref name="defaultStack" />
 9                  <interceptor-ref name="actiontimer" />
10              </interceptor-stack>
11          </interceptors>
12
13          <default-interceptor-ref name="myStack" />
14
15          <action name="GuestBook">
16              <result>jsp/guestBookEntry.jsp</result>
17          </action>
18          <action name="GuestBookSuccess"
                class="com.sharanamvaishali.myApp.action.GuestBookAction">
19              <result name="success">jsp/guestBookView.jsp</result>
20          </action>
21      </package>
22  </struts>
```

Explanation:

Here, there is a single package named guestbook that holds both the actions.

To apply an interceptor, the first step is to declare it:

```
<interceptor name="actiontimer"
class="com.sharanamvaishali.myApp.ActionTimer" />
```

<interceptor> that declares it provides a logical name and maps it to the actual Java class.

After it is declared, a stack named myStack is created that holds the declared interceptor named **actiontimer** along with the **built-in** interceptor named **defaultStack**.

Since the action declares its own interceptor, the action loses its default and therefore, the defaultStack is explicitly referenced using <interceptor-ref>.

This stack is then set as the **default stack** for this package.

150   Struts 2 For Beginners

Process Flow Diagram

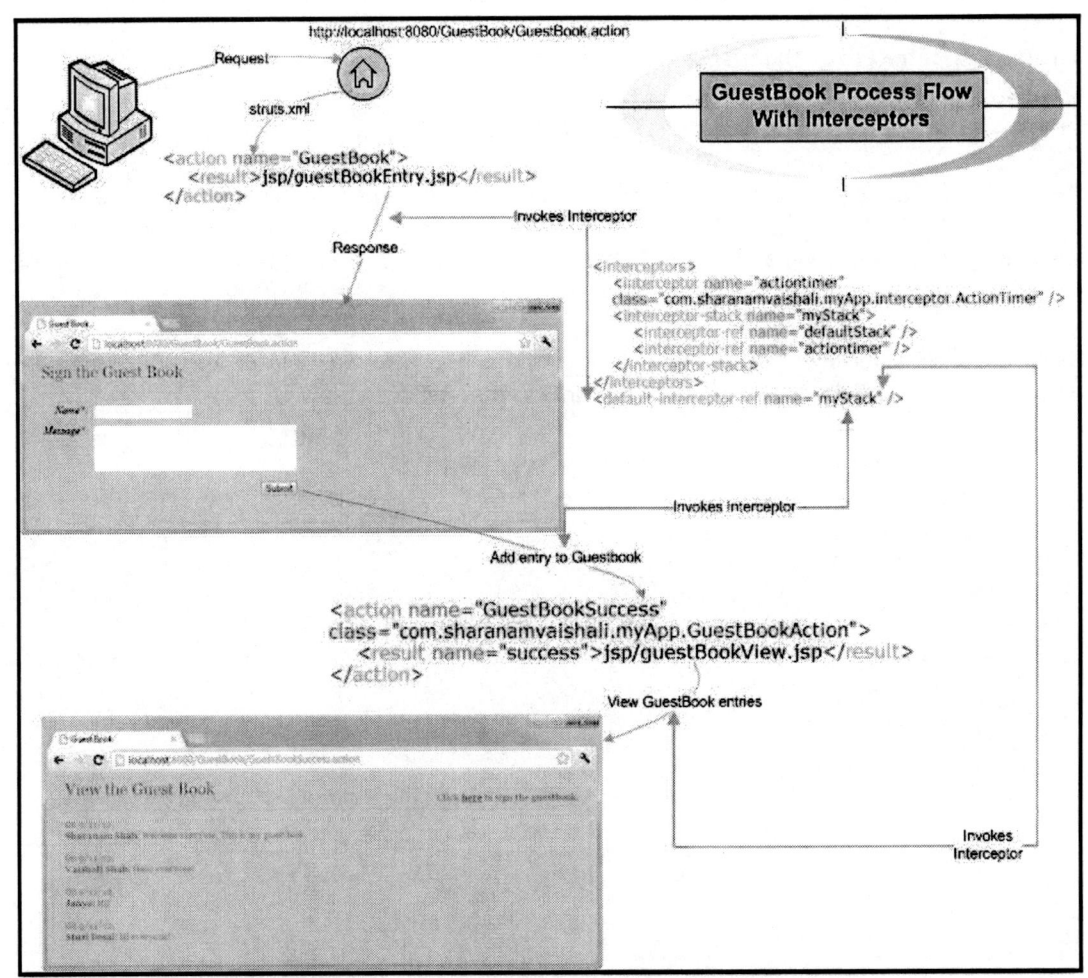

Diagram 9.1: GuestBook Process Flow With Interceptors

Running GuestBook Application

Now that the interceptor is in place. Let's run this application [source code available on the Book's accompanying CDROM].

Build and run the project as shown in the *Chapter 08: Building Views*.

Building Interceptors

index.jsp is rendered in the Web browser, which automatically links to the **GuestBook.action**, as shown in diagram 9.2.

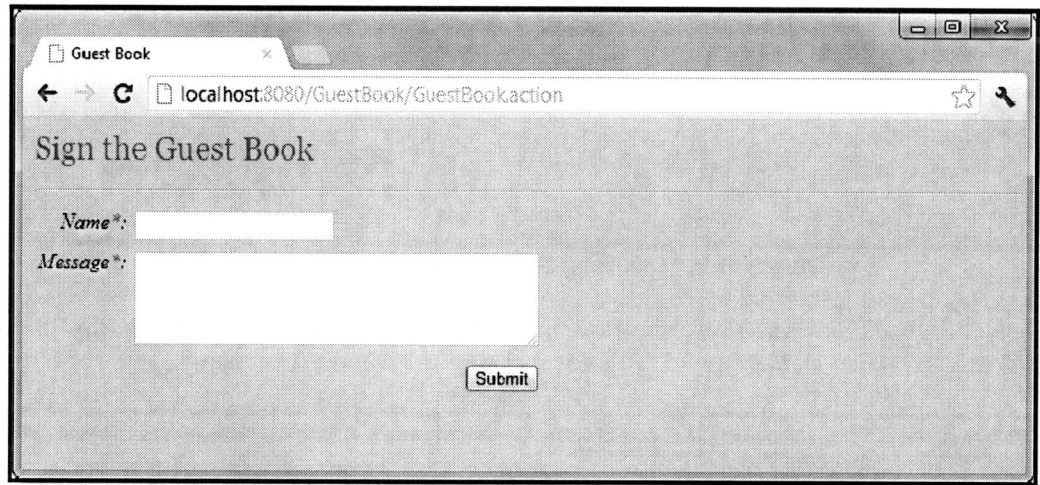

Diagram 9.2: The application run in the Web browser

When GuestBook.action appears, an entry appears in the Output window of the NetBeans, as shown in diagram 9.3. This entry is logged by ActionTimer.java.

Diagram 9.3: The entry logged by the interceptor in the Output window

Now enter the name and the comments in the Name and Message fields. Click Submit. The Guest book view page appears, as shown in diagram 9.4.

152   Struts 2 For Beginners

Diagram 9.4: Viewing the data entered by the user

When GuestBookSuccess.action appears, another entry appears in the Output window of the NetBeans, as shown in diagram 9.5. This entry is logged by ActionTimer.java.

Diagram 9.5: The entry logged by the interceptor in the Output window

When here link is clicked to go back to the Guest Book data entry form, again an entry appears in the Output window of the NetBeans.

Every such entry indicates the time taken for execution.

Now that the actions, views and the interceptors are covered, let's move on to the OGNL that surrounds the data transfer mechanisms of the framework.

Chapter 10

SECTION III: GETTING STARTED WITH STRUTS 2

OGNL And The Value Stack

The earlier chapters covered the action, views and the interceptor components giving a good idea about the role they play in Struts 2 framework. Now let's move further by understanding other important component [Value Stack] that plays a behind the scenes role of transferring and converting data. Struts 2 framework automates these tasks.

The **Value Stack** is a stack of objects. It consists of the following objects in the following order:

1. Temporary Objects: These are objects that are spawned during the execution and placed onto the value stack

2. Model Object: If model objects are being used, the current model object is placed before the action on the value stack

3. Action Object: The action being executed

4. Named Objects: These objects include #application, #session, #request, #attr and #parameters and refer to the corresponding Servlet scopes

Value Stack is a **central component** in Struts 2 framework. All the other core components interact with **Value Stack** which provides access to context information as well as to elements of the execution environment using the OGNL [Object Graph Navigational Language] syntax.

The Value Stack allows an expression language to find property values across multiple Objects.

OGNL is currently the default expression language that allows referencing data from the various regions of the framework in a consistent manner. It provides a mechanism to navigate object graphs using a **dot notation** and **evaluate expressions**, including calling methods on the objects being retrieved.

Value Stack

Value Stack follows a LIFO [Last In First Out] stack. It can hold any number of JavaBeans properties onto the stack. Retrieving a value means querying Value Stack for a property. Value Stack when queried looks through its set of objects, one by one, until it finds property that was queried. The last object put on the stack will be the first one searched.

HINT

> The easiest way to get a property onto the Value Stack is to add it to Action class. The Action is automatically pushed onto the value stack. Once this happens, the Action properties can be accessed directly using their names.

The Value Stack delivers exactly what a server side page wants. When a server side page asks for a property value, the Value Stack does not even know whether that property is on the first bean, second bean or the third bean and so on. It simply serves the value for the property asked for.

When the Value Stack finds what was asked for, the framework automatically converts the value to the target data type i.e. **converts the data** and serves the same i.e. **transfers that data**.

Data Transfer And Type Conversion

One of the most tedious jobs in any Web based application is the moving and converting data from string based HTTP to the different data types of the programming language. This includes conversions from string to other Java data types such as doubles, floats, integer and so on.

Struts 2 framework takes over the job of transferring data and converting the same as required.

For every request:

The framework moves the data from the string based HTTP requests to the JavaBeans properties of different Java data types.

Similarly, whilst rendering the result, some of the data that is available in the JavaBeans properties is transferred and converted for display in the resulting HTML page. This basically means that the data that was previously converted for storage in the JavaBeans properties is now re-converted from the Java data type back to a string format for display on the HTML page.

HINT

> Struts 2 type conversion mechanisms are quite powerful and can be easily extended. It also allows writing custom converters.

OGNL

In the MVC pattern that Struts 2 follows, the View is responsible for displaying the model and other objects. In JSP to access such objects, OGNL is used.

OGNL is an expression and binding language used for retrieving and setting the properties of the Java objects. OGNL acts as a binding language between GUI elements and the model objects.

OGNL helps:
- Bind form fields such as text fields, check boxes and so on to the model objects
- Convert values from one type to another

By:
- Moving data from the request parameters into the action's JavaBeans properties
- Moving data from the action's JavaBeans properties out into rendering HTML pages

To facilitate this movement, OGNL provides an expression language and type converters.

Expression Language

OGNL can be defined as an expression language to interact with Java objects. This is very useful binding language for manipulating and retrieving different properties of Java objects.

OGNL's expression language is typically used in the form input field names and JSP tags.

OGNL has its own syntax which is very simple in structure and hence, easy to learn and use. It also makes code spec more readable. OGNL syntax provides a high level abstraction for navigating object graphs, which means specifying paths through and to JavaBeans properties, collection indices and so on, instead of accessing them directly using Java code spec.

Example

Solution:
Welcome, <s:property value="username" />

Explanation:
Here, a JSP page welcomes a user by displaying the username.

In this code spec, the OGNL expression language is **username** that is held inside double quotes of the value attribute.

<s:property> takes the value from a property named username that is available in one of the Java objects and writes it onto the HTML.

OGNL's expression language allows using a simplified syntax to reference objects that reside in the Java environment.

Type Converters

For the data movement to be valid, OGNL also provides type converters. A type conversion occurs for every data movement.

A conversion could be:
- From the Java data type of the property referenced by the OGNL expression language to the string format of the HTML output
- From the string format of HTML input to the Java data type of the property it belongs to

OGNL And The Value Stack   157

This means every time data moves to or from the Java environment, a translation occurs between the string version of that data that resides in the HTML and the appropriate Java data type. All such conversions are handled by the built-in OGNL type converters.

Built-in Converters

Struts 2 framework comes with several built-in converters between the HTTP native strings and the following list of Java data types:

- String
- boolean/Boolean
- char/Character
- int/Integer
- float/Float
- long/Long
- double/Double
- Date
- array
- List
- Map

These built-in type conversions are automatically applied when an OGNL expression targets a property on the **Value Stack**.

OGNL's Role In Data Transfer And Type Conversion

In Struts 2, to expose a simple JavaBean property that is available in the **Value Stack**, OGNL is used as the expression language. For example, the following code spec extracts the username from the session:

Username: <s:property name="#session.user.username" />

Explanation:

Here, the value of the property named username that belong to the user object available in the session context is being retrieved. This returns the value that would have been returned by invoking **((User) session.get("user")).getUsername()**.

This **accessor pattern** is known as **dot notation** where each property name is separated by a **period [dot]** to provide navigation within an object graph.

An OGNL expression is evaluated in a context that may contain several objects. One of those objects can be designated the root. When referring to a property of the root object, the object being accessed need not be referenced, it can be directly accessed using the property name.

Whilst rendering the result, user.username [available in the JavaBeans properties] is **transferred** and **converted** for display in the resulting HTML page.

This basically means that the data held by that property that was previously converted for storage in the JavaBeans properties is now re-converted from the appropriate Java data type back out to a string format for display on the HTML page.

Accessing Action Context Properties Using

The OGNL context is set to use the framework's own **Action Context**. This context contains references to the standard **Request** and **Session** objects and other key resources.

To access the Action Context's resources the object's name is prefixed with the **# sign**.

The following are the **ActionContext properties** available through Action Context:

Property Name	Description
application	ServletContext as a Map
locale	Java locale object for this client
name	Name of the action
parameters	HttpServletRequest parameters as a Map
session	HttpSession as a Map

Form and OGNL

To take advantage of the automatic data transfer and type conversion when using forms the following needs to be done.

- Write OGNL expressions in the name attribute of the desired form fields
- Create the JavaBeans properties in the Action class to hold the data received

Example

Solution [JSP page that holds a data entry form]:
```
<s:form action="GuestBookSuccess" validate="true">
    <s:textfield label="Birthdate" name="birthdate" />
    <s:textfield label="Name" name="guest" />
    <s:textarea rows="4" cols="36" label="Message" name="message" />
```

```
    <s:submit/>
  </s:form>
```

Solution [Action class that holds JavaBeans Properties]:

```
public class GuestBookAction extends ActionSupport {
    private Date birthdate;
    private String guest;
    private String message;

    @Override
    public String execute() {
       return SUCCESS;
    }

    public Date getBirthdate() {
       return birthdate;
    }
    public void setBirthdate (Date birthdate) {
       this.birthdate = birthdate;
    }

    public String getGuest() {
       return guest;
    }
    public void setGuest(String guest) {
       this.guest = guest;
    }

    public String getMessage() {
       return message;
    }
    public void setMessage(String message) {
       this.message = message;
    }
}
```

How Is An OGNL Expression Resolved

When the request processing begins, the framework places the Action object in the Value Stack. OGNL expressions placed in the JSP page resolve against the Value Stack.

OGNL resolves the expressions as:

```
<s:textfield label="Birthdate" name="birthdate" />
```

In Java, this becomes the following:

```
getGuestBookAction().getBirthdate()
```

OGNL:
- Understands that the birthdate property is of **Date** data type
- Locates the string to Date converter
- Converts the value
- Sets the converted value on the property

Accessing Object Properties

To access the property of an object in the Value Stack, use one of the following:

object.propertyName

OR

object['propertyName']

OR

object["propertyName"]

Accessing Object Properties From The Context Map

To access the property of an object in the Context Map, use one of the following:

#object.propertyName

OR

#object['propertyName']

OR

#object["propertyName"]

Chapter 11

SECTION III: GETTING STARTED WITH STRUTS 2

Validations

Web applications often require user input. This input can range from simple username/password to data entered into a complex form with dependent fields. Such values that enter the application have to be validated prior storage.

One of the fundamental rules of developing applications is:
Do Not Trust User Input

This is true for any language on any platform.

It is very important to ensure that the input that enters the application does not cause the application to crash.

In Java,
- If an object is not initialized, **NullPointerException** is thrown as the exception

- If a number was expected as the input and a String is received instead, a **NumberFormatException** is thrown as the exception

The task of validating user input is often considered quite complex.

In the traditional JSP/Servlet scenario, the problem with adding validation code spec was that it requires maintenance, a recompile and a reinstall of the application, if the business rules change.

One of the core features of Struts 2 framework is its comprehensive built-in validation support which helps simplify the validation code spec. Struts treat form field validation as a configuration which solves the problems that were faced in the traditional JSP/Servlet scenario.

Validation is an important part of any Web framework because it is one of the most painfully repetitive things to have to continually recreate. **Struts 2** framework supports **Server** as well as **Client** side validations including advanced **Ajax** validation. It provides a wide range of validation rules [including regular expression] and plenty of pre-defined validators which can be applied to specific form fields or it can be non-field validations. It is also possible to create custom validators based on project specific validation requirements.

Using predefined validators is quite easy as no initial configuration is required. The framework implements Validation using a **Validation Interceptor** which is configured in the default interceptor stack.

Applying pre-defined validators is as simple as:
- Creating an XML configuration file
- Naming it appropriately
- Placing it in the right directory

The application begins applying these validations by testing the inputs before the action is invoked.

Kinds Of Validations

Struts 2 allows defining validations for an action [Programmatically] or at the domain object level [Declaratively].

To add validation programmatically:

- An action needs to implement **Validateable** interface which holds a method named **validate()** that should contain the actual validations
- An action needs to implement **ValidationAware** interface for reporting validation errors back to the user. This interface provides methods to add validation errors by determining if there are validation errors

HINT

> If the action extends **ActionSupport**, a default implementation for both these interfaces is made available.

Programmatic validations should only be used when the validations are extremely complex. A better approach is to use the other method i.e. provide validations declaratively.

Each action that requires declarative validations will need either annotations on the action class or a corresponding XML file that holds the validation declarations.

Declarative - Domain Object Level Validation

The following code spec depicts the XML validation configuration file:

```
1  <!DOCTYPE validators PUBLIC "-//Apache Struts//XWork Validator 1.0.3//EN"
     "http://struts.apache.org/dtds/xwork-validator-1.0.3.dtd">
2  <validators>
3     <field name="count">
4        <field-validator type="int" short-circuit="true">
5           <param name="min">1</param>
6           <param name="max">100</param>
7           <message key="invalid.count">
8              Value must be between ${min} and ${max}
9           </message>
10       </field-validator>
11    </field>
12
13    <field name="name">
14       <field-validator type="requiredstring">
15          <message>You must enter a name.</message>
16       </field-validator>
17    </field>
18
19    <validator type="expression" short-circuit="true">
20       <param name="expression">email.equals(email2)</param>
21       <message>Email not the same as email2</message>
22    </validator>
23 </validators>
```

Explanation:

In the XML configuration file:
<field-validators> must have a **type** attribute, which refers to a name of the registered Validator with ValidatorFactory.

<validator> may have one or more <param> with name and value attributes to set arbitrary parameters into the Validator instance.

A **<field>** can have one or more **<field-validator>** nodes. Each **<field-validator>** is executed in the order of definition.

The **short-circuit** attribute:

- If set to **true**

AND

- The validation fails

All further validations are skipped and a failed result is returned for that field.

The **key** attribute in the message node is used for determining the message to be displayed to the user from a message bundle.

Validator configuration information [in this case min and max] as well as values from the Value Stack can be used in the validation message by using ${ }.

Validators Scope

Validator scopes indicate whether a Validator can act on a single field accessible through an action or on the full action context which involves more than one field.

Code spec:
```
<field name="count">
   <field-validator type="int" short-circuit="true">
```

Field validators, as the name indicates, act on single fields accessible through an action.

Code spec:
```
<validator type="expression" short-circuit="true">
```

A Validator, in contrast, is more generic and can do validations in the full action context, involving more than one field in the validation rule.

Validators Precedence

<validator> takes precedence over **<field-validator>**. This means <validators> get validated first in the order of the definition and then <field-validator> in the order of their definition.

In the code spec above, the actual execution of validator would be as follows:
1. Validator for email
2. Field Validators for count field
3. Field Validators for name field

Short Circuiting Validations

It is sometimes required that when one validation fails then other dependent validations are not required and hence they should not fire. For example, if an email field is required and it is null, then it does not make sense to check whether it is a valid email address. In order to enable this, a short circuit property is available in the Validation framework. By using this, it is possible to short circuit a stack of validators.

Example

Solution:
```
<validators>
   <field name="enterEmail">
      <field-validator type="requiredString" short-circuit="true">
         <message>Please enter the email address.</message>
      </field-validator>

      <field-validator type="email" short-circuit="true">
         <message>Please enter the valid email address.</message>
      </field-validator>
   </field>
</validator>
```

Explanation:

If the user has not entered the email address i.e. the email address is null or empty the **requiredString** validator is fired but the **email** validator is not fired because the short circuit attribute is set to **true** for the requiredString validator.

Validator Types

The following are the types of validators available in Struts 2 framework.

required

This validator type ensures that the specified is not null.

fieldName

This parameter is mandatory in case of <validator>, however, it is not required in case of <field-validator>.

Example

Solution:
```
<validator type="required">
   <param name="fieldName">username</param>
   <message>Username cannot be null</message>
</validator>

<field name="username">
   <field-validator type="required">
      <message>Username cannot be null</message>
   </field-validator>
</field>
```

requiredstring

This validator type ensures that the string field is not null and has a length > 0 which technically means that it is not String username = "".

fieldName

This parameter is mandatory in case of <validator>, however, it is not required in case of <field-validator>.

trim

This parameter determines whether it will trim the String before performing the length check. If unspecified it holds true i.e. the String will be trimmed.

Example

Solution:
```xml
<validator type="requiredstring">
    <param name="fieldName">username</param>
    <param name="trim">true</param>
    <message>Username is required</message>
</validator>

<field name="username">
    <field-validator type="requiredstring">
        <param name="trim">true</param>
        <message>Username is required</message>
    </field-validator>
</field>
```

stringlength

This validator determines if a String is within a specific length range.

fieldName

This parameter is mandatory in case of <validator>, however, it is not required in case of <field-validator>.

maxLength

If this is specified, it ensures that the String has **at most** that many characters.

minLength

If this is specified, it ensures that String has **at least** that many character.

trim

This parameter determines whether it will trim the String before performing the length check. If unspecified it holds true i.e. the String will be trimmed.

Example

Solution:
```xml
<field name="myPurchaseCode">
```

```xml
    <param name="minLength">10</param>
    <param name="maxLength">10</param>
    <param name="trim">true</param>
    <message>The purchase code needs to be 10 characters long</message>
</field-name>

<validator type="stringlength">
    <param name="fieldName">myPurchaseCode</param>
    <param name="minLength">10</param>
    <param name="maxLength">10</param>
    <param name="trim">true</param>
    <message>The purchase code needs to be 10 characters long</message>
</validator>
```

int

This validator checks whether an integer specified is within a certain range.

For example, the field Employee Age should be validated for the range 18 to 60 i.e. the age of the employee should be more than 18 but less than 60.

fieldName

This parameter is mandatory in case of <validator>, however, it is not required in case of <field-validator>.

max

If this is specified, it ensures that the Integer has the maximum value.

min

If this is specified, it ensures that Integer has the minimum value.

Example

Solution:
```xml
<field name="myAge">
    <field-validator type="int">
        <param name="min">18</param>
        <param name="max">60</param>
        <message> Age needs to be between ${min} and ${max}</message>
    </field-validator>
</field-name>
```

```xml
<validator type="int">
   <param name="fieldName">myAge</param>
   <param name="min">18</param>
   <param name="max">60</param>
   <message>Age needs to be between ${min} and ${max}</message>
</validator>
```

double

This validator checks whether the double specified is within a certain range.

fieldName

This parameter is mandatory in case of <validator>, however, it is not required in case of <field-validator>.

maxInclusive

If this is specified, it ensures that the Integer has the maximum inclusive value in FloatValue specified by Java language.

minInclusive

If this is specified, it ensures that Integer has the minimum inclusive value in FloatValue specified by Java language.

maxExclusive

If this is specified, it ensures that the Integer has the maximum exclusive value in FloatValue specified by Java language.

minExclusive

If this is specified, it ensures that Integer has the minimum exclusive value in FloatValue specified by Java language.

Example

Solution:

```xml
<validator type="double">
   <param name="fieldName">percentage</param>
```

```
    <param name="minInclusive">20</param>
    <param name="maxInclusive">50</param>
    <message>Passing percentage needs to be between ${minInclusive} and
    ${maxInclusive}</message>
</validator>

<field name="percentage">
    <field-validator type="double">
        <param name="minExclusive">20</param>
        <param name="maxExclusive">50</param>
        <message>Passing percentage needs to be between ${minExclusive} and
        ${maxExclusive}</message>
    </field-validator>
</field>
```

date

This validator checks whether the date specified is within a certain range.

fieldName

This parameter is mandatory in case of <validator>, however, it is not required in case of <field-validator>.

max

If this is specified, it ensures that the Date has the maximum value.

min

If this is specified, it ensures that Date has the minimum value.

Example

Solution:
```
<validator type="date">
    <param name="fieldName">anniversary</param>
    <param name="min">01/01/1900</param>
    <param name="max">01/12/2008</param>
    <message>Anniversary date must be within ${min} and ${max}</message>
</validator>

<field name="birthday">
    <field-validator type="date">
        <param name="min">01/01/1900</param>
```

```xml
        <param name="max">01/12/2008</param>
        <message>Birthday must be within ${min} and ${max}</message>
    </field>
</field>
```

expression

This validator evaluates an OGNL expression using the Value Stack. It allows creating powerful validations using just the XML and the existing model.

This validator should be applied when validations are not specific to one field, because it adds action-level error messages.

expression

This parameter is the OGNL expression, which is to be evaluated against the Value Stack. It must be a Boolean value.

> *Example*

Solution:
```xml
<validator type="expression">
    <param name="expression">
        /^\w+([\.-]?\w+)*@\w+([\.-]?\w+)*(\.\w{2,3})+$/
    </param>
    <message>Invalid email address.</message>
</validator>
```

fieldExpression

This validator validates a field using an OGNL expression.

fieldName

This parameter is mandatory in case of <validator>, however, it is not required in case of <field-validator>.

expression

This parameter holds the OGNL expression, which is to be evaluated against the Value Stack and evaluation is in the form of True or False. A value of true means the object or field is valid. A value of false means that the object or field is invalid and causes an error message to be added.

Example

Solution:
```xml
<field name="age">
   <field-validator type="fieldExpression">
      <param name="expression">#age > 18</param>
      <message>The age of marriage for girls should be above 18.</message>
   </field>
</field>
```

email

This validator validates whether a given string field is in a valid email address format.

The OGNL expression used by the email validator to validate whether the string is a valid email address is:

\\b(^[_A-Za-z0-9-](\\.[_A-Za-z0-9-])*@([A-Za-z0-9-])+((\\.com)|(\\.net)|(\\.org)|(\\.info)|(\\.edu)|(\\.mil)|(\\.gov)|(\\.biz)|(\\.ws)|(\\.us)|(\\.tv)|(\\.cc)|(\\.aero)|(\\.arpa)|(\\.coop)|(\\.int)|(\\.jobs)|(\\.museum)|(\\.name)|(\\.pro)|(\\.travel)|(\\.nato)|(\\..{2,3})|(\\..{2,3}\\..{2,3}))$)\\b

fieldName

This parameter is mandatory in case of <validator>, however, it is not required in case of <field-validator>.

Example

Solution:
```xml
<validator type="email">
   <param name="fieldName">emailAddress</param>
   <message>Invalid email address.</message>
</validator>
```

url

This validator validates whether a given field is a string and a valid URL.

fieldName

This parameter is mandatory in case of <validator>, however, it is not required in case of <field-validator>.

Example

Solution:
```
<validator type="url">
   <param name="fieldName">homePage</param>
   <message>Invalid home page URL.</message>
</validator>
```

conversion

This validator validates if a conversion error occurred for a particular field. It checks if a type conversion error had occurred when setting the value on the field and uses the type-conversion framework to create the correct field error message to be added for the field.

fieldName

This parameter is mandatory in case of <validator>, however, it is not required in case of <field-validator>.

Example

Solution:
```
<validator type="conversion">
   <param name="fieldName">myField</param>
   <message>Conversion error occurred.</message>
</validator>
```

regex

This validator validates a string using a regular expression.

fieldName

This parameter is mandatory in case of <validator>, however, it is not required in case of <field-validator>.

expression

This parameter is mandatory. This parameter is the RegExp expression.

caseSensitive

This parameter allows indicating whether the expression should be matched against in a case sensitive way. The default value is true.

trim

This parameter sets whether the expression should be trimmed before matching. The default value is true.

Example

Solution:
```xml
<validator type="regex">
    <param name="fieldName">myStrangePostcode</param>
    <param name="expression">
        <![CDATA[([aAbBcCdD][123][eEfFgG][456])]]>
    </param>
</validator>

<field name="myStrangePostcode">
    <field-validator type="regex">
        <param name="expression">
            <![CDATA[([aAbBcCdD][123][eEfFgG][456])]]>
        </param>
    </field-validator>
</field>
```

visitor

This validator allows forwarding validation to object properties of the action using the object's own validation files.

This allows using ModelDriven development pattern and managing the validations for the models in one place, where they belong, next to the model classes.

For example, model driven actions are used and each has a property called person which is a class Person. If this same model is used across many actions, then the validation information needs to be extracted to re-use it. The visitor validation type allows this functionality.

The visitor validator can handle either simple Object properties, Collections of Objects or Arrays.

fieldName

This parameter is mandatory in case of <validator>, however, it is not required in case of <field-validator>.

context

This parameter is the context of which validation should take place.

appendPrefix

This parameter is the prefix to be added to field.

Example

Solution:
```
<validator type="visitor">
   <param name="fieldName">user</param>
   <param name="context">myContext</param>
   <param name="appendPrefix">true</param>
</validator>

<field name="user">
   <field-validator type="visitor">
      <param name="context">myContext</param>
      <param name="appendPrefix">true</param>
   </field-validator>
</field>
```

Continuing With The Application

Let's continue with GuestBook application to demonstrate validators.

176   Struts 2 For Beginners

This application accepts Visitor's name and comments, as shown in diagram 11.1. <u>Both these inputs are mandatory</u>. Apply validation to this form using declarative method.

Diagram 11.1

Struts 2 framework uses XML based configuration file. This file should be named as: <Action class name>-validation.xml.

To apply the declarative validation to GuestBookAction, create a file **GuestBookAction-validation.xml** in the same directory which holds **GuestBookAction.java**.

To do so, right click **com.sharanamvaishali.myApp.action** package/directory and select **New → XML Document...**, as shown in diagram 11.2.

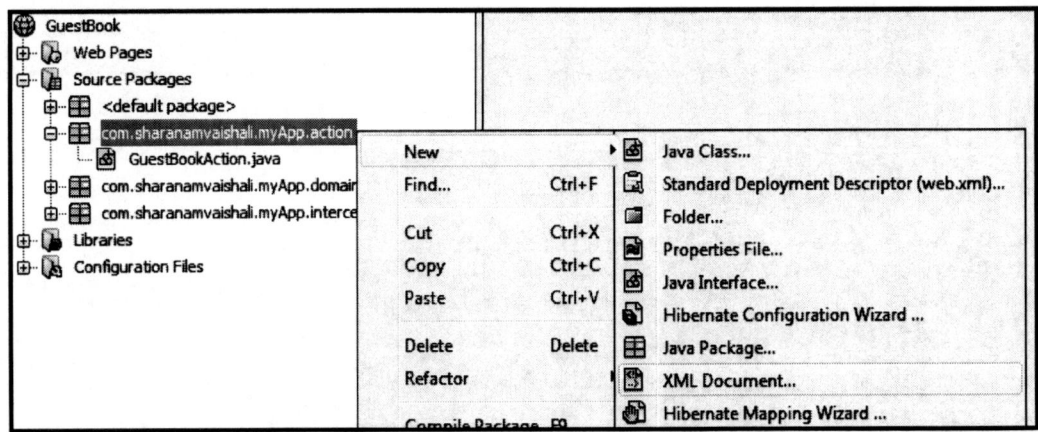

Diagram 11.2: Selecting the XML Document

Enter **GuestBookAction-validation** as the file name, as shown in diagram 11.3.

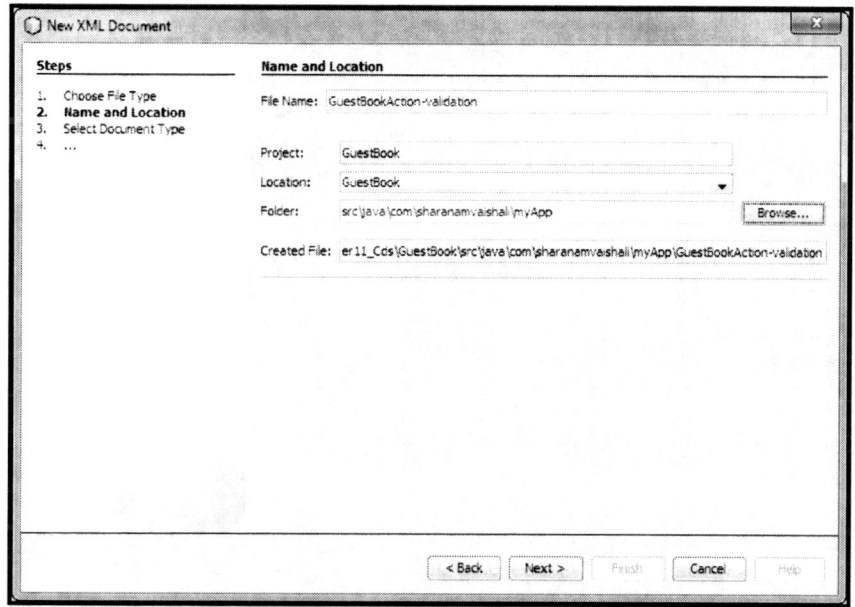

Diagram 11.3: Naming XML Document

Click [Next >]. Select the option **DTD-Constrained Document**, as shown in diagram 11.4.

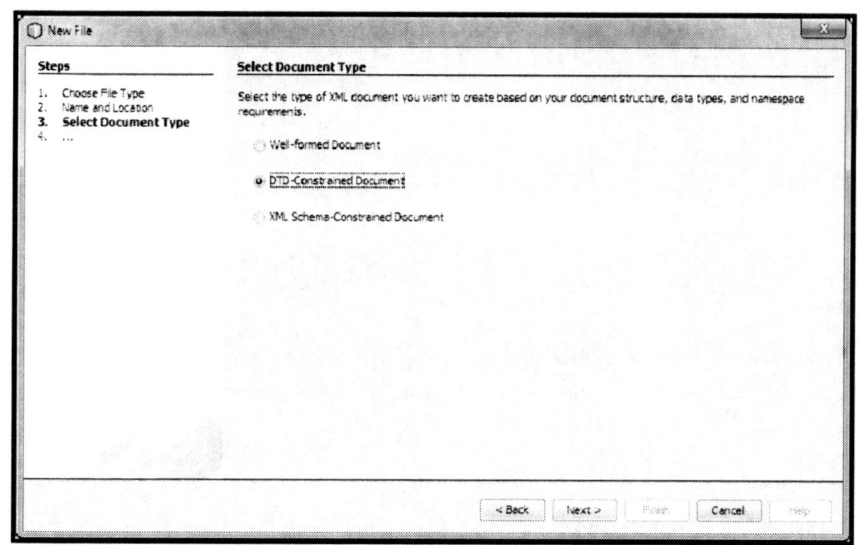

Diagram 11.4: Selecting the document type

178   Struts 2 For Beginners

Click [Next >]. Specify the **DTD Options** for the XML document type, as shown in diagram 11.5. Populate the following fields:

DTD Public ID	-//Apache Struts//XWork Validator 1.0.3//EN
DTD System ID	http://struts.apache.org/dtds/xwork-validator-1.0.3.dtd
Document Root	validators

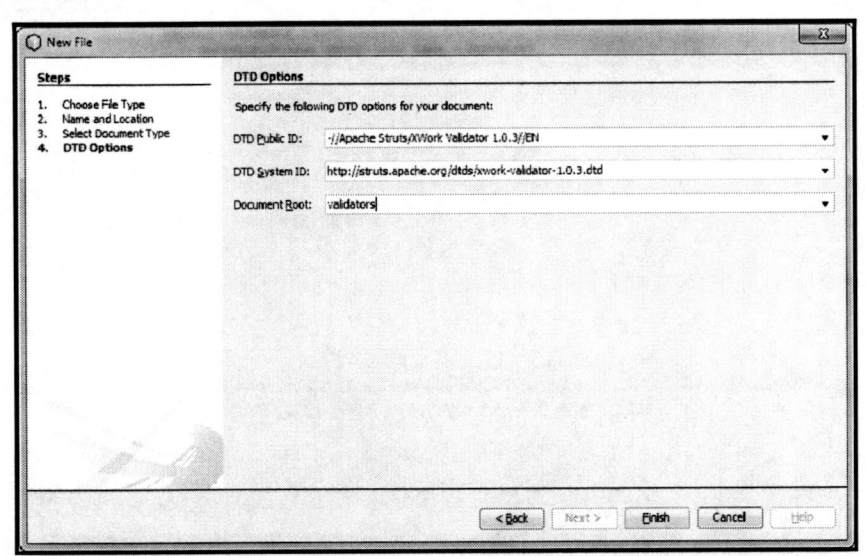

Diagram 11.5: Specifying the DTD options for XML document type

Click [Finish].

Key in the following code spec in **GuestBookAction-validation.xml**:

```
1  <?xml version="1.0" encoding="UTF-8"?>
2  <!DOCTYPE validators PUBLIC "-//Apache Struts//XWork Validator 1.0.3//EN"
   "http://struts.apache.org/dtds/xwork-validator-1.0.3.dtd">
3  <validators>
4    <field name="guest">
5      <field-validator type="requiredstring">
6        <message>Please enter your name.</message>
7      </field-validator>
8    </field>
9    <field name="message">
10     <field-validator type="requiredstring">
11       <message>Please leave a message.</message>
12     </field-validator>
13   </field>
14 </validators>
```

Explanation:

This file and the code spec shows how easy it is to validate the incoming data.

Here, both the inputs requires some sort of validation. Hence, two <field> entries are added.

<field> can contain one or more <field-validator>.

In this case each holds one each as per the application requirements.

The type of validator used for both the input fields is **requiredstring**. This type indicates that something must be present.

If the test fails, an error message is shown using **<message>**.

After the validations are applied, if the visitors skip entering either of them, then the appropriate error messages as defined in the XML file appear, as shown in diagram 11.6.

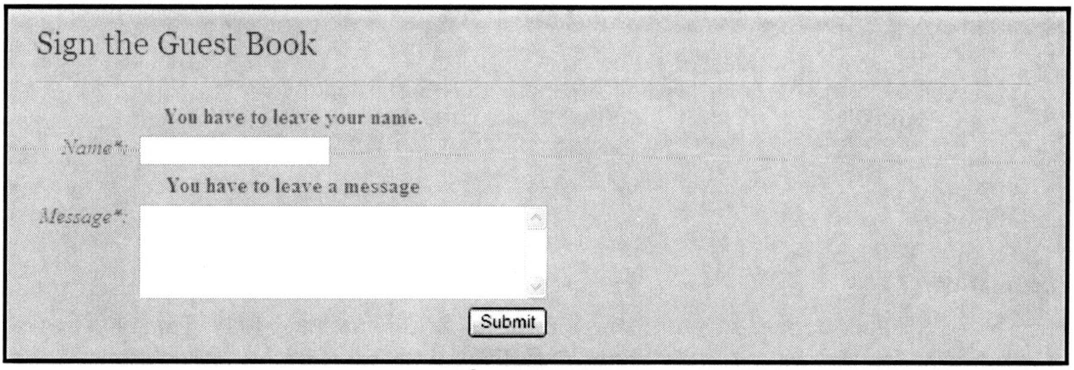

Diagram 11.6

The framework looks for an XML validation configuration, if one exists named as <ActionClass>-validation.xml. In this case it is GuestBookAction-validation.xml.

REMINDER

The validation configuration must be located in the same package as the action class itself.

Next modify struts.xml.

struts.xml Modifications

Code spec:

```xml
 1  <?xml version="1.0" encoding="UTF-8"?>
 2  <!DOCTYPE struts PUBLIC '-//Apache Software Foundation//DTD Commons Validator
    Rules Configuration 2.3//EN' 'http://struts.apache.org/dtds/struts-2.3.dtd'>
 3  <struts>
 4      <package name="guestbook" extends="struts-default">
 5          <interceptors>
 6              <interceptor name="actiontimer"
                    class="com.sharanamvaishali.myApp.interceptor.ActionTimer" />
 7              <interceptor-stack name="myStack">
 8                  <interceptor-ref name="defaultStack" />
 9                  <interceptor-ref name="actiontimer" />
10              </interceptor-stack>
11          </interceptors>
12
13          <default-interceptor-ref name="myStack" />
14
15          <action name="GuestBook">
16              <result>jsp/guestBookEntry.jsp</result>
17          </action>
18          <action name="GuestBookSuccess"
                class="com.sharanamvaishali.myApp.action.GuestBookAction">
19              <result name="input">jsp/guestBookEntry.jsp</result>
20              <result name="success">jsp/guestBookView.jsp</result>
21          </action>
22      </package>
23  </struts>
```

Explanation:

The above code spec defines a result named **input** to indicate the page to be displayed in case of input error. In this case it simply brings back the data entry form [guestBookEntry.jsp] in case of input errors [if any] when the user clicks **Submit**.

Process Flow Diagram

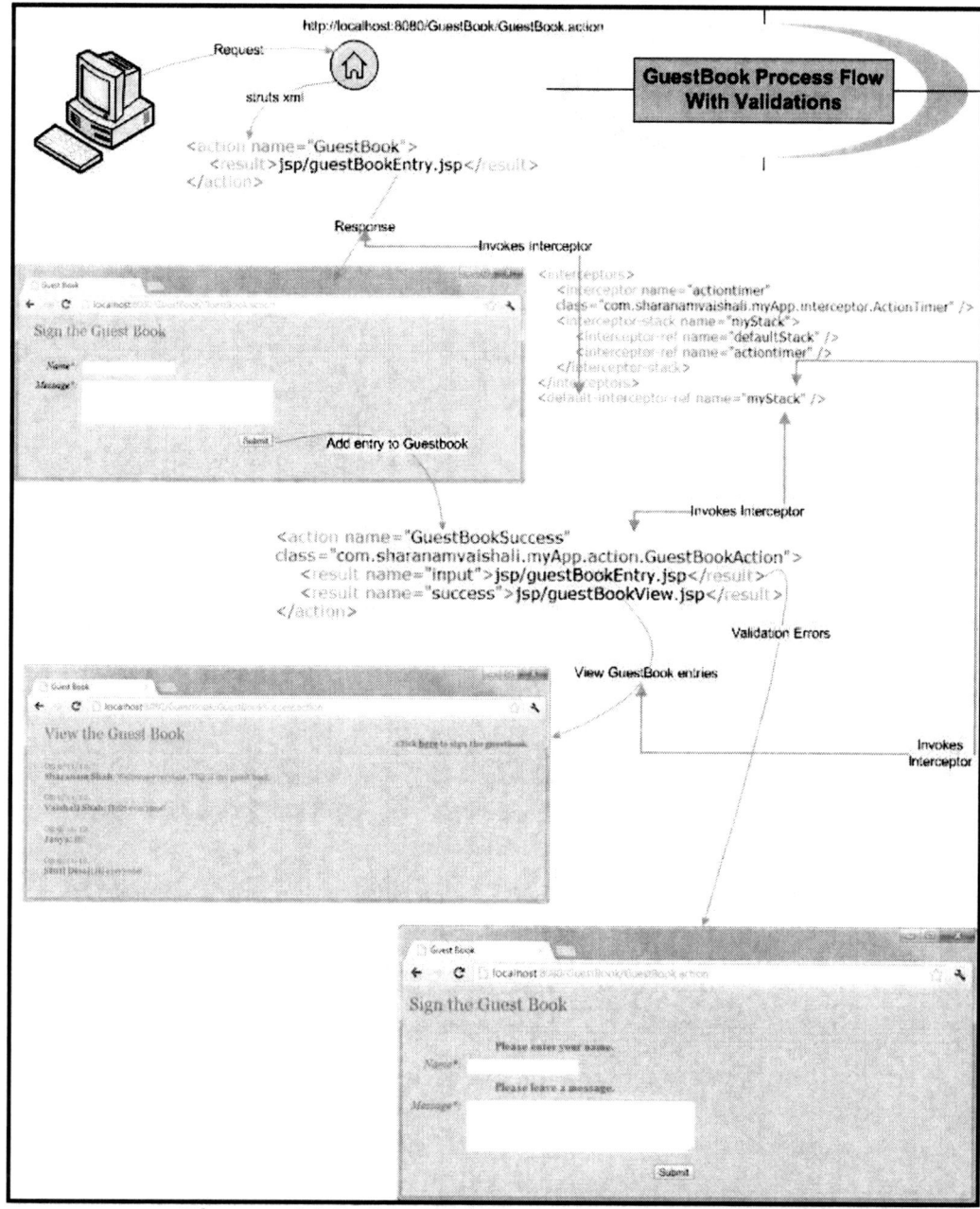

Diagram 11.7: GuestBook Process Flow With Validations

Client Side Validation

Struts 2 supports server side as well as client side validations. In case of client side validations, Struts 2 automatically produces the required JavaScript code spec.

This section describes how the same XML configuration file can be used to apply client side validations. To validate data at the client side, all that needs to be done is:

- Create the XML validation configuration file [same as the one that was created earlier]
- Add **validate=true** to the FORM tag

Struts 2 takes care of the rest by producing the appropriate JavaScript code spec.

Let's convert GuestBook application's validations to client side. To achieve this, add the validate attribute to the form tag in the guestBookEntry.jsp file and set it to true:

```
30      <s:form action="GuestBookSuccess" validate="true">
31          <s:textfield required="true" label="Name" name="guest" />
32          <s:textarea required="true" rows="4" cols="36" label="Message"
                name="message" />
33          <s:submit />
34      </s:form>
```

Since this is client side validation, the error messages appear without the page being refreshed. This is because appropriate JavaScript code spec to do the validation is available on the client side.

JavaScript Code Spec Inclusion

Now when the form renders, view the page source to verify the JavaScript inclusion.

```
31      <td>
32          <script type="text/javascript"
                src="/GuestBook/struts/xhtml/validation.js"></script>
33          <script type="text/javascript"
                src="/GuestBook/struts/utils.js"></script>
34          <form id="GuestBookSuccess" name="GuestBookSuccess"
                onsubmit="return validateForm_GuestBookSuccess();"
                action="/GuestBook/GuestBookSuccess.action" method="post"
                onreset="clearErrorMessages(this);clearErrorLabels(this);">
35              <table class="wwFormTable">
36                  <tr>
37                      <td class="tdLabel"><label for="GuestBookSuccess_guest"
                            class="label">Name<span
                            class="required">*</span>:</label></td>
38                      <td><input type="text" name="guest" value=""
                            id="GuestBookSuccess_guest"/></td>
```

Validations

Here, Struts 2 has set the **onSubmit** attribute of the FORM tag to invoke a JavaScript function. This means prior the form submission, a JavaScript function named **validateForm_GuestBookSuccess()** is invoked which performs the data validation.

If this was a server side validation i.e. validate="true" is absent, in that case, onSubmit is set to "return true;":

```
31          <td>
32              <form id="GuestBookSuccess" name="GuestBookSuccess"
                    onsubmit="return true;"
                    action="/GuestBook/GuestBookSuccess.action" method="post">
33                  <table class="wwFormTable">
34                      <tr>
35                          <td class="tdLabel"><label for="GuestBookSuccess_guest"
                                class="label">Name<span
                                class="required">*</span>:</label></td>
36                          <td><input type="text" name="guest" value=""
                                id="GuestBookSuccess_guest"/></td>
```

validateForm_GuestBookSuccess() is added within <SCRIPT> inside <BODY/>.

```
56          <script type="text/javascript">
57              function validateForm_GuestBookSuccess() {
58                  form = document.getElementById("GuestBookSuccess");
59                  clearErrorMessages(form);
60                  clearErrorLabels(form);
61                  var errors = false;
62                  var continueValidation = true;
63                  if (form.elements['guest']) {
64                      field = form.elements['guest'];
65                      var error = "Please enter your name.";
66                      if (continueValidation && field.value != null && (field.value == "" ||
                            field.value.replace(/^\s+|\s+$/g,"").length == 0)) {
67                          addError(field, error);
68                          errors = true;
69                      }
70                  }
71                  if (form.elements['message']) {
72                      field = form.elements['message'];
73                      var error = "Please leave a message.";
74                      if (continueValidation && field.value != null && (field.value == "" ||
                            field.value.replace(/^\s+|\s+$/g,"").length == 0)) {
75                          addError(field, error);
76                          errors = true;
77                      }
78                  }
79                  return !errors;
80              }
81          </script>
82      </td>
83    </tr>
84  </table>
85 </body>
```

Running GuestBook Application

Now that validators is in place. Let's run this application [source code available on the Book's accompanying CDROM].

Build and run the project using the NetBeans IDE, as shown in the *Chapter 08: Building Views*.

index.jsp appears in the Web browser, which automatically invokes **GuestBook.action**, as shown in diagram 11.8.

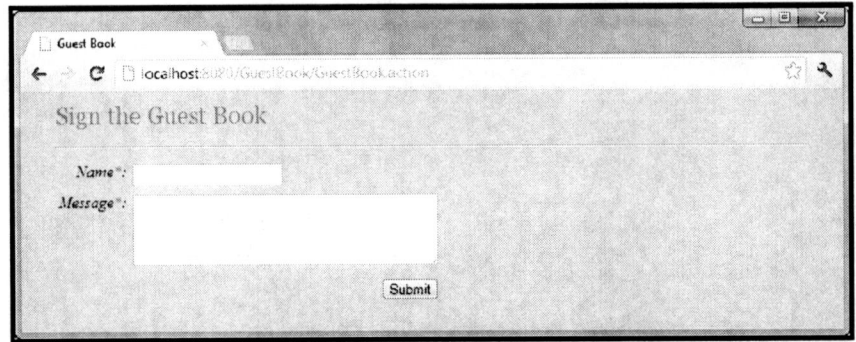

Diagram 11.8: The application run in the Web browser

Click [Submit] without entering any data in the data entry form. The error messages appear in the data entry form, as shown in diagram 11.9.

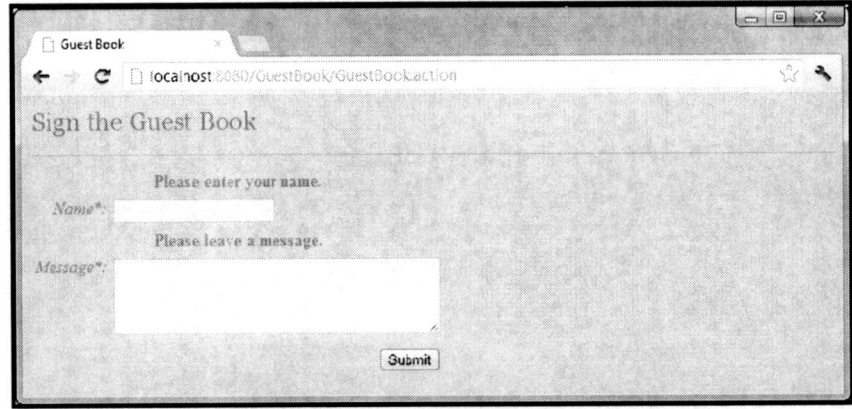

Diagram 11.9: The validation error messages

Enter only the name. Click [Submit]. Only the error message for the message field appears in the data entry form, as shown in diagram 11.10.

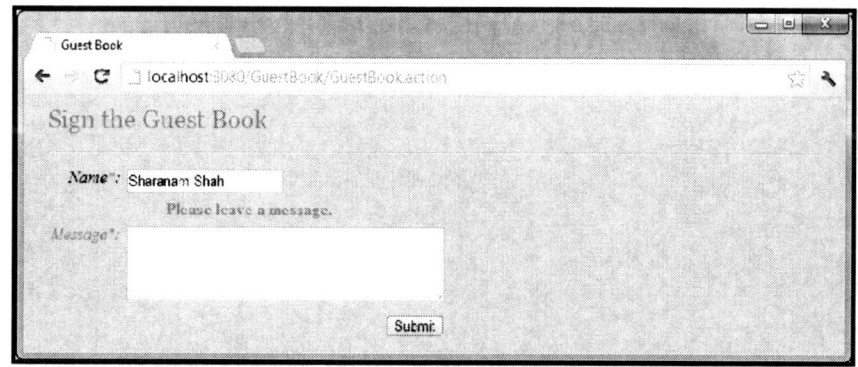

Diagram 11.10: The validation error message

Now enter both the name and the message in the Name and Message fields. Click [Submit]. Guest book view page appears, as shown in diagram 11.11.

Diagram 11.11: Viewing the data entered by the user

This completes GuestBook application.

However, this is not usable in the real world as it does not store the guestbook entries in a permanent data store. To make this application usable, a permanent data store such as MySQL database should be used to hold the entries, which is exactly what the next chapter delves into.

Chapter 12

SECTION III: GETTING STARTED WITH STRUTS 2

Using The Data Store

Now that GuestBook application is up and running. Let's move further and use a data store to hold the Guestbook messages.

Guestbook application, that is built so far uses basic Java techniques that allow tracking messages as they come in. There was no permanent data store used.

The data i.e. visitor's name and the messages were stored temporarily in a class level static ArrayList using a bean object. This means irrespective of the number of GuestBooks instantiated, there will be only one ArrayList store i.e. **messages** which will be shared amongst all the instantiated GuestBooks. Hence, the data that GuestBook application captures does not persist.

This kind of application cannot be used in the real world. To make it usable, a permanent data store is required.

Let's enhance this application by adding a permanent data store.

Application Requirements

The data captured by GuestBook application should be stored in a database table named Guestbook. The database engine will be **MySQL**.

Table Structure

Table Name: GuestBook

Column Definition:

Column Name	Data Type	Width	Description
GuestNo	Integer	11	The identity number of the visitor. Is the primary key. Is auto increment.
Guest	Varchar	50	The name of the visitor who visited the Web site.
Message	Varchar	100	The message of the visitor.
MessageDate	Varchar	40	The date when the visitor left a message.

Continuing With The Application

Ensure that the MySQL database engine [available in this Book's accompanying CDROM] is available on the development machine prior proceeding. This can be downloaded from the website http://dev.mysql.com/downloads/.

Database Creation

Solution:
```
CREATE DATABASE GuestBook;
USE GuestBook;
```

Table Creation

Solution:
```
CREATE TABLE GuestBook(
     GuestNo Int PRIMARY KEY AUTO_INCREMENT,
     Guest varchar(50),
     Message varchar(100),
     MessageDate varchar(40));
```

After the database and the table is created switch to NetBeans to begin the enhancement.

To transfer the captured data to the database, the following needs to be done:
- Add MySQL driver
- Connect to MySQL from the Action class
- Use an INSERT query to add data to the MySQL table
- Use a SELECT query to retrieve data from the MySQL table for display

Add MySQL Driver

MySQL provides connectivity to client applications developed in the Java EE 5 via a JDBC driver named **MySQL Connector/J**.

MySQL Connector/J is a native Java driver that converts JDBC calls into the network protocol used by the MySQL database. MySQL Connector/J is a Type 4 driver, which means that MySQL Connector is pure Java code spec and communicates directly with the MySQL server using the MySQL protocol.

MySQL Connector/J allows the developers working with Java EE 5, to build applications, which interact with MySQL and connect all corporate data even in a heterogeneous environment.

Visit the site **http://dev.mysql.com/downloads/connector/j/** to download the MySQL Connector/J JDBC Driver.

At the time of writing this book the latest version of the **MySQL Connector/J** was **5.1.21** [Available in the Book CDROM].

After it is downloaded, using any unzip utility such as Winzip unzip the contents of the zip file.

Right-click on **Libraries** directory, click **Add JAR/Folder....**

Clicking the **Add JAR/Folder** file displays the dialog box to choose the JAR files. Browse to the **<Drive:>/mysql-connector-java-X.X.X** directory and select **mysql-connector-java-X.X.X-bin.jar** JAR file to add to the project.

Now the mysql-connector JAR file is added to the Libraries directory of the project.

Next modify the action class [GuestBookAction.java].

Action Class Modifications

Solution:

```
1  package com.sharanamvaishali.myApp.action;
2
3  import com.opensymphony.xwork2.ActionSupport;
4  import com.sharanamvaishali.myApp.domain.GuestBook;
5  import java.sql.Connection;
6  import java.sql.DriverManager;
7  import java.sql.ResultSet;
8  import java.sql.Statement;
9  import java.text.DateFormat;
10 import java.text.SimpleDateFormat;
11 import java.util.ArrayList;
12 import java.util.Date;
13
14 public class GuestBookAction extends ActionSupport {
15     private static final long serialVersionUID = -8577843349235520003L;
16     DateFormat dateFormat = new SimpleDateFormat("yyyy/MM/dd");
17     Date date = new Date();
18     private String guest;
19     private String message;
20     private String when = (dateFormat.format(date)).toString();
21     private static ArrayList<GuestBook> messages = new ArrayList<GuestBook>();
22
23     Connection conn = null;
24     Statement stmt = null;
25     ResultSet rs = null;
26
27     private String dbName = "GuestBook";
28     private String host = "localhost";
29     private String username = "root";
30     private String password = "123456";
31
32     @Override
33     public String execute() {
34         try {
35             Class.forName("com.mysql.jdbc.Driver").newInstance();
36             conn = DriverManager.getConnection("jdbc:mysql://" + host + "/" +
                   dbName, username, password);
37             stmt = conn.createStatement();
38
39             String query = "INSERT INTO GuestBook (Guest, Message, MessageDate)
                    VALUES ('" + getGuest() + "', '" + getMessage() + "', '" + getWhen() + "')";
40             stmt.executeUpdate(query);
41
42             query = "SELECT * FROM GuestBook";
43             rs = stmt.executeQuery(query);
44             while (rs.next()) {
45                 GuestBook guestBookMsgs = new GuestBook();
46                 guestBookMsgs.setGuest(rs.getString("Guest"));
```

```
47              guestBookMsgs.setMessage(rs.getString("Message"));
48              guestBookMsgs.setWhen(rs.getString("MessageDate"));
49              messages.add(guestBookMsgs);
50           }
51        } catch (Exception e) {
52        }
53        return SUCCESS;
54    }
55
56    public ArrayList<GuestBook> getMessages() {
57        return messages;
58    }
59    public void setMessages(ArrayList<GuestBook> messages) {
60        this.messages = messages;
61    }
62
63    public String getGuest() {
64        return guest;
65    }
66    public void setGuest(String guest) {
67        this.guest = guest;
68    }
69
70    public String getMessage() {
71        return message;
72    }
73    public void setMessage(String message) {
74        this.message = message;
75    }
76
77    public String getWhen() {
78        return when;
79    }
80    public void setWhen(String when) {
81        this.when = when;
82    }
83 }
```

Explanation:

java.sql Package

java.sql package is used to connect to the MySQL database. java.sql package contains majority of class objects used for database access.

The most important classes inside this package are:

- DriverManager
- Connection

- ResultSet
- Statement

Almost every database driver supports the components of this package.

Objects And Variables Declaration

The following objects are declared and their values set to **null:**
- **Connection:** Is a Java interface which defines a link to a database
- **ResultSet:** Is a Java interface that represents a set of records retrieved from the database
- **Statement:** Is a Java interface that represents how application data requests are sent from Java code spec to the database engine. **Statement** can hold ANSI SQL statements compatible across all database systems

The following four variables of data type String are declared:
- **dbName:** Whose value is set to the database name of the MySQL i.e. **GuestBook**
- **host:** Whose value is set to the name of the machine i.e. **localhost**
- **username:** Whose value is set to the username of the MySQL user i.e. **root**
- **password:** Whose value is set to the password of the MySQL user

Removing static Keyword From ArrayList Declaration

static modifier is removed from ArrayList declaration, as the data is going to be stored and retrieved from the database directly.

Establishing A Connection With The MySQL Database Engine

Class.forName() is used to load the class into memory. It indicates that the JDBC driver from some JDBC vendor has to be loaded into the application.

newInstance() indicates that a new instance of the current class should be created.

Next, to connect to a database, create a JDBC Connection. This acts as a factory for Statement objects that provide the Java application the ability to submit SQL commands to the database.

Creating a Connection involves a single call to **DriverManager**.

getConnection() is overloaded to accept a URL that encodes the username and password.

Then a valid Statement is created via a valid Connection. Connection is used as a factory for generating new statements using **createStatement()**.

Adding The Captured Data To The Database Table

Here, every record that is captured is added to the database table using the INSERT query.

executeUpdate() of **Statement** is used to execute the INSERT statement.

Retrieving The Stored Data From The Database Table

Here, an SQL SELECT query is fired to retrieve the GuestBook entries.

executeQuery() of **Statement** is used to execute an SQL SELECT statement.

Adding The Retrieved Data To The ArrayList

Here, every record that is extracted using an SQL SELECT query is placed in the GuestBook object and then added to the ArrayList for display.

Running GuestBook Application

Now that the data store is in place and integrated with this application. Let's run this application [source code available on the Book's accompanying CDROM].

Ensure that the MySQL password in GuestBookAction.java is set correctly before running this application.

Build and run the project, as shown in the *Chapter 08: Building Views*.

index.jsp is opened in the Web browser, which automatically links to **GuestBook.action** page, as shown in diagram 12.2.

194   Struts 2 For Beginners

Diagram 12.2: The application run in the Web browser

Now enter the name and the comments in the Name and Message fields. Click Submit. The Guest Book view page appears, as shown in diagram 12.3.

Diagram 12.3: Viewing the data entered by the user

When **GuestBookSuccess.action** page appears, the data entered by the user is stored in the MySQL database table named GuestBook that was created earlier.

To ensure that this was done successfully, open MySQL command line utility and query the table to view the following output:

```
+----------------+------------------------------------------+-------------+
| Guest          | Message                                  | MessageDate |
+----------------+------------------------------------------+-------------+
| Sharanam Shah  | Welcome everyone. This is my guest book. | 2012/09/24  |
+----------------+------------------------------------------+-------------+
1 row in set (0.00 sec)
```

Chapter 13

SECTION III: GETTING STARTED WITH STRUTS 2

Integrating Hibernate With Struts 2

Persistence is one of the most vital piece of an application without which all the data is simply lost.

Often when choosing the persistence storage medium the following fundamental qualifiers are considered:

- The length of time data must be persisted
- The volume of data

For example,

- An HTTP session can be considered when the life of a piece of data is limited to the user's session. However, persistence over several sessions or several users, requires a Database

Large amounts of data should not be stored in an HTTP session, instead a database should be considered.

The type of database that is chosen also plays an important influence on the architecture and design.

In today's object-oriented world, data is represented as OBJECTS. This is often called a DOMAIN model. However, the storage medium is based on a RELATIONAL paradigm. These objects have to be persisted to a relational database.

The inevitable mismatch between the object-oriented code spec [DOMAIN model] and the relational database requires writing a lot of code spec that maps one to the other. This code spec is often complex, tedious and costly to develop.

One of the most popular tools to address the mismatch problem is object-relational mappers.

An object-relational mapper is software used to transform an object view of the data into a relational one and provide persistence services such as CREATE, READ, UPDATE and DELETE [CRUD].

One of the most popular object-relational mappers is the open source Hibernate project. Hibernate acts as a layer between the application and the database by taking care of loading and saving of objects.

Hibernate Architecture

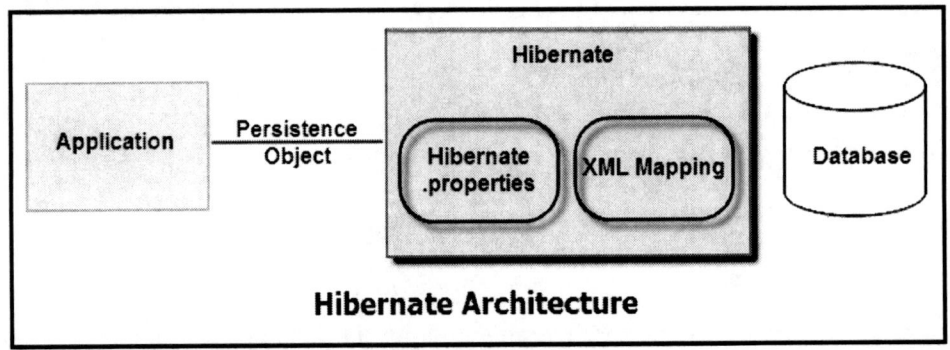

Diagram 13.1

About Hibernate

Hibernate applications are cheaper, more portable and more resilient to change.

Hibernate is a popular, powerful and a free, open source **Object Relational Mapping** library for the Java programming language. It can be used both in standalone Java applications and in Java EE applications using Servlets or EJB - Session Beans.

Hibernate was developed by a team of Java software developers around the world led by Gavin King, JBoss Inc. [now part of Red Hat] and later hired the lead Hibernate developers and worked with them in supporting Hibernate.

Hibernate allows the developer to focus on the objects and features of the application, without having to worry about how to store them or find them later.

Hibernate provides a framework for mapping an object oriented domain model to a traditional relational database.

Hibernate provides mapping between:
- The Java classes and the database tables
- The Java data types and SQL data types

Hibernate also provides data query and retrieval facilities. It generates the SQL calls and relieves the developer from manual result set handling and object conversion, keeping the application portable to all supported SQL databases, with database portability delivered at very little performance overhead.

When dealing with the database programming, it can significantly speed up the productivity and simplify the procedure of development.

To use Hibernate:
- Java bean classes [POJOs] that represents the table in the database are created
- The instance variables of the class are mapped to the columns in the database table

Hibernate allows performing operations SELECT, INSERT, UPDATE and DELETE on the database tables by automatically creating the required SQL query.

Continuing With The Application

GuestBook application that was built earlier in *Chapter 12: Using The Data Store* is capable of interacting with the MySQL database. It accepts guestbook entries, stores it in GuestBook table and displays the same for viewing by other visitors.

This application already has a **persistent bean class** called **GuestBook** which has to be mapped with the database table columns using Hibernate.

Let's integrate this application with Hibernate thus making it portable across all supported SQL databases.

198   Struts 2 For Beginners

From GuestBook application's perspective, Hibernate will be used to provide the object-relational mapping layer for the application, allowing the model to be persisted to a database.

To integrate an application with Hibernate, appropriate library files need to be downloaded and added to this project.

Downloading Hibernate

Download the latest version of Hibernate from **http://www.hibernate.org/downloads**.

From the download page, download the current latest release of Hibernate Core. At the time of writing this book the latest version that was available for download is **4.1.6.FINAL** [available in this Book's accompanying CDROM].

After it is downloaded, using any unzip utility such as Winzip unzip the contents of the zip file.

Adding Hibernate Library Files

Right-click on **Libraries** directory, click **Add JAR/Folder....**

Clicking the **Add JAR/Folder** file displays the dialog box to choose the JAR files.

Browse to the following directories and select the following JAR files to add to the project:

- **<Drive:>/hibernate-release-X.X.X.Final/lib/required** directory:
    - antlr-X.X.X.jar
    - dom4j-X.X.X.jar
    - hibernate-commons-annotations-X.X.X.Final.jar
    - hibernate-core-X.X.X.Final.jar
    - hibernate-jpa-X.X-api-X.X.X.Final.jar
    - javassist-X.X.X-GA.jar
    - jboss-logging-X.X.X.GA.jar
    - jboss-transaction-api_X.X_spec-X.X.X.Final.jar
- **<Drive:>/hibernate-release-X.X.X.Final/lib/jpa** directory:
    - hibernate-entitymanager-X.X.X.Final.jar

Also add the following Struts 2 JAR files from **<Drive:>/struts-X.X.X/lib** directory to GuestBook web application:

- commons-collections-X.X.jar
- struts2-convention-plugin-X.X.X.X.jar
- asm-X.X.jar
- asm-commons-X.X.jar
- asm-tree-X.X.jar

Creating Session Factory

Hibernate's **SessionFactory** interface provides instances of **Session**, which represent connections to the database. Instances of SessionFactory are thread-safe and typically shared throughout an application.

Using NetBeans, create a class called **HibernateUtil** in the **com.sharanamvaishali.myApp.utility** package using the same steps as shown earlier in the *Chapter 07: Working With Actions*.

Key in the following code spec in **HibernateUtil.java**:

```
1  package com.sharanamvaishali.myApp.utility;
2
3  import org.hibernate.HibernateException;
4  import org.hibernate.Session;
5  import org.hibernate.SessionFactory;
6  import org.hibernate.cfg.Configuration;
7  import org.hibernate.service.ServiceRegistry;
8  import org.hibernate.service.ServiceRegistryBuilder;
9
10 public class HibernateUtil {
11     private static SessionFactory sessionFactory;
12     private static ServiceRegistry serviceRegistry;
13
14     public static SessionFactory configureSessionFactory() throws HibernateException {
15         Configuration configuration = new Configuration();
16         configuration.configure();
17         serviceRegistry = new ServiceRegistryBuilder().applySettings(configuration.getProperties()).buildServiceRegistry();
18         sessionFactory = configuration.buildSessionFactory(serviceRegistry);
19         return sessionFactory;
20     }
21
22     public static Session getSession() {
23         return sessionFactory.openSession();
24     }
25 }
```

Explanation:

Imports

The following interfaces/classes are included using the import statement:

org.hibernate.HibernateException

HibernateException is the base Throwable type for Hibernate.

org.hibernate.Session

Session is the main runtime interface between a Java application and Hibernate. This is the central API class abstracting the notion of a persistence service. The main function of the Session is to offer create, read and delete operations for instances of mapped entity classes.

org.hibernate.SessionFactory

SessionFactory allows creating sessions. SessionFactory caches generate SQL statements and other mapping metadata that Hibernate uses at runtime.

org.hibernate.cfg.Configuration

Configuration is used to configure and bootstrap Hibernate. It is meant only as a initialization-time object. The application uses a Configuration instance to specify the location of mapping documents and Hibernate-specific properties and then create SessionFactory.

org.hibernate.service.ServiceRegistry

ServiceRegistry is a registry of services.

org.hibernate.service.ServiceRegistryBuilder

ServiceRegistryBuilder is the builder for standard ServiceRegistry instances.

Objects Declaration

To represent the connections to the database, the following private variables are declared as static:

- sessionFactory
- serviceRegistry

configureSessionFactory()

configureSessionFactory() is defined, which creates the SessionFactory.

An instance of the **Configuration** interface is created. Using it's **configure()**, the session factory is built. This step indicates Hibernate to load **hibernate.cfg.xml**. Using **getProperties()**, all the properties are retrieved from hibernate.cfg.xml.

An instance of ServiceRegistryBuilder interface is created. Using it's applySettings(), groups of incoming setting values are to be applied.

buildServiceRegistry() of ServiceRegistryBuilder builds the service registry accounting for all settings and service initiators and services.

buildSessionFactory() of Configuration creates a SessionFactory using the properties and mappings in the current configuration. SessionFactory will be immutable, so changes made to Configuration after building SessionFactory will not affect it. buildSessionFactory() takes a parameter named ServiceRegistry, which is the registry of services to be used in creating the session factory.

getSession()

getSession(), a getter method, when invoked, returns an instance of Session.

openSession() of SesisonFactory creates an instance of Session. This instance represents the primary interface to the Hibernate framework.

Creating Struts 2 Dispatcher

To integrate this application with Hibernate, a custom Struts 2 dispatcher is created. This class extends StrutsPrepareAndExecuteFilter dispatcher.

Struts2Dispatcher:
- Executes the super classes's **init()**
- Overrides **init()** to create a session factory

This custom class enables the Hibernate support in the application.

Using NetBeans, create one more class called **Struts2Dispatcher** in the package **com.sharanamvaishali.myApp.utility** using the same steps as shown earlier in the *Chapter 07: Working With Actions*.

Key in the following code spec in **Struts2Dispatcher.java**:

```
1  package com.sharanamvaishali.myApp.utility;
2
3  import javax.servlet.FilterConfig;
4  import javax.servlet.ServletException;
5  import org.apache.struts2.dispatcher.ng.filter.StrutsPrepareAndExecuteFilter;
6  import org.hibernate.HibernateException;
7
8  public class Struts2Dispatcher extends StrutsPrepareAndExecuteFilter {
9      @Override
10     public void init(FilterConfig filterConfig) throws ServletException {
11         super.init(filterConfig);
12         try {
13             HibernateUtil.configureSessionFactory();
14             System.out.println("Application successfully initialed.");
15         } catch (HibernateException e) {
16             throw new ServletException();
17         }
18     }
19 }
```

Explanation:

Imports

The following interfaces/classes are included using the import statement:

java.servlet.FilterConfig

FilterConfig is a filter configuration object used by a Servlet container to pass information to a filter during initialization.

java.servlet.ServletException

ServletException defines a general exception a Servlet can throw when it encounters difficulty.

org.apache.struts2.dispatcher.ng.filter.StrutsPrepareAndExecuteFilter

StrutsPrepareAndExecuteFilter handles both the preparation and execution phases of Struts dispatching process. This filter is better to use when there are no another filter that needs access to action context information such as Sitemesh.

StrutsPrepareAndExecuteFilter is used instead of FilterDispatcher, since Struts 2.1.3 FilterDispatcher is deprecated.

org.hibernate.HibernateException

HibernateException is any exception that occurs inside the persistence layer or JDBC driver.

init()

init() is invoked by the Servlet container once when the Servlet filter is placed into service. Filter Configuration passed to this method contains the initialized parameters of the Servlet filter.

In init(), super class's init() is invoked.

A Hibernate session is spawned using **configureSessionFactory()** of **HibernateUtil** class created earlier.

Activating Struts 2 Dispatcher

Now that the custom class called Struts2Dispatcher is available, it needs to be activated. This means Struts 2 framework needs to be informed about the same. To do so, web.xml needs to be updated.

Edit web.xml as shown below:

```
 1  <?xml version="1.0" encoding="UTF-8"?>
 2  <web-app version="3.0" xmlns="http://java.sun.com/xml/ns/javaee"
    xmlns:xsi="http://www.w3.org/2001/XMLSchema-instance"
    xsi:schemaLocation="http://java.sun.com/xml/ns/javaee
    http://java.sun.com/xml/ns/javaee/web-app_3_0.xsd">
 3      <filter>
 4          <filter-name>Struts2Filter</filter-name>
 5          <filter-class>org.apache.struts2.dispatcher.ng.filter.StrutsPrepareAndExecuteFilter</filter-class>
 6          <filter-class>com.sharanamvaishali.myApp.utility.Struts2Dispatcher</filter-class>
 7      </filter>
 8      <filter-mapping>
 9          <filter-name>Struts2Filter</filter-name>
10          <url-pattern>/*</url-pattern>
11      </filter-mapping>
12      <session-config>
13          <session-timeout>
14              30
15          </session-timeout>
16      </session-config>
17  </web-app>
```

(Replace line 5 with line 6)

Explanation:

In web.xml, currently the filter class for struts2 filter is:
org.apache.struts.dispatcher.ng.filter.StrutsPrepareAndExecuteFilter.

Since GuestBook application now has its own custom class that extends **StrutsPrepareAndExecuteFilter**, web.xml needs to be edited to inform Strut 2 framework to begin using **com.sharanamvaishali.myApp.utility.Struts2Dispatcher** instead of org.apache.struts.dispatcher.ng.filter.StrutsPrepareAndExecuteFilter.

Creating Hibernate Configuration File

Hibernate uses **hibernate.cfg.xml** to create the connection pool and setup the required environment. This file is used to provide the information which is necessary for making database connections.

hibernate.cfg.xml configuration defines information such as:

- The database connection
- The transaction factory class
- Resource mappings

And so on.

To do so, right-click the **Source Packages** folder. Select **New** → **Hibernate Configuration Wizard…**, as shown in diagram 13.3.1.

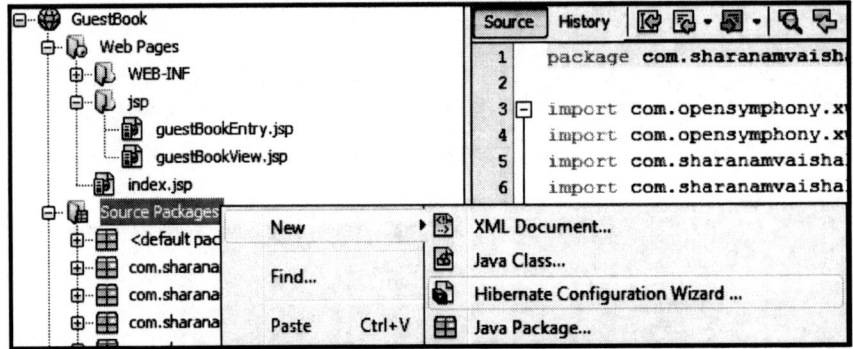

Diagram 13.3.1: Creating hibernate.cfg.xml

New Hibernate Configuration Wizard dialog appears, as shown in diagram 13.3.2. By default, **hibernate.cfg** is already entered as the file name, as shown in diagram 13.3.2.

Integrating Hibernate With Struts 2

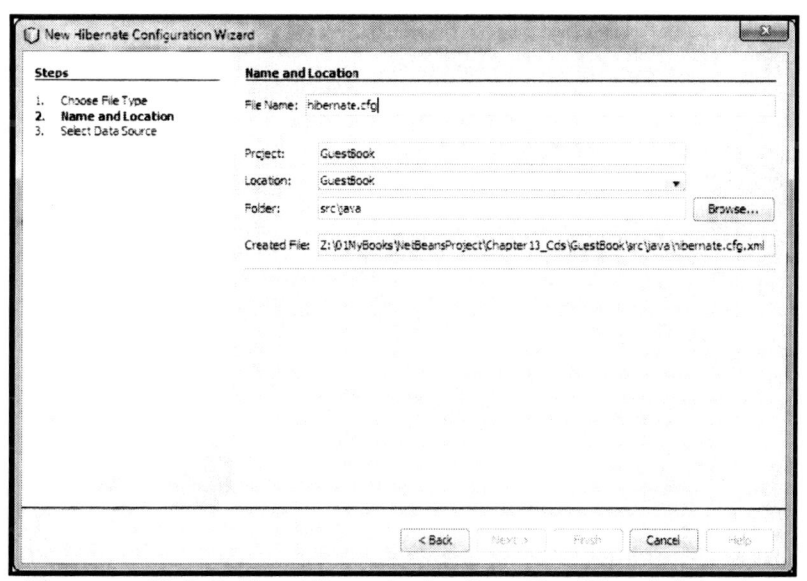

Diagram 13.3.2: New Hibernate Configuration Wizard dialog box

Click [Next >]. **Select Data Source** section of **New Hibernate Configuration Wizard** dialog appears, as shown in diagram 13.3.3.

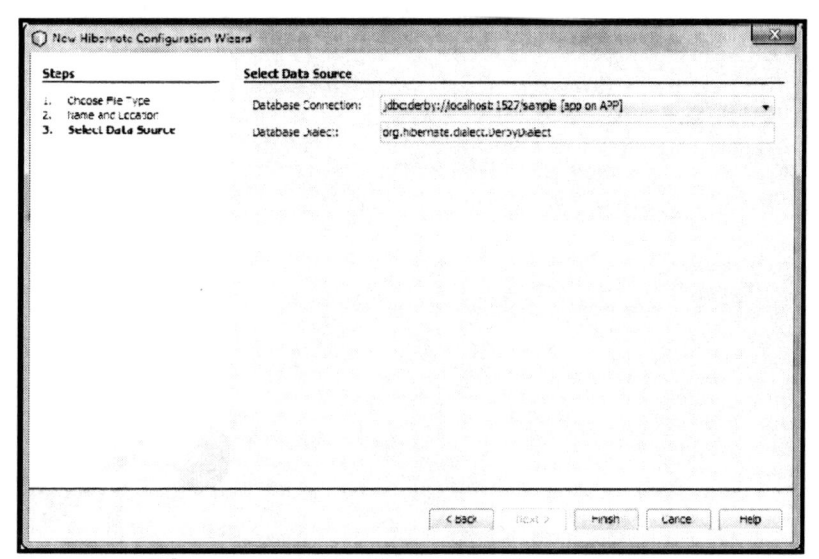

Diagram 13.3.3: Select Data Source section

Select **New Database Connection...** option available in **Database Connection** list box. **New Connection Wizard** dialog box appears, as shown in diagram 13.3.4. Select **MySQL (Connector/J driver)** option available in **Driver** list box, as shown in diagram 13.3.4.

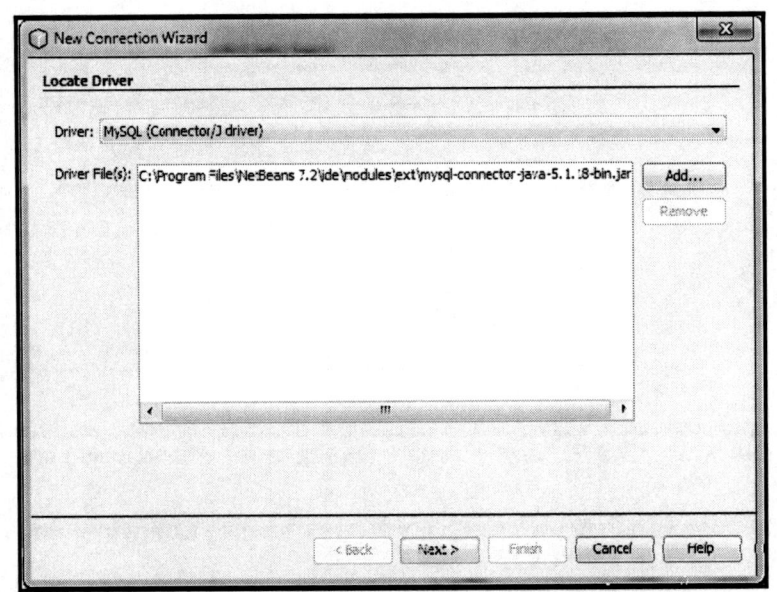

Diagram 13.3.4: New Connection Wizard dialog box

Click **Next >**. **Customize Connection** section of **New Connection Wizard** dialog appears, as shown in diagram 13.3.5. Enter the following details, as shown in diagram 13.3.5:

- The host name
- The port number
- The database name
- The username of the database
- The password of the user

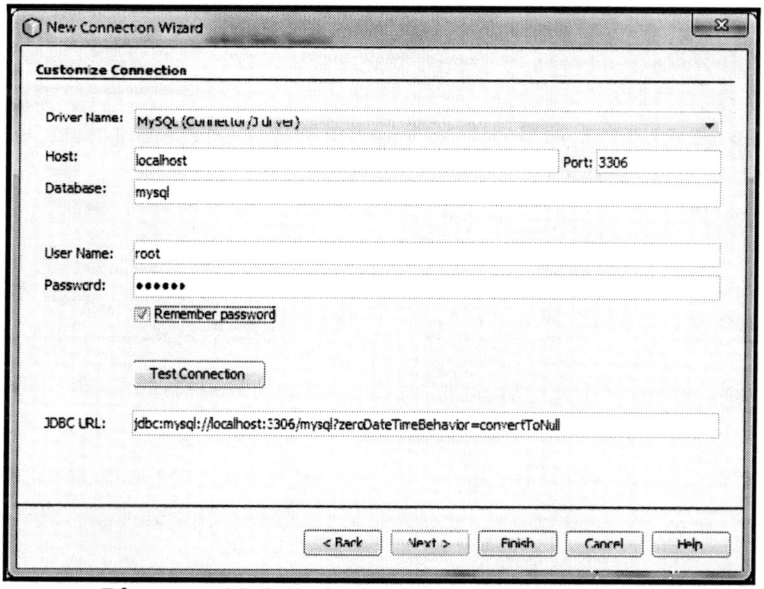

Diagram 13.3.5: Customize Connection section

Click [Finish]. **Select Data Source** of **New Hibernate Configuration Wizard** dialog box again appears, as shown in diagram 13.3.6. Now this section displays the database connection and database dialect details, which were entered in **New Connection Wizard** dialog box.

Click [Finish].

hibernate.cfg.xml should hold the following:

```
1  <?xml version="1.0" encoding="UTF-8"?>
2  <!DOCTYPE hibernate-configuration PUBLIC "-//Hibernate/Hibernate Configuration DTD//EN" "http://www.hibernate.org/dtd/hibernate-configuration-3.0.dtd">
3  <hibernate-configuration>
4   <session-factory>
5    <property name="hibernate.dialect">org.hibernate.dialect.MySQLDialect</property>
6    <property name="hibernate.connection.driver_class">com.mysql.jdbc.Driver</property>
7    <property name="hibernate.connection.url">jdbc:mysql://localhost:3306/GuestBook?zeroDateTimeBehavior=convertToNull</property>
8    <property name="hibernate.connection.username">root</property>
9    <property name="hibernate.connection.password">123456</property>
10   <property name="hibernate.show_sql">true</property>
11  </session-factory>
12 </hibernate-configuration>
```

208   Struts 2 For Beginners

Explanation:

The configuration file requires the following properties:

- **hibernate.dialect:** Is the name of the SQL dialect for the database. It informs Hibernate whether the given database supports identity columns, altering relational tables and unique indexes, among other database specific details

HINT

> Hibernate ships with more than 20 SQL dialects supporting each of the major database vendors including Oracle, DB2, MySQL and PostgreSQL.

- **hibernate.connection.driver_class:** Is the JDBC connection class for the specific database
- **hibernate.connection.url:** Is the full JDBC URL to the database
- **hibernate.connection.username:** Is the username used to connect to the database
- **hibernate.connection.password:** Is the password used to authenticate the username

The connection properties are common to any Java developer who has worked with JDBC in the past.

REMINDER

> Since a connection pool is not specified, Hibernate uses its own rudimentary connection-pooling mechanism. The internal pool is fine for basic testing .

- **hibernate.show_sql:** Enables logging of generated SQL to the console

Modifying GuestBook.java

In hibernate, mapping a bean to a relational database is done either by creating a mapping file in XML or by annotating the bean file itself.

This application is going to annotate the bean class i.e. domain class named GuestBook.java.

Key in the following code spec in **GuestBook.java:**

```
1  package com.sharanamvaishali.myApp.domain;
2
3  import javax.persistence.Column;
4  import javax.persistence.Entity;
5  import javax.persistence.GeneratedValue;
6  import javax.persistence.Id;
7  import javax.persistence.Table;
8
9  @Entity
```

```java
10  @Table(name="GUESTBOOK")
11  public class GuestBook implements java.io.Serializable {
12      @Id
13      @GeneratedValue
14      @Column(name="GUESTNO")
15      private Integer guestNo;
16      @Column(name="GUEST")
17      private String guest;
18      @Column(name="MESSAGE")
19      private String message;
20      @Column(name="MESSAGEDATE")
21      private String when;
22
23      public Integer getGuestNo() {
24          return guestNo;
25      }
26      public void setGuestNo(Integer guestNo) {
27          this.guestNo = guestNo;
28      }
29
30      public String getGuest() {
31          return guest;
32      }
33      public void setGuest(String guest) {
34          this.guest = guest;
35      }
36
37      public String getMessage() {
38          return message;
39      }
40      public void setMessage(String message) {
41          this.message = message;
42      }
43
44      public String getWhen() {
45          return when;
46      }
47      public void setWhen(String when) {
48          this.when = when;
49      }
50  }
```

Explanation:

The earlier GuestBook application did not require a property for the primary key value i.e. **guestNo**. This was handled by MySQL i.e. MySQL used to populate this column on INSERT with a new incremented value.

java.persistence.* Package

JPA entities are plain POJOs i.e. they are Hibernate persistent entities. In Hibernate 4, their mappings are defined through annotations instead of hbm.xml files.

JPA annotations are in the **javax.persistence.*** package.

@Entity

Every persistent POJO class is an entity and is declared using @Entity at the class level.

Therefore, @Entity declares the class as an entity i.e. a persistent POJO class.

@Table

@Table is set at the class level. @Table allows defining the table, catalog and schema names for the entity mapping. If no @Table is defined, then the default values are used i.e. the unqualified class name of the entity.

java.io.Serializable

Serializability of a class is enabled by the class implementing java.io.Serializable interface. All subtypes of a serializable class are themselves serializable. The serialization interface has no methods or fields and serves only to identify the semantics of being serializable.

@Id

@Id declares the identifier property of the entity. The class GuestBook is mapped to the GuestBook table, using the column guestNo as its primary key column.

@GeneratedValue

@GeneratedValue is the identifier generation strategies. The column value is auto incremented.

@Column

The column(s) used for a property mapping can be defined using @Column. The name attribute is the column name of the table. For example: the name attribute of the column guestNo is mapped to GuestNo column of the GuestBook table.

Adding A Mapping Class

Now that the mapping configuration is done, the same needs to be informed to Hibernate. This can be done by adding <mapping> to **hibernate.cfg.xml** created earlier.

Edit **hibernate.cfg.xml** to hold a mapping class as shown below:

```xml
1  <?xml version="1.0" encoding="UTF-8"?>
2  <!DOCTYPE hibernate-configuration PUBLIC "-//Hibernate/Hibernate Configuration DTD//EN" "http://www.hibernate.org/dtd/hibernate-configuration-3.0.dtd">
3  <hibernate-configuration>
4    <session-factory>
5      <property name="hibernate.dialect">org.hibernate.dialect.MySQLDialect</property>
6      <property name="hibernate.connection.driver_class">com.mysql.jdbc.Driver</property>
7      <property name="hibernate.connection.url">jdbc:mysql://localhost:3306/GuestBook?zeroDateTimeBehavior=convertToNull</property>
8      <property name="hibernate.connection.username">root</property>
9      <property name="hibernate.connection.password">123456</property>
10     <property name="hibernate.show_sql">true</property>
11     <mapping class="com.sharanamvaishali.myApp.domain.GuestBook" />
12   </session-factory>
13 </hibernate-configuration>
```

(Add this: line 11)

Explanation:

Hibernate also needs to know the location and names of the mapping class describing the persistent classes. <mapping> provides the name of each mapping class as well as its location relative to the application classpath. Mapping class **GuestBook.java** is included to the configuration file.

Creating Data Access Object

DAO defines the contract between the persistence layer and the classes that will orchestrate the reading/writing and deletion of GuestBook beans.

GuestBookDAO.java

Using NetBeans, create an interface **GuestBookDAO** in the package **com.sharanamvaishali.myApp.dao**.

Right-click **GuestBook** application and select **New → Other…. New File** dialog box appears. Choose **Java** available under **Categories** section and **Java Interface** available under **File Types**.

Name and Location section of **New Java Class** dialog box appears. Enter the **Class Name** as **GuestBookDAO** and **Package** as **com.sharanamvaishali.myApp.dao**.

Click **Finish**. GuestBookDAO.java is created in com.sharanamvaishali.myApp.dao.

212   Struts 2 For Beginners

Key in the following code spec in **GuestBookDAO.java**:

```
1  package com.sharanamvaishali.myApp.dao;
2
3  import com.sharanamvaishali.myApp.domain.GuestBook;
4  import java.util.List;
5
6  public interface GuestBookDAO {
7      public List<GuestBook> listGuestBook();
8      public void saveGuestBook(GuestBook gb);
9  }
```

Explanation:

An **interface** is an abstract type that is used to specify an interface that classes must implement. Interfaces are declared using the **interface** keyword and may only contain method signature and constant declarations [variable declarations that are declared to be both static and final]. An interface may never contain method definitions.

Interfaces cannot be instantiated, but rather are implemented. A class that implements an interface must implement all of the methods described in the interface or be an abstract class.

GuestBookDAOImpl.java

Using NetBeans, create one more class called **GuestBookDAOImpl** in the package **com.sharanamvaishali.myApp.dao**, using the same steps as shown earlier in the *Chapter 07: Working With Actions*.

Key in the following code spec in **GuestBookDAOImpl.java**:

```
1  package com.sharanamvaishali.myApp.dao;
2
3  import com.sharanamvaishali.myApp.domain.GuestBook;
4  import com.sharanamvaishali.myApp.utility.HibernateUtil;
5  import java.util.List;
6  import org.hibernate.Session;
7  import org.hibernate.Transaction;
8
9  public class GuestBookDAOImpl implements GuestBookDAO {
10     Session session = HibernateUtil.getSession();
11     Transaction transaction;
12
13     @Override
14     public List<GuestBook> listGuestBook() {
15         return session.createQuery("FROM GuestBook").list();
16     }
17
18     @Override
19     public void saveGuestBook(GuestBook gb) {
```

```
20        try {
21           transaction = session.beginTransaction();
22           session.save(gb);
23           transaction.commit();
24        } catch (RuntimeException e) {
25           if (gb != null) {
26              transaction.rollback();
27           }
28           throw e;
29        }
30     }
31  }
```

Explanation:

Imports

The following interfaces/classes are included using the import statement:

java.util.List

List is an ordered collection. The user of this interface has precise control over where in the list each element is inserted. The user can access elements by their integer index [position in the list] and search for elements in the list.

org.hibernate.Session

Session is the main runtime interface between a Java application and Hibernate. This is the central API class abstracting the notion of a persistence service. The main function of the Session is to offer create, read and delete operations for instances of mapped entity classes.

org.hibernate.Transaction

Transaction is a package, which abstracts the underlying transaction mechanism [JTA or JDBC] and provides strategies for obtaining application server TransactionManagers.

Objects Declaration

A session object is created. This Hibernate Session is the main runtime interface between a Java application and Hibernate.

The Hibernate Session.SessionFactory allows the application to spawn the Hibernate Session by reading the configuration from **hibernate.cfg.xml**.

A Transaction object is created. This transaction is used to commit the transaction such as An INSERT statement or to rollback such transactions.

listGuestBook()

listGuestBook() is declared, which returns type List of GuestBook.

Using **createQuery()** of Session, the persistent objects are retrieved. HQL statements are object-oriented, meaning that the query on object properties instead of database table and column names.

createQuery() returns a collection of all **GuestBook** instances.

saveGuestBook()

saveGuestBook() is created, which accepts an object of **GuestBook**.

An instance of Transaction is created by invoking **beginTransaction()** of Session.

save() of Session allows saving the information to the database table.

Session then saves the GuestBook list by invoking **save()**. Finally the transaction is committed.

When an object is passed to **save()**, Hibernate reads the state of the variables of that object and executes the required SQL query.

In case of errors, if any, it is determined if the GuestBook object is empty. If not, then the transaction is rolled backed.

Modifying GuestBookAction

Since GuestBook application will now use Hibernate, the following code spec needs to be removed:

- The CONNECTION code spec
- The INSERT query code spec
- The SELECT query code spec

Instead of a **ArrayList**, a **LIST** object of type **GuestBook** is used to hold the guestbook entries returned by **listGuestBook()** of DAO.

Integrating Hibernate With Struts 2   215

GuestBookAction also implements **ModelDriven** interface.

Key in the following code spec in GuestBookAction.java:

```
1  package com.sharanamvaishali.myApp.action;
2
3  import com.opensymphony.xwork2.ActionSupport;
4  import com.opensymphony.xwork2.ModelDriven;                    [Add this]
5  import com.sharanamvaishali.myApp.dao.GuestBookDAO;
6  import com.sharanamvaishali.myApp.dao.GuestBookDAOImpl;
7  import com.sharanamvaishali.myApp.domain.GuestBook;
8  import java.sql.Connection;
9  import java.sql.DriverManager;                                 [Remove this]
10 import java.sql.ResultSet;
11 import java.sql.Statement;
12 import java.text.DateFormat;
13 import java.text.SimpleDateFormat;
14 import java.util.ArrayList;
15 import java.util.Date;
16 import java.util.List;                                         [Add this]
17
18 public class GuestBookAction extends ActionSupport implements  [Add this]
   ModelDriven<GuestBook> {
19     private static final long serialVersionUID = -8577843349235520003L;
20     DateFormat dateFormat = new SimpleDateFormat("yyyy/MM/dd");
21     Date date = new Date();
22     private String guest;
23     private String message;
24     private String when = (dateFormat.format(date)).toString();
25     private ArrayList<GuestBook> messages = new ArrayList<GuestBook>();
26
27     private GuestBook guestBook = new GuestBook();
28     private List<GuestBook> messages = new ArrayList<GuestBook>();   [Replace this with]
29     private GuestBookDAO guestBookDAO = new GuestBookDAOImpl();
30
31
32     Connection conn = null;
33     Statement stmt = null;
34     ResultSet rs = null;
35                                                                 [Remove this]
36     private String dbName = "GuestBook";
37     private String host = "localhost";
38     private String username = "root";
39     private String password = "123456";
40
41     @Override
42     public GuestBook getModel() {                               [Add this]
43         return guestBook;
44     }
45
46     @Override
47     public String execute() {
48         try {
49             Class.forName("com.mysql.jdbc.Driver").newInstance();
```

```java
            conn = DriverManager.getConnection("jdbc:mysql://" + host + "/" + dbName,
                username, password);
            stmt = conn.createStatement();

            String query = "INSERT INTO GuestBook (Guest, Message, MessageDate)
                VALUES ('" + getGuest() + "', '" + getMessage() + "', '" + getWhen() + "')";
            stmt.executeUpdate(query);

            query = "SELECT * FROM GuestBook";
            rs = stmt.executeQuery(query);
            while (rs.next()) {
                GuestBook guestBookMsgs = new GuestBook();
                guestBookMsgs.setGuest(rs.getString("Guest"));
                guestBookMsgs.setMessage(rs.getString("Message"));
                guestBookMsgs.setWhen(rs.getString("MessageDate"));
                messages.add(guestBookMsgs);
            }
        } catch (Exception e) {
        }
```

Replace this with:
```java
        guestBook.setWhen(dateFormat.format(date).toString());
        guestBookDAO.saveGuestBook(guestBook);
        messages = guestBookDAO.listGuestBook();
        return SUCCESS;
    }
```

Remove this:
```java
    public ArrayList<GuestBook> getMessages() {
        return messages;
    }
    public void setMessages(ArrayList<GuestBook> messages) {
        this.messages = messages;
    }

    public String getGuest() {
        return guest;
    }
    public void setGuest(String guest) {
        this.guest = guest;
    }

    public String getMessage() {
        return message;
    }
    public void setMessage(String message) {
        this.message = message;
    }

    public String getWhen() {
        return when;
    }
    public void setWhen(String when) {
        this.when = when;
    }
```

```
102    public List<GuestBook> getMessages() {
103        return messages;
104    }
105    public void setMessages(List<GuestBook> messages) {
106        this.messages = messages;
107    }
108
109    public GuestBook getGuestBook() {
110        return guestBook;
111    }
112    public void setGuestBook(GuestBook guestBook) {
113        this.guestBook = guestBook;
114    }
115 }
```

Add this

Explanation:

Implements ModelDriven

Struts 2 does not have **forms** like Struts 1 did.

In Struts 2 request parameters are bound directly to fields in the actions class and this class is placed on top of the stack when the action is executed.

ModelDriven Actions provide a model object to be pushed onto the ValueStack in addition to the Action itself.

REMINDER

To use ModelDriven Actions, make sure that the Model Driven Interceptor is applied to the application. This interceptor is part of the default interceptor stack defaultStack so it is applied to all actions by default.

Objects And Variables Declarations

The following objects/variables are declared:
- An instance of GuestBook POJO entity
- A **list** object of type **GuestBook** is created to hold the guestbook entries for view purpose
- An instance of GuestBookDAO interface

getModel()

If an action class implements the interface **com.opensymphony.xwork2.ModelDriven**, then it needs to return an object from **getModel()**.

Struts will then populate the fields of this object with the request parameters and this object will be placed on top of the stack once the action is executed. Validation will also be performed on this model object, instead of the action.

getModel() is the model [in this case GuestBook POJO entity] to be pushed onto the ValueStack instead of the Action itself.

execute()

The entry that was captured by the data entry form is saved to the MySQL database table using **saveGuestBook()** of **GuestBookDAO**. This method is passed populated object of the GuestBook POJO entity.

After the new entry is saved in the database table, the existing entries are retrieved and stored in the **messages** List object.

Getter/Setter Methods

Getter/Setter methods for the list object [messages] and GuestBook POJO entity are set.

Running The Application

Let's run this application [source code available on the Book's accompanying CDROM].

Build and run the project as shown in the *Chapter 08: Building Views*.

index.jsp appears in the Web browser, which automatically redirects to the **GuestBook.action** page, as shown in diagram 13.5.

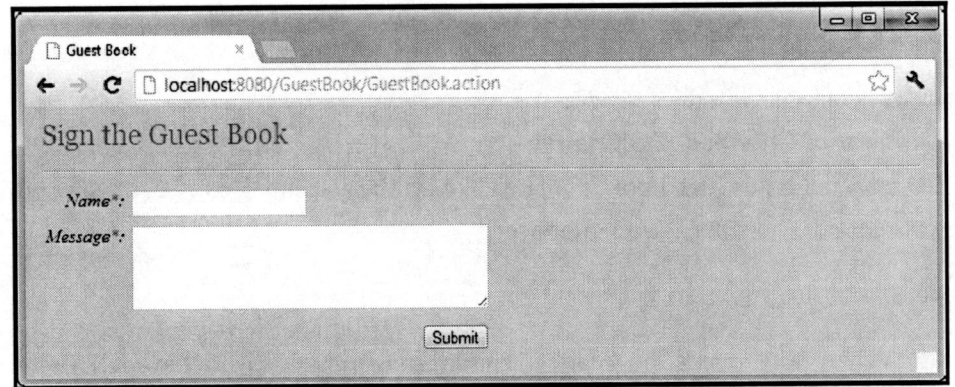

Diagram 13.5: The application run in the Web browser

Now enter the name and the comments in the Name and Message fields. Click [Submit]. The Guest Book view page appears, as shown in diagram 13.6.

Diagram 13.6: Viewing the data entered by the user

When GuestBookSuccess.action appears, the data entered by the user is stored in the MySQL database table named GuestBook that was created earlier.

To ensure that this was done successfully, open MySQL command line utility and query the table to view the following output.

```
+----------------+------------------------------------------+------------+
| Guest          | Message                                  | MessageDate|
+----------------+------------------------------------------+------------+
| Sharanam Shah  | Welcome everyone, This is my guest book. | 2012/09/24 |
| Janya          | Hello everyone!!!                        | 2012/09/25 |
+----------------+------------------------------------------+------------+
2 rows in set (0.00 sec)
```

Chapter 14

SECTION IV: APPLICATION DEVELOPMENT USING STRUTS 2

Defining The Project And Its Requirements

Now since the fundamentals of Struts 2 are in place. Let's do something practical.

To make the practical interesting, let's bind it to a real world business model.

Business Model

Our client is a large book seller. It has to compete with a large number of similar businesses in this business space.

Profit margins in this space do not permit a large degree of price point manipulation. Hence, to remain competitive in this space and provide its customers the best deals, our book seller decided to implement a computerized book shop system.

Workflow

The workflow begins as follows:

A visitor visits the book shop.

The book seller gathers the visitor's requirements.

The visitor/buyer may provide the following parameters to explain the requirements:
- Book Name
- Author Name(s)
- ISBN
- An idea about the contents of the book

The book seller based on the inputs received from the visitor and the domain knowledge that the book seller possesses, searches the book and provides it to the visitor.

The book seller also accepts orders over the telephone. Orders accepted over the telephone are served as follows:
- The buyer calls the book shop
- Enquires about a book usually by its name or an ISBN number
- The book seller accepts the order, indicates the invoice amount and the shipping charges
- Delivers the book(s) and collects the payment [by cash]

Using the current workflow, the book seller cannot:
- Do an efficient and quick physical search of the book(s) that map to the buyer requirements
- Categorize books [such as Database, Web Programming, .Net, Java and so on], due to such a large number of books, regularly hitting the market

The book seller has therefore proposed to computerize the business workflow. This will help track and maintain the book details.

Application Requirements

This section describes the application requirements. This document is intended to be used by the project team that will design and implement the system.

Defining The Project And Its Requirements

The application must:

- Provide a **secure login mechanism** which allows the system users to login and access the book's data store
- Provide **User Interfaces** that allows:
    - Managing book in the data store. This includes Adding, Editing and Deleting Books
    - Searching existing books using either of the following search criteria:
        - Book Name
        - ISBN
        - Author Name(s)
        - Publisher Name
        - Category
        - Synopsis
        - About Authors
        - Topics Covered
        - Contents Of CDROM
    - Viewing a book's details
- Session Management

    Ability to maintain session across all the modules

Based on these requirements, the following can be defined:

- Data Store
- User Interfaces and Data Entry Forms
- Actions i.e. what happens when a user clicks a button on such User Interfaces

Intended Users

This application is intended to be used by book shop's internal resources, employees as well as the bookshop owner for administrative and search purposes

This application is expected to run on both an intranet as well as an extranet.

Operating Environment

Operating System

Windows: All flavors that support NetBeans 7.2 & MySQL 5.5.27

External Software Applications

Java SE Development Kit [JDK] 7 Update 6
MySQL Community Server 5.5.27
MySQL Connector/J 5.1.21

Framework

Struts 2.3.4.1

User Interface And Data Entry Form Requirements

After going through the application requirements, it appears that the following user interfaces are required:

User Login

Diagram 14.1

This will be the entry point to the application. The user provides the username and the appropriate password and clicks **Login**.

Objective	To allow a user to login to the application
Actors	Book shop employee, Book shop owner
Pre-Condition	- -
Post-Condition	Actors successfully authenticate themselves and log in to the application

Steps

1. User navigates to the login page
2. System displays a data entry form to capture the following:

Form Field	Type	Unique	Alphanumeric	Required	Max Size
Username	Text box	Yes	Yes	Yes	25
Password	Text box	Yes	Yes	Yes	8

3. User enters the username and the password [Refer A-1]
4. User clicks Login [Refer A-2]
5. System authenticates the username and password. If found valid, the system displays the search page

Alternate Steps

A-1: Empty Input fields

System displays a message indicating that the username or password is not entered.

A-2: Invalid User

System displays a message indicating that the username or password is not valid.

Search Books

Diagram 14.2

After the user logs in successfully, the search book page appears.

Objective	To allow a user to search for the required books
Actors	Book shop employee, Book shop owner
Pre-Condition	User logs in successfully
Post-Condition	Actors successfully retrieves the required information if it is available in the system

Steps

1. User logs in, reaches the homepage
2. System displays a data entry form to capture the following:

Form Field	Type	Unique	Alphanumeric	Required	Max Size
Search	Text box	Yes	Yes	Yes	75

3. User enters the required information and clicks BookShop Search [Refer A-1]
4. System fetches the required information from the database based on the keyword entered by the user and displays the same on the Search page

Alternate Steps

A-1: Empty Input Fields

System displays a message indicating that the search criteria is not entered.

Manage Books

Diagram 14.3

This interface should allow managing [viewing, adding, updating, deleting] books authored and published.

View Books

	Book	ISBN	Synopsis	Author
✗	Oracle For Professionals	978-81-8404-526	Designed for new and experienced developers this book is an essential guide for putting Oracle SQL and PL/SQL to work. It provides all of the basics you would expect to find in an introductory text and at the same time serves those who want to harness the unexploited overlooked power of Oracle SQL and PLSQL with an easy to follow format and numerous real examples based on most commonly used business database models.	Sharanam Shah
✗	Practical Java Project For Beginners	10: 81-8404-342-2	This book can be useful for students pursuing B.E. M.C.A M.Sc. IGNOU BCA B.Sc. courses who have to make and submit a project as part of their curriculum.	Anil Kumar
✗	JavaServer Pages For Beginners	10: 81-8404-359-7	The book has been written to provide genuine knowledge to programmers who wish to learn Java Server side Web based application development using Java Server Pages. Learning web development is done through a set of examples and hands on exercises	Sharanam Shah

Diagram 14.4

Objective	To view a list of all Books
Actors	Book shop employee, Book shop owner
Pre-Condition	At least one Book exists
Post-Condition	Actors view all the available books

Steps

1. User logs in successfully
2. System displays the search book page with Manage Books as one of the menu options
3. User selects Manage Books to view existing books
5. System displays a data entry form to capture the following:

Form Field	Type	Unique	Alphanumeric	Required	Max Size
ISBN	Text box	Yes	Yes	Yes	20
Book Name	Text box	Yes	Yes	Yes	20

6. User enters the required information and clicks Find
7. System fetches the required information from the database based on the keyword entered by the user and displays the same on the Manage Books page
8. System displays a list of all books currently in the system with the following information:
   - Name of the Book
   - ISBN of the Book

- Synopsis of the Book
- Name of the Author

Add Books

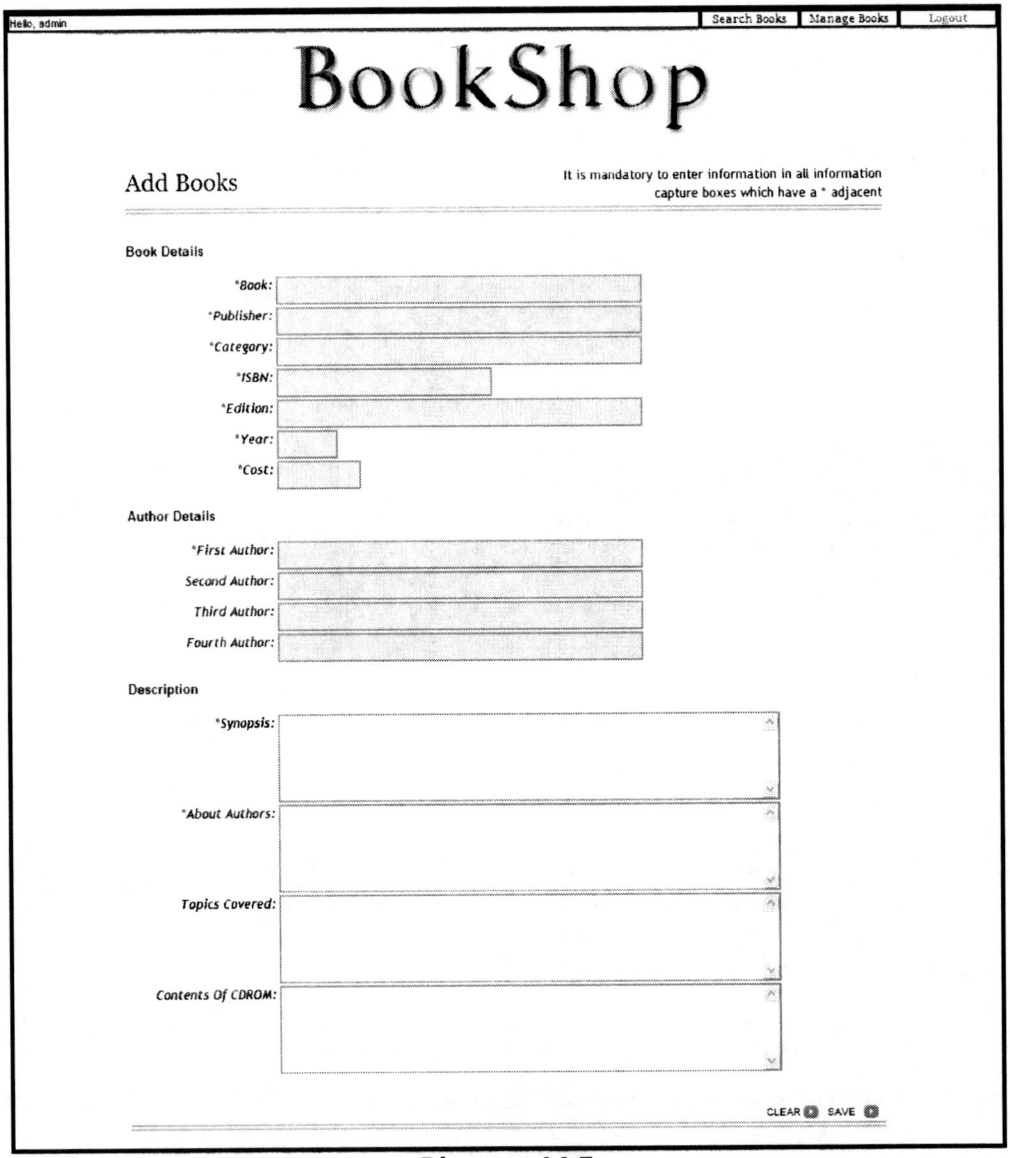

Diagram 14.5

Objective	To add a new Book
Actors	Book shop employee, Book shop owner
Pre-Condition	Users should log in successfully
Post-Condition	Actors successfully adds a new book

Steps

1. User logs in successfully
2. System displays the search book page with Manage Books as one of the menu options
3. User selects Manage Books
4. User clicks Add to add a new book
5. System displays a data entry form to capture the following:

Form Field	Type	Unique	Alphanumeric	Required	Max Size
Book	Text box	No	No	Yes	25
Publisher	Text box	No	No	Yes	25
Category	Text box	No	No	Yes	25
ISBN	Text box	Yes	Yes	Yes	15
Edition	Text box	No	No	Yes	25
Year	Text box	No	No	Yes	4
Cost	Text box	No	No	Yes	8
First Author	Text box	No	No	Yes	25
Second Author	Text box	No	No	No	25
Third Author	Text box	No	No	No	25
Fourth Author	Text box	No	No	No	25
Synopsis	Text area	No	Yes	Yes	80 cols 5 rows
About Authors	Text area	No	Yes	Yes	80 cols 5 rows
Topics Covered	Text area	No	Yes	No	80 cols 5 rows
Contents of CDROM	Text area	No	Yes	No	80 cols 5 rows

6. User enters all required information in the fields [Refer A-1]
7. User selects option to save data [Refer A-2]
8. System saves data and creates the new book
9. System takes the user back to the Manage Books page

Alternate Steps

A-1: Empty input fields

System displays a message indicating that the required fields are not entered.

A-2: User selects Clear

System does not save any user entered data.
System does not create a new book.

Edit Books

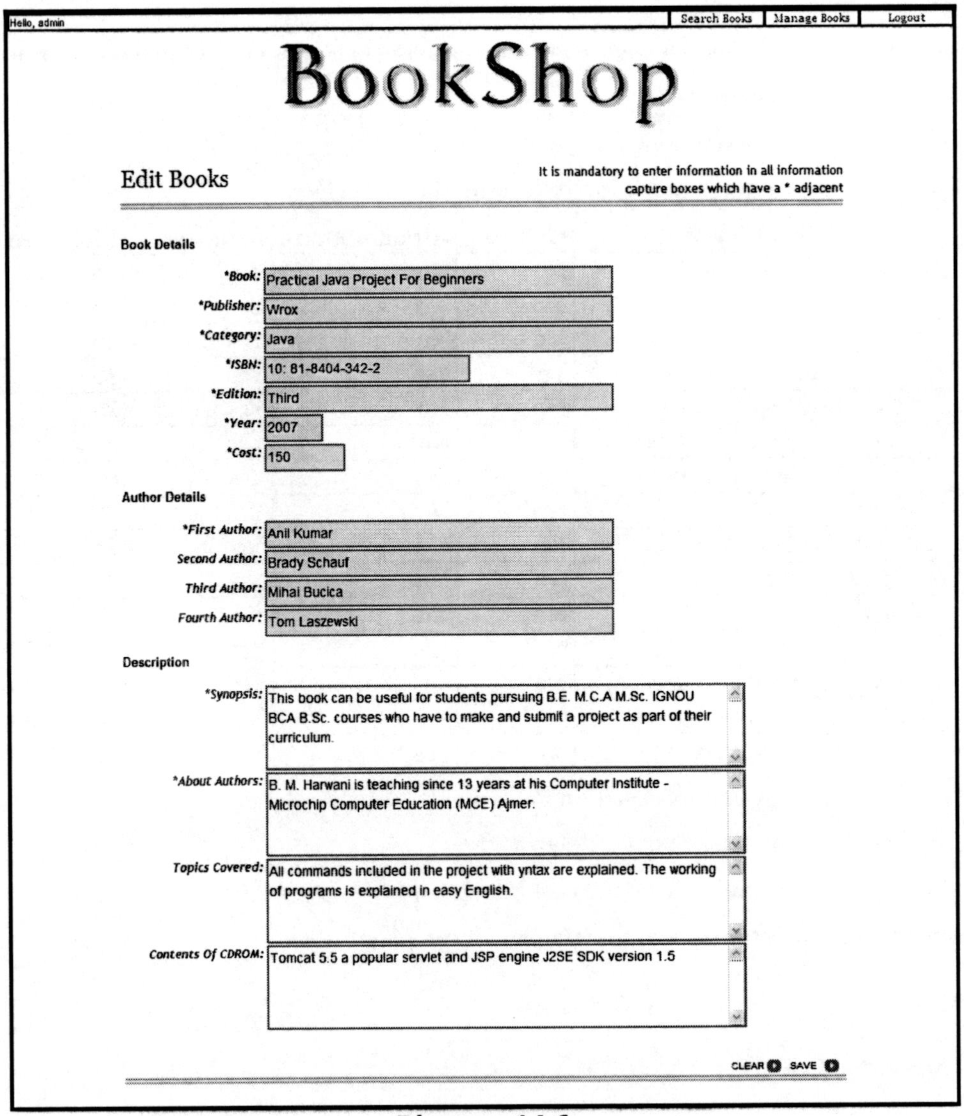

Diagram 14.6

Objective	To edit an existing Book
Actors	Book shop employee, Book shop owner
Pre-Condition	Users logs in successfully
Post-Condition	Actors successfully edit an existing book

Steps

1. User logs in successfully
2. System displays the home page with Manage Books as one of the menu options
3. User selects Manage Books to view and edit existing books [Refer A-1]
4. System displays a data entry form to capture the following:

Form Field	Type	Unique	Alphanumeric	Required	Max Size
ISBN	Text box	Yes	Yes	Yes	20
Book Name	Text box	Yes	Yes	Yes	20

5. User enters the required information and clicks Find
6. System fetches the required information from the database based on the keyword entered by the user and displays the same on the Manage Books page
7. System displays a list of all books currently in the system with the following information:
    - Name of the Book
    - ISBN of the Book
    - Synopsis of the Book
    - The image of the Cover Page of the Book
8. Users clicks the desired book for editing
9. System displays a data entry form pre-populated with the existing form data
10. User edits the desired information in the fields [Refer A-1]
11. User selects option to save data [Refer A-2]
12. System saves data and updates the existing book
13. System takes the user back to the Manage Books page

Alternate Steps

A-1: Empty input fields

System displays a message indicating that the required fields are not entered.

A-2: User selects Clear

System does not save any user entered data.
System does not update the book.

Delete Books

	Book	ISBN	Synopsis	Author
✖	Oracle For Professionals	978-81-8404-526	Designed for new and experienced developers this book is an essential guide for putting Oracle SQL and PL/SQL to work. It provides all of the basics you would expect to find in an introductory text and at the same time serves those who want to harness the unexploited overlooked power of Oracle SQL and PLSQL with an easy to follow format and numerous real examples based on most commonly used business database models.	Sharanam Shah
✖	Practical Java Project For Beginners	10: 81-8404-342-2	This book can be useful for students pursuing B.E. M.C.A M.Sc. IGNOU BCA B.Sc. courses who have to make and submit a project as part of their curriculum.	Anil Kumar
✖	JavaServer Pages For Beginners	10: 81-8404-359-7	The book has been written to provide genuine knowledge to programmers who wish to learn Java Server side Web based application development using Java Server Pages. Learning web development is done through a set of examples and hands on exercises	Sharanam Shah

Diagram 14.7

Objective	To delete an existing Book
Actors	Book shop employee, Book shop owner
Pre-Condition	Users logs in successfully
Post-Condition	Actors successfully deletes an existing book

Steps

1. User logs in successfully
2. System displays the home page with Manage Books as one of the menu options
3. User selects Manage Books to view and delete existing books [Refer A-1]
4. System displays a data entry form to capture the following:

Form Field	Type	Unique	Alphanumeric	Required	Max Size
ISBN	Text box	Yes	Yes	Yes	20
Book Name	Text box	Yes	Yes	Yes	20

5. User enters the required information and clicks Find

6. System fetches the required information from the database based on the keyword entered by the user and displays the same on the Manage Books page
7. System displays a list of all books currently in the system with the following information:
    - Name of the Book
    - ISBN of the Book
    - Synopsis of the Book
    - The image of the Cover Page of the Book
8. Users chooses the desired book for deletion and clicks **X**
9. System deletes the selected books
10. System refreshes the page to reflect the updated list of books

Proposed Actions

After the User Interfaces are defined the next most logical step in the development process is to define the Actions necessary in this application.

Actions will be processes that will be fired whilst a user interacts with the interfaces. An Action will take place for each situation or activity, possible in the application.

For this application after going through the User Interfaces, the following Actions are required:

LoginAction

Once the user logs in, this action compares the username and password to those in a database. If the username and password match, then returns **success**, otherwise, returns **error**.

InsertBookAction

Picks up the necessary information from the JSP and inserts a new record into the database table.

EditBookAction

Picks up the necessary information from the database and populates the Update Books data entry form so that the user can update the book details.

UpdateBookAction

Picks up the necessary information from the JSP and updates the existing record in the database table.

DeleteBookAction

Picks up the Book's IDentity number from the JSP and deletes the record identified by the IDentity number from the database table.

ManageSearchBooksAction

Picks up the ISBN or Book name or both, fires an SQL SELECT query to retrieve the appropriate records and then returns the records that match the given ISBN or book name or both.

SearchBooksAction

Picks up the search criteria, fires an SQL SELECT query to retrieve the appropriate records and then returns the records that match the given search criteria.

LogoffAction

Performs the necessary steps to log the current user off the system.

Chapter 15

SECTION IV: APPLICATION DEVELOPMENT USING STRUTS 2

Project Specifications

Based on the software requirements specifications defined in *Chapter 14: Defining The Project And Its Requirements*, the application will comprise of the following:

Java Server Pages

File Name	Description
index.jsp	Application's homepage
login.jsp	Login form
menu.jsp	Menu bar [included in JSPs that require a menu bar]
manageBooks.jsp	Manage Books form
addBooks.jsp	Add Books data entry form
updateBooks.jsp	Update Books data entry form
searchBooks.jsp	Search Books form

Actions

File Name	Description
`loginAction.java`	Login Action class
`searchBooksAction.java`	Search Books Action class
`manageSearchBooksAction.java`	Manage Search Books Action class
`insertBookAction.java`	Insert Books Action class
`editBookAction.java`	Edit Books Action class
`updateBookAction.java`	Update Books Action class
`deleteBookAction.java`	Delete Books Action class
`logOffAction.java`	Logout Action class

Interceptors

File Name	Description
`AuthenticationInterceptor.java`	Authentication Interceptor class

CSS

File Name	Description
`stylesheet.css`	Cascading Style Sheet

Beans

File Name	Description
`Book.java`	Book Bean class
`dbConnection.java`	Database connection class

Configuration [struts.xml]

Code Spec:

```
1  <?xml version="1.0" encoding="UTF-8"?>
2  <!DOCTYPE struts PUBLIC '-//Apache Software Foundation//DTD Commons Validator Rules
   Configuration 2.3//EN' 'http://struts.apache.org/dtds/struts-2.3.dtd'>
3  <struts>
4     <package name="bookShop" extends="struts-default">
5        <interceptors>
6           <interceptor name="loginInterceptor"
                 class="com.sharanamvaishali.bookShop.interceptor.AuthenticationInterceptor" />
7           <interceptor-stack name="myStack">
8              <interceptor-ref name="defaultStack" />
```

```xml
 9            <interceptor-ref name="loginInterceptor" />
10         </interceptor-stack>
11      </interceptors>
12
13      <global-results>
14         <result name="loginAction" type="redirectAction">index</result>
15      </global-results>
16
17      <action name="index">
18         <result>bookShop/login.jsp</result>
19      </action>
20      <action name="doLogin"
        class="com.sharanamvaishali.bookShop.action.loginAction">
21         <result name="success" type="redirectAction">showSearchBooks</result>
22         <result name="error">bookShop/login.jsp</result>
23         <result name="input">bookShop/login.jsp</result>
24      </action>
25      <action name="showSearchBooks">
26            <interceptor-ref name="myStack"/>
27            <result>bookShop/searchBooks.jsp</result>
28      </action>
29      <action name="showManageBooks">
30         <interceptor-ref name="myStack" />
31         <result>bookShop/manageBooks.jsp</result>
32      </action>
33      <action name="doLogout"
        class="com.sharanamvaishali.bookShop.action.logOffAction">
34         <result type="redirectAction">index</result>
35      </action>
36
37      <action name="showAddBooks">
38         <interceptor-ref name="myStack" />
39         <result type="redirect">bookShop/addBooks.jsp</result>
40      </action>
41      <action name="doInsertBooks"
        class="com.sharanamvaishali.bookShop.action.insertBookAction">
42         <interceptor-ref name="myStack" />
43         <result name="success">/bookShop/manageBooks.jsp</result>
44         <result name="input">/bookShop/addBooks.jsp</result>
45      </action>
46
47      <action name="showEditBooks"
        class="com.sharanamvaishali.bookShop.action.editBookAction">
48         <interceptor-ref name="myStack" />
49         <result name="success">bookShop/updateBooks.jsp</result>
50      </action>
51      <action name="doUpdateBooks"
        class="com.sharanamvaishali.bookShop.action.updateBookAction">
52         <interceptor-ref name="myStack" />
53         <result name="success">/bookShop/manageBooks.jsp</result>
54         <result name="input">/bookShop/updateBooks.jsp</result>
55      </action>
56
57      <action name="doDeleteBooks"
        class="com.sharanamvaishali.bookShop.action.deleteBookAction">
```

```xml
58            <interceptor-ref name="myStack" />
59            <result name="success">bookShop/manageBooks.jsp</result>
60        </action>
61
62        <action name="doManageSearchBooks"
          class="com.sharanamvaishali.bookShop.action.manageSearchBooksAction">
63            <interceptor-ref name="myStack" />
64            <result name="success">/bookShop/manageBooks.jsp</result>
65        </action>
66        <action name="doSearchBooks"
          class="com.sharanamvaishali.bookShop.action.searchBooksAction">
67            <interceptor-ref name="myStack" />
68            <result name="success">/bookShop/searchBooks.jsp</result>
69            <result name="input">/bookShop/searchBooks.jsp</result>
70        </action>
71    </package>
72 </struts>
```

Process Flow Diagrams

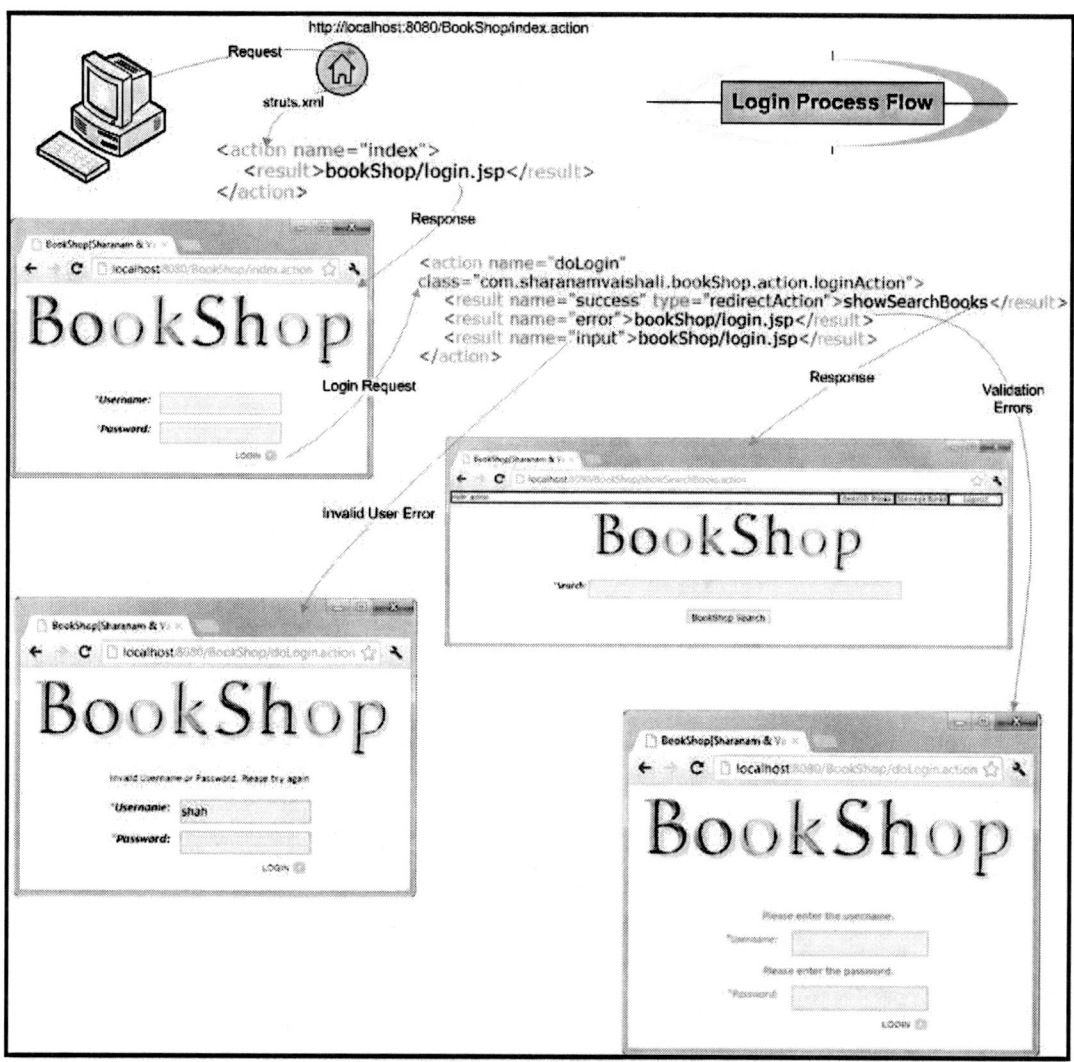

Diagram 15.1: Login Process Flow

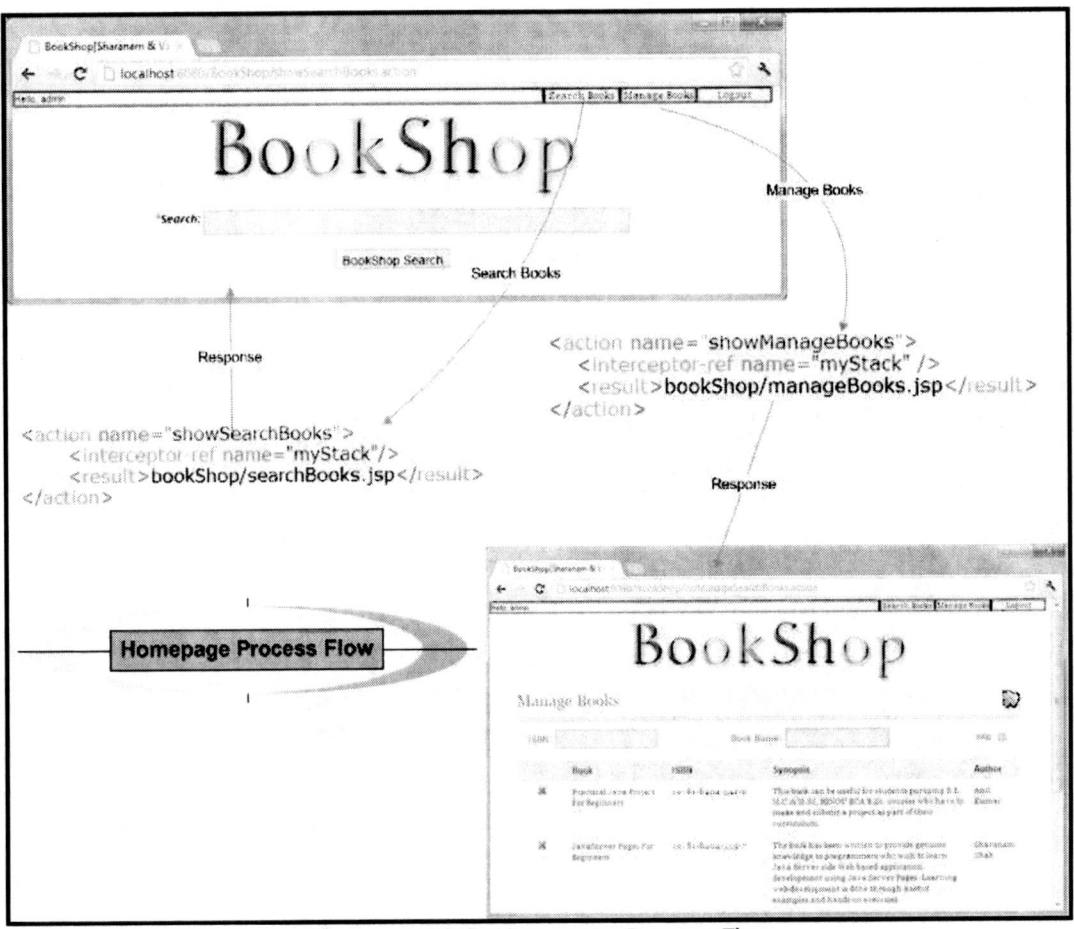

Diagram 15.2: Homepage Process Flow

Project Specifications 241

```xml
<action name="doSearchBooks"
class="com.sharanamvaishali.bookShop.action.searchBooksAction">
    <interceptor-ref name="myStack" />
    <result name="success">/bookShop/searchBooks.jsp</result>
    <result name="input">/bookShop/searchBooks.jsp</result>
</action>
```

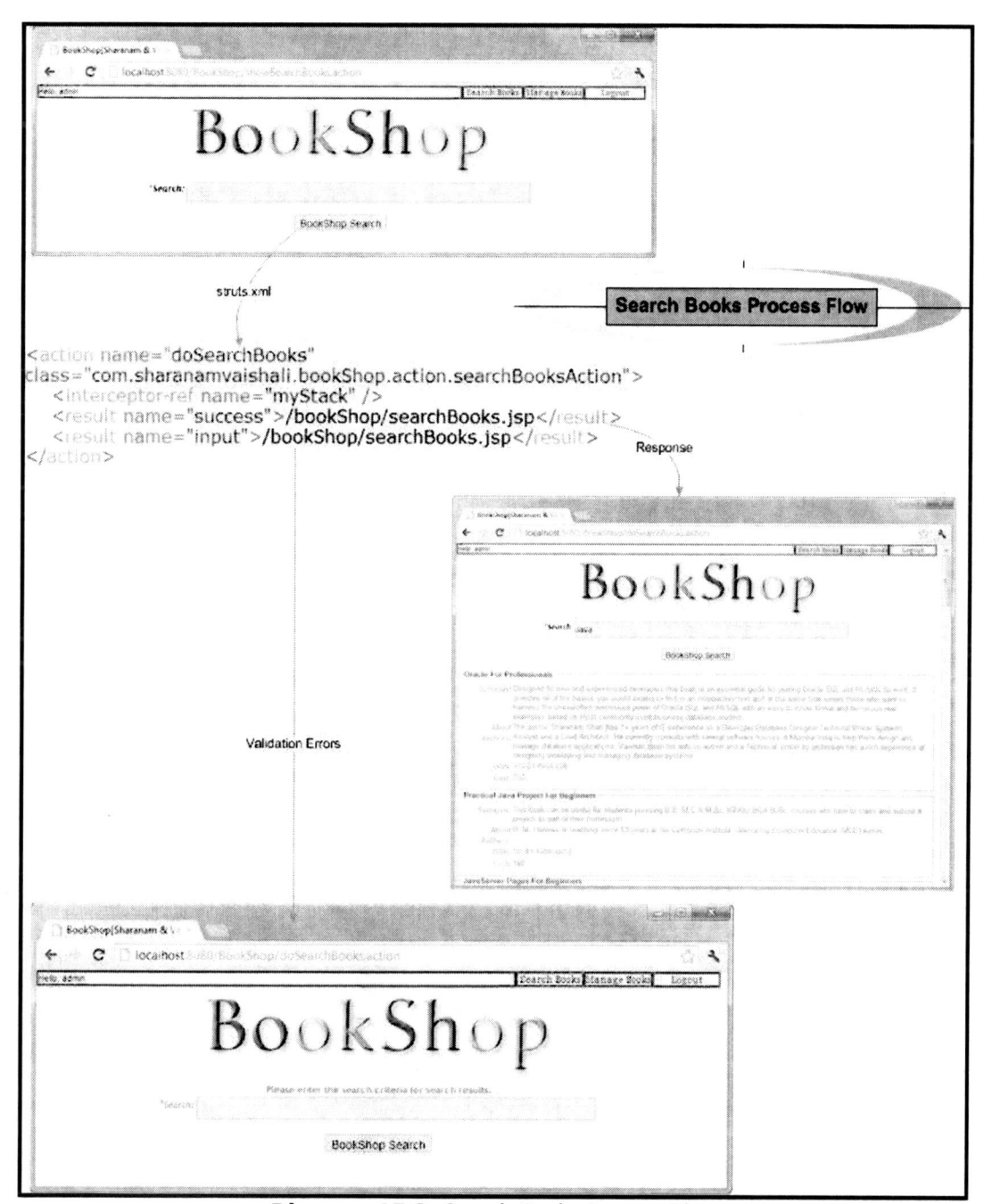

Diagram 15.3: Search Books Process Flow

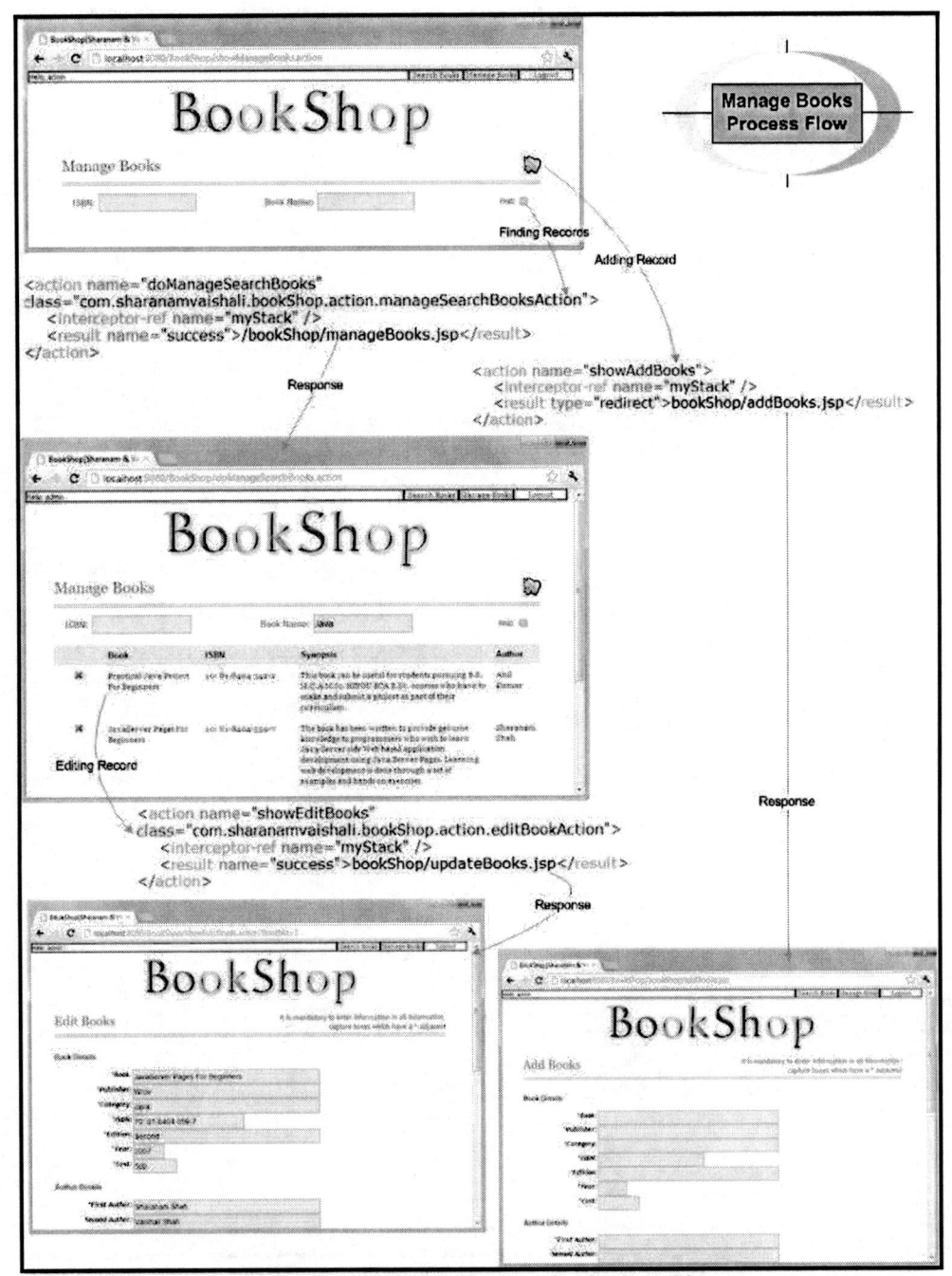

Diagram 15.4: Manage Books Process Flow

Project Specifications 243

```
<action name="doInsertBooks"
 class="com.sharanamvaishali.bookShop.action.insertBookAction">
    <interceptor-ref name="myStack" />
    <result name="success">/bookShop/manageBooks.jsp</result>
    <result name="input">/bookShop/addBooks.jsp</result>
</action>
```

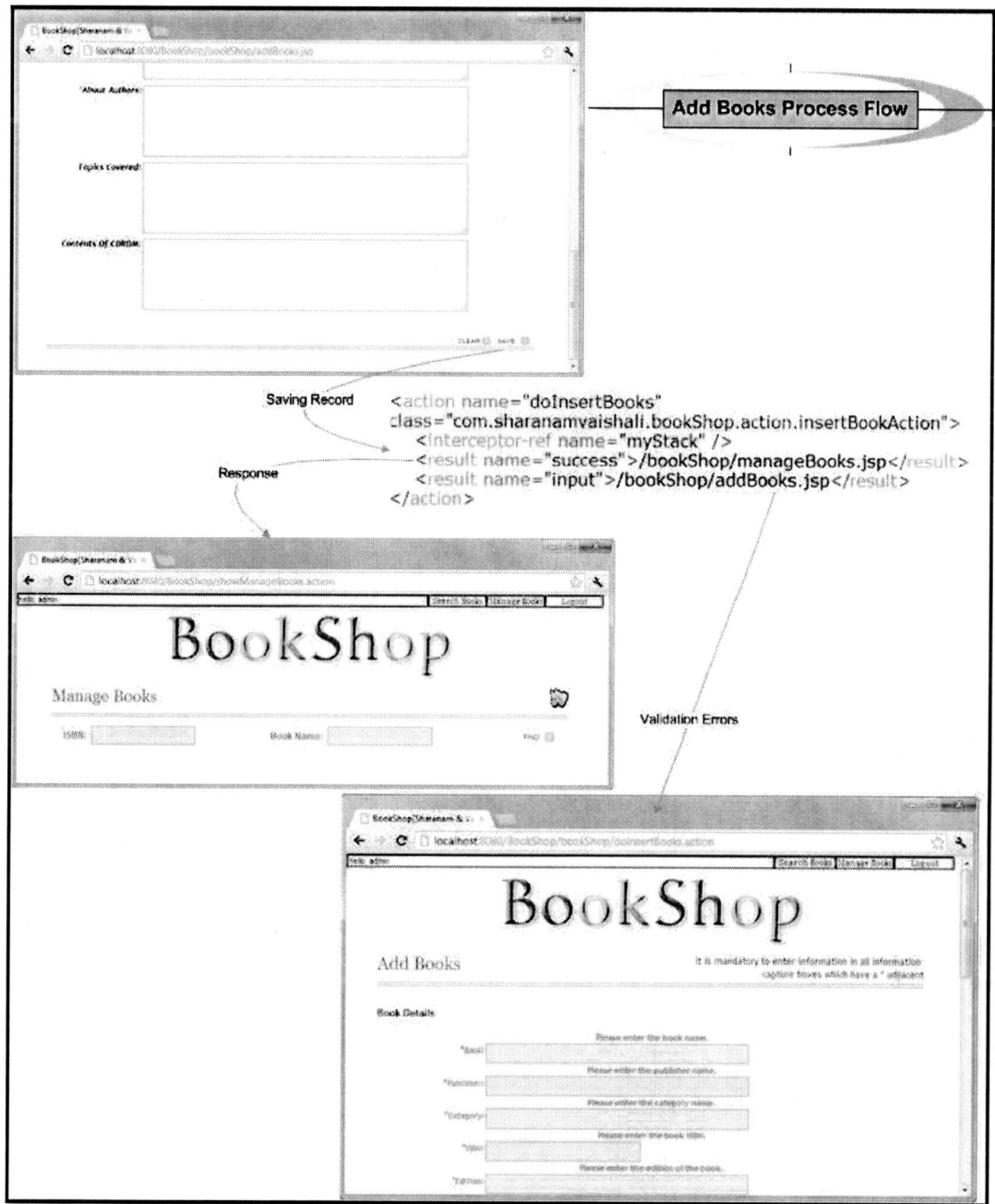

Diagram 15.5: Add Books Process Flow

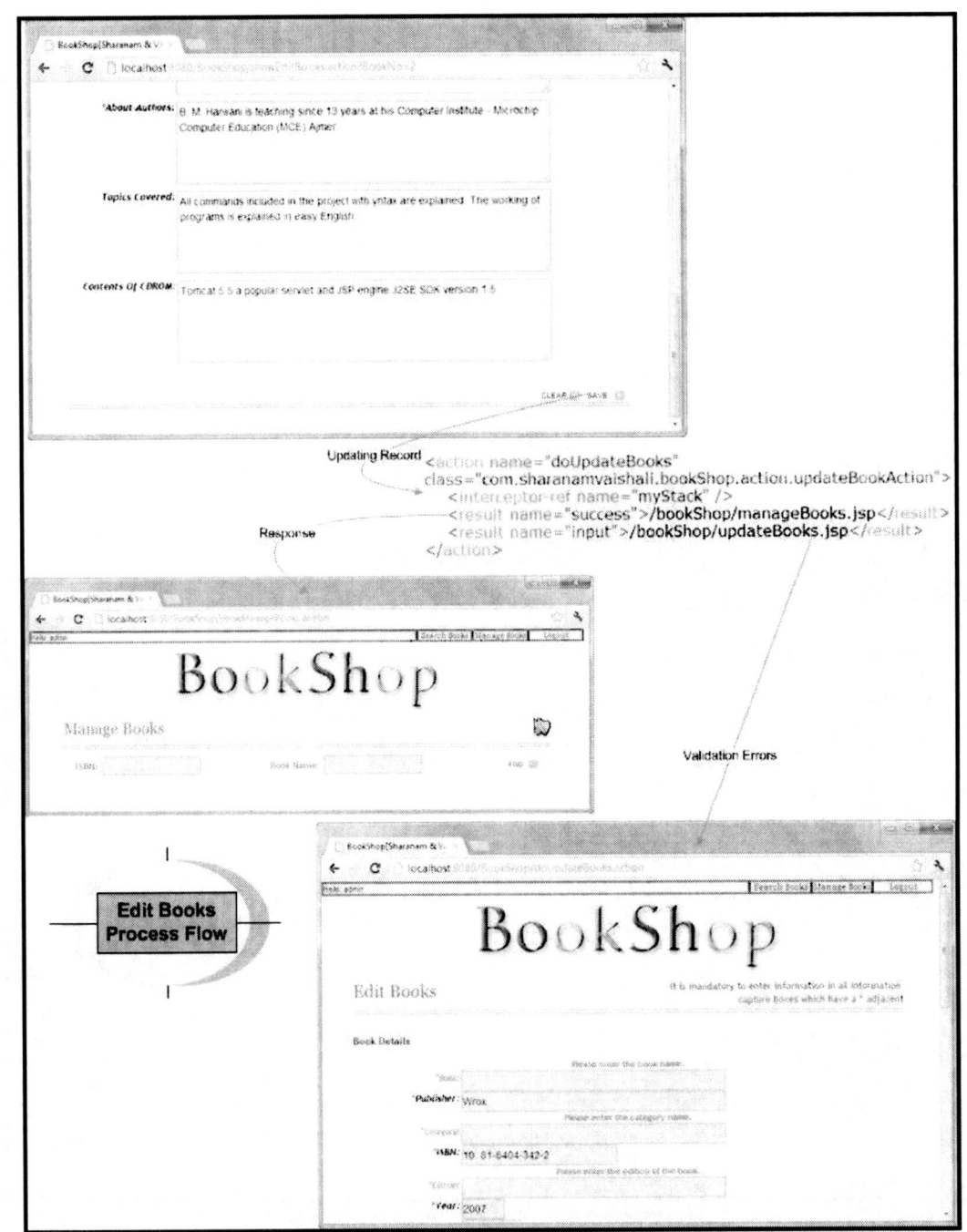

Diagram 15.6: Edit Books Process Flow

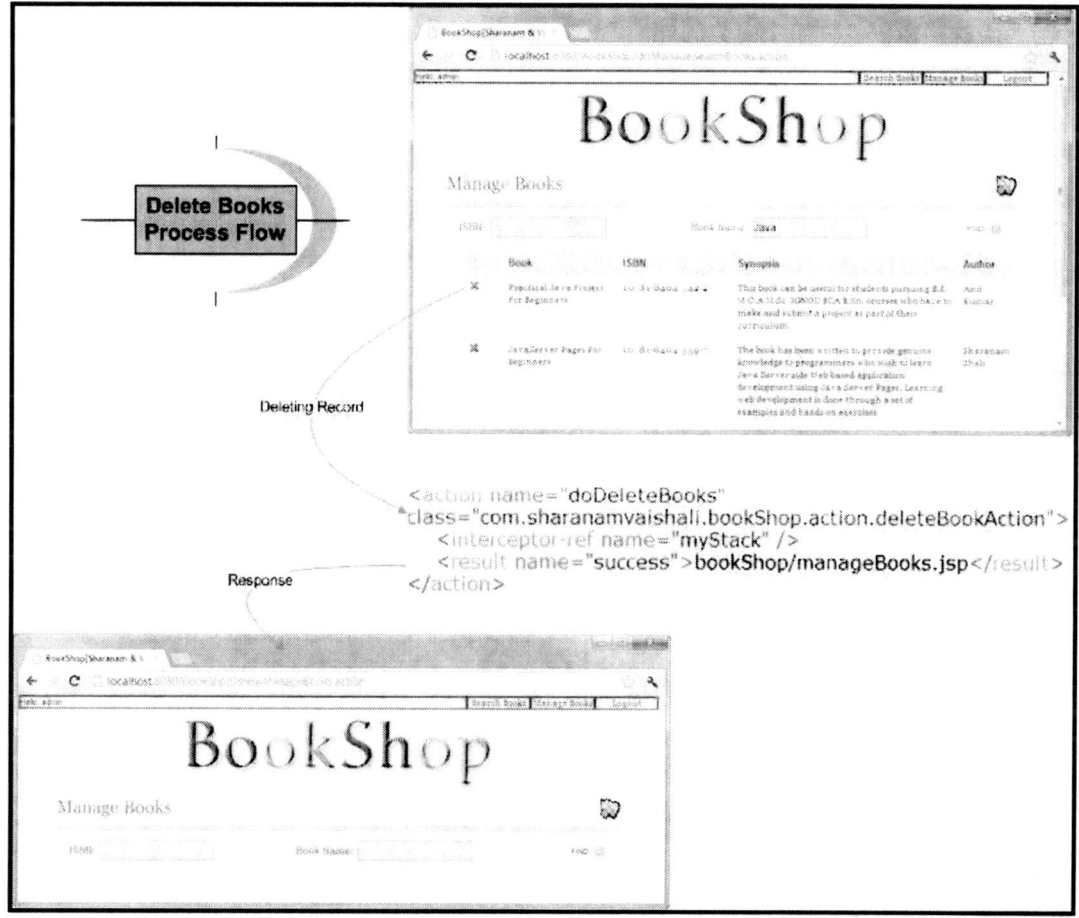

Diagram 15.7: Delete Books Process Flow

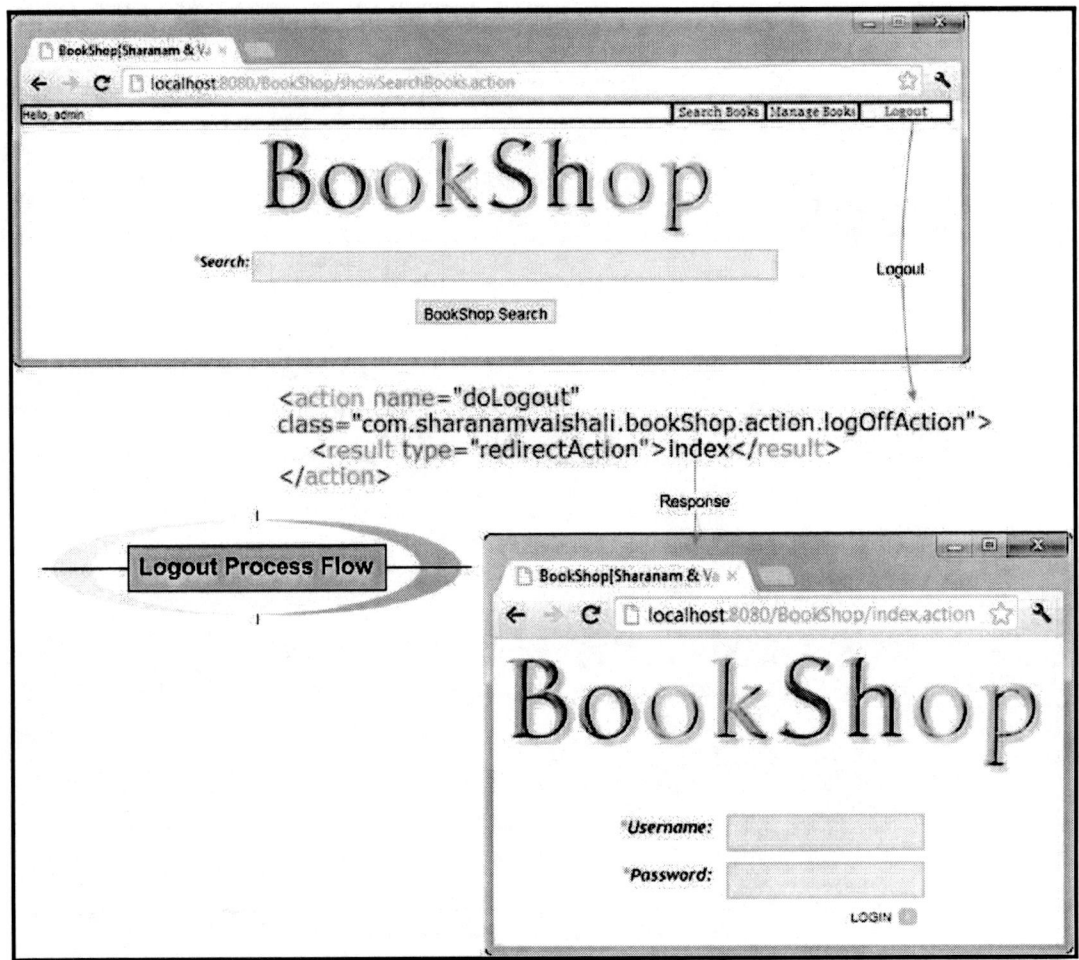

Diagram 15.8: Logout Process Flow

Validations

loginAction-validation.xml

Field Name	Validation Type	Message
username	requiredstring	Please enter the username.
password	requiredstring	Please enter the password.

Project Specifications

searchBookAction-validation.xml

Field Name	Validation Type	Message
`searchCriteria`	requiredstring	Please enter the search criteria for search results.

insertBookAction-validation.xml

Field Name	Validation Type	Message
`BookName`	requiredstring	Please enter the book name.
`PublisherName`	requiredstring	Please enter the publisher name.
`Category`	requiredstring	Please enter the category name.
`ISBN`	requiredstring	Please enter the book ISBN.
`Edition`	requiredstring	Please enter the edition of the book.
`Year`	requiredstring	Please enter the year when the book was published.
	int	Please enter a numeric value.
`Cost`	requiredstring	Please enter the cost of the book.
	int	Please enter a numeric value.
`FirstAuthor`	requiredstring	Please enter the name of the first author.
`Synopsis`	requiredstring	Please enter the synopsis of the book.
`AboutAuthors`	requiredstring	Please enter the about the author details.

updateBookAction-validation.xml

Field Name	Validation Type	Message
`BookName`	requiredstring	Please enter the book name.
`PublisherName`	requiredstring	Please enter the publisher name.
`Category`	requiredstring	Please enter the category name.
`ISBN`	requiredstring	Please enter the book ISBN.
`Edition`	requiredstring	Please enter the edition of the book.
`Year`	requiredstring	Please enter the year when the book was published.
	int	Please enter a numeric value.
`Cost`	requiredstring	Please enter the cost of the book.
	int	Please enter a numeric value.
`FirstAuthor`	requiredstring	Please enter the name of the first author.
`Synopsis`	requiredstring	Please enter the synopsis of the book.
`AboutAuthors`	requiredstring	Please enter the about the author details.

Libraries

- antlr-2.7.2.jar

- commons-fileupload-1.2.2.jar
- commons-io-2.0.1.jar
- commons-lang3-3.1.jar
- commons-logging-1.1.1.jar
- freemarker-2.3.19.jar
- ognl-3.0.5.jar
- struts2-core-2.3.4.1.jar
- javassist-3.11.0.GA.jar
- xwork-core-2.3.4.1.jar
- struts2-dojo-plugin-2.3.4.1.jar
- mysql-connector-java-5.1.21-bin.jar

Table Structure

Database Name

Code spec:
CREATE DATABASE BookShop;
USE BookShop;

Table Definitions

SystemUsers

This table stores the system user details.

Column Name	Data Type	Size	Null	Default	Constraints
UserNo	Integer	10	No	- -	Primary key
Description	An identity number of the system user					
Username	Varchar	30	No	- -	Unique key
Description	The username of the system user					
Password	Varchar	30	No	- -	- -
Description	The password of the system user					

Code spec:
```
CREATE TABLE SystemUsers(
    UserNo int(10) NOT NULL,
    Username varchar(30) NOT NULL,
    Password varchar(30) NOT NULL,
    PRIMARY KEY (UserNo),
    UNIQUE KEY Username(Username));
```

REMINDER

> Ensure that few records are available in this table to allow login. Login form authenticate users against the records available in this table.

Books

This table stores the book details captured using the Add Books d/e form.

Column Name	Data Type	Size	Null	Default	Constraints
BookNo	Integer	10	No	- -	Primary Key
Description	An identity number of the book					
BookName	Varchar	255	No	- -	- -
Description	The name of the book					
FirstAuthor	Varchar	60	No	- -	- -
Description	The name of the first author					
SecondAuthor	Varchar	60	Yes	NULL	- -
Description	The name of the second author					
ThirdAuthor	Varchar	60	Yes	NULL	- -
Description	The name of the third author					
FourthAuthor	Varchar	60	Yes	NULL	- -
Description	The name of the fourth author					
PublisherName	Varchar	100	No	- -	- -
Description	The name of the publisher					
Category	Varchar	100	No	- -	- -
Description	The name of the category					
ISBN	Varchar	20	No	- -	Unique key
Description	The ISBN of the book					
Edition	Varchar	20	No	- -	- -
Description	The edition of the book					

Column Name	Data Type	Size	Null	Default	Constraints
Year	Integer	4	No	- -	- -
Description	The year when the book was published					
Cost	Integer	12	No	- -	- -
Description	The cost of the book					
Synopsis	Varchar	4000	No	- -	- -
Description	The synopsis of the book					
AboutAuthors	Varchar	4000	No	- -	- -
Description	The information about the book authors					
TopicsCovered	Varchar	4000	Yes	NULL	- -
Description	The topics covered in the book					
ContentsCDROM	Varchar	4000	Yes	NULL	- -
Description	The contents of the CDROM of the book					

Code spec:

```
CREATE TABLE Books(
    BookNo int(10) NOT NULL,
    BookName varchar(255) NOT NULL,
    FirstAuthor varchar(60) NOT NULL,
    SecondAuthor varchar(60) DEFAULT NULL,
    ThirdAuthor varchar(60) DEFAULT NULL,
    FourthAuthor varchar(60) DEFAULT NULL,
    PublisherName varchar(100) NOT NULL,
    Category varchar(100) NOT NULL,
    ISBN varchar(20) NOT NULL,
    Edition varchar(20) NOT NULL,
    Year int(4) NOT NULL,
    Cost int(12) NOT NULL,
    Synopsis varchar(4000) NOT NULL,
    AboutAuthors varchar(4000) NOT NULL,
    TopicsCovered varchar(4000) NOT NULL,
    ContentsCDROM varchar(4000) NOT NULL,
    PRIMARY KEY (BookNo),
    UNIQUE KEY ISBN(ISBN));
```

REMINDER

The Book's accompanying CDROM holds an SQL file called bookshop.sql. This file can be used to create the database, tables and a few records to start with. This file can be imported into the MySQL database engine using the **source** command.

Chapter 16

SECTION IV: APPLICATION DEVELOPMENT USING STRUTS 2

The Administration Home Page [index.jsp]

The application begins with the homepage i.e. **index.jsp**. This file holds a redirect statement which redirects to **index.action**.

Code Spec

```
1   <% response.sendRedirect ("index.action"); %>
```

struts.xml holds a mapping to help the redirection:

```
17      <action name="index">
18          <result>bookShop/login.jsp</result>
19      </action>
```

Using this mapping the control shifts to login.jsp and Login data entry form is served, as shown in diagram 16.1.

BookShop

Diagram 16.1: Login Form

Login Form [login.jsp]

This is a simple JSP that holds a data entry form with the following specifications.

Form Specifications

File Name	login.jsp
Title	BookShop[Sharanam & Vaishali Shah] - Login
Bound To Table	SystemUsers
Form Name	frmLogin
Action	doLogin
Method	Post

Data Fields

Label	Name	Bound To	Validation Rules
Username	username	SystemUsers.Username	Cannot be left blank
Password	password	SystemUsers.Password	Cannot be left blank

Data Controls

Object	Label	Name
Button	Login	login

Micro-Help For Form Fields

Form Field	Micro Help Statement
username	Enter Username
password	Enter Password

The Administration Home Page [index.jsp]

Code Spec

```jsp
1  <%@page contentType="text/html" pageEncoding="UTF-8"%>
2  <%@ taglib prefix="s" uri="/struts-tags" %>
3  <!DOCTYPE html>
4  <html>
5    <head>
6      <meta http-equiv="Content-Type" content="text/html; charset=UTF-8">
7      <title>BookShop[Sharanam & Vaishali Shah] - Login</title>
8      <link href="/BookShop/css/stylesheet.css" type="text/css" rel="stylesheet">
9      <s:head />
10   </head>
11   <body>
12     <s:form id="frmLogin" name="frmLogin" method="post" action="doLogin" >
13       <table border="0" cellpadding="0" cellspacing="0" align="center" width="100%">
14         <tr>
15           <td align="center">
16             <img src="/BookShop/images/b.gif"/>
17             <img src="/BookShop/images/o1.gif"/>
18             <img src="/BookShop/images/o2.gif"/>
19             <img src="/BookShop/images/k.gif"/>
20             <img src="/BookShop/images/s.gif"/>
21             <img src="/BookShop/images/h.gif"/>
22             <img src="/BookShop/images/o2.gif"/>
23             <img src="/BookShop/images/p.gif"/>
24           </td>
25         </tr>
26       </table>
27       <table border="0" cellpadding="4" cellspacing="0" width="248px" align="center">
28         <tbody>
29           <tr>
30             <td colspan="2" align="left">
31               <s:property value="message" />
32             </td>
33           </tr>
34           <tr>
35             <td valign="middle" class="formContent">
36               <s:textfield required="true" requiredposition="left" maxLength="25" label="Username" name="username" title="Enter Username" />
37               <s:password required="true" requiredposition="left" maxLength="8" label="Password" name="password" title="Enter Password" />
38               <s:submit cssClass="buttonText" cssStyle="background:url(/BookShop/images/submit_bg.gif) no-repeat scroll 37px 0px;" name="login" value="Login" />
39             </td>
40           </tr>
41         </tbody>
```

254 Struts 2 For Beginners

```
42          </table>
43        </s:form>
44      </body>
45    </html>
```

Process Flow

After the user keys in the username and password and clicks LOGIN ▶, the form is submitted to the action named **doLogin**.

struts.xml holds a mapping to help the form submission:

```
20      <action name="doLogin"
           class="com.sharanamvaishali.bookShop.action.loginAction">
21        <result name="success" type="redirectAction">showSearchBooks</result>
22        <result name="error">bookShop/login.jsp</result>
23        <result name="input">bookShop/login.jsp</result>
24      </action>
```

This means the values [username and password] captured by the login form are passed on to the action doLogin → bookShop.loginAction.

doLogin [loginAction.java]

This is an action class with the following specifications.

Class Name	Package	Extends	Implements
loginAction	bookShop	ActionSupport	SessionAware

Properties			
Property Name	Property Type	Methods	
username	String	getUsername()	setUsername()
password	String	getPassword()	setPassword()
message	String	getMessage()	setMessage()
session	Map	getSession()	setSession()

Methods	
Method Name	Return Values
execute()	SUCCESS / ERROR

Code Spec

```
1  package com.sharanamvaishali.bookShop.action;
2
3  import com.opensymphony.xwork2.ActionContext;
4  import com.opensymphony.xwork2.ActionSupport;
5  import com.sharanamvaishali.bookShop.dbConnection.dbConnection;
6  import java.sql.*;
```

The Administration Home Page [index.jsp]

```java
 7  import java.util.*;
 8  import org.apache.struts2.interceptor.SessionAware;
 9
10  public class loginAction extends ActionSupport implements SessionAware {
11      private String username, password, message;
12      private ResultSet rs;
13      private Map session;
14
15      public Map getSession() {
16          return session;
17      }
18      public void setSession(Map session) {
19          this.session = session;
20      }
21
22      public String getUsername() {
23          return username;
24      }
25      public void setUsername(String username) {
26          this.username = username;
27      }
28
29      public String getPassword() {
30          return password;
31      }
32      public void setPassword(String password) {
33          this.password = password;
34      }
35
36      public String getMessage() {
37          return message;
38      }
39
40      @Override
41      public String execute() throws Exception {
42          dbConnection db = new dbConnection();
43          db.getConnection();
44          String SQL = "SELECT Username, Password FROM SystemUsers WHERE Username='" + username + "' AND Password='" + password + "'";
45          rs = db.stmt.executeQuery(SQL);
46
47          if(rs.next()){
48              session = ActionContext.getContext().getSession();
49              session.put("username", username);
50              db.removeConnection();
51              return SUCCESS;
52          } else {
53              db.removeConnection();
54              message = "Invalid Username or Password. Please try again";
55              return ERROR;
56          }
57      }
58  }
```

Explanation:

As soon as this action takes charge, **execute()**, does the following:

Establishes a database connection as:
- Spawns an object of class **dbConnectionAction**
- Invokes **getConnection()** of that class

Fires an SQL SELECT query using **executeQuery()** of the Statement object:

```
SELECT Username, Password FROM SystemUsers WHERE
Username='" + username + "' AND Password='" + password + ""
```

The results are held in a ResultSet object.

This SELECT query attempts to retrieve a record from the **SystemUsers** table identified by username and password that were captured by the Login form and passed on to this action.

HINT

Currently in this application users are authenticated against the records available in the SystemUsers table. There is no data entry form to allow additions of new users. This has to be done manually using INSERT SQL query. A pre-defined user called **admin** [password=admin] is already available for demonstration purpose.

If this query retrieves a record, then:
- The username is stored in the session
- The database connection is destroyed
- SUCCESS is returned

struts.xml holds a mapping to help the **SUCCESS** result:

```
20      <action name="doLogin"
            class="com.sharanamvaishali.bookShop.action.loginAction">
21          <result name="success" type="redirectAction">showSearchBooks</result>
22          <result name="error">bookShop/login.jsp</result>
23          <result name="input">bookShop/login.jsp</result>
24      </action>
```

Since SUCCESS is returned, searchBooks.jsp [identified by the action named showSearchBooks] will be served which is the first page [an entry point] to begin working with this application.

The Administration Home Page [index.jsp]

struts.xml holds a mapping for the action named showSearchBooks:

```
25      <action name="showSearchBooks">
26          <interceptor-ref name="myStack"/>
27          <result>bookShop/searchBooks.jsp</result>
28      </action>
```

If this query does not retrieve a record, then:

- The database connection is destroyed
- An error message to indicate the issue is stored in a property that will be displayed on Login form, as shown in diagram 16.2
- ERROR is returned

struts.xml holds a mapping to help the **ERROR** result:

```
20      <action name="doLogin"
            class="com.sharanamvaishali.bookShop.action.loginAction">
21          <result name="success" type="redirectAction">showSearchBooks</result>
22          <result name="error">bookShop/login.jsp</result>
23          <result name="input">bookShop/login.jsp</result>
24      </action>
```

Since ERROR is returned, login.jsp will be served along with the error message, as shown in diagram 16.2.

Diagram 16.2: Invalid username or password error message

Validations [loginAction-validation.xml]

If the required **input** fields are kept empty whilst submitting the form loginAction-validation.xml takes care of the validations.

Code Spec

```
1  <?xml version="1.0" encoding="UTF-8"?>
2  <!DOCTYPE validators PUBLIC "-//Apache Struts//XWork Validator 1.0.3//EN"
   "http://struts.apache.org/dtds/xwork-validator-1.0.3.dtd">
3  <validators>
4    <field name="username">
5      <field-validator type="requiredstring">
6        <message>Please enter the username.</message>
7      </field-validator>
8    </field>
9
10   <field name="password">
11     <field-validator type="requiredstring">
12       <message>Please enter the password.</message>
13     </field-validator>
14   </field>
15 </validators>
```

After the errors, if any, are detected the login data entry form is served again with appropriate error messages, as shown in diagram 16.3.

struts.xml holds a mapping to serve the data entry form:

```
20       <action name="doLogin"
            class="com.sharanamvaishali.bookShop.action.loginAction">
21         <result name="success" type="redirectAction">showSearchBooks</result>
22         <result name="error">bookShop/login.jsp</result>
23         <result name="input">bookShop/login.jsp</result>
24       </action>
```

Diagram 16.3: Empty fields' error message

Chapter 17

SECTION IV: APPLICATION DEVELOPMENT USING STRUTS 2

Search Books [searchBooks.jsp]

This is a JSP that is served immediately after a successful login. It holds a data entry form to capture the search criteria, as shown in diagram 17.1.

Diagram 17.1: Search Books form

The search results are generated dynamically and displayed, as shown in diagram 17.2.

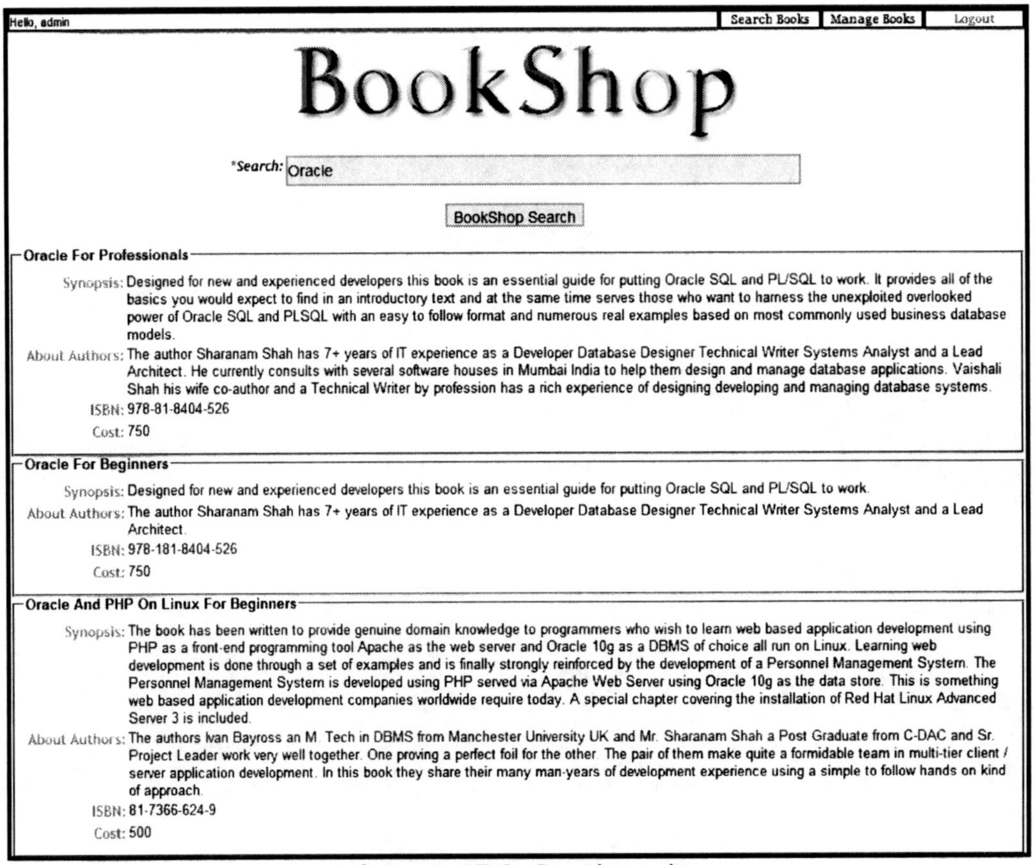

Diagram 17.2: Search results

Form Specifications

File Name	searchBooks.jsp
Title	BookShop[Sharanam & Vaishali Shah] - Search Books
Bound To Table	Books
Form Name	frmSearch
Action	doSearchBooks
Method	Post

Data Fields

Label	Name	Bound To	Validation Rules
Search	searchCriteria	Books.*	Cannot be left blank

Data Controls

Object	Label	Name
Button	BookShop Search	cmdBook

Micro-Help For Form Fields

Form Field	Micro Help Statement
searchCriteria	Enter the Search Criteria

Code Spec

```
1   <%@page contentType="text/html" pageEncoding="UTF-8"%>
2   <%@ taglib prefix="s" uri="/struts-tags" %>
3   <!DOCTYPE html>
4   <html>
5     <head>
6       <meta http-equiv="Content-Type" content="text/html; charset=UTF-8">
7       <title>BookShop[Sharanam & Vaishali Shah] - Search Books</title>
8       <link href="/BookShop/css/stylesheet.css" type="text/css" rel="stylesheet">
9       <s:head />
10    </head>
11    <body>
12      <s:include value="menu.jsp" />
13      <s:form id="frmSearch" name="frmSearch" method="post" action="doSearchBooks">
14        <table border="0" cellpadding="0" cellspacing="0" align="center">
15          <s:textfield label="Search" required="true" requiredposition="left" name="searchCriteria" id="searchCriteria" title="Enter the search criteria" size="75" />
16        </table>
17        <table border="0" cellpadding="0" cellspacing="0" width="100%">
18          <tr><td> </td></tr>
19          <tr>
20            <td align="center">
21              <s:submit theme="simple" id="cmdBook" value="BookShop Search"/>
22            </td>
23          </tr>
24          <tr><td> </td></tr>
25          <tr>
26            <td>
27              <s:iterator value="book">
28                <table width="100%" cellpadding="0" cellspacing="0">
29                  <tr>
30                    <td>
31                      <fieldset>
32                        <legend align="left" class="Arial13BrownB"><s:property
```

```
33                          value="BookName"/></legend>
                            <table width="100%" align="left" border="0"
                            cellspacing="2" cellpadding="0">
34                            <tr>
35                              <td valign="top" align="left" width="85%">
36                                <table width="100%" border="0"
                                  cellpadding="0" cellspacing="2" align="left">
37                                  <tr>
38                                    <td valign="top" width="10%"
                                    align="right">
39                                      <s:label theme="simple"
                                        name="Synopsis"
                                        cssClass="mandatory"
                                        value="Synopsis: "/>
40                                    </td>
41                                    <td width="90%" valign="top"
                                    class="Arial13GrayN">
42                                      <s:property value="Synopsis"/>
43                                    </td>
44                                  </tr>
45                                  <tr>
46                                    <td valign="top" width="10%"
                                    align="right">
47                                      <s:label theme="simple"
                                        name="AboutAuthors"
                                        cssClass="mandatory" value="About
                                        Authors: "/>
48                                    </td>
49                                    <td width="90%" valign="top"
                                    class="Arial13GrayN">
50                                      <s:property value="AboutAuthors"/>
51                                    </td>
52                                  </tr>
53                                  <tr>
54                                    <td valign="top" width="10%"
                                    align="right">
55                                      <s:label theme="simple"
                                        name="ISBN" cssClass="mandatory"
                                        value="ISBN: "/>
56                                    </td>
57                                    <td width="90%" valign="top"
                                    class="Arial13GrayN">
58                                      <s:property value="ISBN"/>
59                                    </td>
60                                  </tr>
61                                  <tr>
62                                    <td valign="top" width="10%"
                                    align="right">
63                                      <s:label theme="simple"
                                        name="Cost" cssClass="mandatory"
                                        value="Cost: "/>
64                                    </td>
65                                    <td width="90%" valign="top"
```

Search Books [searchBooks.jsp]

```
66                              class="Arial13GrayN">
67                                  <s:property value="Cost"/>
68                              </td>
69                          </tr>
70                      </table>
71                  </td>
72              </tr>
73          </table>
74      </fieldset>
75  </td>
76  </tr>
77  </table>
78  </s:iterator>
79  </td>
80  </tr>
81  </table>
82  </s:form>
83  </body>
84  </html>
```

Process Flow

After the user keys in the search criteria and clicks [BookShop Search], the form is submitted to the action named **doSearchBooks**.

struts.xml holds a mapping to help the form submission:

```
66      <action name="doSearchBooks"
            class="com.sharanamvaishali.bookShop.action.searchBooksAction">
67          <interceptor-ref name="myStack" />
68          <result name="success">/bookShop/searchBooks.jsp</result>
69          <result name="input">/bookShop/searchBooks.jsp</result>
70      </action>
```

This means the search criteria captured by Search Books form are passed on to the action **doSearchBooks → bookshop.searchBooksAction**.

doSearchBooks [searchBooksAction.java]

This is an action class with the following specifications.

Class Name	Package	Extends	Implements
searchBooksAction	bookShop	ActionSupport	- -

Properties			
Property Name	**Property Type**	**Methods**	
searchCriteria	String	getSearchCriteria()	setSearchCriteria()
book	ArrayList	getBook()	setBook()

Methods

Method Name	Return Values
execute()	SUCCESS

Code Spec

```
1   package com.sharanamvaishali.bookShop.action;
2
3   import com.opensymphony.xwork2.ActionSupport;
4   import com.sharanamvaishali.bookShop.dbConnection.dbConnection;
5   import com.sharanamvaishali.bookShop.domain.Book;
6   import java.sql.*;
7   import java.util.ArrayList;
8
9   public class searchBooksAction extends ActionSupport {
10      private String searchCriteria;
11      private ResultSet rs;
12      private ArrayList<Book> book = new ArrayList<Book>();
13
14      public String getSearchCriteria() {
15          return searchCriteria;
16      }
17      public void setSearchCriteria(String searchCriteria) {
18          this.searchCriteria = searchCriteria;
19      }
20
21      public ArrayList getBook() {
22          return book;
23      }
24      public void setBook(ArrayList book) {
25          this.book = book;
26      }
27
28      @Override
29      public String execute() throws Exception{
30          dbConnection db = new dbConnection();
31          db.getConnection();
32          String SQL = "SELECT * FROM Books WHERE BookName LIKE '%" +
            searchCriteria + "%' OR ISBN LIKE '%" + searchCriteria + "%' OR Edition LIKE
            '%" + searchCriteria + "%' OR Year LIKE '%" + searchCriteria + "%' OR Synopsis
            LIKE '%" + searchCriteria + "%' OR AboutAuthors LIKE '%" + searchCriteria +
            "%' OR TopicsCovered LIKE '%" + searchCriteria + "%' OR ContentsCDROM LIKE
            '%" + searchCriteria + "%' OR Cost LIKE '%" + searchCriteria  + "%' OR
            FirstAuthor LIKE '%" + searchCriteria + "%' OR SecondAuthor LIKE '%" +
            searchCriteria + "%' OR ThirdAuthor LIKE '%" + searchCriteria + "%' OR
            FourthAuthor LIKE '%" + searchCriteria + "%'";
33          System.out.println(SQL);
34          rs = db.stmt.executeQuery(SQL);
35          while(rs.next()){
36              Book bk = new Book(rs.getInt("BookNo"), rs.getString("BookName"),
                rs.getString("PublisherName"), rs.getString("Category"), rs.getString("ISBN"),
```

```
                rs.getString("Edition"), rs.getString("FirstAuthor"),
                rs.getString("SecondAuthor"), rs.getString("ThirdAuthor"),
                rs.getString("FourthAuthor"), rs.getString("Synopsis"),
                rs.getString("AboutAuthors"), rs.getString("TopicsCovered"),
                rs.getString("ContentsCDROM"), rs.getInt("Year"), rs.getInt("Cost"));
37          book.add(bk);
38       }
39       db.removeConnection();
40       return SUCCESS;
41    }
42 }
```

Explanation:

As soon as this action takes charge, **execute()**, does the following:

Establishes a database connection as:

- Spawns an object of class **dbConnectionAction**
- Invokes **getConnection()** of that class

Fires an SQL SELECT query using **executeQuery()** of the Statement object:

```
SELECT * FROM Books
    WHERE BookName LIKE '%" + searchCriteria + "%'
        OR ISBN LIKE '%" + searchCriteria + "%'
        OR Edition LIKE '%" + searchCriteria + "%'
        OR Year LIKE '%" + searchCriteria + "%'
        OR Synopsis LIKE '%" + searchCriteria + "%'
        OR AboutAuthors LIKE '%" + searchCriteria + "%'
        OR TopicsCovered LIKE '%" + searchCriteria + "%'
        OR ContentsCDROM LIKE '%" + searchCriteria + "%'
        OR Cost LIKE '%" + searchCriteria  + "%'
        OR FirstAuthor LIKE '%" + searchCriteria + "%'
        OR SecondAuthor LIKE '%" + searchCriteria + "%'
        OR ThirdAuthor LIKE '%" + searchCriteria + "%'
        OR FourthAuthor LIKE '%" + searchCriteria + "%'"
```

The results are held in a ResultSet object.

This SELECT query attempts to retrieve records from the Books table identified by the search criteria that were captured by the Search Books form and passed on to this action.

All the records that the query retrieves are extracted using a **WHILE** loop which does the following:

- Spawns an object of Book bean class using the parameterized constructor
- This constructor is passed all column values of the current record in the loop
- Finally, this object is added to **book ArrayList**

The database connection is destroyed. SUCCESS is returned.

struts.xml holds a mapping to help the SUCCESS result:

```
66      <action name="doSearchBooks"
             class="com.sharanamvaishali.bookShop.action.searchBooksAction">
67        <interceptor-ref name="myStack" />
68        <result name="success">/bookShop/searchBooks.jsp</result>
69        <result name="input">/bookShop/searchBooks.jsp</result>
70      </action>
```

Since SUCCESS is returned, searchBooks.jsp will be served again with the populated ArrayList object **book**.

searchBooks.jsp on taking charge uses the **iterator** tag to iterate over the contents of the ArrayList object **book**:

```
<s:iterator value="book">
    <table width="100%" cellpadding="0" cellspacing="0">
       <tr>
          <td>
             <fieldset>
                <legend align="left"
                class="Arial13BrownB"><s:property
                value="BookName"/></legend>
```

The **book** object holds all those records [meeting the search criteria] retrieved by the SQL query.

Each record's column values are extracted using **<s:property>**.

```
<table width="100%" border="0" cellpadding="0" cellspacing="2" align="left">
   <tr>
      <td valign="top" width="10%" align="right">
         <s:label theme="simple" name="Synopsis" cssClass="mandatory"
         value="Synopsis: "/>
      </td>
      <td width="90%" valign="top" class="Arial13GrayN">
         <s:property value="Synopsis"/>
      </td>
   </tr>
   <tr>
      <td valign="top" width="10%" align="right">
         <s:label theme="simple" name="AboutAuthors" cssClass="mandatory"
         value="About Authors: "/>
      </td>
      <td width="90%" valign="top" class="Arial13GrayN">
         <s:property value="AboutAuthors"/>
```

Validations [searchBooksAction-validation.xml]

If the required **input** field is kept empty whilst submitting the form, searchBooksAction-validation.xml takes care of the validations.

Code Spec

```
1  <?xml version="1.0" encoding="UTF-8"?>
2  <!DOCTYPE validators PUBLIC "-//Apache Struts//XWork Validator 1.0.3//EN"
   "http://struts.apache.org/dtds/xwork-validator-1.0.3.dtd">
3  <validators>
4    <field name="searchCriteria">
5      <field-validator type="requiredstring">
6        <message>Please enter the search criteria for search results.</message>
7      </field-validator>
8    </field>
9  </validators>
```

After the errors, if any, are detected search book data entry form is served again with appropriate error messages, as shown in diagram 17.3.

struts.xml holds a mapping to serve the data entry form:

```
66    <action name="doSearchBooks"
           class="com.sharanamvaishali.bookShop.action.searchBooksAction">
67      <interceptor-ref name="myStack" />
68      <result name="success">/bookShop/searchBooks.jsp</result>
69      <result name="input">/bookShop/searchBooks.jsp</result>
70    </action>
```

Diagram 17.3: Empty fields' error message

Chapter 18

SECTION IV: APPLICATION DEVELOPMENT USING STRUTS 2

Manage Books [manageBooks.jsp]

This is a JSP, as shown in diagram 18.1 that allows the following:
- **Adding** a new book
- **Searching** for existing books
    - **Modifying** an existing book
    - **Deleting** an existing book

Diagram 18.1: Manage Books form

Add Books [addBooks.jsp]

This is a JSP that holds a data entry form, as shown in diagram 18.2. This form appears when the user clicks ![icon], from Manage Books form.

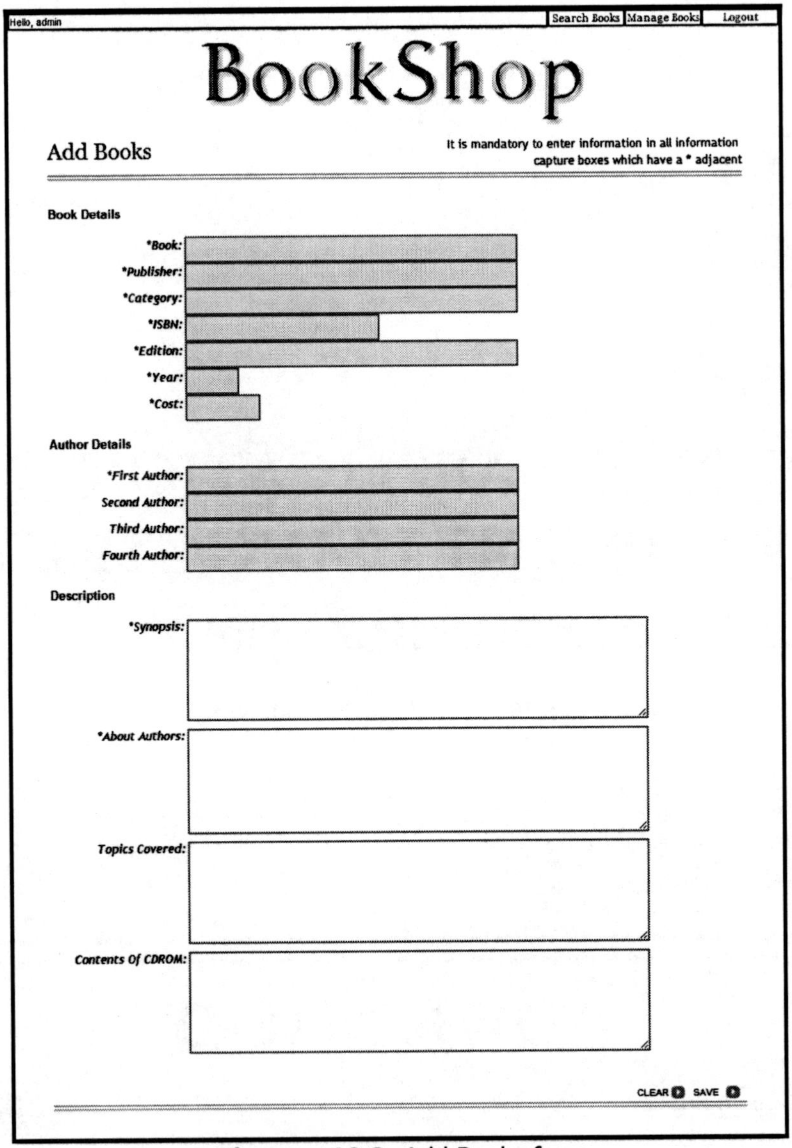

Diagram 18.2: Add Books form

struts.xml holds a mapping to help the redirect to Add Books:

```
37      <action name="showAddBooks">
38          <interceptor-ref name="myStack" />
39          <result type="redirect">bookShop/addBooks.jsp</result>
40      </action>
```

Form Specifications

File Name	addBooks.jsp
Title	BookShop[Sharanam & Vaishali Shah] - Add Books
Bound To Table	Books
Form Name	frmBooks
Action	doInsertBooks
Method	Post

Data Fields

Book Details			
Label	Name	Bound To	Validation Rules
Book	BookName	Books.BookName	Cannot be left blank
Publisher	PublisherName	Books.PublisherName	Cannot be left blank
Category	Category	Books.Category	Cannot be left blank
ISBN	ISBN	Books.ISBN	Cannot be left blank
Edition	Edition	Books.Edition	Cannot be left blank
Year	Year	Books.Year	Cannot be left blank / Must be an integer
Cost	Cost	Books.Cost	Cannot be left blank / Must be an integer

Author Details			
Label	Name	Bound To	Validation Rules
First Author	FirstAuthor	Books.FirstAuthor	Cannot be left blank
Second Author	SecondAuthor	Books.SecondAuthor	*Optional*
Third Author	ThirdAuthor	Books.ThirdAuthor	*Optional*
Fourth Author	FourthAuthor	Books.FourthAuthor	*Optional*

Description			
Label	Name	Bound To	Validation Rules
Synopsis	Synopsis	Books.Synopsis	Cannot be left blank
About Authors	AboutAuthors	Books.AboutAuthors	Cannot be left blank
Topics Covered	TopicsCovered	Books.TopicsCovered	*Optional*
Contents Of CDROM	ContentsCDROM	Books.ContentsCDROM	*Optional*

Data Controls

Object	Label	Name
Button	Save	btnSubmit
Button	Clear	btnReset

Micro-Help For Form Fields

Book Details

Form Field	Micro Help Statement
BookName	Enter the book name
PublisherName	Enter the publisher name
Category	Enter the category name
ISBN	Enter the ISBN
Edition	Enter the edition of the book
Year	Enter the year
Cost	Enter the cost of the book

Author Details

Form Field	Micro Help Statement
FirstAuthor	Enter the name of the author
SecondAuthor	Enter the name of the author
ThirdAuthor	Enter the name of the author
FourthAuthor	Enter the name of the author

Description

Form Field	Micro Help Statement
Synopsis	Enter the synopsis
AboutAuthors	Enter the about author details
TopicsCovered	Enter the topics covered in the book
ContentsCDROM	Enter the contents of CDROM

Code Spec

```
1   <%@page contentType="text/html" pageEncoding="UTF-8"%>
2   <%@ taglib prefix="s" uri="/struts-tags" %>
3   <!DOCTYPE html>
4   <html>
5     <head>
6       <meta http-equiv="Content-Type" content="text/html; charset=UTF-8">
7       <title>BookShop[Sharanam & Vaishali Shah] - Add Books</title>
8       <link href="/BookShop/css/stylesheet.css" type="text/css" rel="stylesheet">
9       <s:head />
10    </head>
```

```
11    <body>
12      <s:include value="menu.jsp" />
13      <s:form id="frmBooks" name="frmBooks" action="doInsertBooks"
        method="post">
14        <table width="760" border="0" align="center" cellpadding="0"
          cellspacing="0">
15          <tr>
16            <td>
17              <table border="0" cellpadding="0" cellspacing="0" width="100%">
18                <tr>
19                  <td valign="top" align="left" style="font:24px
                    Georgia;color:#786e4e;height:37px;">
20                    Add Books
21                  </td>
22                  <td class="treb13blacknormal" valign="top" align="right">
23                    It is mandatory to enter information in all information
                    <br>capture boxes which have a <span
                    class="mandatory">*</span> adjacent
24                  </td>
25                </tr>
26              </table>
27            </td>
28          </tr>
29          <tr align="left" valign="top">
30            <td height="20">
31              <img src="/BookShop/images/hr.jpg"/>
32            </td>
33          </tr>
34          <tr align="left" valign="top">
35            <td>
36              <table width="100%" border="0" align="center" cellpadding="0"
                cellspacing="0">
37                <tr>
38                  <td>
39                    <table width="100%" border="0" cellpadding="0"
                      cellspacing="0">
40                      <tr>
41                        <td class="Arial13BrownB">
42                          <br />Book Details<br /><br />
43                        </td>
44                      </tr>
45                      <s:textfield required="true" requiredposition="left"
                        id="BookName" label="Book" name="BookName"
                        title="Enter the book name" maxLength="25"
                        size="55"/>
46                      <s:textfield required="true" requiredposition="left"
                        id="PublisherName" label="Publisher"
                        name="PublisherName" title="Enter the publisher name"
                        maxLength="25" size="55"/>
47                      <s:textfield required="true" requiredposition="left"
                        id="Category" label="Category" name="Category"
                        title="Enter the category name" maxLength="25"
                        size="55"/>
```

```
48      <s:textfield required="true" requiredposition="left"
        id="ISBN" label="ISBN" name="ISBN" title="Enter the
        ISBN" maxLength="15" size="30"/>
49      <s:textfield required="true" requiredposition="left"
        id="Edition" label="Edition" name="Edition" title="Enter
        the edition of the book" maxLength="25" size="55"/>
50      <s:textfield required="true" requiredposition="left"
        id="Year" label="Year" name="Year" title="Enter the
        year" maxLength="4" size="4"/>
51      <s:textfield required="true" requiredposition="left"
        id="Cost" label="Cost" name="Cost" title="Enter the cost
        of the book" maxLength="8" size="8"/>
52      <tr>
53         <td class="Arial13BrownB">
54            <br />Author Details<br /><br />
55         </td>
56      </tr>
57      <s:textfield required="true" requiredposition="left"
        id="FirstAuthor" label="First Author" name="FirstAuthor"
        title="Enter the name of the author" maxLength="25"
        size="55"/>
58      <s:textfield id="SecondAuthor" label="Second Author"
        name="SecondAuthor" title="Enter the name of the
        author" maxLength="25" size="55"/>
59      <s:textfield id="ThirdAuthor" label="Third Author"
        name="ThirdAuthor" title="Enter the name of the author"
        maxLength="25" size="55"/>
60      <s:textfield id="FourthAuthor" label="Fourth Author"
        name="FourthAuthor" title="Enter the name of the
        author" maxLength="25" size="55"/>
61      <tr>
62         <td class="Arial13BrownB">
63            <br />Description<br /><br />
64         </td>
65      </tr>
66      <s:textarea required="true" requiredposition="left"
        id="Synopsis" label="Synopsis" name="Synopsis"
        title="Enter the synopsis" cols="80"
        rows="5"></s:textarea>
67      <s:textarea required="true" requiredposition="left"
        id="AboutAuthors" label="About Authors"
        name="AboutAuthors" title="Enter the about author
        details" cols="80" rows="5"></s:textarea>
68      <s:textarea id="TopicsCovered" label="Topics Covered"
        name="TopicsCovered" title="Enter the topics covered in
        the book" cols="80" rows="5"></s:textarea>
69      <s:textarea id="ContentsCDROM" label="Contents Of
        CDROM" name="ContentsCDROM" title="Enter the
        contents of CDROM" cols="80" rows="5"></s:textarea>
70         </table>
71      </td>
72  </tr>
```

Manage Books [manageBooks.jsp]

```
73                    <tr>
74                       <td>
75                          <br /><br />
76                          <s:submit theme="simple"
                            cssStyle="background:url(/BookShop/images/submit_bg.gif)
                            no-repeat scroll 37px 0px;" cssClass="buttonText"
                            name="btnSubmit" id="btnSubmit" value="Save" />
77                          <s:reset theme="simple"
                            cssStyle="background:url(/BookShop/images/submit_bg.gif)
                            no-repeat scroll 37px 0px;" cssClass="buttonText"
                            name="btnReset" id="btnReset" value="Clear" />
78                       </td>
79                    </tr>
80                 </table>
81              </td>
82           </tr>
83           <tr align="left" valign="top">
84              <td>
85                 <img src="/BookShop/images/hr.jpg"/>
86              </td>
87           </tr>
88           <tr>
89              <td>
90                 <br>
91              </td>
92           </tr>
93        </table>
94     </s:form>
95   </body>
96 </html>
```

Process Flow

After the user keys in the required inputs and clicks SAVE ▶, the form is submitted to the action named **doInsertBooks**.

struts.xml holds a mapping to help the form submission:

```
41      <action name="doInsertBooks"
        class="com.sharanamvaishali.bookShop.action.insertBookAction">
42         <interceptor-ref name="myStack" />
43         <result name="success">/bookShop/manageBooks.jsp</result>
44         <result name="input">/bookShop/addBooks.jsp</result>
45      </action>
```

This means the input values captured by Add Books form are passed on to the action **doInsertBooks → bookShop.insertBookAction**.

doInsertBooks [insertBookAction.java]

This is an action class with the following specifications.

Class Name	Package	Extends	Implements
insertBookAction	bookshop	ActionSupport	- -

Properties

Property Name	Property Type	Methods	
BookName	String	getBookName()	setBookName()
PublisherName	String	getPublisherName()	setPublisherName()
Category	String	getCategory()	setCategory()
ISBN	String	getISBN()	setISBN()
Edition	String	getEdition()	setEdition()
FirstAuthor	String	getFirstAuthor()	setFirstAuthor()
SecondAuthor	String	getSecondAuthor()	setSecondAuthor()
ThirdAuthor	String	getThirdAuthor()	setThirdAuthor()
FourthAuthor	String	getFourthAuthor()	setFourthAuthor()
Synopsis	String	getSynopsis()	setSynopsis()
AboutAuthors	String	getAboutAuthors()	setAboutAuthors()
TopicsCovered	String	getTopicsCovered()	setTopicsCovered()
ContentsCDROM	String	getContentsCDROM()	setContentsCDROM()
BookNo	int	getBookNo()	setBookNo()
Year	int	getYear()	setYear()
Cost	int	getCost()	setCost()

Methods

Method Name	Return Values
execute()	SUCCESS

Code Spec

```
1  package com.sharanamvaishali.bookShop.action;
2
3  import com.opensymphony.xwork2.ActionSupport;
4  import com.sharanamvaishali.bookShop.dbConnection.dbConnection;
5  import java.sql.*;
6
7  public class insertBookAction extends ActionSupport {
8      private ResultSet rs;
9      private String BookName, PublisherName, Category, ISBN, Edition, FirstAuthor,
           SecondAuthor, ThirdAuthor, FourthAuthor, Synopsis, AboutAuthors, TopicsCovered,
           ContentsCDROM;
10     private int BookNo, Year, Cost;
11
12     public String getAboutAuthors() {
13         return AboutAuthors;
```

Manage Books [manageBooks.jsp]

```
14      }
15      public void setAboutAuthors(String AboutAuthors) {
16          this.AboutAuthors = AboutAuthors;
17      }
18
19      public String getBookName() {
20          return BookName;
21      }
22      public void setBookName(String BookName) {
23          this.BookName = BookName;
24      }
25
26      public int getBookNo() {
27          return BookNo;
28      }
29      public void setBookNo(int BookNo) {
30          this.BookNo = BookNo;
31      }
32
33      public String getCategory() {
34          return Category;
35      }
36      public void setCategory(String Category) {
37          this.Category = Category;
38      }
39
40      public String getContentsCDROM() {
41          return ContentsCDROM;
42      }
43      public void setContentsCDROM(String ContentsCDROM) {
44          this.ContentsCDROM = ContentsCDROM;
45      }
46
47      public int getCost() {
48          return Cost;
49      }
50      public void setCost(int Cost) {
51          this.Cost = Cost;
52      }
53
54      public String getEdition() {
55          return Edition;
56      }
57      public void setEdition(String Edition) {
58          this.Edition = Edition;
59      }
60
61      public String getFirstAuthor() {
62          return FirstAuthor;
63      }
64      public void setFirstAuthor(String FirstAuthor) {
65          this.FirstAuthor = FirstAuthor;
66      }
67
```

```java
68      public String getFourthAuthor() {
69          return FourthAuthor;
70      }
71      public void setFourthAuthor(String FourthAuthor) {
72          this.FourthAuthor = FourthAuthor;
73      }
74
75      public String getISBN() {
76          return ISBN;
77      }
78      public void setISBN(String ISBN) {
79          this.ISBN = ISBN;
80      }
81
82      public String getPublisherName() {
83          return PublisherName;
84      }
85      public void setPublisherName(String PublisherName) {
86          this.PublisherName = PublisherName;
87      }
88
89      public String getSecondAuthor() {
90          return SecondAuthor;
91      }
92      public void setSecondAuthor(String SecondAuthor) {
93          this.SecondAuthor = SecondAuthor;
94      }
95
96      public String getSynopsis() {
97          return Synopsis;
98      }
99      public void setSynopsis(String Synopsis) {
100         this.Synopsis = Synopsis;
101     }
102
103     public String getThirdAuthor() {
104         return ThirdAuthor;
105     }
106     public void setThirdAuthor(String ThirdAuthor) {
107         this.ThirdAuthor = ThirdAuthor;
108     }
109
110     public String getTopicsCovered() {
111         return TopicsCovered;
112     }
113     public void setTopicsCovered(String TopicsCovered) {
114         this.TopicsCovered = TopicsCovered;
115     }
116
117     public int getYear() {
118         return Year;
119     }
120     public void setYear(int Year) {
121         this.Year = Year;
```

```
122        }
123
124        @Override
125        public String execute() throws Exception {
126            dbConnection db = new dbConnection();
127            db.getConnection();
128            String SQL = "SELECT MAX(BookNo) + 1 AS 'BookNo' FROM Books";
129            rs = db.stmt.executeQuery(SQL);
130            rs.next();
131            if(rs.getString("BookNo") != null) {
132                BookNo = rs.getInt("BookNo");
133            }
134            SQL = "INSERT INTO Books (BookNo, BookName, FirstAuthor, SecondAuthor,
               ThirdAuthor, FourthAuthor, PublisherName, Category, ISBN, Edition, Year, Cost,
               Synopsis, AboutAuthors, TopicsCovered, ContentsCDROM) VALUES ("+ BookNo
               + ",'" + BookName + "','" + FirstAuthor + "','" + SecondAuthor + "','" +
               ThirdAuthor + "','" + FourthAuthor + "','" + PublisherName + "','" + Category +
               "','" + ISBN + "','" + Edition + "'," + Year + "," + Cost + ",'" + Synopsis + "','"
               + AboutAuthors + "','" + TopicsCovered + "','" + ContentsCDROM + "')";
135            db.stmt.executeUpdate(SQL);
136            db.removeConnection();
137            return SUCCESS;
138        }
139    }
```

Process Flow

As soon as this action takes charge, **execute()**, does the following:

Establishes a database connection as:

- Spawns an object of the class **dbConnectionAction**
- Invokes **getConnection()** of that class

Fires an SQL SELECT query using **executeQuery()** of the Statement object:

SELECT MAX(BookNo) + 1 AS 'BookNo' FROM Books

The results are held in a ResultSet object.

This SELECT query retrieves the next book number from the Books table. This means a **Primary Key** is being generated for the Books table prior record insertion.

After the primary key is generated, it is stored in a memory variable.

An SQL INSERT query is fired to perform the actual INSERT operation. This query is passed values that were captured by Add Books form which are available to the action via the JavaBeans properties.

```
INSERT INTO Books (BookNo, BookName, FirstAuthor, SecondAuthor, ThirdAuthor,
            FourthAuthor, PublisherName, Category, ISBN, Edition, Year,
            Cost, Synopsis, AboutAuthors, TopicsCovered, ContentsCDROM)
    VALUES ("+ BookNo + ", '" + BookName + "', '" + FirstAuthor + "',
        '" + SecondAuthor + "', '" + ThirdAuthor + "', '" + FourthAuthor + "',
        '" + PublisherName + "', '" + Category + "', '" + ISBN + "',
        '" + Edition + "', " + Year + ", " + Cost + ", '" + Synopsis + "',
        '" + AboutAuthors + "', '" + TopicsCovered + "',
        '" + ContentsCDROM + "')
```

After the record is inserted:

- The database connection is destroyed
- SUCCESS is returned

struts.xml holds a mapping to help the **SUCCESS** result:

```
41      <action name="doInsertBooks"
            class="com.sharanamvaishali.bookShop.action.insertBookAction">
42          <interceptor-ref name="myStack" />
43          <result name="success">/bookShop/manageBooks.jsp</result>
44          <result name="input">/bookShop/addBooks.jsp</result>
45      </action>
```

Since SUCCESS is returned, manageBooks.jsp is served again.

Validations [insertBooksAction-validation.xml]

If the required **input** fields are kept empty whilst submitting the form, insertBooksAction-validation.xml takes care of the validations.

Code Spec

```
1   <?xml version="1.0" encoding="UTF-8"?>
2   <!DOCTYPE validators PUBLIC "-//Apache Struts//XWork Validator 1.0.3//EN"
    "http://struts.apache.org/dtds/xwork-validator-1.0.3.dtd">
3   <validators>
4       <field name="BookName">
5           <field-validator type="requiredstring">
6               <message>Please enter the book name.</message>
7           </field-validator>
8       </field>
9
10      <field name="PublisherName">
11          <field-validator type="requiredstring">
```

```
12            <message>Please enter the publisher name.</message>
13         </field-validator>
14      </field>
15
16      <field name="Category">
17         <field-validator type="requiredstring">
18            <message>Please enter the category name.</message>
19         </field-validator>
20      </field>
21
22      <field name="ISBN">
23         <field-validator type="requiredstring">
24            <message>Please enter the book ISBN.</message>
25         </field-validator>
26      </field>
27
28      <field name="Edition">
29         <field-validator type="requiredstring">
30            <message>Please enter the edition of the book.</message>
31         </field-validator>
32      </field>
33
34      <field name="Year">
35         <field-validator type="required" short-circuit="true">
36            <message>Please enter the year when the book was published.</message>
37         </field-validator>
38         <field-validator type="int" short-circuit="true">
39            <message>Enter a numeric value</message>
40         </field-validator>
41      </field>
42
43      <field name="Cost">
44         <field-validator type="required" short-circuit="true">
45            <message>Please enter the cost of the book.</message>
46         </field-validator>
47         <field-validator type="int" short-circuit="true">
48            <message>Enter a numeric value</message>
49         </field-validator>
50      </field>
51
52      <field name="FirstAuthor">
53         <field-validator type="requiredstring">
54            <message>Please enter the name of the first author.</message>
55         </field-validator>
56      </field>
57
58      <field name="Synopsis">
59         <field-validator type="requiredstring">
60            <message>Please enter the synopsis of the book.</message>
61         </field-validator>
62      </field>
63
64      <field name="AboutAuthors">
```

```
65          <field-validator type="requiredstring">
66              <message>Please enter the about the author details.</message>
67          </field-validator>
68      </field>
69  </validators>
```

After the errors, if any, are detected the add book data entry form is served again with appropriate error messages, as shown in diagram 18.3.

struts.xml holds a mapping to serve the data entry form:

```
41      <action name="doInsertBooks"
            class="com.sharanamvaishali.bookShop.action.insertBookAction">
42          <interceptor-ref name="myStack" />
43          <result name="success">/bookShop/manageBooks.jsp</result>
44          <result name="input">/bookShop/addBooks.jsp</result>
45      </action>
```

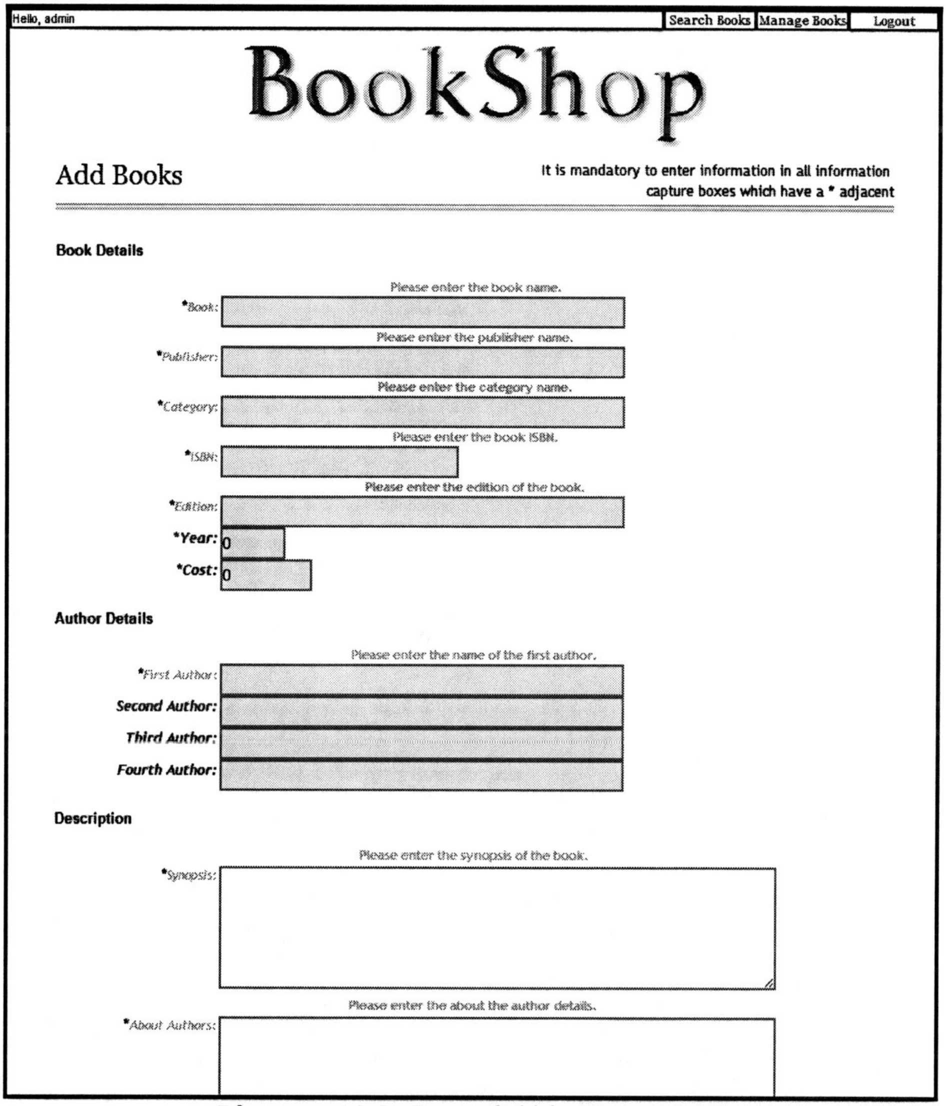

Manage Books [manageBooks.jsp]

Diagram 18.3: Empty fields' error message

Search Results [manageBooks.jsp]

The search results are displayed when the user keys in the ISBN and/or Book Name and clicks FIND, as shown in diagram 18.4.

284 Struts 2 For Beginners

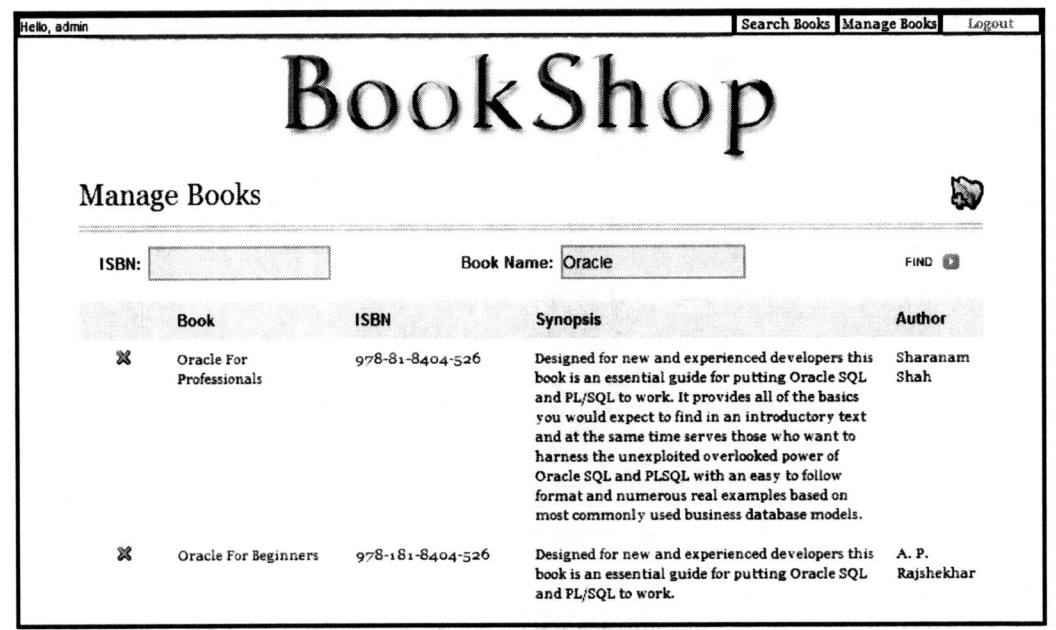

Diagram 18.4: Manage Books results

Code Spec

```
1   <%@page contentType="text/html" pageEncoding="UTF-8"%>
2   <%@ taglib prefix="s" uri="/struts-tags" %>
3   <!DOCTYPE html>
4   <html>
5     <head>
6       <meta http-equiv="Content-Type" content="text/html; charset=UTF-8">
7       <title>BookShop[Sharanam & Vaishali Shah] - Manage Books</title>
8       <link href="/BookShop/css/stylesheet.css" type="text/css" rel="stylesheet">
9       <s:head />
10    </head>
11    <body>
12      <s:include value="menu.jsp" />
13      <s:form id="frmSearch" name="frmSearch" method="post"
              action="doManageSearchBooks">
14        <table border="0" cellpadding="0" cellspacing="0" align="center"
             width="760">
15          <tr>
16            <td>
17              <table border="0" cellpadding="0" cellspacing="0" width="100%">
18                <tr>
19                  <td valign="top" align="left" style="padding-right:0px;
                      padding-left:0px; padding-bottom:0px; font:24px Georgia;
                      width:228px; color:#786e4e; padding-top:0px; height:37px;">
20                    Manage Books
```

Manage Books [manageBooks.jsp]

```
21                    </td>
22                    <td align="right">
23                       <s:a href="showAddBooks.action" ><img
                         src="/BookShop/images/AddIcon.png" border="0" alt="Add
                         Book" style="cursor:pointer;"/></s:a>
24                    </td>
25                 </tr>
26              </table>
27           </td>
28        </tr>
29        <tr align="left" valign="top">
30           <td height="20">
31              <img src="/BookShop/images/hr.jpg"/>
32           </td>
33        </tr>
34        <tr>
35           <td>
36              <table border="0" cellpadding="0" cellspacing="0" width="100%">
37                 <tr>
38                    <td align="right" valign="middle" class="Arial13GrayB">
39                       <s:label theme="simple" id="lblISBN"
                         name="lblISBN">ISBN: </s:label>
40                    </td>
41                    <td align="left" valign="top">
42                       <s:textfield theme="simple" name="searchISBN"
                         id="searchISBN" title="Enter the ISBN" size="20" />
43                    </td>
44                    <td align="right" valign="middle" class="Arial13GrayB">
45                       <s:label theme="simple" id="lblBook"
                         name="lblBook">Book Name: </s:label>
46                    </td>
47                    <td align="left" valign="top">
48                       <s:textfield theme="simple" name="searchBookName"
                         id="searchBookName" title="Enter the book name"
                         size="20" />
49                    </td>
50                    <td valign="middle">
51                       <s:submit theme="simple"
                         cssStyle="background:url(/BookShop/images/submit_bg.gif)
                         no-repeat 35px 0px; margin:2px 10px 0px 15px;"
                         cssClass="buttonText" id="cmdBook" value="Find"/>
52                    </td>
53                 </tr>
54              </table>
55           </td>
56        </tr>
57        <tr><td> </td></tr>
58     </table>
59   </s:form>
60   <table align="center" cellspacing="0" cellpadding="8" width="760">
61      <s:if test="book.size()>0">
62         <tr bgcolor="#EFEBDE">
63            <td width="10%" align="center"> </td>
```

```
64                <td width="20%" class="Arial13BrownB" align="left">Book</td>
65                <td width="20%" class="Arial13BrownB" align="left">ISBN</td>
66                <td width="40%" class="Arial13BrownB" align="left">Synopsis</td>
67                <td width="10%" class="Arial13BrownB" align="left">Author</td>
68            </tr>
69        </s:if>
70        <s:iterator value="book">
71          <tr title="Click to edit">
72            <td valign="top">
73              <a href="<s:url action="doDeleteBooks"><s:param name="BookNo" value="BookNo" /></s:url>">
74                <img src="/BookShop/images/TrashIcon.png" border="0" alt="Delete" style="cursor:pointer;"/>
75              </a>
76            </td>
77            <td valign="top" align="left" style="cursor:pointer;" onmousedown=">
78              <a href="<s:url action="showEditBooks"><s:param name="BookNo" value="BookNo" /></s:url>">
79                <s:property value="BookName"/>
80              </a>
81            </td>
82            <td valign="top" align="left" style="cursor:pointer;" onmousedown=">
83              <a href="<s:url action="showEditBooks"><s:param name="BookNo" value="BookNo" /></s:url>">
84                <s:property value="ISBN"/>
85              </a>
86            </td>
87            <td valign="top" align="left" style="cursor:pointer;" onmousedown=">
88              <a href="<s:url action="showEditBooks"><s:param name="BookNo" value="BookNo" /></s:url>">
89                <s:property value="Synopsis"/>
90              </a>
91            </td>
92            <td valign="top" align="left" style="cursor:pointer;" onmousedown=">
93              <a href="<s:url action="showEditBooks"><s:param name="BookNo" value="BookNo" /></s:url>">
94                <s:property value="FirstAuthor"/>
95              </a>
96            </td>
97          </tr>
98        </s:iterator>
99      </table>
100   </body>
101 </html>
```

Process Flow

After the user keys in the ISBN and/or Book Name clicks FIND , the form is submitted to the action named **doManageSearchBooks**.

Manage Books [manageBooks.jsp]

struts.xml holds a mapping to help the form submission:

```
62      <action name="doManageSearchBooks"
            class="com.sharanamvaishali.bookShop.action.manageSearchBooksAction">
63          <interceptor-ref name="myStack" />
64          <result name="success">/bookShop/manageBooks.jsp</result>
65      </action>
```

This means the search criteria captured by Manage Books form are passed on to the action **doManageSearchBooks** → **bookShop.manageSearchBooksAction**.

doManageSearchBooks [manageSearchBooksAction.java]

This is an action class with the following specifications.

Class Name	Package	Extends	Implements
manageSearchBooksAction	bookshop	ActionSupport	- -

Properties			
Property Name	**Property Type**	colspan Methods	
searchISBN	String	getSearchISBN()	setSearchISBN()
searchBookName	String	getSearchBookName()	setSearchBookName()
book	ArrayList	getBook()	setBook()

Methods	
Method Name	**Return Values**
execute()	SUCCESS

Code Spec

```
1   package com.sharanamvaishali.bookShop.action;
2
3   import com.opensymphony.xwork2.ActionSupport;
4   import com.sharanamvaishali.bookShop.dbConnection.dbConnection;
5   import com.sharanamvaishali.bookShop.domain.Book;
6   import java.sql.*;
7   import java.util.ArrayList;
8
9   public class manageSearchBooksAction extends ActionSupport {
10      private String searchISBN, searchBookName;
11      private ResultSet rs;
12      private ArrayList<Book> book = new ArrayList<Book>();
13
14      public String getSearchBookName() {
15          return searchBookName;
16      }
17      public void setSearchBookName(String searchBookName) {
```

288   Struts 2 For Beginners

```
18          this.searchBookName = searchBookName;
19      }
20
21      public String getSearchISBN() {
22          return searchISBN;
23      }
24      public void setSearchISBN(String searchISBN) {
25          this.searchISBN = searchISBN;
26      }
27
28      public ArrayList getBook() {
29          return book;
30      }
31      public void setBook(ArrayList book) {
32          this.book = book;
33      }
34
35      @Override
36      public String execute() throws Exception{
37          dbConnection db = new dbConnection();
38          db.getConnection();
39          String SQL = "";
40          if (searchISBN == null) {
41              SQL = "SELECT * FROM Books WHERE BookName LIKE '%" + searchBookName + "%'";
42          } else if(searchBookName == null) {
43              SQL = "SELECT * FROM Books WHERE ISBN LIKE '%" + searchISBN + "%'";
44          } else if(searchBookName != null && searchISBN != null) {
45              SQL = "SELECT * FROM Books WHERE ISBN LIKE '%" + searchISBN + "%' AND BookName LIKE '%" + searchBookName + "%'";
46          }
47          System.out.println(SQL);
48          rs = db.stmt.executeQuery(SQL);
49          while(rs.next()){
50              Book bk = new Book(rs.getInt("BookNo"), rs.getString("BookName"),
                    rs.getString("PublisherName"), rs.getString("Category"), rs.getString("ISBN"),
                    rs.getString("Edition"), rs.getString("FirstAuthor"),
                    rs.getString("SecondAuthor"), rs.getString("ThirdAuthor"),
                    rs.getString("FourthAuthor"), rs.getString("Synopsis"),
                    rs.getString("AboutAuthors"), rs.getString("TopicsCovered"),
                    rs.getString("ContentsCDROM"), rs.getInt("Year"), rs.getInt("Cost"));
51              book.add(bk);
52          }
53          db.removeConnection();
54          return SUCCESS;
55      }
56  }
```

Process Flow

As soon as this action takes charge, **execute()**, does the following:

Manage Books [manageBooks.jsp]

Establishes a database connection as:
- Spawns an object of the class **dbConnectionAction**
- Invokes **getConnection()** of that class

Based on the search criteria, fires an SQL SELECT query using **executeQuery()** of Statement.

If the user has not keyed in the ISBN criteria:

SELECT * FROM Books WHERE BookName LIKE '%" + searchBookName + "%'"

If the user has not keyed in the Book Name criteria:

SELECT * FROM Books WHERE ISBN LIKE '%" + searchISBN + "%'"

If the user has keyed in both the criteria:

SELECT * FROM Books WHERE ISBN LIKE '%" + searchISBN + "%'
    AND BookName LIKE '%" + searchBookName + "%'"

The results are held in a ResultSet object.

This SELECT query attempts to retrieve records from the Books table identified by the search criteria that were captured by the Manage Books form and passed on to this action.

All the records that the query retrieves are extracted using a **WHILE** loop which does the following:
- Spawns an object of the bean class **Book** using the parameterized constructor
- This constructor is passed all column values of the current record in the loop
- Finally, this object is added to **ArrayList** object **book**

The database connection is destroyed. SUCCESS is returned.

struts.xml holds a mapping to help the **SUCCESS** result:

```
62      <action name="doManageSearchBooks"
            class="com.sharanamvaishali.bookShop.action.manageSearchBooksAction">
63          <interceptor-ref name="myStack" />
64          <result name="success">/bookShop/manageBooks.jsp</result>
65      </action>
```

Since SUCCESS is returned, manageBooks.jsp will be served again with the populated ArrayList object **book**.

The JSP i.e. manageBooks.jsp on taking charge uses **<s:iterator>** to iterate over the contents of ArrayList object **book**.

```
<s:iterator value="book">
   <tr title="Click to edit">
      <td valign="top">
         <a href="<s:url action="doDeleteBooks"><s:param name="BookNo" value="[
            <img src="/BookShop/images/TrashIcon.png" border="0" alt="Delete" style
         </a>
      </td>
      <td valign="top" align="left" style="cursor:pointer;" onmousedown="">
         <a href="<s:url action="showEditBooks"><s:param name="BookNo" value="[
            <s:property value="BookName"/>
```

The book object holds all those records [meeting the search criteria] retrieved by the SQL query.

Each record's column values are extracted using **<s:property>**.

```
<s:iterator value="book">
   <tr title="Click to edit">
      <td valign="top">
         <a href="<s:url action="doDeleteBooks"><s:param name="BookNo" value="[
            <img src="/BookShop/images/TrashIcon.png" border="0" alt="Delete" style
         </a>
      </td>
      <td valign="top" align="left" style="cursor:pointer;" onmousedown="">
         <a href="<s:url action="showEditBooks"><s:param name="BookNo" value="[
            <s:property value="BookName"/>
```

Update Books Form [updateBooks.jsp]

This is a JSP that holds a data entry form, as shown in diagram 18.5. This form appears when the user clicks a record from the search result on Manage Books form.

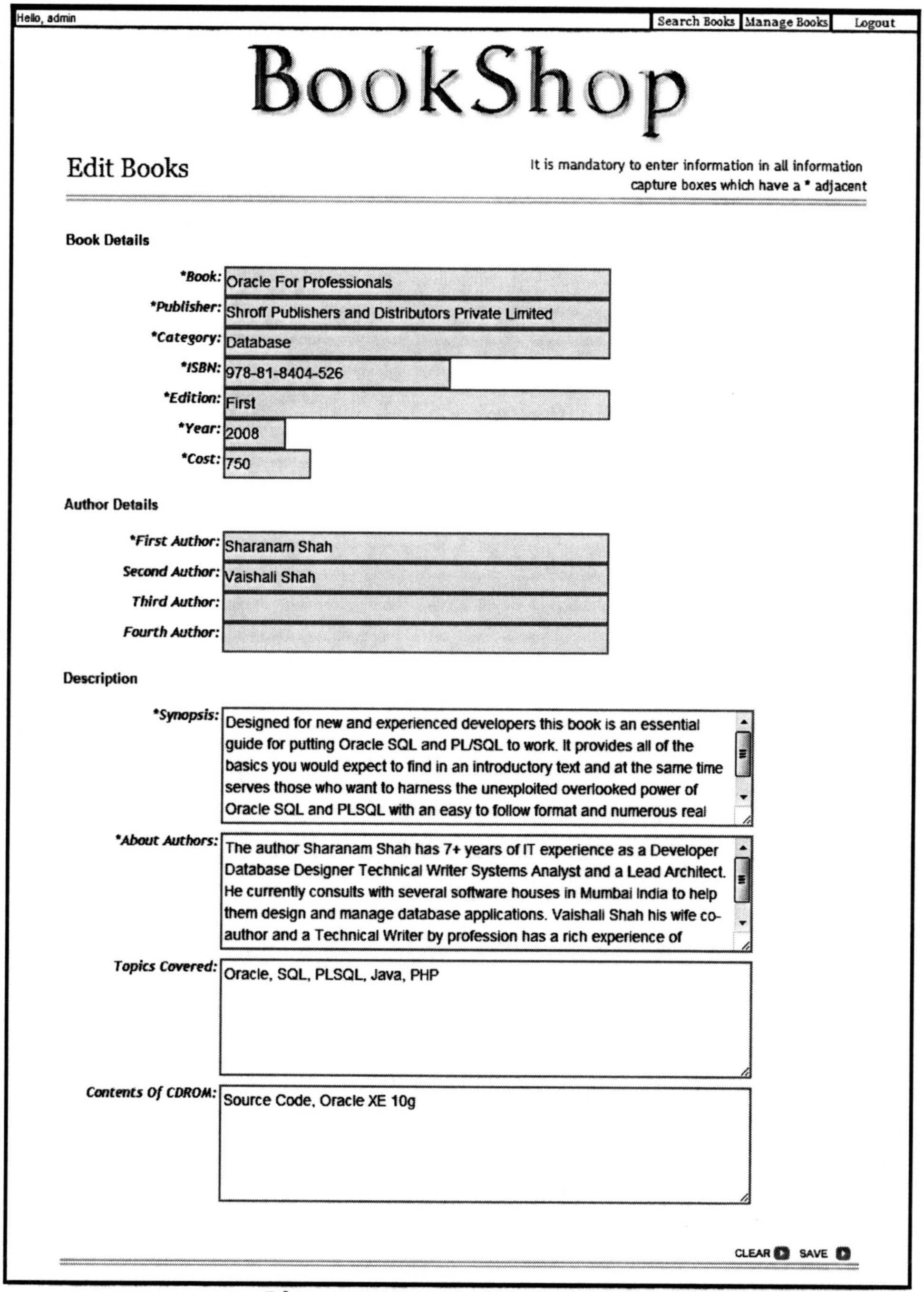

Hello, admin
Search Books
Manage Books
Logout
BookShop
Edit Books
It is mandatory to enter information in all information capture boxes which have a * adjacent
Book Details
*Book: Oracle For Professionals
*Publisher: Shroff Publishers and Distributors Private Limited
*Category: Database
*ISBN: 978-81-8404-526
*Edition: First
*Year: 2008
*Cost: 750
Author Details
*First Author: Sharanam Shah
Second Author: Vaishali Shah
Third Author:
Fourth Author:
Description
*Synopsis: Designed for new and experienced developers this book is an essential guide for putting Oracle SQL and PL/SQL to work. It provides all of the basics you would expect to find in an introductory text and at the same time serves those who want to harness the unexploited overlooked power of Oracle SQL and PLSQL with an easy to follow format and numerous real
*About Authors: The author Sharanam Shah has 7+ years of IT experience as a Developer Database Designer Technical Writer Systems Analyst and a Lead Architect. He currently consults with several software houses in Mumbai India to help them design and manage database applications. Vaishali Shah his wife co-author and a Technical Writer by profession has a rich experience of
Topics Covered: Oracle, SQL, PLSQL, Java, PHP
Contents Of CDROM: Source Code, Oracle XE 10g
CLEAR
SAVE

Diagram 18.5: Update Books form

The form is pre-populated with the selected record. The user can simply make the desired changes and Save.

struts.xml holds a mapping to help the invocation of the Update Books form:

```
47      <action name="showEditBooks"
            class="com.sharanamvaishali.bookShop.action.editBookAction">
48          <interceptor-ref name="myStack" />
49          <result name="success">bookShop/updateBooks.jsp</result>
50      </action>
```

Form Specifications

File Name	updateBooks.jsp
Title	BookShop[Sharanam & Vaishali Shah] - Edit Book
Bound To Table	Books
Form Name	frmBooks
Action	doUpdateBooks
Method	Post

Data Fields

Book Details

Label	Name	Bound To	Validation Rules
Book	BookName	Books.BookName	Cannot be left blank
Publisher	PublisherName	Books.PublisherName	Cannot be left blank
Category	Category	Books.Category	Cannot be left blank
ISBN	ISBN	Books.ISBN	Cannot be left blank
Edition	Edition	Books.Edition	Cannot be left blank
Year	Year	Books.Year	Cannot be left blank Must be an integer
Cost	Cost	Books.Cost	Cannot be left blank Must be an integer

Author Details

Label	Name	Bound To	Validation Rules
First Author	FirstAuthor	Books.FirstAuthor	Cannot be left blank
Second Author	SecondAuthor	Books.SecondAuthor	*Optional*
Third Author	ThirdAuthor	Books.ThirdAuthor	*Optional*
Fourth Author	FourthAuthor	Books.FourthAuthor	*Optional*

Description

Label	Name	Bound To	Validation Rules
Synopsis	Synopsis	Books.Synopsis	Cannot be left blank
About Authors	AboutAuthors	Books.AboutAuthors	Cannot be left blank
Topics Covered	TopicsCovered	Books.TopicsCovered	*Optional*
Contents Of CDROM	ContentsCDROM	Books.ContentsCDROM	*Optional*

Data Controls

Object	Label	Name
Button	Save	btnSubmit
Button	Clear	btnReset

Micro-Help For Form Fields

Book Details

Form Field	Micro Help Statement
BookName	Enter the book name
PublisherName	Enter the publisher name
Category	Enter the category name
ISBN	Enter the ISBN
Edition	Enter the edition of the book
Year	Enter the year
Cost	Enter the cost of the book

Author Details

Form Field	Micro Help Statement
FirstAuthor	Enter the name of the author
SecondAuthor	Enter the name of the author
ThirdAuthor	Enter the name of the author
FourthAuthor	Enter the name of the author

Description

Form Field	Micro Help Statement
Synopsis	Enter the synopsis
AboutAuthors	Enter the about author details
TopicsCovered	Enter the topics covered in the book
ContentsCDROM	Enter the contents of CDROM

Code Spec

```
1  <%@page contentType="text/html" pageEncoding="UTF-8"%>
2  <%@ taglib prefix="s" uri="/struts-tags" %>
```

```
3   <!DOCTYPE html>
4   <html>
5     <head>
6       <meta http-equiv="Content-Type" content="text/html; charset=UTF-8">
7       <title>BookShop[Sharanam & Vaishali Shah] - Edit Book</title>
8       <link href="/BookShop/css/stylesheet.css" type="text/css" rel="stylesheet">
9       <s:head />
10    </head>
11    <body>
12      <s:include value="menu.jsp" />
13      <s:form id="frmBooks" name="frmBooks" action="doUpdateBooks"
        method="post">
14        <s:hidden name="BookNo" id="BookNo"/>
15        <table width="760" border="0" align="center" cellpadding="0"
          cellspacing="0">
16          <tr>
17            <td>
18              <table border="0" cellpadding="0" cellspacing="0" width="100%">
19                <tr>
20                  <td valign="top" align="left" style="font:24px
                    Georgia;color:#786e4e;height:37px;">
21                    Edit Books
22                  </td>
23                  <td class="treb13blacknormal" valign="top" align="right">
24                    It is mandatory to enter information in all information
                    <br>capture boxes which have a <span
                    class="mandatory">*</span> adjacent
25                  </td>
26                </tr>
27              </table>
28            </td>
29          </tr>
30          <tr align="left" valign="top">
31            <td height="20">
32              <img src="/BookShop/images/hr.jpg"/>
33            </td>
34          </tr>
35          <tr align="left" valign="top">
36            <td>
37              <table width="100%" border="0" align="center" cellpadding="0"
                cellspacing="0">
38                <tr>
39                  <td>
40                    <table width="100%" border="0" cellpadding="0"
                      cellspacing="0">
41                      <tr>
42                        <td class="Arial13BrownB">
43                          <br />Book Details<br /><br />
44                        </td>
45                      </tr>
46                      <s:textfield required="true" requiredposition="left"
                        id="BookName" label="Book" name="BookName"
                        title="Enter the book name" maxLength="25"
                        size="55"/>
```

```
47  <s:textfield required="true" requiredposition="left"
    id="PublisherName" label="Publisher"
    name="PublisherName" title="Enter the publisher name"
    maxLength="25" size="55"/>
48  <s:textfield required="true" requiredposition="left"
    id="Category" label="Category" name="Category"
    title="Enter the category name" maxLength="25"
    size="55"/>
49  <s:textfield required="true" requiredposition="left"
    id="ISBN" label="ISBN" name="ISBN" title="Enter the
    ISBN" maxLength="15" size="30"/>
50  <s:textfield required="true" requiredposition="left"
    id="Edition" label="Edition" name="Edition" title="Enter
    the edition of the book" maxLength="25" size="55"/>
51  <s:textfield required="true" requiredposition="left"
    id="Year" label="Year" name="Year" title="Enter the
    year" maxLength="4" size="4"/>
52  <s:textfield required="true" requiredposition="left"
    id="Cost" label="Cost" name="Cost" title="Enter the cost
    of the book" maxLength="8" size="8"/>
53  <tr>
54     <td class="Arial13BrownB">
55        <br />Author Details<br /><br />
56     </td>
57  </tr>
58  <s:textfield required="true" requiredposition="left"
    id="FirstAuthor" label="First Author" name="FirstAuthor"
    title="Enter the name of the author" maxLength="25"
    size="55"/>
59  <s:textfield id="SecondAuthor" label="Second Author"
    name="SecondAuthor" title="Enter the name of the
    author" maxLength="25" size="55"/>
60  <s:textfield id="ThirdAuthor" label="Third Author"
    name="ThirdAuthor" title="Enter the name of the author"
    maxLength="25" size="55"/>
61  <s:textfield id="FourthAuthor" label="Fourth Author"
    name="FourthAuthor" title="Enter the name of the
    author" maxLength="25" size="55"/>
62  <tr>
63     <td class="Arial13BrownB">
64        <br />Description<br /><br />
65     </td>
66  </tr>
67  <s:textarea required="true" requiredposition="left"
    id="Synopsis" label="Synopsis" name="Synopsis"
    title="Enter the synopsis" cols="80"
    rows="5"></s:textarea>
68  <s:textarea required="true" requiredposition="left"
    id="AboutAuthors" label="About Authors"
    name="AboutAuthors" title="Enter the about author
    details" cols="80" rows="5"></s:textarea>
69  <s:textarea id="TopicsCovered" label="Topics Covered"
    name="TopicsCovered" title="Enter the topics covered in
```

```
70                              the book" cols="80" rows="5"></s:textarea>
                                <s:textarea id="ContentsCDROM" label="Contents Of
                                CDROM" name="ContentsCDROM" title="Enter the
                                contents of CDROM" cols="80" rows="5"></s:textarea>
71                          </table>
72                      </td>
73                  </tr>
74                  <tr>
75                      <td>
76                          <br /><br />
77                          <s:submit theme="simple"
                            cssStyle="background:url(/BookShop/images/submit_bg.gif)
                            no-repeat scroll 37px 0px;" cssClass="buttonText"
                            name="btnSubmit" id="btnSubmit" value="Save" />
78                          <s:reset theme="simple"
                            cssStyle="background:url(/BookShop/images/submit_bg.gif)
                            no-repeat scroll 37px 0px;" cssClass="buttonText"
                            name="btnReset" id="btnReset" value="Clear" />
79                      </td>
80                  </tr>
81              </table>
82          </td>
83      </tr>
84      <tr align="left" valign="top">
85          <td>
86              <img src="/BookShop/images/hr.jpg"/>
87          </td>
88      </tr>
89      <tr>
90          <td>
91              <br>
92          </td>
93      </tr>
94  </table>
95  </s:form>
96  </body>
97  </html>
```

Process Flow

After the user clicks the desired record from the search results in Manage Books form, the control shifts to the action named **doUpdateBooks**.

struts.xml holds a mapping to help the form submission:

```
51      <action name="doUpdateBooks"
            class="com.sharanamvaishali.bookShop.action.updateBookAction">
52          <interceptor-ref name="myStack" />
53          <result name="success">/bookShop/manageBooks.jsp</result>
54          <result name="input">/bookShop/updateBooks.jsp</result>
55      </action>
```

showEditBooks [editBookAction.java]

This is an action class with the following specifications.

Class Name	Package	Extends	Implements
updateBookAction	bookShop	ActionSupport	- -

Properties

Property Name	Property Type	Methods	
BookName	String	getBookName()	setBookName()
PublisherName	String	getPublisherName()	setPublisherName()
Category	String	getCategory()	setCategory()
ISBN	String	getISBN()	setISBN()
Edition	String	getEdition()	setEdition()
FirstAuthor	String	getFirstAuthor()	setFirstAuthor()
SecondAuthor	String	getSecondAuthor()	setSecondAuthor()
ThirdAuthor	String	getThirdAuthor()	setThirdAuthor()
FourthAuthor	String	getFourthAuthor()	setFourthAuthor()
Synopsis	String	getSynopsis()	setSynopsis()
AboutAuthors	String	getAboutAuthors()	setAboutAuthors()
TopicsCovered	String	getTopicsCovered()	setTopicsCovered()
ContentsCDROM	String	getContentsCDROM()	setContentsCDROM()
BookNo	int	getBookNo()	setBookNo()
Year	int	getYear()	setYear()
Cost	int	getCost()	setCost()

Methods

Method Name	Return Values
execute()	SUCCESS

Code Spec

```
1  package com.sharanamvaishali.bookShop.action;
2
3  import com.opensymphony.xwork2.ActionSupport;
4  import com.sharanamvaishali.bookShop.dbConnection.dbConnection;
5  import java.sql.*;
6
7  public class editBookAction extends ActionSupport {
8      private ResultSet rs;
9      private String BookName, PublisherName, Category, ISBN, Edition, FirstAuthor,
         SecondAuthor, ThirdAuthor, FourthAuthor, Synopsis, AboutAuthors, TopicsCovered,
         ContentsCDROM;
10     private int BookNo, Year, Cost;
11
12     public String getAboutAuthors() {
13         return AboutAuthors;
14     }
```

```java
15      public void setAboutAuthors(String AboutAuthors) {
16          this.AboutAuthors = AboutAuthors;
17      }
18
19      public String getBookName() {
20          return BookName;
21      }
22      public void setBookName(String BookName) {
23          this.BookName = BookName;
24      }
25
26      public int getBookNo() {
27          return BookNo;
28      }
29      public void setBookNo(int BookNo) {
30          this.BookNo = BookNo;
31      }
32
33      public String getCategory() {
34          return Category;
35      }
36      public void setCategory(String Category) {
37          this.Category = Category;
38      }
39
40      public String getContentsCDROM() {
41          return ContentsCDROM;
42      }
43      public void setContentsCDROM(String ContentsCDROM) {
44          this.ContentsCDROM = ContentsCDROM;
45      }
46
47      public int getCost() {
48          return Cost;
49      }
50      public void setCost(int Cost) {
51          this.Cost = Cost;
52      }
53
54      public String getEdition() {
55          return Edition;
56      }
57      public void setEdition(String Edition) {
58          this.Edition = Edition;
59      }
60
61      public String getFirstAuthor() {
62          return FirstAuthor;
63      }
64      public void setFirstAuthor(String FirstAuthor) {
65          this.FirstAuthor = FirstAuthor;
66      }
67
68      public String getFourthAuthor() {
```

```java
69            return FourthAuthor;
70        }
71        public void setFourthAuthor(String FourthAuthor) {
72            this.FourthAuthor = FourthAuthor;
73        }
74
75        public String getISBN() {
76            return ISBN;
77        }
78        public void setISBN(String ISBN) {
79            this.ISBN = ISBN;
80        }
81
82        public String getPublisherName() {
83            return PublisherName;
84        }
85        public void setPublisherName(String PublisherName) {
86            this.PublisherName = PublisherName;
87        }
88
89        public String getSecondAuthor() {
90            return SecondAuthor;
91        }
92        public void setSecondAuthor(String SecondAuthor) {
93            this.SecondAuthor = SecondAuthor;
94        }
95
96        public String getSynopsis() {
97            return Synopsis;
98        }
99        public void setSynopsis(String Synopsis) {
100            this.Synopsis = Synopsis;
101        }
102
103        public String getThirdAuthor() {
104            return ThirdAuthor;
105        }
106        public void setThirdAuthor(String ThirdAuthor) {
107            this.ThirdAuthor = ThirdAuthor;
108        }
109
110        public String getTopicsCovered() {
111            return TopicsCovered;
112        }
113        public void setTopicsCovered(String TopicsCovered) {
114            this.TopicsCovered = TopicsCovered;
115        }
116
117        public int getYear() {
118            return Year;
119        }
120        public void setYear(int Year) {
121            this.Year = Year;
122        }
```

```
123
124     @Override
125     public String execute() throws Exception {
126         dbConnection db = new dbConnection();
127         db.getConnection();
128         String SQL = "SELECT * FROM Books WHERE BookNo = " + getBookNo();
129         rs = db.stmt.executeQuery(SQL);
130         while(rs.next()){
131             setBookNo(rs.getInt("BookNo"));
132             setBookName(rs.getString("BookName"));
133             setAboutAuthors(rs.getString("AboutAuthors"));
134             setCategory(rs.getString("Category"));
135             setContentsCDROM(rs.getString("ContentsCDROM"));
136             setCost(rs.getInt("Cost"));
137             setEdition(rs.getString("Edition"));
138             setFirstAuthor(rs.getString("FirstAuthor"));
139             setFourthAuthor(rs.getString("FourthAuthor"));
140             setISBN(rs.getString("ISBN"));
141             setPublisherName(rs.getString("PublisherName"));
142             setSecondAuthor(rs.getString("SecondAuthor"));
143             setSynopsis(rs.getString("Synopsis"));
144             setThirdAuthor(rs.getString("ThirdAuthor"));
145             setTopicsCovered(rs.getString("TopicsCovered"));
146             setYear(rs.getInt("Year"));
147         }
148         db.removeConnection();
149         return SUCCESS;
150     }
151 }
```

Process Flow

As soon as this action takes charge, **execute()**, does the following:

Establishes a database connection as:

- Spawns an object of the class **dbConnectionAction**
- Invokes **getConnection()** of that class

Fires an SQL SELECT query using **executeQuery()** of Statement:

SELECT * FROM Books WHERE BookNo = " + getBookNo()

The results are held in a ResultSet object.

This SELECT query retrieves the complete record for the selected book using book number as the criteria.

Manage Books [manageBooks.jsp]

The record that the query retrieves is extracted using a **WHILE** loop which does the following:

- Using the setter methods assigns the column values to JavaBeans properties
- The database connection is destroyed
- SUCCESS is returned

struts.xml holds a mapping to help the SUCCESS result.

```
47      <action name="showEditBooks"
             class="com.sharanamvaishali.bookShop.action.editBookAction">
48         <interceptor-ref name="myStack" />
49         <result name="success">bookShop/updateBooks.jsp</result>
50      </action>
```

Since SUCCESS is returned, updateBooks.jsp is served with pre-populated data that the SQL query in the action class retrieved.

After the user makes the desired changes and clicks SAVE, the form is submitted to the action named **doUpdateBooks** → **bookShop.updateBookAction**.

struts.xml holds a mapping to help the form submission:

```
51      <action name="doUpdateBooks"
             class="com.sharanamvaishali.bookShop.action.updateBookAction">
52         <interceptor-ref name="myStack" />
53         <result name="success">/bookShop/manageBooks.jsp</result>
54         <result name="input">/bookShop/updateBooks.jsp</result>
55      </action>
```

This means the input values captured by Update Books form are passed on to the action **doUpdateBooks** → **bookShop.updateBookAction**.

doUpdateBooks [updateBookAction.java]

This is an action class with the following specifications.

Class Name	Package	Extends	Implements
updateBookAction	bookShop	ActionSupport	- -
Properties			
Property Name	Property Type	Methods	
BookName	String	getBookName()	setBookName()
PublisherName	String	getPublisherName()	setPublisherName()
Category	String	getCategory()	setCategory()
ISBN	String	getISBN()	setISBN()

Properties			
Property Name	Property Type	Methods	
Edition	String	getEdition()	setEdition()
FirstAuthor	String	getFirstAuthor()	setFirstAuthor()
SecondAuthor	String	getSecondAuthor()	setSecondAuthor()
ThirdAuthor	String	getThirdAuthor()	setThirdAuthor()
FourthAuthor	String	getFourthAuthor()	setFourthAuthor()
Synopsis	String	getSynopsis()	setSynopsis()
AboutAuthors	String	getAboutAuthors()	setAboutAuthors()
TopicsCovered	String	getTopicsCovered()	setTopicsCovered()
ContentsCDROM	String	getContentsCDROM()	setContentsCDROM()
BookNo	int	getBookNo()	setBookNo()
Year	int	getYear()	setYear()
Cost	int	getCost()	setCost()

Methods	
Method Name	Return Values
execute()	SUCCESS

Code Spec

```
1   package com.sharanamvaishali.bookShop.action;
2
3   import com.opensymphony.xwork2.ActionSupport;
4   import com.sharanamvaishali.bookShop.dbConnection.dbConnection;
5
6   public class updateBookAction extends ActionSupport{
7       private String BookName, PublisherName, Category, ISBN, Edition, FirstAuthor,
            SecondAuthor, ThirdAuthor, FourthAuthor, Synopsis, AboutAuthors, TopicsCovered,
            ContentsCDROM;
8       private int BookNo, Year, Cost;
9
10      public String getAboutAuthors() {
11          return AboutAuthors;
12      }
13      public void setAboutAuthors(String AboutAuthors) {
14          this.AboutAuthors = AboutAuthors;
15      }
16
17      public String getBookName() {
18          return BookName;
19      }
20      public void setBookName(String BookName) {
21          this.BookName = BookName;
22      }
23
24      public int getBookNo() {
25          return BookNo;
26      }
27      public void setBookNo(int BookNo) {
```

```
28          this.BookNo = BookNo;
29       }
30
31       public String getCategory() {
32          return Category;
33       }
34       public void setCategory(String Category) {
35          this.Category = Category;
36       }
37
38       public String getContentsCDROM() {
39          return ContentsCDROM;
40       }
41       public void setContentsCDROM(String ContentsCDROM) {
42          this.ContentsCDROM = ContentsCDROM;
43       }
44
45       public int getCost() {
46          return Cost;
47       }
48       public void setCost(int Cost) {
49          this.Cost = Cost;
50       }
51
52       public String getEdition() {
53          return Edition;
54       }
55       public void setEdition(String Edition) {
56          this.Edition = Edition;
57       }
58
59       public String getFirstAuthor() {
60          return FirstAuthor;
61       }
62       public void setFirstAuthor(String FirstAuthor) {
63          this.FirstAuthor = FirstAuthor;
64       }
65
66       public String getFourthAuthor() {
67          return FourthAuthor;
68       }
69       public void setFourthAuthor(String FourthAuthor) {
70          this.FourthAuthor = FourthAuthor;
71       }
72
73       public String getISBN() {
74          return ISBN;
75       }
76       public void setISBN(String ISBN) {
77          this.ISBN = ISBN;
78       }
79
80       public String getPublisherName() {
81          return PublisherName;
```

```java
82      }
83      public void setPublisherName(String PublisherName) {
84          this.PublisherName = PublisherName;
85      }
86
87      public String getSecondAuthor() {
88          return SecondAuthor;
89      }
90      public void setSecondAuthor(String SecondAuthor) {
91          this.SecondAuthor = SecondAuthor;
92      }
93
94      public String getSynopsis() {
95          return Synopsis;
96      }
97      public void setSynopsis(String Synopsis) {
98          this.Synopsis = Synopsis;
99      }
100
101     public String getThirdAuthor() {
102         return ThirdAuthor;
103     }
104     public void setThirdAuthor(String ThirdAuthor) {
105         this.ThirdAuthor = ThirdAuthor;
106     }
107
108     public String getTopicsCovered() {
109         return TopicsCovered;
110     }
111     public void setTopicsCovered(String TopicsCovered) {
112         this.TopicsCovered = TopicsCovered;
113     }
114
115     public int getYear() {
116         return Year;
117     }
118     public void setYear(int Year) {
119         this.Year = Year;
120     }
121
122     @Override
123     public String execute() throws Exception{
124         dbConnection db = new dbConnection();
125         db.getConnection();
126         String SQL = "UPDATE Books SET BookName ='" + BookName + "', FirstAuthor
            = '" + FirstAuthor + "', SecondAuthor = '" + SecondAuthor + "', ThirdAuthor = '"
            + ThirdAuthor + "', FourthAuthor ='" + FourthAuthor + "', PublisherName = '" +
            PublisherName + "', Category = '" + Category + "', ISBN = '" + ISBN + "',
            Edition ='" + Edition + "', Year = " + Year + ", Cost = " + Cost + ", Synopsis =
            '" + Synopsis + "', AboutAuthors = '" + AboutAuthors + "', TopicsCovered = '" +
            TopicsCovered + "', ContentsCDROM = '" + ContentsCDROM + "' WHERE
            BookNo = " + BookNo;
127         db.stmt.executeUpdate(SQL);
128         db.removeConnection();
```

```
129        return SUCCESS;
130    }
131 }
```

Process Flow

As soon as this action takes charge, **execute()**, does the following:

Establishes a database connection as:

- Spawns an object of the class **dbConnectionAction**
- Invokes **getConnection()** of that class

Fires an SQL UPDATE query using **executeUpdate()** of Statement:

```
UPDATE Books SET BookName ='" + BookName + "',
   FirstAuthor = '" + FirstAuthor + "', SecondAuthor = '" + SecondAuthor + "',
   ThirdAuthor = '" + ThirdAuthor + "', FourthAuthor ='" + FourthAuthor + "',
   PublisherName = '" + PublisherName + "', Category = '" + Category + "',
   ISBN = '" + ISBN + "', Edition ='" + Edition + "', Year = " + Year + ",
   Cost = " + Cost + ", Synopsis = '" + Synopsis + "',
   AboutAuthors = '" + AboutAuthors + "', TopicsCovered = '" + TopicsCovered + "',
   ContentsCDROM = '" + ContentsCDROM + "' WHERE BookNo = " + BookNo;
```

The SQL UPDATE query is fired to perform the actual UPDATE operation. This query is passed values that were captured by Update Books form which are available to the action via the JavaBeans properties.

After the record is updated:

- The database connection is destroyed
- SUCCESS is returned

struts.xml holds a mapping to help the **SUCCESS** result:

```
51      <action name="doUpdateBooks"
        class="com.sharanamvaishali.bookShop.action.updateBookAction">
52         <interceptor-ref name="myStack" />
53         <result name="success">/bookShop/manageBooks.jsp</result>
54         <result name="input">/bookShop/updateBooks.jsp</result>
55      </action>
```

Since SUCCESS is returned, manageBooks.jsp is served again.

Validations [insertBooksAction-validation.xml]

If the required input fields are kept empty whilst submitting the form, updateBooksAction-validation.xml takes care of the validations.

Code Spec

```xml
1  <?xml version="1.0" encoding="UTF-8"?>
2  <!DOCTYPE validators PUBLIC "-//Apache Struts//XWork Validator 1.0.3//EN"
   "http://struts.apache.org/dtds/xwork-validator-1.0.3.dtd">
3  <validators>
4    <field name="BookName">
5      <field-validator type="requiredstring">
6        <message>Please enter the book name.</message>
7      </field-validator>
8    </field>
9  
10   <field name="PublisherName">
11     <field-validator type="requiredstring">
12       <message>Please enter the publisher name.</message>
13     </field-validator>
14   </field>
15  
16   <field name="Category">
17     <field-validator type="requiredstring">
18       <message>Please enter the category name.</message>
19     </field-validator>
20   </field>
21  
22   <field name="ISBN">
23     <field-validator type="requiredstring">
24       <message>Please enter the book ISBN.</message>
25     </field-validator>
26   </field>
27  
28   <field name="Edition">
29     <field-validator type="requiredstring">
30       <message>Please enter the edition of the book.</message>
31     </field-validator>
32   </field>
33  
34   <field name="Year">
35     <field-validator type="required" short-circuit="true">
36       <message>Please enter the year when the book was published.</message>
37     </field-validator>
38     <field-validator type="int" short-circuit="true">
39       <message>Enter a numeric value</message>
40     </field-validator>
41   </field>
42  
43   <field name="Cost">
```

Manage Books [manageBooks.jsp]

```
44            <field-validator type="required" short-circuit="true">
45               <message>Please enter the cost of the book.</message>
46            </field-validator>
47            <field-validator type="int" short-circuit="true">
48               <message>Enter a numeric value</message>
49            </field-validator>
50         </field>
51
52         <field name="FirstAuthor">
53            <field-validator type="requiredstring">
54               <message>Please enter the book name.</message>
55            </field-validator>
56         </field>
57
58         <field name="Synopsis">
59            <field-validator type="requiredstring">
60               <message>Please enter the book name.</message>
61            </field-validator>
62         </field>
63
64         <field name="AboutAuthors">
65            <field-validator type="requiredstring">
66               <message>Please enter the book name.</message>
67            </field-validator>
68         </field>
69   </validators>
```

After the errors, if any, are detected the add book data entry form is served again with appropriate error messages, as shown in diagram 18.6.

struts.xml holds a mapping to serve the data entry form:

```
51        <action name="doUpdateBooks"
          class="com.sharanamvaishali.bookShop.action.updateBookAction">
52           <interceptor-ref name="myStack" />
53           <result name="success">/bookShop/manageBooks.jsp</result>
54           <result name="input">/bookShop/updateBooks.jsp</result>
55        </action>
```

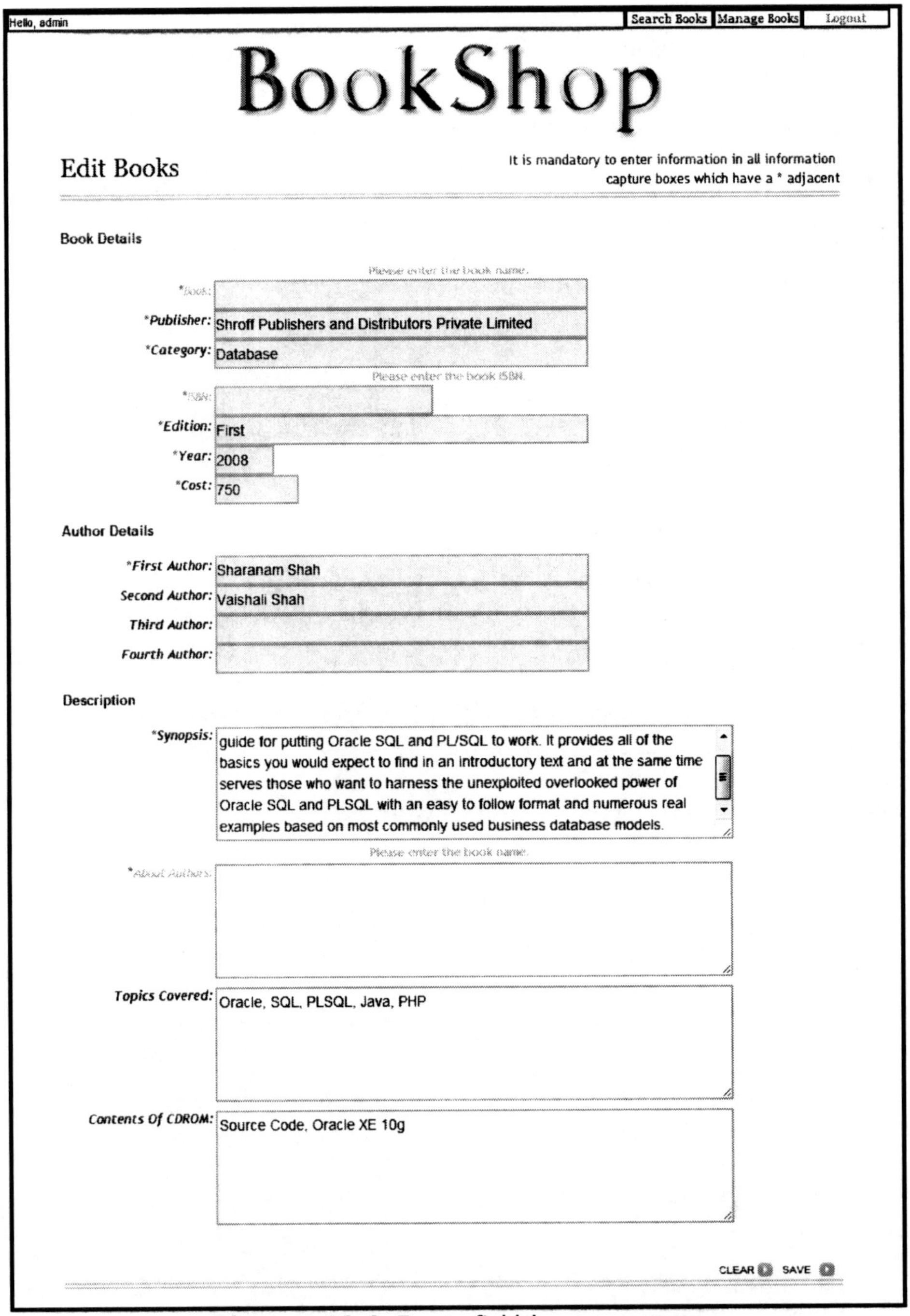

BookShop

Hello, admin   Search Books | Manage Books | Logout

Edit Books

It is mandatory to enter information in all information capture boxes which have a * adjacent

Book Details

Please enter the book name.
- *Book:
- *Publisher: Shroff Publishers and Distributors Private Limited
- *Category: Database

Please enter the book ISBN.
- *ISBN:
- *Edition: First
- *Year: 2008
- *Cost: 750

Author Details
- *First Author: Sharanam Shah
- Second Author: Vaishali Shah
- Third Author:
- Fourth Author:

Description
- *Synopsis: guide for putting Oracle SQL and PL/SQL to work. It provides all of the basics you would expect to find in an introductory text and at the same time serves those who want to harness the unexploited overlooked power of Oracle SQL and PLSQL with an easy to follow format and numerous real examples based on most commonly used business database models.

Please enter the book name.
- *About Authors:

- Topics Covered: Oracle, SQL, PLSQL, Java, PHP

- Contents Of CDROM: Source Code, Oracle XE 10g

CLEAR ● SAVE ●

Diagram 18.6: Empty fields' error message

Delete Books [manageBooks.jsp]

To delete an existing record, the user needs to click ✘ adjacent to the desired record from the search results, as shown in diagram 18.7.

	Book	ISBN	Synopsis	Author
✘	Practical Java Project For Beginners	10: 81-8404-342-2	This book can be useful for students pursuing B.E. M.C.A M.Sc. IGNOU BCA B.Sc. courses who have to make and submit a project as part of their curriculum.	Anil Kumar
✘	JavaServer Pages For Beginners	10: 81-8404-359-7	The book has been written to provide genuine knowledge to programmers who wish to learn Java Server side Web based application development using Java Server Pages. Learning web development is done through a set of examples and hands on exercises	Sharanam Shah
✘	Java Server Pages	81-7774-359-7	The book has been written to provide genuine knowledge to programmers who wish to learn Java Server side Web based application development using Java Server Pages. Learning web development is done through a set of examples and hands on exercises	Vaishali Shah

Diagram 18.7: Grid of book details

Process Flow

After the user clicks ✘, the control shifts to the action named **doDeleteBooks**.

struts.xml holds a mapping to help the form submission:

```
57      <action name="doDeleteBooks"
              class="com.sharanamvaishali.bookShop.action.deleteBookAction">
58          <interceptor-ref name="myStack" />
59          <result name="success">bookShop/manageBooks.jsp</result>
60      </action>
```

doDeleteBooks [deleteBookAction.java]

This is an action class with the following specifications.

Class Name	Package	Extends	Implements
deleteBookAction	bookShop	ActionSupport	- -
Properties			
Property Name	**Property Type**	**Methods**	
BookNo	int	getBookNo()	setBookNo()

Methods

Method Name	Return Values
execute()	SUCCESS

Code Spec

```
1  package com.sharanamvaishali.bookShop.action;
2
3  import com.opensymphony.xwork2.ActionSupport;
4  import com.sharanamvaishali.bookShop.dbConnection.dbConnection;
5
6  public class deleteBookAction extends ActionSupport {
7      private int BookNo;
8
9      public int getBookNo() {
10         return BookNo;
11     }
12     public void setBookNo(int BookNo) {
13         this.BookNo = BookNo;
14     }
15
16     @Override
17     public String execute() throws Exception {
18         dbConnection db = new dbConnection();
19         db.getConnection();
20         String SQL = "DELETE FROM Books WHERE BookNo ="+BookNo;
21         db.stmt.executeUpdate(SQL);
22         db.removeConnection();
23         return SUCCESS;
24     }
25 }
```

Process Flow

As soon as this action takes charge, **execute()**, does the following:

Establishes a database connection as:

- Spawns an object of the class **dbConnectionAction**
- Invokes **getConnection()** of that class

Fires an SQL DELETE query using **executeUpdate()** of Statement:

DELETE FROM Books WHERE BookNo ="+BookNo

After the record is deleted, the database connection is destroyed and SUCCESS is returned.

struts.xml holds a mapping to help the **SUCCESS** result:

```
57      <action name="doDeleteBooks"
            class="com.sharanamvaishali.bookShop.action.deleteBookAction">
58          <interceptor-ref name="myStack" />
59          <result name="success">bookShop/manageBooks.jsp</result>
60      </action>
```

Since SUCCESS is returned, manageBooks.jsp is served.

Chapter 19

SECTION IV: APPLICATION DEVELOPMENT USING STRUTS 2

Logout

This is a menu available on all the forms.

Logout when clicked destroys the session and redirects to Login form.

Process Flow

After the user clicks [Logout], the action named **logoutAction** is invoked.

struts.xml holds a mapping to help the form submission:

```
33      <action name="doLogout"
            class="com.sharanamvaishali.bookShop.action.logOffAction">
34          <result type="redirectAction">index</result>
35      </action>
```

doLogout [logOffAction.java]

This is an action class with the following specifications.

Class Name	Package	Extends	Implements
logOffAction	bookShop	ActionSupport	SessionAware

Properties			
Property Name	Property Type	Methods	
session	Map	getSession()	setSession()

Methods	
Method Name	Return Values
execute()	SUCCESS

Code Spec

```
1  package com.sharanamvaishali.bookShop.action;
2
3  import com.opensymphony.xwork2.ActionContext;
4  import com.opensymphony.xwork2.ActionSupport;
5  import java.util.*;
6  import org.apache.struts2.interceptor.SessionAware;
7
8  public class logOffAction extends ActionSupport implements SessionAware {
9      private Map session;
10
11     public Map getSession() {
12         return session;
13     }
14     public void setSession(Map session) {
15         this.session = session;
16     }
17
18     @Override
19     public String execute() throws Exception {
20         session = ActionContext.getContext().getSession();
21         session.remove("username");
22         session.clear();
23         return SUCCESS;
24     }
25 }
```

Process Flow

As soon as this action takes charge, **execute()**, does the following:

- Destroys the existing session
- SUCCESS is returned

struts.xml holds a mapping to help the SUCCESS result:

```
33      <action name="doLogout"
            class="com.sharanamvaishali.bookShop.action.logOffAction">
34          <result type="redirectAction">index</result>
35      </action>
```

Since SUCCESS is returned, login.jsp will be served.

Chapter 20

SECTION IV: APPLICATION DEVELOPMENT USING STRUTS 2

Beans And Interceptors

Book Bean Class

This is a bean class created to store the records that are retrieved from the Books tables. An object of this class is then added to an ArrayList object and passed onto the Value Stack thus making it available to Search Books and Manage Books forms for displaying search results.

Class Specifications

Class Name	Package	Extends	Implements
Books	bookShop	- -	- -

Properties			
Property Name	**Property Type**	**Methods**	
BookName	String	getBookName()	setBookName()
PublisherName	String	getPublisherName()	setPublisherName()
Category	String	getCategory()	setCategory()

Properties

Property Name	Property Type	Methods	
ISBN	String	getISBN()	setISBN()
Edition	String	getEdition()	setEdition()
FirstAuthor	String	getFirstAuthor()	setFirstAuthor()
SecondAuthor	String	getSecondAuthor()	setSecondAuthor()
ThirdAuthor	String	getThirdAuthor()	setThirdAuthor()
FourthAuthor	String	getFourthAuthor()	setFourthAuthor()
Synopsis	String	getSynopsis()	setSynopsis()
AboutAuthors	String	getAboutAuthors()	setAboutAuthors()
TopicsCovered	String	getTopicsCovered()	setTopicsCovered()
ContentsCDROM	String	getContentsCDROM()	setContentsCDROM()
BookNo	int	getBookNo()	setBookNo()
Year	int	getYear()	setYear()
Cost	int	getCost()	setCost()

Methods

Constructor Name	Parameter Values
Book()	- -
Book()	int BookNo String BookName String PublisherName String Category String CoverPage String ISBN String Edition String FirstAuthor String SecondAuthor String ThirdAuthor String FourthAuthor String Synopsis String AboutAuthors String TopicsCovered String ContentsCDROM int Year int Cost

Code Spec

```
1  package com.sharanamvaishali.bookShop.domain;
2
3  public class Book {
4      private String BookName, PublisherName, Category, ISBN, Edition, FirstAuthor,
         SecondAuthor, ThirdAuthor, FourthAuthor, Synopsis, AboutAuthors, TopicsCovered,
         ContentsCDROM;
```

```java
5      private int BookNo, Year, Cost;
6
7      public Book() {
8      }
9
10     public Book(int BookNo, String BookName, String PublisherName, String Category,
           String ISBN, String Edition, String FirstAuthor, String SecondAuthor, String
           ThirdAuthor, String FourthAuthor, String Synopsis, String AboutAuthors, String
           TopicsCovered, String ContentsCDROM, int Year, int Cost) {
11         this.BookNo = BookNo;
12         this.BookName = BookName;
13         this.PublisherName = PublisherName;
14         this.Category = Category;
15         this.ISBN = ISBN;
16         this.Edition = Edition;
17         this.FirstAuthor = FirstAuthor;
18         this.SecondAuthor = SecondAuthor;
19         this.ThirdAuthor = ThirdAuthor;
20         this.FourthAuthor = FourthAuthor;
21         this.Synopsis = Synopsis;
22         this.AboutAuthors = AboutAuthors;
23         this.TopicsCovered = TopicsCovered;
24         this.ContentsCDROM = ContentsCDROM;
25         this.Year = Year;
26         this.Cost = Cost;
27     }
28
29     public String getAboutAuthors() {
30         return AboutAuthors;
31     }
32     public void setAboutAuthors(String AboutAuthors) {
33         this.AboutAuthors = AboutAuthors;
34     }
35
36     public String getBookName() {
37         return BookName;
38     }
39     public void setBookName(String BookName) {
40         this.BookName = BookName;
41     }
42
43     public int getBookNo() {
44         return BookNo;
45     }
46     public void setBookNo(int BookNo) {
47         this.BookNo = BookNo;
48     }
49
50     public String getCategory() {
51         return Category;
52     }
53     public void setCategory(String Category) {
54         this.Category = Category;
```

```java
55      }
56
57      public String getContentsCDROM() {
58          return ContentsCDROM;
59      }
60      public void setContentsCDROM(String ContentsCDROM) {
61          this.ContentsCDROM = ContentsCDROM;
62      }
63
64      public int getCost() {
65          return Cost;
66      }
67      public void setCost(int Cost) {
68          this.Cost = Cost;
69      }
70
71      public String getEdition() {
72          return Edition;
73      }
74      public void setEdition(String Edition) {
75          this.Edition = Edition;
76      }
77
78      public String getFirstAuthor() {
79          return FirstAuthor;
80      }
81      public void setFirstAuthor(String FirstAuthor) {
82          this.FirstAuthor = FirstAuthor;
83      }
84
85      public String getFourthAuthor() {
86          return FourthAuthor;
87      }
88      public void setFourthAuthor(String FourthAuthor) {
89          this.FourthAuthor = FourthAuthor;
90      }
91
92      public String getISBN() {
93          return ISBN;
94      }
95      public void setISBN(String ISBN) {
96          this.ISBN = ISBN;
97      }
98
99      public String getPublisherName() {
100         return PublisherName;
101     }
102     public void setPublisherName(String PublisherName) {
103         this.PublisherName = PublisherName;
104     }
105
106     public String getSecondAuthor() {
107         return SecondAuthor;
```

```
108     }
109     public void setSecondAuthor(String SecondAuthor) {
110         this.SecondAuthor = SecondAuthor;
111     }
112
113     public String getSynopsis() {
114         return Synopsis;
115     }
116     public void setSynopsis(String Synopsis) {
117         this.Synopsis = Synopsis;
118     }
119
120     public String getThirdAuthor() {
121         return ThirdAuthor;
122     }
123     public void setThirdAuthor(String ThirdAuthor) {
124         this.ThirdAuthor = ThirdAuthor;
125     }
126
127     public String getTopicsCovered() {
128         return TopicsCovered;
129     }
130     public void setTopicsCovered(String TopicsCovered) {
131         this.TopicsCovered = TopicsCovered;
132     }
133
134     public int getYear() {
135         return Year;
136     }
137     public void setYear(int Year) {
138         this.Year = Year;
139     }
140 }
```

dbConnection

This is a **POJO** created to expose methods that help establish and destroy database connections.

An object of this class is created by other action classes that require database interaction.

Class Specifications

Class Name	Package	Extends	Implements
dbConnection	bookShop	- -	- -

Properties				
Property Name	Property Type	Methods	
- -	- -	- -	- -

Methods	
Constructor Name	Parameter Values
getConnection()	- -
removeConnection()	- -

Code Spec

```
1  package com.sharanamvaishali.bookShop.dbConnection;
2
3  import java.sql.Connection;
4  import java.sql.DriverManager;
5  import java.sql.PreparedStatement;
6  import java.sql.SQLException;
7  import java.sql.Statement;
8
9  public class dbConnection {
10     public Connection conn = null;
11     public Statement stmt = null;
12     public PreparedStatement pstmt = null;
13
14     String dbName = "BookShop";
15     String host = "localhost";
16     String username = "root";
17     String password = "123456";
18
19     public Connection getConnection() throws Exception, SQLException {
20         try {
21             Class.forName("com.mysql.jdbc.Driver").newInstance();
22             conn = DriverManager.getConnection("jdbc:mysql://" + host + "/" + dbName,
                    username, password);
23             stmt = conn.createStatement();
24         }
25         catch(Exception e) {
26             System.out.println(e.getMessage());
27         }
28         return conn;
29     }
30
31     public void removeConnection() throws SQLException {
32         conn.close();
33     }
34 }
```

AuthenticationInterceptor

This is an **interceptor** class created to prevent unauthenticated users from using the application. This means, users who have not logged in cannot reach the following forms:

❏ Search Books

- Manage Books
    - Add Books
    - Edit Books

If a user attempts to access these forms without logging in [using direct URLs] then the interceptor automatically redirects to the login page.

Class Specifications

Class Name	Package	Extends	Implements
AuthenticationInterceptor	bookShop	- -	Interceptor

Methods	
Method Name	Parameter Values
destroy()	- -
init()	
intercept()	ActionInvocation

Code Spec

```
1  package com.sharanamvaishali.bookShop.interceptor;
2
3  import com.opensymphony.xwork2.ActionInvocation;
4  import com.opensymphony.xwork2.interceptor.Interceptor;
5  import java.util.Map;
6
7  public class AuthenticationInterceptor implements Interceptor {
8      @Override
9      public void destroy() {
10     }
11
12     @Override
13     public void init() {
14     }
15
16     @Override
17     public String intercept(ActionInvocation actionInvocation) throws Exception {
18         Map session = actionInvocation.getInvocationContext().getSession();
19         if (session.get("username") == null) {
20             return "loginAction";
21         }
22         else {
23             return actionInvocation.invoke();
24         }
25     }
26 }
```

Process Flow

This Interceptor is executed as follows:

1. The framework receives a **request** and decides on the **Action** the URL maps to
2. The framework consults the application's configuration file [struts.xml], to discover the interceptor to be fired
3. The framework starts the invocation process by executing the **Interceptor**
4. After the interceptor is invoked, the framework causes the Action itself to be **executed**

For this application the interceptor fires for the following actions as defined in struts.xml:

```xml
1  <?xml version="1.0" encoding="UTF-8"?>
2  <!DOCTYPE struts PUBLIC '-//Apache Software Foundation//DTD Commons Validator Rules Configuration 2.3//EN' 'http://struts.apache.org/dtds/struts-2.3.dtd'>
3  <struts>
4      <package name="bookShop" extends="struts-default">
5          <interceptors>
6              <interceptor name="loginInterceptor"
                   class="com.sharanamvaishali.bookShop.interceptor.AuthenticationInterceptor" />
7              <interceptor-stack name="myStack">
8                  <interceptor-ref name="defaultStack" />
9                  <interceptor-ref name="loginInterceptor" />          Interceptor Declaration
10             </interceptor-stack>
11         </interceptors>
12
13         <global-results>
14             <result name="loginAction" type="redirectAction">index</result>
15         </global-results>
16
17         <action name="index">
18             <result>bookShop/login.jsp</result>
19         </action>
20         <action name="doLogin"
                class="com.sharanamvaishali.bookShop.action.loginAction">
21             <result name="success" type="redirectAction">showSearchBooks</result>
22             <result name="error">bookShop/login.jsp</result>
23             <result name="input">bookShop/login.jsp</result>
24         </action>
25         <action name="showSearchBooks">
26             <interceptor-ref name="myStack"/>
27             <result>bookShop/searchBooks.jsp</result>
28         </action>
29         <action name="showManageBooks">
30             <interceptor-ref name="myStack" />
31             <result>bookShop/manageBooks.jsp</result>
32         </action>
33         <action name="doLogout"
                class="com.sharanamvaishali.bookShop.action.logOffAction">
34             <result type="redirectAction">index</result>
35         </action>
```

```xml
36
37      <action name="showAddBooks">
38        <interceptor-ref name="myStack" />
39        <result type="redirect">bookShop/addBooks.jsp</result>
40      </action>
41      <action name="doInsertBooks"
        class="com.sharanamvaishali.bookShop.action.insertBookAction">
42        <interceptor-ref name="myStack" />
43        <result name="success">/bookShop/manageBooks.jsp</result>
44        <result name="input">/bookShop/addBooks.jsp</result>
45      </action>
46
47      <action name="showEditBooks"
        class="com.sharanamvaishali.bookShop.action.editBookAction">
48        <interceptor-ref name="myStack" />
49        <result name="success">bookShop/updateBooks.jsp</result>
50      </action>
51      <action name="doUpdateBooks"
        class="com.sharanamvaishali.bookShop.action.updateBookAction">
52        <interceptor-ref name="myStack" />
53        <result name="success">/bookShop/manageBooks.jsp</result>
54        <result name="input">/bookShop/updateBooks.jsp</result>
55      </action>
56
57      <action name="doDeleteBooks"
        class="com.sharanamvaishali.bookShop.action.deleteBookAction">
58        <interceptor-ref name="myStack" />
59        <result name="success">bookShop/manageBooks.jsp</result>
60      </action>
61
62      <action name="doManageSearchBooks"
        class="com.sharanamvaishali.bookShop.action.manageSearchBooksAction">
63        <interceptor-ref name="myStack" />
64        <result name="success">/bookShop/manageBooks.jsp</result>
65      </action>
66      <action name="doSearchBooks"
        class="com.sharanamvaishali.bookShop.action.searchBooksAction">
67        <interceptor-ref name="myStack" />
68        <result name="success">/bookShop/searchBooks.jsp</result>
69        <result name="input">/bookShop/searchBooks.jsp</result>
70      </action>
71    </package>
72  </struts>
```

intercept()

Using getSession() from the current action's Invocation Context, the current session is extracted.

If this session holds a valid value for the username attribute [that was stored whilst logging in], the current action is invoked to resume the execution.

If this session does not hold a valid value for the username attribute, loginAction is returned.

struts.xml holds a mapping to help the **loginAction global result:**

```
13      <global-results>
14          <result name="loginAction" type="redirectAction">index</result>
15      </global-results>
```

This result redirects to the action named **index**, which delivers the login form.

struts.xml holds a mapping to help the redirection:

```
17      <action name="index">
18          <result>bookShop/login.jsp</result>
19      </action>
```

Chapter 21

SECTION IV: APPLICATION DEVELOPMENT USING STRUTS 2

Running The Application

Now that BookShop application [source code available on the Book's accompanying CDROM] is created using the NetBeans IDE, let's build and run this application, to understand the way it functions.

Open the project using NetBeans IDE and follow the instructions to build and run it:

Begin by building the project using NetBeans IDE.

To do so, right click **BookShop** project and select **Build**, as shown in diagram 21.1.

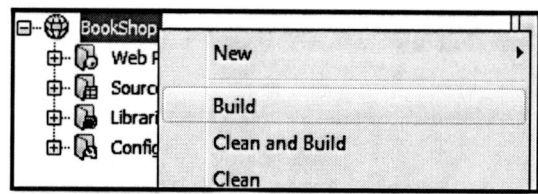

Diagram 21.1: Building the project

Then run the application by right clicking **BookShop** project and selecting **Run**, as shown in diagram 21.2.

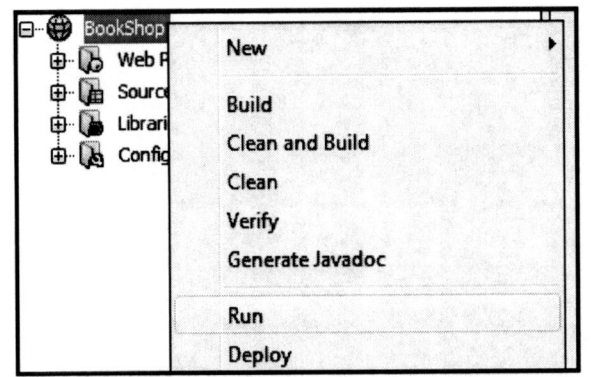

Diagram 21.2: Running the project

Login

This brings up BookShop application in the Web browser, as shown in diagram 21.3.

Diagram 21.3

Key in the admin as the username as well as the password and click LOGIN.

This authenticates the username and password and if found valid displays the Homepage [Search Books], as shown in diagram 21.4.

Diagram 21.4

If the username or password entered are found to be invalid an error is displayed, as shown in diagram 21.5.

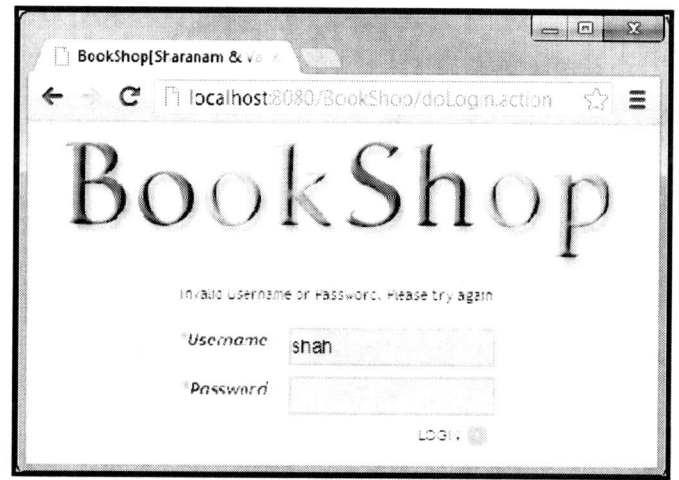

Diagram 21.5

If either of the inputs i.e. username or password are left empty and the user clicks LOGIN appropriate error messages appear due to validation failure, as shown in diagram 21.6.

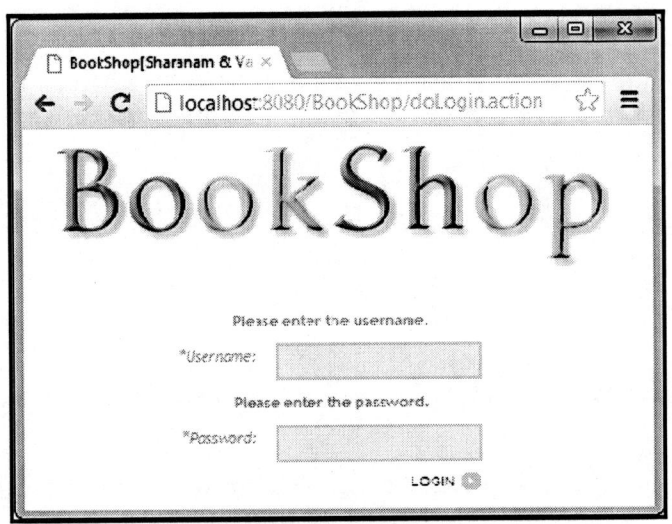

Diagram 21.6

Search Books

Diagram 21.7

Key in the desired search criteria and click `BookShop Search`. This performs the search operation and displays the search results, as shown in diagram 21.8.

Running The Application 331

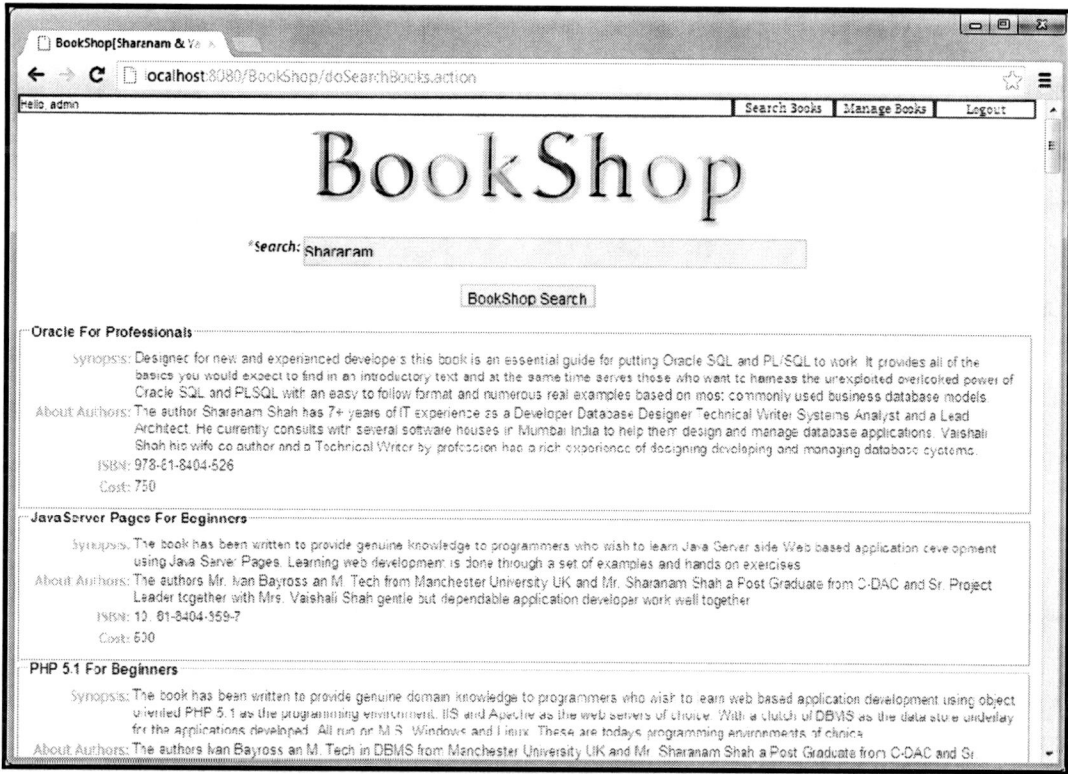

Diagram 21.8

If the search criteria is left empty and the user clicks [BookShop Search] an error message due to validation failure appears, as shown in diagram 21.9.

Diagram 21.9

Manage Books

To access Manage books form click **Manage Books**. This displays Manage Books form, as shown in diagram 21.10.

Diagram 21.10

Add Books

To add a new book, click . This displays Add Books data entry form, as shown in diagram 21.11.

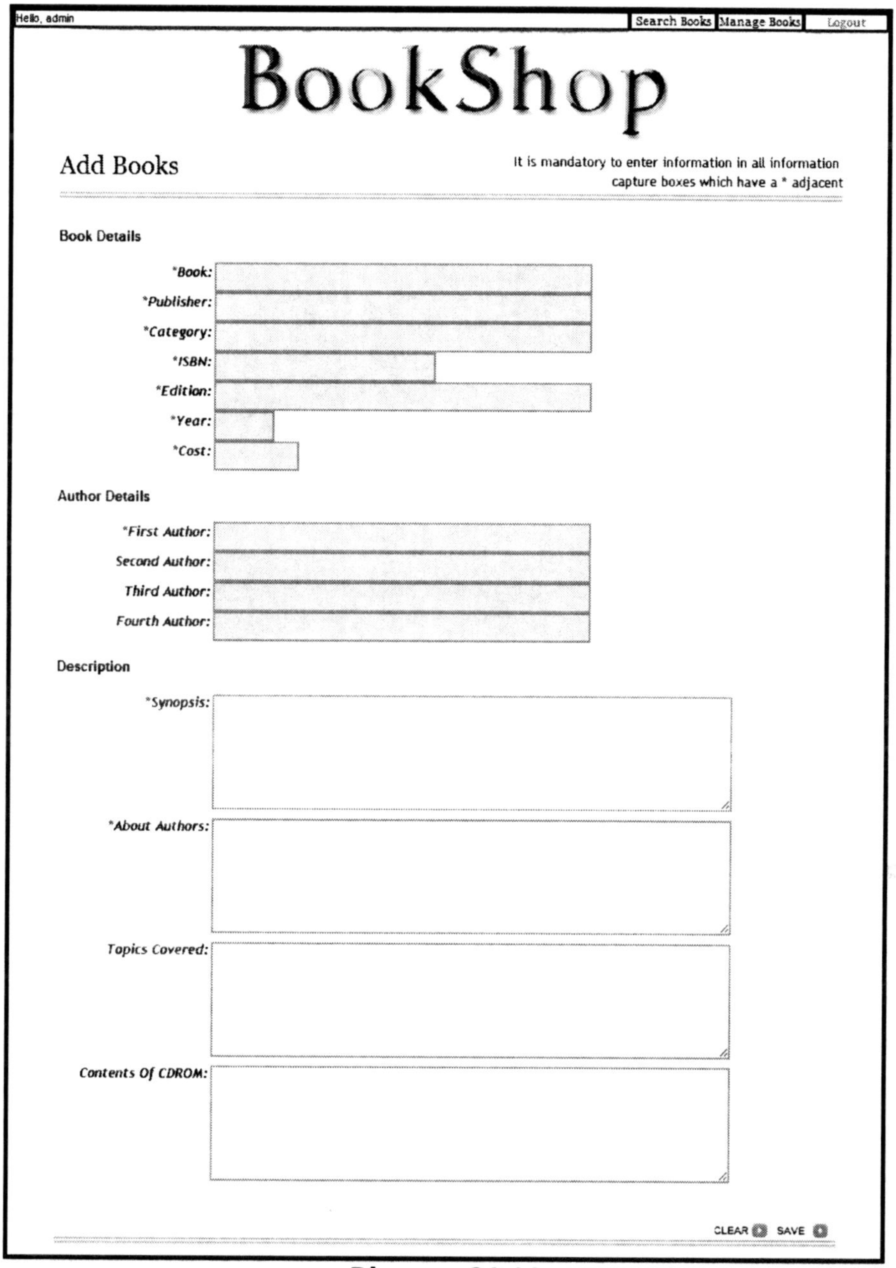

Running The Application 333

Diagram 21.11

Key in the required data and click SAVE ▶. This saves the data to the database and brings back Manage Books form, as shown in diagram 21.10.

334   Struts 2 For Beginners

If the required data is left empty and the user clicks SAVE ▶ error messages due to validation failure appear, as shown in diagram 21.12.

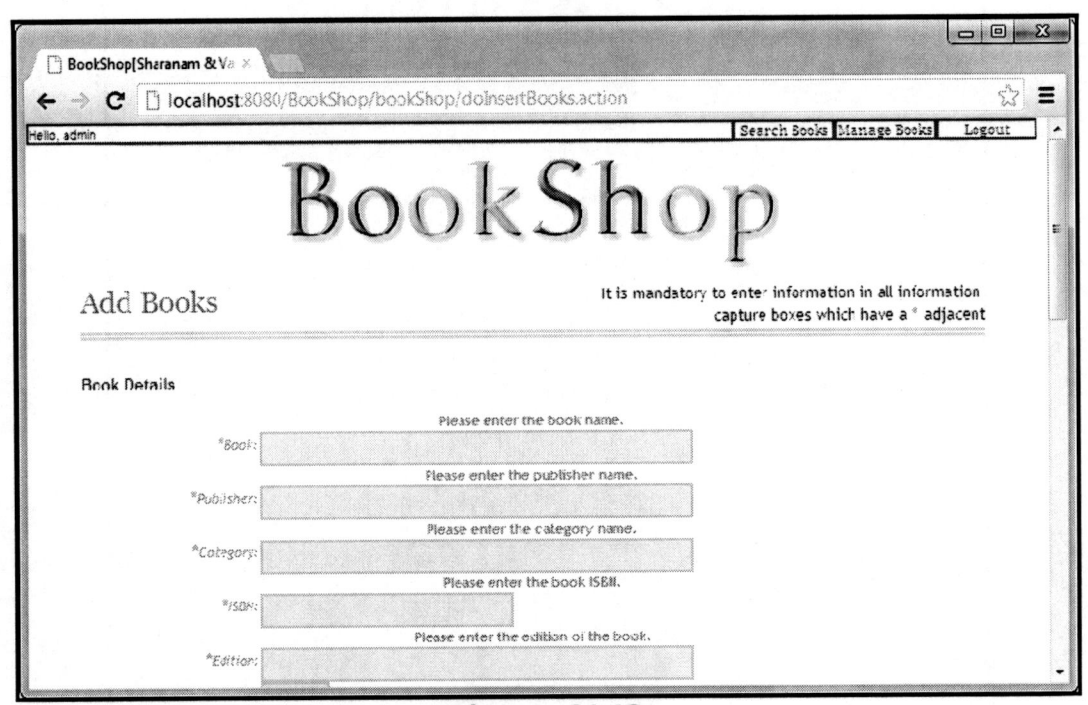

Diagram 21.12

Edit Books

To edit an existing book, key in a book name or an ISBN and click FIND ▶. This displays search results, as shown in diagram 21.13.

Running The Application 335

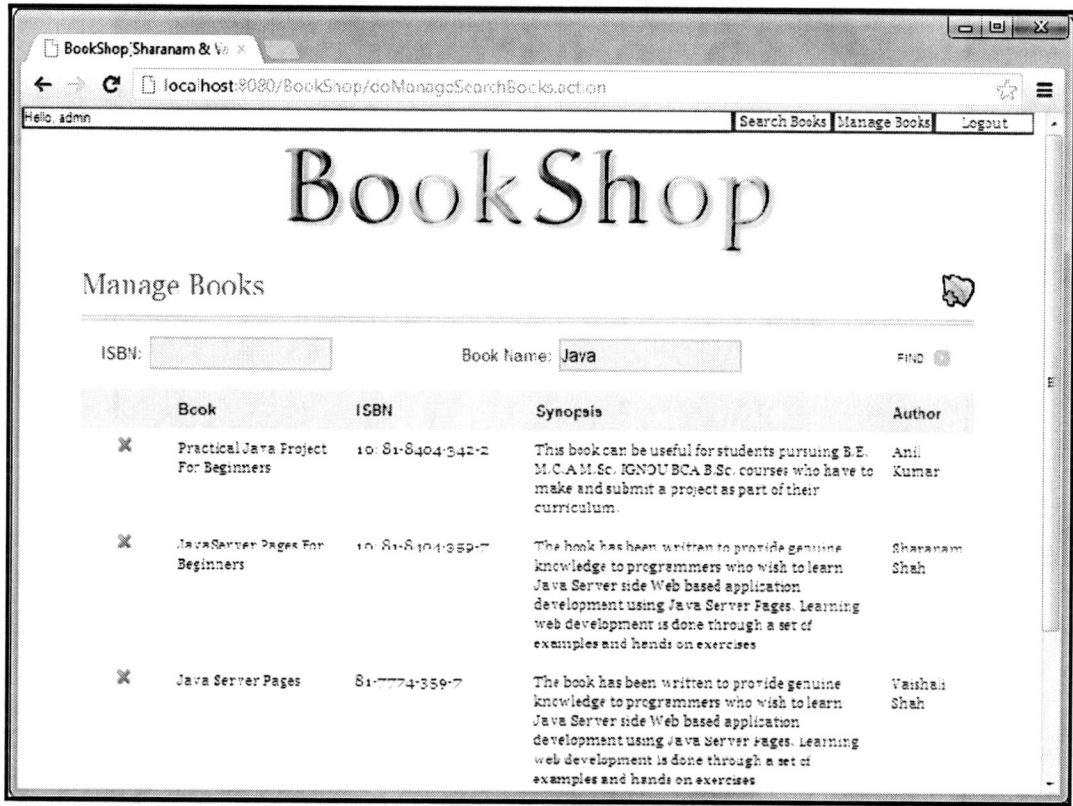

Diagram 21.13

Click a record from the search results to edit. This displays Edit Books form [pre-populated] with the chosen record's data, as shown in diagram 21.14.

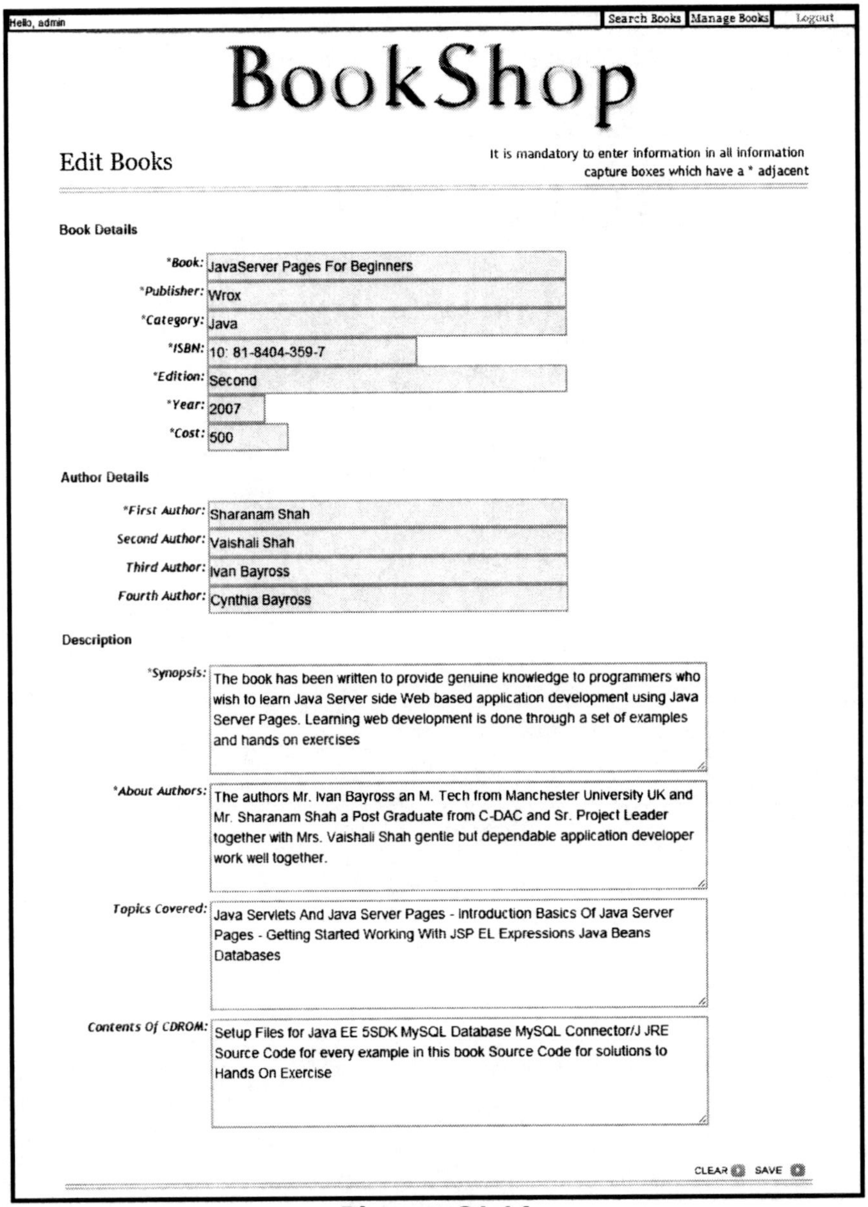

Diagram 21.14

Make the desired changes and click SAVE ▶. This makes the changes permanent and brings back Manage Books form, as shown in diagram 21.10.

Running The Application

If the required data is left empty whilst editing the book details and the user clicks SAVE ▶ error messages due to validation failure appear, as shown in diagram 21.15.

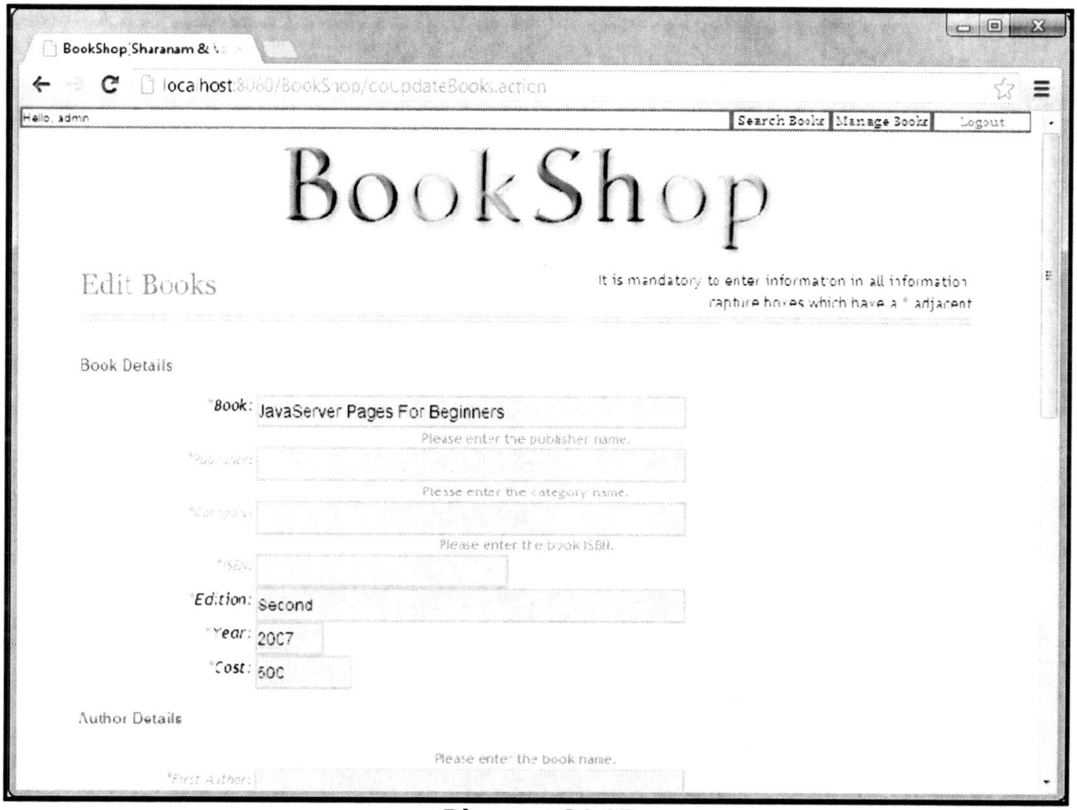

Diagram 21.15

Delete Books

To delete an existing book, key in a book name or an ISBN and click FIND ▶. This displays search results, as shown in diagram 21.16.

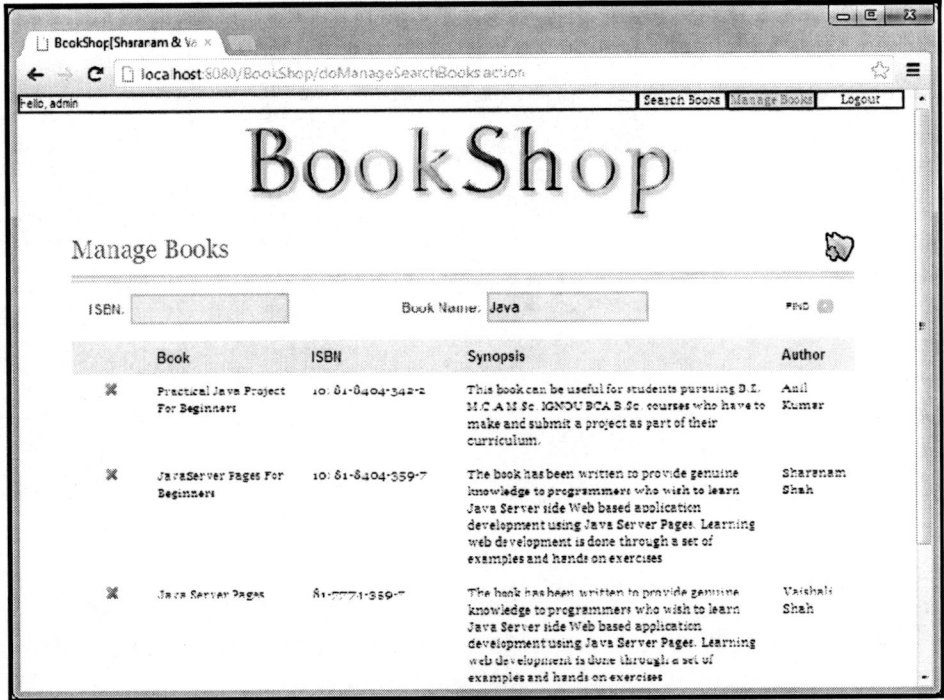

Diagram 21.16

Click ✖ adjacent to the desired record to delete that record. This deletes the record and brings back Manage Books form, as shown in diagram 21.10.

Logout

To logout, click [Logout]. This destroys the session and brings back the login page, as shown in diagram 21.3.

If after the session is destroyed, a user attempts to reach Search Books, Manage Books, Add Books or Edit Books directly using the following URLs, the application does not allow this.

- http://localhost:8080/BookShop/showSearchBooks.action
- http://localhost:8080/BookShop/showManageBooks.action
- http://localhost:8080/BookShop/bookShop/addBooks.jsp
- http://localhost:8080/BookShop/showEditBooks.action?BookNo=1

It simply redirects to the login page, as shown in diagram 21.3. This means that the user cannot use the application without logging in.

Chapter 22

SECTION V: APPLICATION DEVELOPMENT USING STRUTS 2.X.X AND HIBERNATE 4

Defining The Project And Its Requirements

Now that concepts are in place, let's build an application that helps re-enforce the learning that took place.

This chapter uses Struts 2.x.x to demonstrate building **Customer** application with Hibernate 4 as the ORM tool.

Hibernate can be used in just about any kind of Java application. It may run inside a Servlet, JSP, JSF, a Swing client and so on. It can also be used along with Model-View-Controller [MVC] Web application frameworks such as Struts, Spring, Tapestry and so on.

Technically, this application will use:
- JSP as the delivery mechanism
- **Struts 2.x.x** as the Web application framework

- **Hibernate** as the ORM tool
- **DAO** as the design pattern
- **MySQL** as the database
- **Ajax** wherever required

All the code spec will be built and deployed using **NetBeans IDE**.

Database Tables

Entity Relationship Diagram

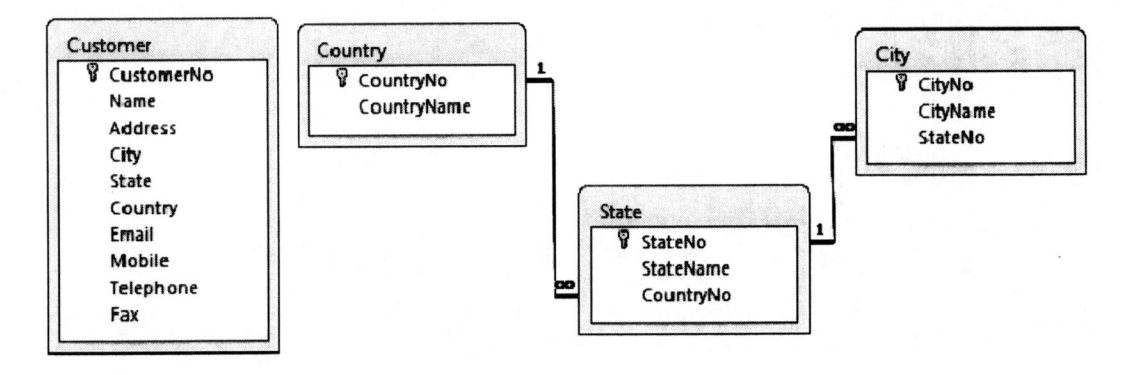

Table Specifications

City

```
+-----------+-------------+------+-----+---------+----------------+
| Field     | Type        | Null | Key | Default | Extra          |
+-----------+-------------+------+-----+---------+----------------+
| CITYNO    | int(11)     | NO   | PRI | NULL    | auto_increment |
| CITYNAME  | varchar(50) | YES  |     | NULL    |                |
| STATENO   | int(11)     | YES  | MUL | NULL    |                |
+-----------+-------------+------+-----+---------+----------------+
```

State

```
+-----------+-------------+------+-----+---------+----------------+
| Field     | Type        | Null | Key | Default | Extra          |
+-----------+-------------+------+-----+---------+----------------+
| STATENO   | int(11)     | NO   | PRI | NULL    | auto_increment |
| STATENAME | varchar(50) | YES  |     | NULL    |                |
| COUNTRYNO | int(11)     | YES  | MUL | NULL    |                |
+-----------+-------------+------+-----+---------+----------------+
```

Country

```
+-------------+-------------+------+-----+---------+----------------+
| Field       | Type        | Null | Key | Default | Extra          |
+-------------+-------------+------+-----+---------+----------------+
| COUNTRYNO   | int(11)     | NO   | PRI | NULL    | auto_increment |
| COUNTRYNAME | varchar(50) | YES  |     | NULL    |                |
+-------------+-------------+------+-----+---------+----------------+
```

Customer

```
+------------+--------------+------+-----+---------+----------------+
| Field      | Type         | Null | Key | Default | Extra          |
+------------+--------------+------+-----+---------+----------------+
| CUSTOMERNO | int(11)      | NO   | PRI | NULL    | auto_increment |
| NAME       | varchar(50)  | YES  |     | NULL    |                |
| ADDRESS    | varchar(150) | YES  |     | NULL    |                |
| CITY       | varchar(25)  | YES  |     | NULL    |                |
| STATE      | varchar(25)  | YES  |     | NULL    |                |
| COUNTRY    | varchar(25)  | YES  |     | NULL    |                |
| EMAIL      | varchar(75)  | YES  |     | NULL    |                |
| MOBILE     | varchar(15)  | YES  |     | NULL    |                |
| TELEPHONE  | varchar(15)  | YES  |     | NULL    |                |
| FAX        | varchar(15)  | YES  |     | NULL    |                |
+------------+--------------+------+-----+---------+----------------+
```

The table creation code spec is available as an SQL script [**Customer.sql**] in this Book's accompanying CDROM.

These tables allow holding:

- Multiple Customers [Customer]
- Each customer's address is made up of a Country, State and City

Using MySQL's command line utility:

- Create a database called CustomerDB
- Create the above defined tables within this database

Data Entry Form

The application holds a single data entry form, as shown in diagram 22.1 which is also the entry point to this application.

This form allows:

- Accepting the customer details
- Editing an existing customer's details
- Deleting an existing customer

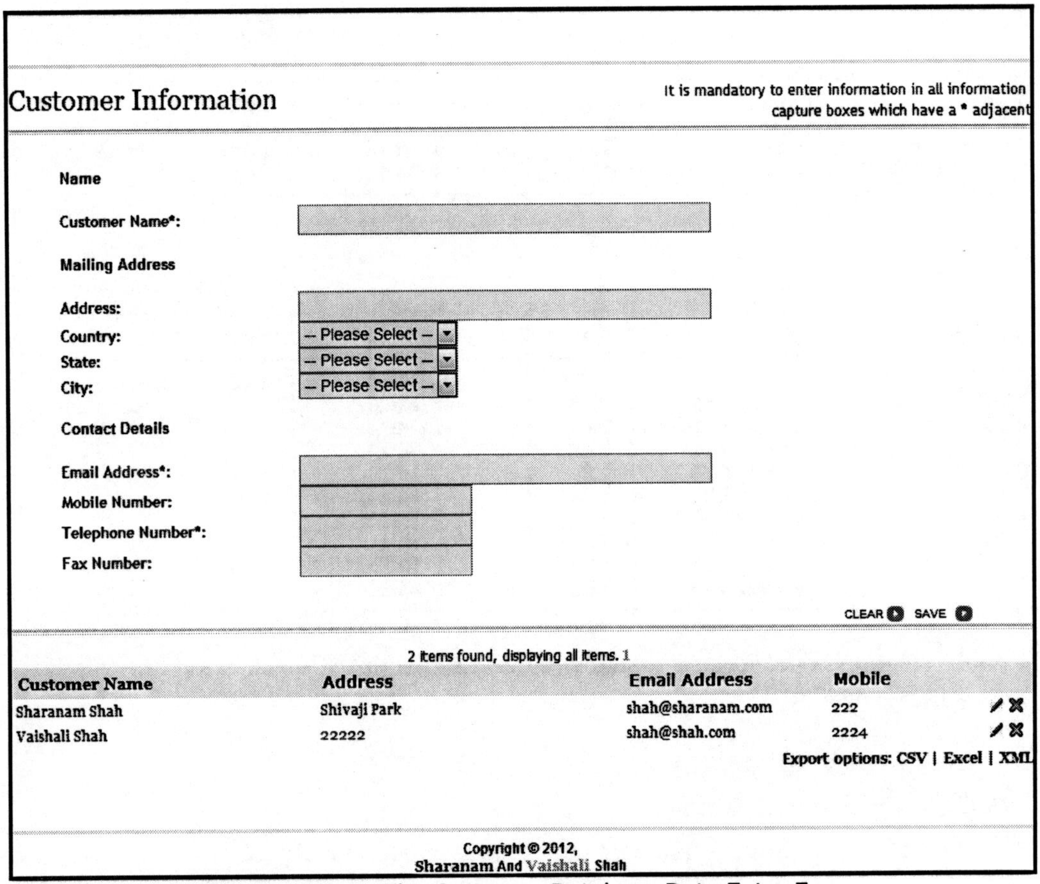

Diagram 22.1: The Customer Database Data Entry Form

As soon as the application is executed, this form is delivered.

To insert a new customer, the user can key in the customer details using the data entry form and click SAVE.

The data grid [created using Display Tag library] on this form allows viewing existing records. Every record in this grid provides links that allow editing or deleting that record. ✎ when clicked populates the data entry form with that customer's details. The user can make the desired changes and click SAVE.

✖ when clicked deletes that customer and all the associated email addresses from the underlying database tables.

Chapter 23

SECTION V: APPLICATION DEVELOPMENT USING STRUTS 2.X.X AND HIBERNATE 4

Building The Application

Since NetBeans is the IDE of choice throughout this book. Use it to create a new Web Application Project called **Customer**.

Run NetBeans IDE and create a new **Web Application** project by selecting File → New Project.... **New Project** dialog box appears, as shown in diagram 23.1.1.

Select **Java Web** option available under **Categories** list box and **Web Application** option available under the **Projects** list box, as shown in diagram 23.1.1.

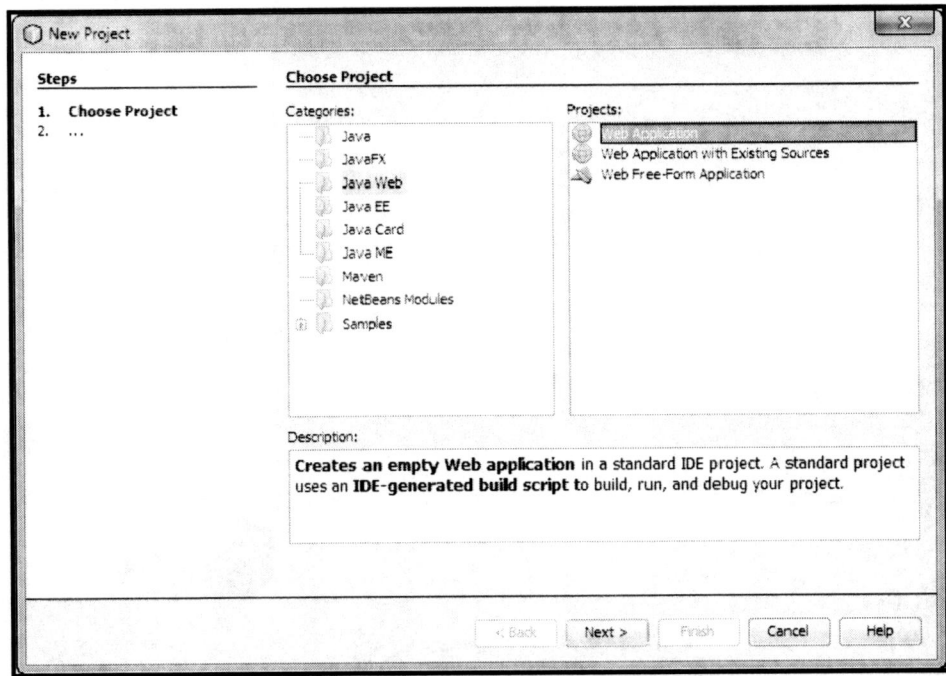

Diagram 23.1.1: New Project dialog box

Click [Next >].

New Web Application dialog box appears, as shown in diagram 23.1.2.

Enter the name of the Web application as **Customer** and select the checkbox **Use Dedicated Folder for Storing Libraries**, as shown in diagram 23.1.2.

Building The Application 345

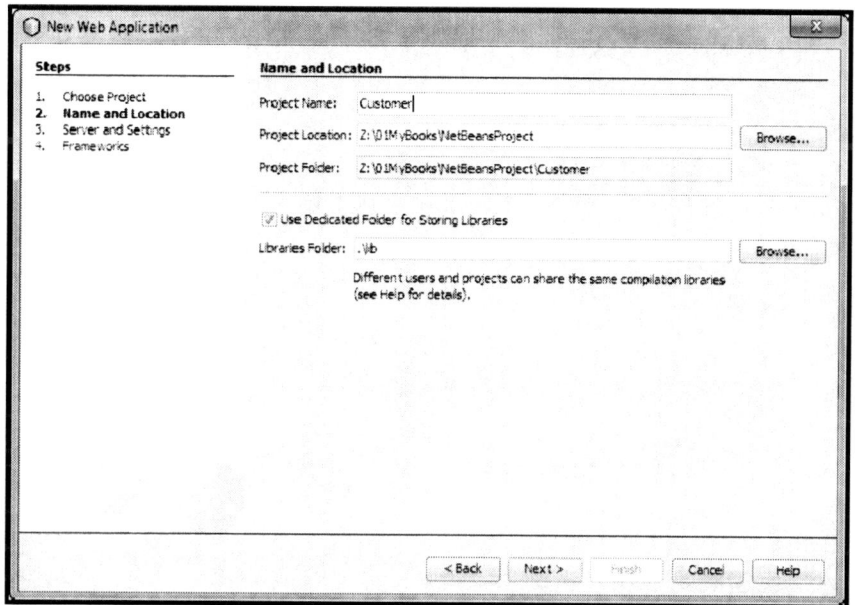

Diagram 23.1.2: Name and Location section of Web Application dialog box

Click **Next >**. **Server and Settings** section of **New Web Application** dialog box appears, as shown in diagram 23.1.3. Keep the defaults as it is.

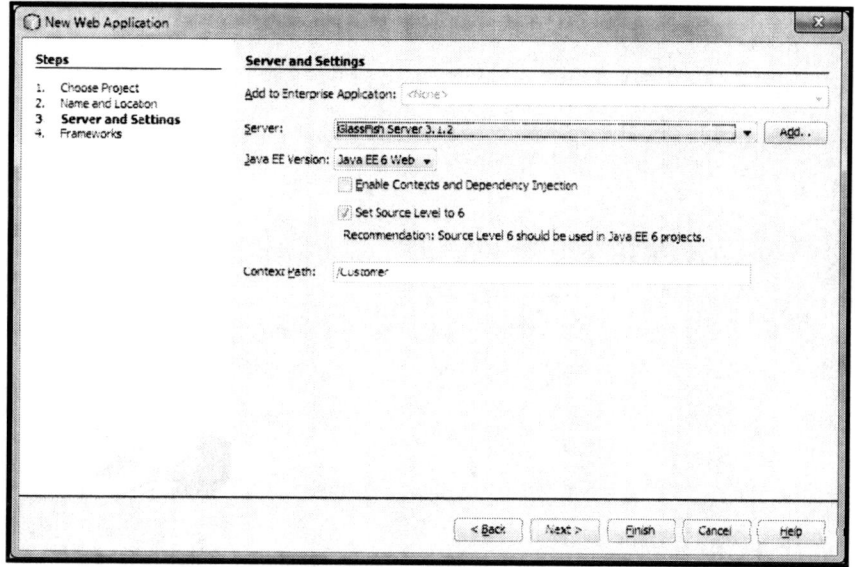

Diagram 24.1.3: Server and Settings section of New Web Application dialog box

Struts 2 For Beginners

Click [Next >]. **Frameworks** section of **New Web Application** dialog box appears, as shown in diagram 23.1.4. <u>Do not choose a framework, in the Frameworks dialog box.</u>

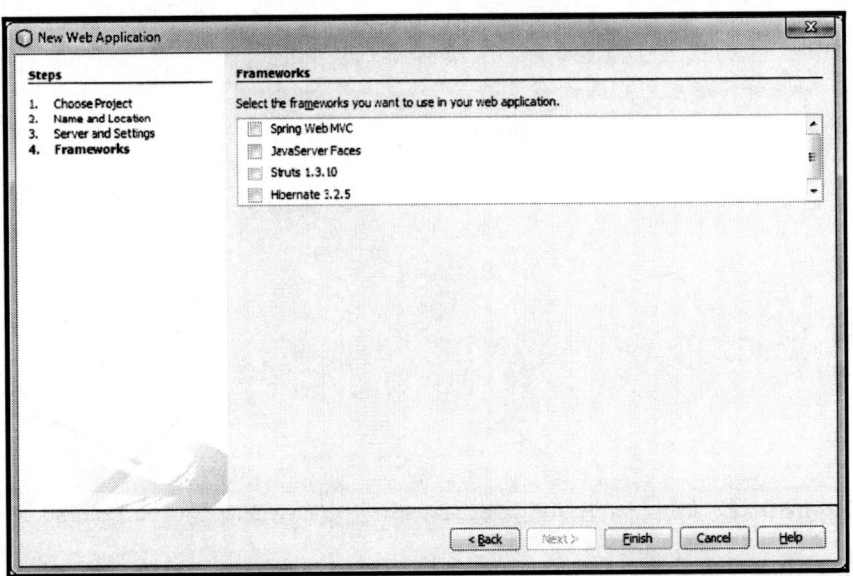

Diagram 23.1.4: Frameworks section of New Web Application dialog box

Click [Finish].

Customer application is created in NetBeans IDE, as shown in diagram 23.1.4.

Building The Application 347

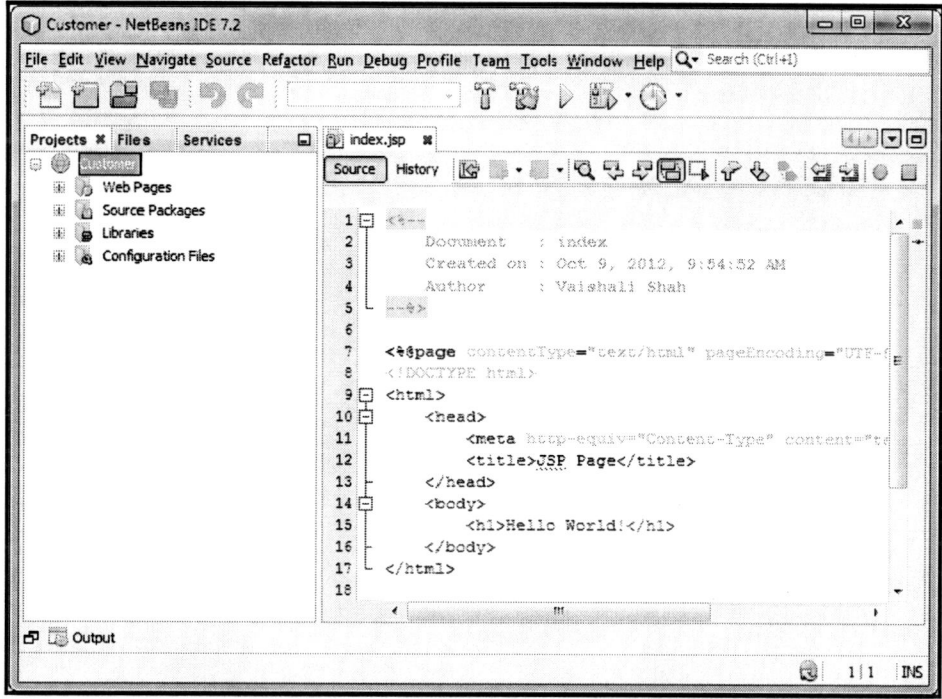

Diagram 23.1.4: Customer in NetBeans IDE

Once NetBeans IDE brings up **Customer** application, the next step is to add the required library files [JDBC driver, Hibernate, Struts 2, DisplayTag] to Customer application.

Chapter 24

SECTION V: APPLICATION DEVELOPMENT USING STRUTS 2.X.X AND HIBERNATE 4

Adding The Library Files To The Project

This application uses Hibernate, Struts 2, a JDBC driver and Display Tag. Hence, appropriate library files have to be added to the project.

Downloading The Required Library Files

This application requires the following:

Hibernate

The Hibernate ORM tool. This can be downloaded from http://www.hibernate.org/downloads.

MySQL JDBC Driver

The JDBC driver to interact with the MySQL database. This can be downloaded from http://dev.mysql.com/downloads/connector/j/.

Display Tag

Display tag library is an open source suite of custom tags that provide high-level Web presentation patterns which will work in an MVC model. The library provides a significant amount of functionality while still being easy to use.

This library helps produce the data grid that is used in **Customer** data entry form.

Customer Name	Address	Email Address	Mobile	
		2 items found, displaying all items. 1		
Sharanam Shah	Shivaji Park	shah@sharanam.com	222	✎ ✕
Vaishali Shah	Dadar	shah@shah.com	2224	✎ ✕
			Export options: CSV | Excel | XML	

This can be downloaded from http://www.displaytag.org/10/download.html.

Simple Logging Facade for Java [SLF4J]

SLF4J serves as a simple facade or abstraction for various logging frameworks, for example, java.util.logging, log4j and logback, allowing the end user to plug in the desired logging framework at deployment time.

This can be downloaded from http://www.slf4j.org/download.html.

Struts 2.x.x

The Struts 2.x.x framework. This can be downloaded from http://struts.apache.org/download.cgi.

REMINDER

All of these library files are available in this book's accompanying CDROM.

A Dedicated Library Directory

While creating Customer application, **Use Dedicated Folder for Storing Libraries** option was selected, which means, that whichever library file added to Customer application will be stored in that lib directory of the application, by default.

Adding Library Files To The Application

Follow the steps shown in the *Chapter 05: Installing And Setting Up Struts 2*, to add the following library files to Customer Application:

Hibernate

- From **<Drive:>/hibernate-release-4.1.6.Final/lib/required** directory:
    - antlr-2.7.7.jar
    - dom4j-1.6.1.jar
    - hibernate-commons-annotations-4.0.1.FINAL.jar
    - hibernate-core-4.1.6.FINAL.jar
    - hibernate-jpa-2.0-api-1.0.1.FINAL.jar
    - javassist-3.15.0.GA.jar
    - jboss-logging-3.1.0.GA.jar
    - jboss-transaction-api_1.1_spec-1.0.0.FINAL.jar
    - commons-collections-3.1.jar
    - dom4j-1.6.1.jar
- From **<Drive:>/hibernate-release-4.1.6.Final/lib/jpa** directory:
    - hibernate-entitymanager-4.1.6.Final.jar

Struts

- From **<Drive:>/struts-2.3.4.1/lib** directory:
    - asm-3.3.jar
    - asm-commons-3.3.jar
    - asm-tree-3.3.jar
    - commons-beanutils-1.8.0.jar
    - commons-collections-3.1.jar

- commons-fileupload-1.2.2.jar
- commons-io-2.0.1.jar
- commons-lang-2.4.jar
- commons-lang3-3.1.jar
- commons-logging-1.1.1.jar
- freemarker-2.3.19.jar
- ognl-3.0.5.jar
- struts2-convention-plugin-2.3.4.1.jar
- struts2-core-2.3.4.1.jar
- struts2-dojo-plugin-2.3.4.1.jar
- struts2-pell-multipart-plugin-2.3.4.1.jar
- xwork-core-2.3.4.1.jar

MySQL Connector/J

- From **<Drive:>/mysql-connector-java-5.1.21** directory:
    - mysql-connector-java-5.1.21-bin.jar

Display Tags

- From **<Drive:>/displaytag-1.2/** directory:
    - displaytag-1.2.jar
    - displaytag-export-poi-1.2.jar
    - displaytag-portlet-1.2.jar

SLF4J

- From **<Drive:>/ slf4j-1.6.4/** directory:
    - slf4j-api-1.6.4.jar
    - slf4j-simple-1.6.4.jar

Chapter 25

SECTION V: APPLICATION DEVELOPMENT USING STRUTS 2.X.X AND HIBERNATE 4

Hibernate And Struts Configuration

Since Hibernate is the ORM of choice for this application, it is necessary to have a configuration file that defines connection and the mapping resources.

Using NetBeans IDE, create an XML based configuration file named hibernate.cfg.xml by following the steps shown in *Chapter 13: Integrating Hibernate With Struts 2*.

Now hibernate.cfg.xml will hold the following code spec:

```
1  <?xml version="1.0" encoding="UTF-8"?>
2  <!DOCTYPE hibernate-configuration PUBLIC "-//Hibernate/Hibernate Configuration DTD //EN" "http://www.hibernate.org/dtd/hibernate-configuration-3.0.dtd">
3  <hibernate-configuration>
4    <session-factory>
5      <property name="hibernate.dialect">org.hibernate.dialect.MySQLDialect</property>
```

354   Struts 2 For Beginners

```
6    <property
     name="hibernate.connection.driver_class">com.mysql.jdbc.Driver</property>
7    <property
     name="hibernate.connection.url">jdbc:mysql://localhost:3306/CustomerDB?zeroDat
     eTimeBehavior=convertToNull</property>
8    <property name="hibernate.connection.username">root</property>
9    <property name="hibernate.connection.password">123456</property>
10   <property name="hibernate.default_catalog">CustomerDB</property>
11   <!-- Mapping class will be placed here. -->
12   </session-factory>
13 </hibernate-configuration>
```

This file informs Hibernate to use **MySQL** as the **dialect** and **CustomerDB** as the **database**.

The resource classes will be inserted later.

com.sharanamvaishali.development.utility Package

Hibernate Utility Class

SessionFactory is considered one of the most important components in Hibernate API. It is responsible for the generation of Hibernate Session objects that are required to interact with database.

The standard and the most recommended practice is to have a helper class called **HibernateUtil** that manages SessionFactory component for the entire application.

Using the NetBeans IDE, add **Java class** [as shown in diagram 25.1.1] named **HibernateUtil.java** under a **package** called **com.sharanamvaishali.development.utility** as shown in diagram 25.1.2.

Diagram 25.1.1: Selecting the option Java Class...

Hibernate And Struts Configuration 355

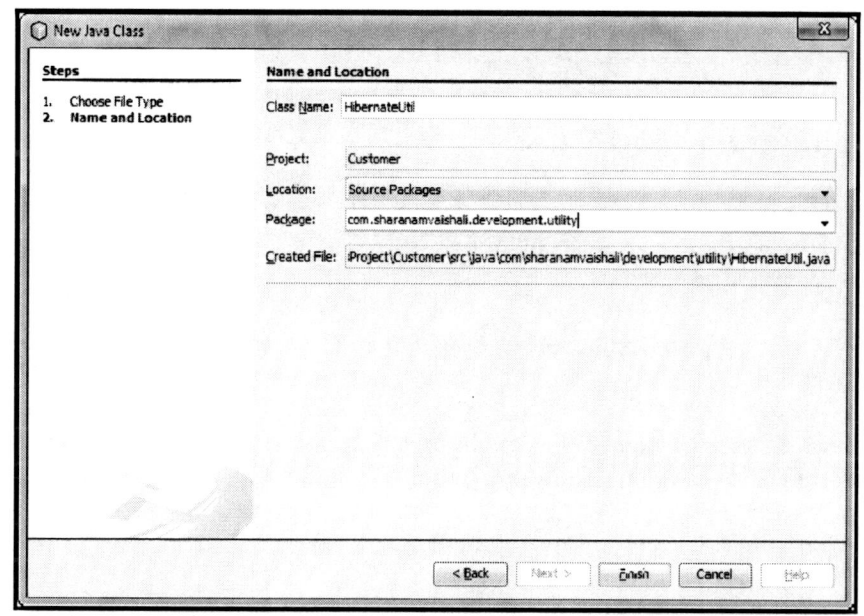

Diagram 25.1.2: Creating HibernateUtil class

HibernateUtil.java is created under the package com.sharanamvaishali.development.utility.

Key in the following code spec in HibernateUtil.java:

```
1  package com.sharanamvaishali.development.utility;
2
3  import org.hibernate.HibernateException;
4  import org.hibernate.Session;
5  import org.hibernate.SessionFactory;
6  import org.hibernate.cfg.Configuration;
7  import org.hibernate.service.ServiceRegistry;
8  import org.hibernate.service.ServiceRegistryBuilder;
9
10 public class HibernateUtil {
11     private static SessionFactory sessionFactory;
12     private static ServiceRegistry serviceRegistry;
13
14     public static SessionFactory configureSessionFactory() throws HibernateException {
15         Configuration configuration = new Configuration();
16         configuration.configure();
17         serviceRegistry = new
           ServiceRegistryBuilder().applySettings(configuration.getProperties()).buildService
           Registry();
18         sessionFactory = configuration.buildSessionFactory(serviceRegistry);
19         return sessionFactory;
20     }
21
22     public static Session getSession() {
```

```
23          return sessionFactory.openSession();
24     }
25 }
```

Development Support Class

This application uses AJAX to retrieve States [for a country] and Cities [for a state], which requires an HttpServletResponse to obtain a PrintWriter. This PrintWriter will be used to return a list of states and cities.

To make available HttpServletResponse, an action class is required with appropriate getter and setter methods.

Create Java class named DevelopmentSupport.java under the package com.sharanamvaishali.development.utility by following the steps shown above.

Key in the following code spec in DevelopmentSupport.java:

```
1  package com.sharanamvaishali.development.utility;
2
3  import com.opensymphony.xwork2.ActionSupport;
4  import javax.servlet.http.HttpServletRequest;
5  import javax.servlet.http.HttpServletResponse;
6  import javax.servlet.http.HttpSession;
7  import org.apache.struts2.ServletActionContext;
8  import org.apache.struts2.interceptor.ServletRequestAware;
9  import org.apache.struts2.interceptor.ServletResponseAware;
10
11 public class DevelopmentSupport extends ActionSupport implements ServletRequestAware, ServletResponseAware {
12     private static final long serialVersionUID = 3515078654701117288L;
13     private HttpServletRequest request;
14     private HttpServletResponse response;
15
16     public HttpServletRequest getRequest() {
17         if (request == null) {
18             request = ServletActionContext.getRequest();
19         }
20         return request;
21     }
22     @Override
23     public void setServletRequest(HttpServletRequest request) {
24         this.request = request;
25     }
26
27     public HttpServletResponse getResponse() {
28         if (response == null) {
29             response = ServletActionContext.getResponse();
30         }
```

```
31          return response;
32      }
33      @Override
34      public void setServletResponse(HttpServletResponse response) {
35          this.response = response;
36      }
37
38      public HttpSession getSession() {
39          return getRequest().getSession();
40      }
41  }
```

Struts 2 Dispatcher Class

To integrate this application with Hibernate, a custom Struts 2 dispatcher is created. This class extends StrutsPrepareAndExecuteFilter dispatcher.

Struts2Dispatcher:

❑ Executes the super classes's **init()**

❑ Overrides **init()** to create a session factory

This custom class enables the Hibernate support in the application.

Create Java class named Struts2Dispatcher.java under the package com.sharanamvaishali.development.utility by following the steps shown above.

Key in the following code spec in Struts2Dispatcher.java:

```
1   package com.sharanamvaishali.development.utility;
2
3   import javax.servlet.FilterConfig;
4   import javax.servlet.ServletException;
5   import org.apache.struts2.dispatcher.ng.filter.StrutsPrepareAndExecuteFilter;
6   import org.hibernate.HibernateException;
7
8   public class Struts2Dispatcher extends StrutsPrepareAndExecuteFilter {
9       @Override
10      public void init(FilterConfig filterConfig) throws ServletException {
11          super.init(filterConfig);
12          try {
13              HibernateUtil.configureSessionFactory();
14              System.out.println("Application successfully initialized.");
15          } catch (HibernateException e) {
16              throw new ServletException();
17          }
18      }
19  }
```

Chapter 26

SECTION V: APPLICATION DEVELOPMENT USING STRUTS 2.X.X AND HIBERNATE 4

POJOs And DAOs

This application uses the following tables:
- City
- State
- Country
- Customer

Customer data entry form holds drop down list boxes where the user can choose a country, state and a city to define the customer's address.

Appropriate POJO that represent these tables have to be created.

All the code spec that allows performing database operations such as Create, Read, Update, and Delete will be placed in the DAO.

com.sharanamvaishali.development.domain Package

City

Create a Java class called **City** under the package **com.sharanamvaishali.development.domain** with the following code spec:

```
1  package com.sharanamvaishali.development.domain;
2
3  import javax.persistence.CascadeType;
4  import javax.persistence.Column;
5  import javax.persistence.Entity;
6  import javax.persistence.GeneratedValue;
7  import javax.persistence.Id;
8  import javax.persistence.JoinColumn;
9  import javax.persistence.ManyToOne;
10 import javax.persistence.Table;
11
12 @Entity
13 @Table(name="CITY")
14 public class City implements java.io.Serializable {
15    @Id
16    @GeneratedValue
17    @Column(name="CITYNO")
18    private Integer cityNo;
19    @Column(name="CITYNAME")
20    private String cityName;
21    @ManyToOne(cascade= CascadeType.ALL)
22    @JoinColumn(name="stateNo")
23    private State state;
24
25    public City() {
26    }
27
28    public City(State state, String cityName) {
29       this.state = state;
30       this.cityName = cityName;
31    }
32
33    public Integer getCityNo() {
34       return cityNo;
35    }
36    public void setCityNo(Integer cityNo) {
37       this.cityNo = cityNo;
38    }
39
40    public String getCityName() {
41       return cityName;
42    }
43    public void setCityName(String cityName) {
44       this.cityName = cityName;
```

```
45      }
46
47      public State getState() {
48          return state;
49      }
50      public void setState(State state) {
51          this.state = state;
52      }
53  }
```

Explanation:

City POJO is connected to the database table named **City**.

@ManyToOne

@ManyToOne is used to create the <u>many-to-one relationship</u> between the City and State entities. The **cascade** attribute is used to cascade the required operations to the associated entity. If the cascade attribute is set to **CascadeType.ALL** then all the operations will be cascaded. For instance when a City object is saved, the associated State object will also be saved automatically.

@JoinColumn

@JoinColumn indicate the owning side of the relationship, it is responsible for updating the database column. It will create **StateNo** column on the database table City.

State

Create a Java class called **State** under the package **com.sharanamvaishali.development.domain** with the following code spec:

```
1   package com.sharanamvaishali.development.domain;
2
3   import java.util.HashSet;
4   import java.util.Set;
5   import javax.persistence.CascadeType;
6   import javax.persistence.Column;
7   import javax.persistence.Entity;
8   import javax.persistence.FetchType;
9   import javax.persistence.GeneratedValue;
10  import javax.persistence.Id;
11  import javax.persistence.JoinColumn;
12  import javax.persistence.ManyToOne;
13  import javax.persistence.OneToMany;
14  import javax.persistence.Table;
15
16  @Entity
```

```java
17  @Table(name="STATE")
18  public class State implements java.io.Serializable {
19      @Id
20      @GeneratedValue
21      @Column(name="STATENO")
22      private Integer stateNo;
23      @Column(name="STATENAME")
24      private String stateName;
25      @ManyToOne(cascade= CascadeType.ALL)
26      @JoinColumn(name="countryNo")
27      private Country country;
28      @OneToMany(cascade= CascadeType.ALL, mappedBy="state", fetch=
        FetchType.LAZY)
29      private Set<City> cities = new HashSet<City>(0);
30
31      public State() {
32      }
33
34      public State(Country country, String stateName, Set<City> cities) {
35          this.country = country;
36          this.stateName = stateName;
37          this.cities = cities;
38      }
39
40      public Integer getStateNo() {
41          return stateNo;
42      }
43      public void setStateNo(Integer stateNo) {
44          this.stateNo = stateNo;
45      }
46
47      public String getStateName() {
48          return stateName;
49      }
50      public void setStateName(String stateName) {
51          this.stateName = stateName;
52      }
53
54      public Country getCountry() {
55          return country;
56      }
57      public void setCountry(Country country) {
58          this.country = country;
59      }
60
61      public Set<City> getCities() {
62          return cities;
63      }
64      public void setCities(Set<City> cities) {
65          this.cities = cities;
66      }
67  }
```

Explanation:

State POJO is connected to the database table named **State**.

@OneToMany

@OneToMany is used to create the <u>one-to-many relationship</u> between the City and State entities. It indicates that one state can have multiple cities.

The **mappedBy** attribute refers to the property name of the association of the owner side. In this case is **state**, which was declared in **City** entity:

State Entity
28   @OneToMany(cascade= CascadeType.ALL, mappedBy="state", fetch= FetchType.LAZY)
29   private Set<City> cities = new HashSet<City>(0);

City Entity
21   @ManyToOne(cascade= CascadeType.ALL)
22   @JoinColumn(name="stateNo")
23   private State state;

The **fetch** attribute is used to choose between Outer-Join fetching or Sequential SELECT fetching. If the fetch attribute is set to **FetchType.LAZY**, then it triggers a SELECT when the associated object is accessed for the first time.

Country

Create a Java class called **Country** under the package **com.sharanamvaishali.development.domain** with the following code spec:

```
1  package com.sharanamvaishali.development.domain;
2
3  import java.util.HashSet;
4  import java.util.Set;
5  import javax.persistence.CascadeType;
6  import javax.persistence.Column;
7  import javax.persistence.Entity;
8  import javax.persistence.FetchType;
9  import javax.persistence.GeneratedValue;
10 import javax.persistence.Id;
11 import javax.persistence.OneToMany;
12 import javax.persistence.Table;
13
14 @Entity
15 @Table(name="COUNTRY")
16 public class Country implements java.io.Serializable {
```

```
17    @Id
18    @GeneratedValue
19    @Column(name="COUNTRYNO")
20    private Integer countryNo;
21    @Column(name="COUNTRYNAME")
22    private String countryName;
23    @OneToMany(cascade= CascadeType.ALL, mappedBy="country", fetch=
      FetchType.LAZY)
24    private Set<State> states = new HashSet<State>(0);
25
26    public Country() {
27    }
28
29    public Country(String countryName, Set<State> states) {
30        this.countryName = countryName;
31        this.states = states;
32    }
33
34    public Integer getCountryNo() {
35        return countryNo;
36    }
37    public void setCountryNo(Integer countryNo) {
38        this.countryNo = countryNo;
39    }
40
41    public String getCountryName() {
42        return countryName;
43    }
44    public void setCountryName(String countryName) {
45        this.countryName = countryName;
46    }
47
48    public Set<State> getStates() {
49        return states;
50    }
51    public void setStates(Set<State> states) {
52        this.states = states;
53    }
54 }
```

Explanation:

Country POJO is connected to the database table named **Country**.

Customer

Create a Java class called **Customer** under the package **com.sharanamvaishali.development.domain** with the following code spec:

```
1  package com.sharanamvaishali.development.domain;
2
3  import javax.persistence.Column;
```

```java
import javax.persistence.Entity;
import javax.persistence.GeneratedValue;
import javax.persistence.Id;
import javax.persistence.Table;

@Entity
@Table(name="CUSTOMER")
public class Customer implements java.io.Serializable {
    @Id
    @GeneratedValue
    @Column(name="CUSTOMERNO")
    private Integer customerNo;
    @Column(name="NAME")
    private String name;
    @Column(name="ADDRESS")
    private String address;
    @Column(name="CITY")
    private String city;
    @Column(name="STATE")
    private String state;
    @Column(name="COUNTRY")
    private String country;
    @Column(name="EMAIL")
    private String email;
    @Column(name="MOBILE")
    private String mobile;
    @Column(name="TELEPHONE")
    private String telephone;
    @Column(name="FAX")
    private String fax;

    public Customer() {
    }

    public Customer(String name, String address, String city, String state, String country, String email, String mobile, String telephone, String fax) {
        this.name = name;
        this.address = address;
        this.city = city;
        this.state = state;
        this.country = country;
        this.email = email;
        this.mobile = mobile;
        this.telephone = telephone;
        this.fax = fax;
    }

    public Integer getCustomerNo() {
        return customerNo;
    }
    public void setCustomerNo(Integer customerNo) {
        this.customerNo = customerNo;
    }
```

```java
 56
 57    public String getName() {
 58        return name;
 59    }
 60    public void setName(String name) {
 61        this.name = name;
 62    }
 63
 64    public String getAddress() {
 65        return address;
 66    }
 67    public void setAddress(String address) {
 68        this.address = address;
 69    }
 70
 71    public String getCity() {
 72        return city;
 73    }
 74    public void setCity(String city) {
 75        this.city = city;
 76    }
 77
 78    public String getEmail() {
 79        return email;
 80    }
 81    public void setEmail(String email) {
 82        this.email = email;
 83    }
 84
 85    public String getState() {
 86        return state;
 87    }
 88    public void setState(String state) {
 89        this.state = state;
 90    }
 91
 92    public String getCountry() {
 93        return country;
 94    }
 95    public void setCountry(String country) {
 96        this.country = country;
 97    }
 98
 99    public String getMobile() {
100        return mobile;
101    }
102    public void setMobile(String mobile) {
103        this.mobile = mobile;
104    }
105
106    public String getTelephone() {
107        return telephone;
108    }
```

```
109      public void setTelephone(String telephone) {
110          this.telephone = telephone;
111      }
112
113      public String getFax() {
114          return fax;
115      }
116      public void setFax(String fax) {
117          this.fax = fax;
118      }
119  }
```

Explanation:

Customer POJO is connected to the database table named **Customer**.

com.sharanamvaishali.development.dao Package

City

CityDAO

Create an interface named **CityDAO.java** under **com.sharanamvaishali.development.dao** by following the steps shown in *Chapter 13: Integrating Hibernate With Struts 2*.

Key in the following code spec in CityDAO.java:

```
1  package com.sharanamvaishali.development.dao;
2
3  import com.sharanamvaishali.development.domain.City;
4  import java.util.List;
5
6  public interface CityDAO {
7      public List<City> listCity();
8      public List<City> listCityByState(Integer stateNo);
9  }
```

CityDAOImpl

Create a Java class named **CityDAOImpl.java** under **com.sharanamvaishali.development.dao** by following the steps shown above.

Key in the following code spec in CityDAOImpl.java:

```
1  package com.sharanamvaishali.development.dao;
2
3  import com.sharanamvaishali.development.domain.City;
4  import com.sharanamvaishali.development.utility.HibernateUtil;
5  import java.util.List;
```

368   Struts 2 For Beginners

```
 6  import org.hibernate.Session;
 7
 8  public class CityDAOImpl implements CityDAO {
 9      Session session = HibernateUtil.getSession();
10
11      @Override
12      public List<City> listCity() {
13          return session.createQuery("FROM City").list();
14      }
15
16      @Override
17      public List<City> listCityByState(Integer stateNo) {
18          return session.createQuery("SELECT c FROM City c WHERE c.state.stateNo = :stateNo").setParameter("stateNo", stateNo).list();
19      }
20  }
```

Explanation:

CityDAOImpl class implements **CityDAO**.

This class provides the following methods that allow database operations:

listCity()

listCity() fires an HQL SELECT query on the City object and returns the query result as a list.

listCityByState()

listCityByState() accepts StateNo, fires an HQL SELECT query with a condition using a WHERE clause on the City object and returns the query result as a list

State

StateDAO

Create an interface named **StateDAO.java** under **com.sharanamvaishali.development.dao** by following the steps shown in *Chapter 13: Integrating Hibernate With Struts 2*.

Key in the following code spec in StateDAO.java:

```
1  package com.sharanamvaishali.development.dao;
2
3  import com.sharanamvaishali.development.domain.State;
4  import java.util.List;
5
6  public interface StateDAO {
7      public List<State> listState();
```

```
8     public List<State> listStateByCountry(Integer countryNo);
9 }
```

StateDAOImpl

Create a Java class named **StateDAOImpl.java** under **com.sharanamvaishali.development.dao** by following the steps shown above.

Key in the following code spec in StateDAOImpl.java:

```
1  package com.sharanamvaishali.development.dao;
2
3  import com.sharanamvaishali.development.domain.State;
4  import com.sharanamvaishali.development.utility.HibernateUtil;
5  import java.util.List;
6  import org.hibernate.Session;
7
8  public class StateDAOImpl implements StateDAO {
9    Session session = HibernateUtil.getSession();
10
11   @Override
12   public List<State> listState() {
13     return session.createQuery("FROM State").list();
14   }
15
16   @Override
17   public List<State> listStateByCountry(Integer countryNo) {
18     return session.createQuery("SELECT s FROM State s WHERE s.country.countryNo
          = :countryNo").setParameter("countryNo", countryNo).list();
19   }
20 }
```

Explanation:

StateDAOImpl class implements **StateDAO**.

This class provides the following methods that allow database operations:

listState()

listState() fires an HQL SELECT query on the State object and returns the query result as a list.

listStateByCountry()

listStateByCountry() accepts CountryNo, fires an HQL SELECT query with a condition using a WHERE clause on the State object and returns the query result as a list

Country

CountryDAO

Create an interface named **CountryDAO.java** under **com.sharanamvaishali.development.dao** by following the steps shown in *Chapter 13: Integrating Hibernate With Struts 2*.

Key in the following code spec in CountryDAO.java:

```
1  package com.sharanamvaishali.development.dao;
2
3  import com.sharanamvaishali.development.domain.Country;
4  import java.util.List;
5
6  public interface CountryDAO {
7      public List<Country> listCountry();
8  }
```

CountryDAOImpl

Create a Java class named **CountryDAOImpl.java** under **com.sharanamvaishali.development.dao** by following the steps shown above.

Key in the following code spec in CountryDAOImpl.java:

```
1  package com.sharanamvaishali.development.dao;
2
3  import com.sharanamvaishali.development.domain.Country;
4  import com.sharanamvaishali.development.utility.HibernateUtil;
5  import java.util.List;
6  import org.hibernate.Session;
7
8  public class CountryDAOImpl implements CountryDAO {
9      Session session = HibernateUtil.getSession();
10
11     @Override
12     public List<Country> listCountry() {
13         session.beginTransaction();
14         return session.createQuery("FROM Country").list();
15     }
16 }
```

Explanation:

CountryDAOImpl class implements **CountryDAO**.

This class provides the following methods that allow database operations:

listCountry()

listCountry() fires an HQL SELECT query on the Country object and returns the query result as a list.

Customer

CustomerDAO

Create an interface named **CustomerDAO.java** under **com.sharanamvaishali.development.dao** by following the steps shown in *Chapter 13: Integrating Hibernate With Struts 2*.

Key in the following code spec in CustomerDAO.java:

```
1   package com.sharanamvaishali.development.dao;
2
3   import com.sharanamvaishali.development.domain.Customer;
4   import java.util.List;
5
6   public interface CustomerDAO {
7       public void saveCustomer(Customer customer);
8       public void deleteCustomer(Customer customer);
9       public List<Customer> listCustomer();
10      public Customer listCustomerByCustomerNo(Integer customerNo);
11  }
```

CustomerDAOImpl

Create a Java class named **CustomerDAOImpl.java** under **com.sharanamvaishali.development.dao** by following the steps shown above.

Key in the following code spec in CustomerDAOImpl.java:

```
1   package com.sharanamvaishali.development.dao;
2
3   import com.sharanamvaishali.development.domain.Customer;
4   import com.sharanamvaishali.development.utility.HibernateUtil;
5   import java.util.List;
6   import org.hibernate.Session;
7   import org.hibernate.Transaction;
8
9   public class CustomerDAOImpl implements CustomerDAO {
10      Session session = HibernateUtil.getSession();
11      Transaction transaction;
12
13      @Override
14      public void saveCustomer(Customer customer) {
```

```
15      try {
16          transaction = session.beginTransaction();
17          session.merge(customer);
18          transaction.commit();
19      } catch(RuntimeException e) {
20          if (customer != null) {
21              transaction.rollback();
22          }
23          throw e;
24      }
25  }
26
27  @Override
28  public void deleteCustomer(Customer customer) {
29      transaction = session.beginTransaction();
30      session.delete(customer);
31      transaction.commit();
32  }
33
34  @Override
35  public List<Customer> listCustomer() {
36      return session.createQuery("SELECT c FROM Customer c").list();
37  }
38
39  @Override
40  public Customer listCustomerByCustomerNo(Integer customerNo) {
41      return (Customer) session.load(Customer.class, customerNo);
42  }
43 }
```

Explanation:

CountryDAOImpl class implements **CountryDAO**.

This class provides the following methods that allow database operations:

saveCustomer()

saveCustomer() accepts an object of the **Customer** POJO. saveCustomer() when invoked, begins a transaction, saves the object it receives using **merge()** of Session and finally commits the transaction.

merge() of Session saves as well as updates the Customer details entered by the user.

If the Customer detail is found to be empty then the transaction is roll backed.

POJOs And DAOs

deleteCustomer()

deleteCustomer() accepts an object of the **Customer** POJO. deleteCustomer() when invoked, begins a transaction, deletes the object it receives using **delete()** of Session and finally commits the transaction.

listCustomer()

listCustomer() fires an HQL SELECT query on the Customer object and returns the query result as a list.

listCustomerByCustomerNo()

listCustomerByCustomerNo() accepts CustomerNo, fires an HQL SELECT query with a condition using a WHERE clause on the Customer object and returns the query result as a list.

Mapping POJOs In Hibernate Configuration

Add the following mapping class in **hibernate.cfg.xml**:

```
1  <?xml version="1.0" encoding="UTF-8"?>
2  <!DOCTYPE hibernate-configuration PUBLIC "-//Hibernate/Hibernate Configuration DTD
   //EN" "http://www.hibernate.org/dtd/hibernate-configuration-3.0.dtd">
3  <hibernate-configuration>
4    <session-factory>
5      <property name="hibernate.dialect">org.hibernate.dialect.MySQLDialect</property>
6      <property name="hibernate.connection.driver_class">com.mysql.jdbc.Driver</property>
7      <property name="hibernate.connection.url">jdbc:mysql://localhost:3306/CustomerDB?zeroDateTimeBehavior=convertToNull</property>
8      <property name="hibernate.connection.username">root</property>
9      <property name="hibernate.connection.password">123456</property>
10     <property name="hibernate.default_catalog">CustomerDB</property>
11     <mapping class="com.sharanamvaishali.development.domain.State" />
12     <mapping class="com.sharanamvaishali.development.domain.Country" />
13     <mapping class="com.sharanamvaishali.development.domain.City" />
14     <mapping class="com.sharanamvaishali.development.domain.Customer" />
15   </session-factory>
16 </hibernate-configuration>
```

Chapter 27

SECTION V: APPLICATION DEVELOPMENT USING STRUTS 2.X.X AND HIBERNATE 4

Action Classes

AjaxAction

This application uses Ajax to retrieve States [for a Country] and Cities [for a State]. This class holds the code spec that helps retrieve states and cities.

Create **AjaxAction.java** under **com.sharanamvaishali.development.action** and key in the following code spec:

```
1  package com.sharanamvaishali.development.action;
2
3  import com.opensymphony.xwork2.Action;
4  import com.sharanamvaishali.development.dao.CityDAO;
5  import com.sharanamvaishali.development.dao.CityDAOImpl;
6  import com.sharanamvaishali.development.dao.StateDAO;
7  import com.sharanamvaishali.development.dao.StateDAOImpl;
```

```java
 8   import com.sharanamvaishali.development.domain.City;
 9   import com.sharanamvaishali.development.domain.State;
10   import com.sharanamvaishali.development.utility.DevelopmentSupport;
11   import java.io.PrintWriter;
12   import java.util.List;
13
14   public class AjaxAction extends DevelopmentSupport {
15       private String outstr = "";
16       private String searchValue;
17       private List<State> stateList = null;
18       private List<City> cityList = null;
19       private StateDAO stateDAO = new StateDAOImpl();
20       private CityDAO cityDAO = new CityDAOImpl();
21
22       public String getOutstr() {
23           return outstr;
24       }
25       public void setOutstr(String outstr) {
26           this.outstr = outstr;
27       }
28
29       public String getSearchValue() {
30           return searchValue;
31       }
32       public void setSearchValue(String searchValue) {
33           this.searchValue = searchValue;
34       }
35
36       public String getStateList() throws Exception {
37           PrintWriter out = getResponse().getWriter();
38           if (searchValue.length() > 0) {
39               try {
40                   stateList = stateDAO.listStateByCountry(Integer.parseInt(searchValue));
41                   if (stateList != null && !stateList.isEmpty()) {
42                       for (State state : stateList) {
43                           Integer val = state.getStateNo();
44                           String str = state.getStateName();
45                           if (outstr.length() == 0) {
46                               outstr = val + "|" + str;
47                           } else {
48                               outstr += "," + val + "|" + str;
49                           }
50                       }
51                   }
52               } catch (Exception e) {
53               }
54               out.print(outstr);
55               out.flush();
56               out.close();
57           }
58           return Action.SUCCESS;
59       }
60
61       public String getCityList() throws Exception {
```

```
62              PrintWriter out = getResponse().getWriter();
63              if (searchValue.length() > 0) {
64                  try {
65                      cityList = cityDAO.listCityByState(Integer.parseInt(searchValue));
66                      if (cityList != null && !cityList.isEmpty()) {
67                          for (City city : cityList) {
68                              Integer val = city.getCityNo();
69                              String str = city.getCityName();
70                              if (outstr.length() == 0) {
71                                  outstr = val + "|" + str;
72                              } else {
73                                  outstr += "," + val + "|" + str;
74                              }
75                          }
76                      }
77                  }
78                  catch (Exception e) {
79                  }
80                  out.print(outstr);
81                  out.flush();
82                  out.close();
83              }
84              return Action.SUCCESS;
85          }
86      }
```

Explanation:

getStateList()

- Receives CountryNo as a request parameter via Ajax [searchValue]
- Passes CountryNo to StateDAO object's listStateByCountry()
    - listStateByCountry() returns a list of states for that country
- Prints the list to PrintWriter for Ajax to receive

getCityList()

- Receives StateNo as a request parameter via Ajax [searchValue]
- Passes StateNo to CityDAO object's listCityByState()
    - listCityByState() returns a list of cities for that state
- Prints the list to PrintWriter for Ajax to receive

CustomerIndexAction

Customer data entry form when invoked requires the following initialization:

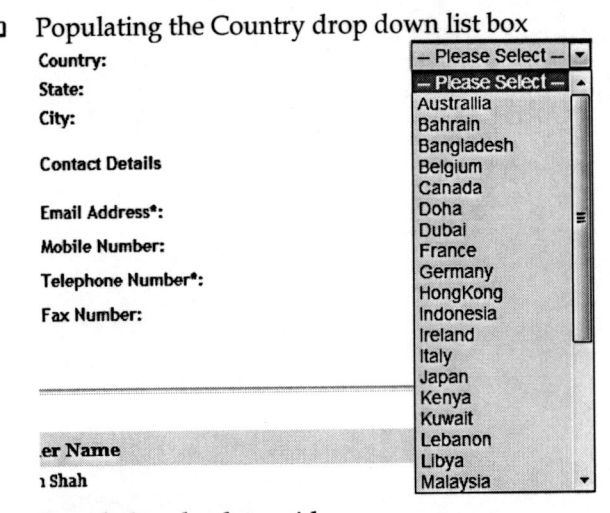

- Populating the Country drop down list box

- Populating the data grid

This class holds the code spec that helps retrieve these.

Create CustomerIndexAction.java under com.sharanamvaishali.development.action and key in the following code spec:

```
1  package com.sharanamvaishali.development.action;
2
3  import com.sharanamvaishali.development.dao.CountryDAO;
4  import com.sharanamvaishali.development.dao.CountryDAOImpl;
5  import com.sharanamvaishali.development.dao.CustomerDAO;
6  import com.sharanamvaishali.development.dao.CustomerDAOImpl;
7  import com.sharanamvaishali.development.domain.City;
8  import com.sharanamvaishali.development.domain.Country;
9  import com.sharanamvaishali.development.domain.Customer;
10 import com.sharanamvaishali.development.domain.State;
11 import com.sharanamvaishali.development.utility.DevelopmentSupport;
12 import java.util.ArrayList;
13 import java.util.List;
14
15 public class CustomerIndexAction extends DevelopmentSupport {
16     private List<Country> countryList = new ArrayList<Country>();
17     private List<State> stateList = new ArrayList<State>();
18     private List<City> cityList = new ArrayList<City>();
19     private List<Customer> customerList = new ArrayList<Customer>();
20     private CountryDAO countryDAO = new CountryDAOImpl();
```

```java
21      private CustomerDAO customerDAO = new CustomerDAOImpl();
22
23      public List<Country> getCountryList() {
24          return countryList;
25      }
26      public void setCountryList(List<Country> countryList) {
27          this.countryList = countryList;
28      }
29
30      public List<State> getStateList() {
31          return stateList;
32      }
33      public void setStateList(List<State> stateList) {
34          this.stateList = stateList;
35      }
36
37      public List<City> getCityList() {
38          return cityList;
39      }
40      public void setCityList(List<City> cityList) {
41          this.cityList = cityList;
42      }
43
44      public List<Customer> getCustomerList() {
45          return customerList;
46      }
47      public void setCustomerList(List<Customer> customerList) {
48          this.customerList = customerList;
49      }
50
51      @Override
52      public String execute() throws Exception {
53          countryList = countryDAO.listCountry();
54          customerList = customerDAO.listCustomer();
55          return SUCCESS;
56      }
57  }
```

Explanation:

This Action class is invoked when Customer data entry form [JSP] appears. **execute()** uses the methods of **CountryDAO** and **CustomerDAO** classes to retrieve the required data.

This data is made available the JSP using getter/setter methods.

CustomerAction

This action class is invoked by Customer data entry form to perform database operations when the user clicks Save, Edit, Delete or Clear.

Struts 2 For Beginners

Create **CustomerAction.java** under **com.sharanamvaishali.development.action** and key in the following code spec:

```
1  package com.sharanamvaishali.development.action;
2
3  import com.sharanamvaishali.development.dao.CityDAO;
4  import com.sharanamvaishali.development.dao.CityDAOImpl;
5  import com.sharanamvaishali.development.dao.CountryDAO;
6  import com.sharanamvaishali.development.dao.CountryDAOImpl;
7  import com.sharanamvaishali.development.dao.CustomerDAO;
8  import com.sharanamvaishali.development.dao.CustomerDAOImpl;
9  import com.sharanamvaishali.development.dao.StateDAO;
10 import com.sharanamvaishali.development.dao.StateDAOImpl;
11 import com.sharanamvaishali.development.domain.City;
12 import com.sharanamvaishali.development.domain.Country;
13 import com.sharanamvaishali.development.domain.Customer;
14 import com.sharanamvaishali.development.domain.State;
15 import com.sharanamvaishali.development.utility.DevelopmentSupport;
16 import java.util.ArrayList;
17 import java.util.List;
18
19 public class CustomerAction extends DevelopmentSupport {
20     private String customerNo;
21     private String editFlag;
22     private Customer customer;
23     private List<Customer> customerList = new ArrayList<Customer>();
24     private List<Country> countryList = new ArrayList<Country>();
25     private List<State> stateList = new ArrayList<State>();
26     private List<City> cityList = new ArrayList<City>();
27     private CountryDAO countryDAO = new CountryDAOImpl();
28     private CustomerDAO customerDAO = new CustomerDAOImpl();
29     private StateDAO stateDAO = new StateDAOImpl();
30     private CityDAO cityDAO = new CityDAOImpl();
31
32     public String getCustomerNo() {
33         return customerNo;
34     }
35     public void setCustomerNo(String customerNo) {
36         this.customerNo = customerNo;
37     }
38
39     public String getEditFlag() {
40         return editFlag;
41     }
42     public void setEditFlag(String editFlag) {
43         this.editFlag = editFlag;
44     }
45
46     public Customer getCustomer() {
47         return customer;
48     }
49     public void setCustomer(Customer customer) {
50         this.customer = customer;
```

```java
51      }
52
53      public List<Customer> getCustomerList() {
54          return customerList;
55      }
56      public void setCustomerList(List<Customer> customerList) {
57          this.customerList = customerList;
58      }
59
60      public List<Country> getCountryList() {
61          return countryList;
62      }
63      public void setCountryList(List<Country> countryList) {
64          this.countryList = countryList;
65      }
66
67      public List<State> getStateList() {
68          return stateList;
69      }
70      public void setStateList(List<State> stateList) {
71          this.stateList = stateList;
72      }
73
74      public List<City> getCityList() {
75          return cityList;
76      }
77      public void setCityList(List<City> cityList) {
78          this.cityList = cityList;
79      }
80
81      @Override
82      public String execute() throws Exception {
83          if (editFlag != null && editFlag.equals("Y")) {
84              customer.setCustomerNo(Integer.parseInt(customerNo));
85              customerDAO.saveCustomer(customer);
86          }
87          else {
88              customerDAO.saveCustomer(customer);
89          }
90          customer = new Customer();
91          countryList = countryDAO.listCountry();
92          customerList = customerDAO.listCustomer();
93          return SUCCESS;
94      }
95
96      public String edit() {
97          countryList = countryDAO.listCountry();
98          customer =
              customerDAO.listCustomerByCustomerNo(Integer.parseInt(getCustomerNo()));
99          stateList =
              stateDAO.listStateByCountry(Integer.parseInt(customer.getCountry()));
100         cityList = cityDAO.listCityByState(Integer.parseInt(customer.getState()));
101         customerList = customerDAO.listCustomer();
```

```
102         return SUCCESS;
103     }
104
105     public String delete() {
106         countryList = countryDAO.listCountry();
107         Customer customerForDelete =
                customerDAO.listCustomerByCustomerNo(Integer.parseInt(getCustomerNo()));
108         customerDAO.deleteCustomer(customerForDelete);
109         customerList = customerDAO.listCustomer();
110         return SUCCESS;
111     }
112
113     public String clear() {
114         customer = new Customer();
115         editFlag = "";
116         customerNo = "";
117         countryList = countryDAO.listCountry();
118         customerList = customerDAO.listCustomer();
119         return SUCCESS;
120     }
121 }
```

Explanation:

This Action class is invoked when the user clicks Save, Edit, Delete or Clear.

execute()

When Save is clicked **execute()** is invoked. This method based on the value available in **editFlag**, determines whether to **update** or **insert**.

if (editFlag != null && editFlag.equals("Y")) {

If the mode is update:

The existing customer identity is set:

customer.setCustomerNo(Integer.parseInt(customerNo));

The customer object is updated using:

customerDAO.saveCustomer(customer);

If the mode is insert:

The customer object is saved using:

customerDAO.saveCustomer(customer);

Finally, the customer object is re-initialized and **countryList** and **customerList** List objects are re-populated to serve fresh data to the user.

edit()

Edit when clicked invokes edit(). This method populates the customer object with the appropriate customer's data based on CustomerNo.

customer = customerDAO.listCustomerByCustomerNo(Integer.parseInt(getCustomerNo()));

Country, State and City drop down List objects are populated based on the customer's country, state and city.

Finally, **customerList** object is re-populated to serve fresh data in the data grid.

delete()

Delete when clicked invokes delete(). This method populates the customer object with the appropriate customer's data based on CustomerNo.

Customer customerForDelete = customerDAO.listCustomerByCustomerNo(Integer.parseInt(getCustomerNo()));

Invokes the DAO object's method to delete that object:

customerDAO.deleteCustomer(customerForDelete);

Chapter 28

SECTION V: APPLICATION DEVELOPMENT USING STRUTS 2.X.X AND HIBERNATE 4

JSP, JavaScript And CSS

JSP

Now that all the required functionality is in place, let's build the view.

customer.jsp [/jsp]

- Holds a data entry form
    - To accept fresh customer data
    - To edit existing customer's data
- Holds a data grid
    - To view existing customers

- To initiate
  - Edit
  - Delete
- Holds a footer [/jsp/footer.jsp]

Technically, this JSP will allow:
- Insert
- Update
- Delete
- View

All these actions are submitted to the appropriate action class for processing.

These actions are bifurcated as:
- Application Initialization & View Operation [handled by CustomerIndexAction.java → execute()]
- Save Operation [handled by CustomerAction.java → execute()]
- Edit Operation [handled by CustomerAction.java → edit()]
- Delete Operation [handled by CustomerAction.java → delete()]

Once the action is determined, DAO object's methods are invoked to perform the appropriate database operation.

Create a JSP called **customer** under the directory **jsp** with the following code spec:

```
1  <%@page contentType="text/html" pageEncoding="UTF-8"%>
2  <%@ taglib prefix="s" uri="/struts-tags"%>
3  <%@ taglib uri="http://displaytag.sf.net" prefix="display"%>
4  <!DOCTYPE html>
5  <html>
6    <head>
7      <title>Customer Information</title>
8      <script language="JavaScript" type="text/JavaScript"
            src="../javaScript/jquery2.js"></script>
9      <script language="JavaScript" type="text/JavaScript"
            src="../javaScript/customer.js"></script>
10     <link href="../css/stylesheet.css" type="text/css" rel="stylesheet">
11   </head>
12   <body>
13     <div id="header"></div>
14     <s:form action="SaveCustomer" validate="true">
15       <s:hidden name="editFlag" />
16       <s:hidden name="customerNo" />
```

```
17          <table width="100%" border="0" align="center" cellpadding="0"
            cellspacing="0">
18            <tr>
19              <td>
20                <table border="0" cellpadding="0" cellspacing="0" width="100%">
21                  <tr>
22                    <td width="50%" valign="top" align="left"
                      class="spanHeader">
23                      <span>Customer Information</span>
24                    </td>
25                    <td width="50%" class="treb13blacknormal" valign="top"
                      align="right">
26                      It is mandatory to enter information in all information
                      <br>capture boxes which have a <span
                      class="mandatory">*</span> adjacent
27                    </td>
28                  </tr>
29                </table>
30              </td>
31            </tr>
32            <tr align="left" valign="top">
33              <td height="20" style="background:url('../images/hr.jpg')
                repeat-x;"> </td>
34            </tr>
35            <tr align="left" valign="top">
36              <td>
37                <table width="90%" border="0" align="center" cellpadding="0"
                  cellspacing="0">
38                  <tr>
39                    <td>
40                      <table width="100%" border="0" cellpadding="0"
                        cellspacing="0">
41                        <tr>
42                          <td class="Arial13BrownB">
43                            <br />Name<br /><br />
44                          </td>
45                        </tr>
46                        <s:textfield required="true" requiredposition="right"
                          label="Customer Name" name="customer.name"
                          title="Enter the customer name" maxLength="48"
                          size="55"/>
47                        <tr>
48                          <td class="Arial13BrownB">
49                            <br />Mailing Address<br /><br />
50                          </td>
51                        </tr>
52                        <s:textfield label="Address" name="customer.address"
                          title="Enter the street address" maxLength="148"
                          size="55"/>
53                        <s:select label="Country" name="customer.country"
                          headerKey="" headerValue="-- Please Select --"
                          list="countryList" listKey="countryNo"
                          listValue="countryName" onchange="getStateList()"/>
```

```
54                          <s:select label="State" name="customer.state"
                            headerKey="" headerValue="-- Please Select --"
                            list="stateList" listKey="stateNo"
                            listValue="stateName" onchange="getCityList()"/>
55                          <s:select label="City" name="customer.city"
                            headerKey="" headerValue="-- Please Select --"
                            list="cityList" listKey="cityNo" listValue="cityName" />
56                          <tr>
57                             <td class="Arial13BrownB">
58                                <br />Contact Details<br /><br />
59                             </td>
60                          </tr>
61                          <s:textfield required="true" requiredposition="right"
                            label="Email Address" name="customer.email"
                            title="Enter the email address" maxLength="73"
                            size="55" />
62                          <s:textfield label="Mobile Number"
                            name="customer.mobile" title="Enter the mobile
                            number" maxLength="10" />
63                          <s:textfield required="true" requiredposition="right"
                            label="Telephone Number" name="customer.telephone"
                            title="Enter the telephone number" maxLength="10" />
64                          <s:textfield label="Fax Number" name="customer.fax"
                            title="Enter the fax number" maxLength="10" />
65                       </table>
66                    </td>
67                 </tr>
68                 <tr>
69                    <td>
70                       <br /><br />
71                       <s:submit theme="simple"
                         cssStyle="background:url(../images/submit_bg.gif)
                         no-repeat scroll 37px 0px;" cssClass="buttonText"
                         name="btnSubmit" value="Save" />
72                       <s:submit theme="simple"
                         cssStyle="background:url(../images/submit_bg.gif)
                         no-repeat scroll 37px 0px;" cssClass="buttonText"
                         name="btnReset" value="Clear"
                         onclick="javascript:clearCustomerFields();" />
73                    </td>
74                 </tr>
75              </table>
76           </td>
77        </tr>
78        <tr align="left" valign="top">
79           <td height="20" style="background:url('../images/hr.jpg')
             repeat-x;"> </td>
80        </tr>
81     </table>
82     <table width="100%" border="0" cellspacing="0" cellpadding="0">
83        <display:table style="width:100%" name="customerList" pagesize="15"
          excludedParams="*" export="true" cellpadding="0" cellspacing="0"
          requestURI="/customer/Index.action">
```

```
84          <display:column property="name" title="Customer Name"
                maxLength="35" headerClass="gridheader" class="griddata"
                style="width:30%" sortable="true"/>
85          <display:column property="address" title="Address" maxLength="35"
                headerClass="gridheader" class="griddata" style="width:30%"/>
86          <display:column property="email" title="Email Address"
                headerClass="gridheader" class="griddata" style="width:20%"/>
87          <display:column property="mobile" title="Mobile"
                headerClass="gridheader" class="griddata" style="width:15%"/>
88          <display:column paramId="customerNo" paramProperty="customerNo"
                href="/Customer/customer/Edit.action?editFlag=Y"
                headerClass="gridheader" class="griddata" media="html">
89              <img align="right" src="../images/edit.jpg" border="0" alt="Edit"
                    style="cursor:pointer;"/>
90          </display:column>
91          <display:column paramId="customerNo" paramProperty="customerNo"
                href="/Customer/customer/Delete.action" headerClass="gridheader"
                class="griddata" media="html">
92              <img align="left" src="../images/TrashIcon.png" border="0"
                    alt="Delete" style="cursor:pointer;"/>
93          </display:column>
94        </display:table>
95      </table>
96    </s:form>
97    <s:include value="/jsp/footer.jsp" />
98  </body>
99 </html>
```

footer.jsp [/jsp]

Create a JSP called **footer** under the directory **/jsp** with the following code spec:

```
1  <%@page contentType="text/html" pageEncoding="UTF-8"%>
2  <%@ taglib prefix="s" uri="/struts-tags" %>
3  <table align="center" width="100%" border="0" cellspacing="0" cellpadding="0">
4    <tr height="50px">
5      <td align="center"> </td>
6    </tr>
7    <tr height="50px" id="footer">
8      <td align="center">
9        <strong>Copyright © 2012,<br> <a
           href="http://www.sharanamshah.com">Sharanam</a> And <a
           href="http://www.vaishalishahonline.com">Vaishali</a> Shah</strong>
10     </td>
11   </tr>
12 </table>
```

This file is included in customer.jsp.

```
97          <s:include value="/jsp/footer.jsp" />
```

ajax.jsp [/jsp]

Create a JSP called **ajax** under the directory **/jsp** with no code spec. This is a blank file required to emulate a result type when returning state and city list using Ajax.

JavaScript

customer [/javaScript]

This script holds the following functions:

- clearCustomerFields()
- getStateList()
- getCityList()

These functions are invoked by customer.jsp to:

- Clear form fields when the user clicks **Clear**
- Populate states when the user chooses a Country
- Populate cities when the user chooses a State

```
9    <script language="JavaScript" type="text/JavaScript"
     src="../javaScript/customer.js"></script>
```

Create a JavaScript file called **customer** under the directory **javaScript** with the following code spec:

```
1   function clearCustomerFields(){
2       document.forms[0].action = "/Customer/customer/Clear.action";
3       document.forms[0].submit();
4       return false;
5   }
6
7   function getStateList() {
8       var searchValue = document.getElementById("SaveCustomer_customer_country").value;
9       if (searchValue != "") {
10          var msg = $.ajax({
11              url:"/Customer/ajax/getStateList.action?searchValue=" + searchValue,
12              async:false
13          }).responseText;
14          var listText = unescape(msg);
15          var TypeArray = new Array();
16          var TypeArrayInfo = new Array();
17          TypeArray = listText.split(",");
18          document.getElementById("SaveCustomer_customer_state").options.length = 0;
```

```
19        document.getElementById("SaveCustomer_customer_state").options.add(new
          Option("-- Please Select --", ""));
20        for (i = 0; i < TypeArray.length; i++) {
21            TypeArrayInfo = TypeArray[i].split("|");
22            document.getElementById("SaveCustomer_customer_state").options.add(new
              Option(TypeArrayInfo[1], TypeArrayInfo[0]));
23        }
24    } else{
25        document.getElementById("SaveCustomer_customer_state").options.length = 0;
26        document.getElementById("SaveCustomer_customer_state").options.add(new
          Option("-- Please Select --", ""));
27        document.getElementById("SaveCustomer_customer_city").options.length = 0;
28        document.getElementById("SaveCustomer_customer_city").options.add(new
          Option("-- Please Select --", ""));
29    }
30 }
31
32 function getCityList() {
33     var searchValue =
       document.getElementById("SaveCustomer_customer_state").value;
34     if (searchValue != "") {
35         var msg = $.ajax({
36             url:"/Customer/ajax/getCityList.action?searchValue=" + searchValue,
37             async:false
38         }).responseText;
39         var listText = unescape(msg);
40         var TypeArray = new Array();
41         var TypeArrayInfo = new Array();
42         TypeArray = listText.split(",");
43         document.getElementById("SaveCustomer_customer_city").options.length = 0;
44         document.getElementById("SaveCustomer_customer_city").options.add(new
           Option("-- Please Select --", ""));
45         for (i = 0; i < TypeArray.length; i++) {
46             TypeArrayInfo = TypeArray[i].split("|");
47             document.getElementById("SaveCustomer_customer_city").options.add(new
               Option(TypeArrayInfo[1], TypeArrayInfo[0]));
48         }
49     } else{
50         document.getElementById("SaveCustomer_customer_city").options.length = 0;
51         document.getElementById("SaveCustomer_customer_city").options.add(new
           Option("-- Please Select --", ""));
52     }
53 }
```

jquery2 [/javaScript]

jQuery is a lightweight JavaScript library that emphasizes interaction between JavaScript and HTML. It is great library for developing Ajax based application.

This file can be downloaded from:
http://jquery.com/download/.

Download it and place it under **javaScript**.

```
javaScript
├── customer.js
└── jquery2.js
```

CSS

The application uses a CSS file stylesheet.css to style JSP.

customer.jsp uses it.

```
10          <link href="../css/stylesheet.css" type="text/css" rel="stylesheet">
```

This file is available on this book's accompanying CDROM. Place it under **css**.

```
WEB-INF
css
└── stylesheet.css
```

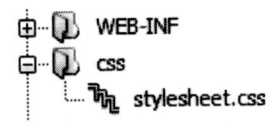

Images

The application uses a few images to style JSP. customer.jsp uses it. These files are available on this book's accompanying CDROM.

Copy these files and place then under **images**.

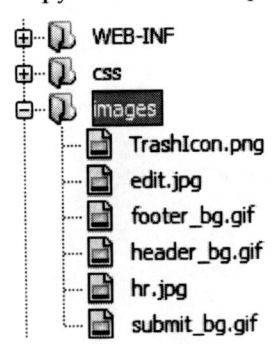

```
WEB-INF
css
images
├── TrashIcon.png
├── edit.jpg
├── footer_bg.gif
├── header_bg.gif
├── hr.jpg
└── submit_bg.gif
```

Index Page

This application uses an index.html file to invoke the application. Create this file under /, if it is not available.

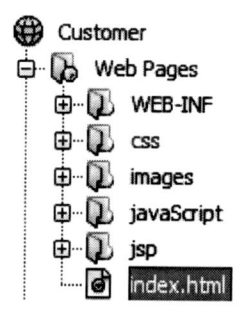

- Customer
  - Web Pages
    - WEB-INF
    - css
    - images
    - javaScript
    - jsp
    - index.html

Add the following code spec in this file:

```
1  <!DOCTYPE html>
2  <html>
3     <head>
4        <meta http-equiv="Refresh" content="0; URL=customer/Index.action">
5     </head>
6     <body>
7        <p>Loading ...</p>
8     </body>
9  </html>
```

Chapter 29

SECTION V: APPLICATION DEVELOPMENT USING STRUTS 2.X.X AND HIBERNATE 4

Configuration

Display Tag Properties

Since this application uses Display Tag to produce a data grid to display the existing customers, a few properties need to be set.

This can be done using a properties file called **displaytag.properties**.

Create a properties file called **displaytag.properties** under the directory **src\java** with the following code spec:

```
1  export.types=csv excel xml
2  export.excel=true
3  export.csv=true
4  export.xml=true
```

```
5  export.excel.filename=customer.xls
6  export.xml.filename=customer.xml
7  export.csv.filename=customer.csv
```

Struts XML Configuration Files

Now that the JSP and Actions classes are in place, let's bind the two together using struts.xml.

Create **struts.xml** under /

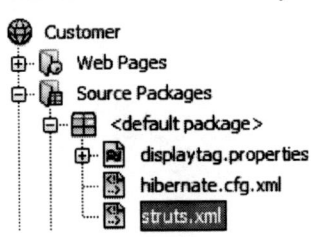

```
Customer
├── Web Pages
└── Source Packages
    └── <default package>
        ├── displaytag.properties
        ├── hibernate.cfg.xml
        └── struts.xml
```

Add the following code spec:

```
1  <?xml version="1.0" encoding="UTF-8"?>
2  <!DOCTYPE struts PUBLIC '-//Apache Software Foundation//DTD Commons Validator
   Rules Configuration 2.3//EN' 'http://struts.apache.org/dtds/struts-2.3.dtd'>
3  <struts>
4      <include file="/com/sharanamvaishali/development/action/customer.xml" />
5      <include file="/com/sharanamvaishali/development/action/ajax.xml" />
6  </struts>
```

Create **customer.xml** under **com.sharanamvaishali.development.action** package

```
Customer
├── Web Pages
└── Source Packages
    ├── <default package>
    └── com.sharanamvaishali.development.action
        ├── AjaxAction.java
        ├── CustomerAction.java
        ├── CustomerIndexAction.java
        ├── ajax.xml
        └── customer.xml
```

Add the following code spec:

```
1  <?xml version="1.0" encoding="UTF-8"?>
2  <!DOCTYPE struts PUBLIC '-//Apache Software Foundation//DTD Commons Validator
   Rules Configuration 2.3//EN' 'http://struts.apache.org/dtds/struts-2.3.dtd'>
3  <struts>
4      <package name="customer" namespace="/customer" extends="struts-default">
```

```
5        <action name="Index"
         class="com.sharanamvaishali.development.action.CustomerIndexAction">
6            <result name="success">/jsp/customer.jsp</result>
7        </action>
8
9        <action name="SaveCustomer"
         class="com.sharanamvaishali.development.action.CustomerAction">
10           <result type="redirectAction">Index</result>
11       </action>
12
13       <action name="Edit" method="edit"
         class="com.sharanamvaishali.development.action.CustomerAction">
14           <result>/jsp/customer.jsp</result>
15       </action>
16
17       <action name="Delete" method="delete"
         class="com.sharanamvaishali.development.action.CustomerAction">
18           <result>/jsp/customer.jsp</result>
19       </action>
20
21       <action name="Clear" method="clear"
         class="com.sharanamvaishali.development.action.CustomerAction">
22           <result>/jsp/customer.jsp</result>
23       </action>
24   </package>
25 </struts>
```

Create **ajax.xml** under **com.sharanamvaishali.development.action** package

- Customer
  - Web Pages
  - Source Packages
    - <default package>
    - com.sharanamvaishali.development.action
      - AjaxAction.java
      - CustomerAction.java
      - CustomerIndexAction.java
      - **ajax.xml**
      - customer.xml

Add the following code spec:

```
1  <?xml version="1.0" encoding="UTF-8"?>
2  <!DOCTYPE struts PUBLIC '-//Apache Software Foundation//DTD Commons Validator
   Rules Configuration 2.3//EN' 'http://struts.apache.org/dtds/struts-2.3.dtd'>
3  <struts>
4    <package name="ajax" namespace="/ajax" extends="struts-default">
5        <action name="getStateList" method="getStateList"
         class="com.sharanamvaishali.development.action.AjaxAction">
6            <result name="success">/jsp/ajax.jsp</result>
7        </action>
8
```

Struts 2 For Beginners

```xml
 9      <action name="getCityList" method="getCityList"
            class="com.sharanamvaishali.development.action.AjaxAction">
10          <result name="success">/jsp/ajax.jsp</result>
11      </action>
12    </package>
13  </struts>
```

web.xml

This application uses Struts and Display Tag library which requires creating a few filters mappings for Struts and Display Tag.

```
Customer
└── Web Pages
    └── WEB-INF
        └── web.xml
```

Create web.xml and key in the following code spec:

```xml
 1  <?xml version="1.0" encoding="UTF-8"?>
 2  <web-app version="3.0" xmlns="http://java.sun.com/xml/ns/javaee"
        xmlns:xsi="http://www.w3.org/2001/XMLSchema-instance"
        xsi:schemaLocation="http://java.sun.com/xml/ns/javaee
        http://java.sun.com/xml/ns/javaee/web-app_3_0.xsd">
 3      <filter>
 4          <filter-name>struts2</filter-name>
 5          <filter-class>com.sharanamvaishali.development.utility.Struts2Dispatcher</filter-class>
 6      </filter>
 7      <filter-mapping>
 8          <filter-name>struts2</filter-name>
 9          <url-pattern>/*</url-pattern>
10      </filter-mapping>
11      <filter>
12          <filter-name>ResponseOverrideFilter</filter-name>
13          <filter-class>org.displaytag.filter.ResponseOverrideFilter</filter-class>
14      </filter>
15      <filter-mapping>
16          <filter-name>ResponseOverrideFilter</filter-name>
17          <url-pattern>*.action</url-pattern>
18      </filter-mapping>
19      <filter-mapping>
20          <filter-name>ResponseOverrideFilter</filter-name>
21          <url-pattern>*.jsp</url-pattern>
22      </filter-mapping>
23      <session-config>
24          <session-timeout>30</session-timeout>
25      </session-config>
26      <welcome-file-list>
27          <welcome-file>index.html</welcome-file>
28      </welcome-file-list>
29  </web-app>
```

(Struts 2 Dispatcher)
(Display Tags)
(Index Page that invokes Customer form)

This completes building the application using NetBeans IDE.

Chapter 30

SECTION V: APPLICATION DEVELOPMENT USING STRUTS 2.X.X AND HIBERNATE 4

Running The Application

Run the application. To do so, right click the application and select **Clean and Build**.

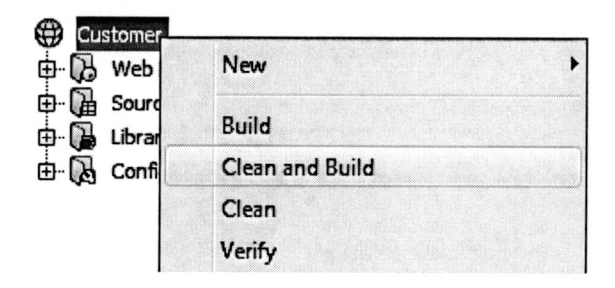

Once done, right click the application and select **Run**.

400   Struts 2 For Beginners

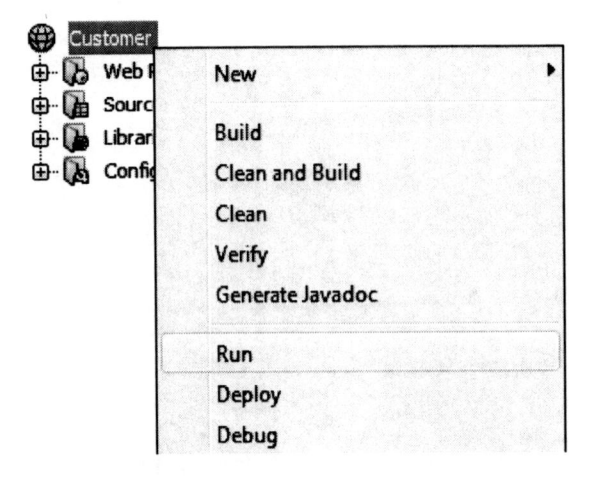

This brings up the application in the default web browser, as shown in diagram 30.1.

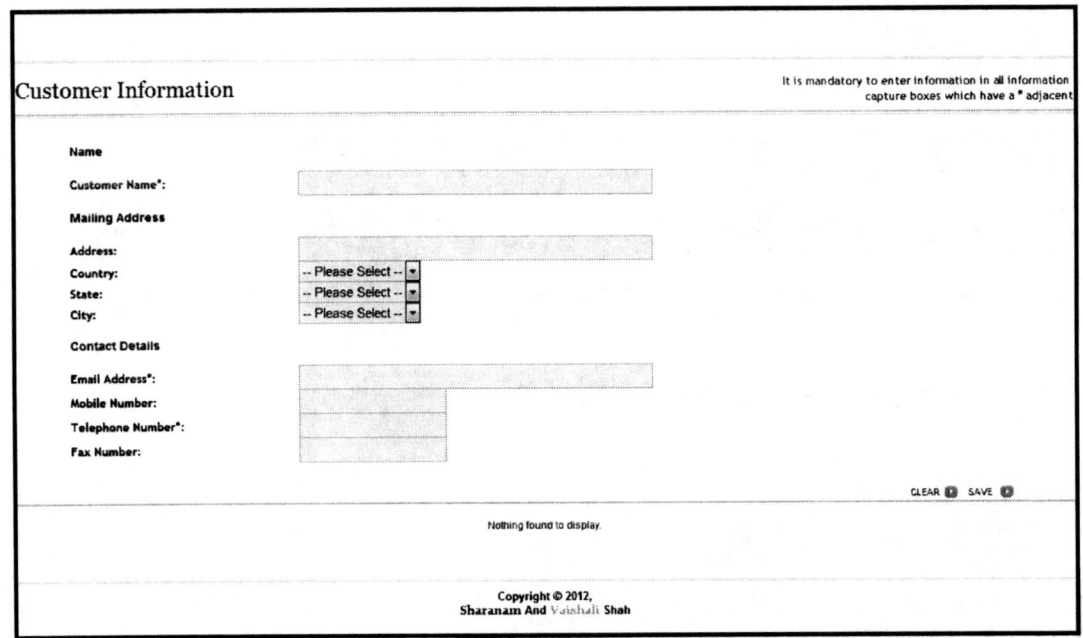

Diagram 30.1

Process Flow

Diagrammatically this process can be represented as show in diagram 30.2.1 and 30.2.2.

Running The Application

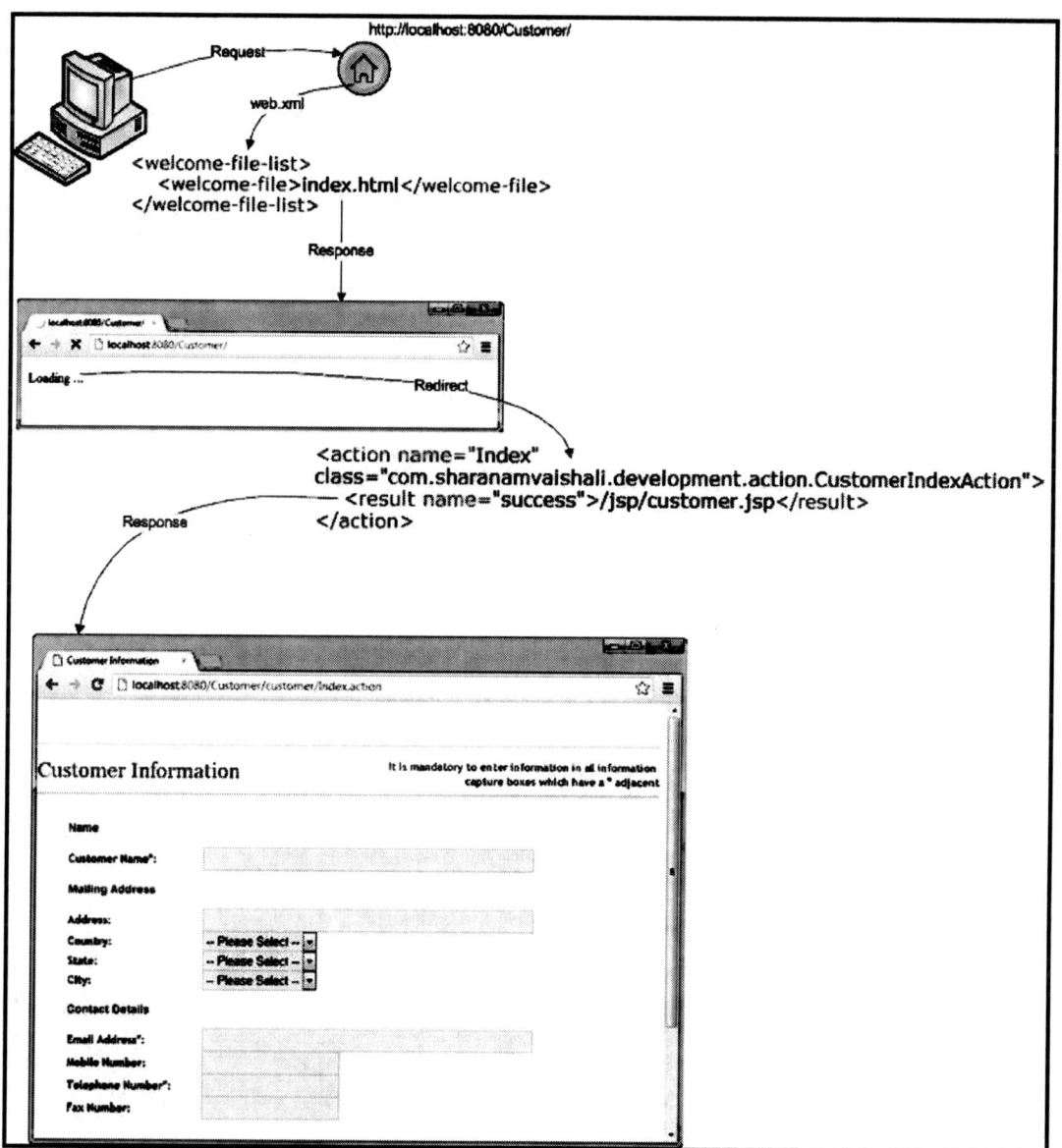

Diagram 30.2.1: Customer Database Invocation

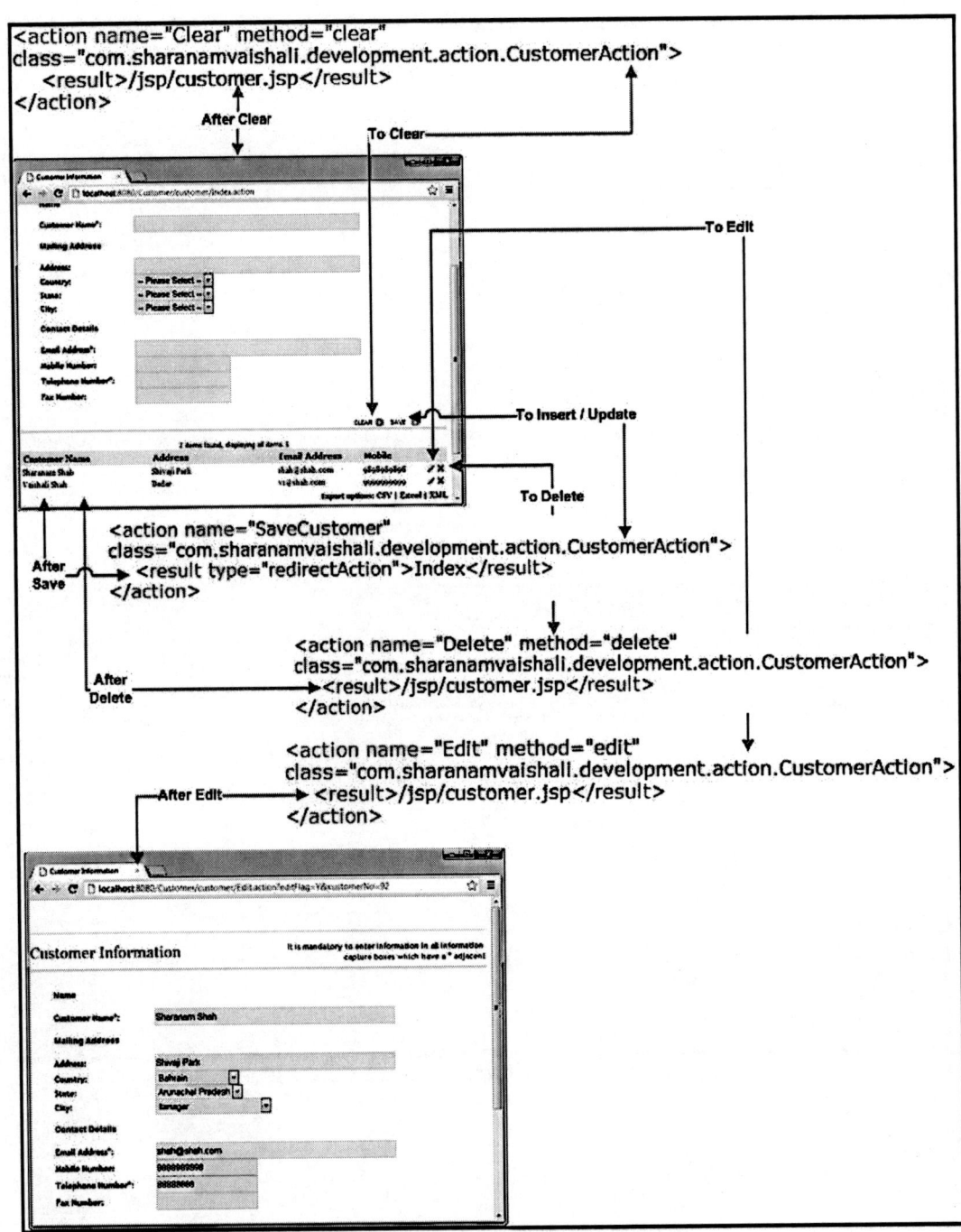

Diagram 30.2.2: Database Operations

Index

.

.properties extension 99

@

@Column 210
@Entity 210
@GeneratedValue 210
@Id 210
@JoinColumn 361
@ManyToOne 361
@OneToMany 363
@Override 84
@Table 210

<

<package> Attributes
    The abstract Attribute 75
    The extends Attribute 74
    The name Attribute 74
    The namespace Attribute 74
<action> Attributes
    The class Attribute 75
    The method Attribute 76
    The name Attribute 75
<include> Attributes
    The file Attribute 76
<mapping> 211
<result> Attributes
    The name Attribute 76
    The type Attribute 76
<s:form> 125
<s:head> 124
<s:iterator> 127
<s:property> 127

A

Accessor Pattern 157
Action 19
    Data carrier 20
    Model 19
Action Class 19, 65
Action Component 10

Action Context 158
Action Interface 19
ActionContext Properties 158
   application 158
   locale 158
   name 158
   parameters 158
   session 158
ActionInvocation 16, 141
ActionInvocation.invoke() 146
ActionMapper 15
ActionProxy 15
Actions 4, 65
AJAX 356
Apache Jakarta Project 5
ArrayList's add() 84

B

Built-in Converters 157
Built-in Interceptors 134
   Alias Interceptor [alias] 134
   Chaining Interceptor [chaining] 135
   Checkbox Interceptor [checkbox] 135
   Conversion Error Interceptor [conversionError] 135
   Create Session Interceptor [createSession] 135
   Debugging Interceptor [debugging] 135
   Exception Interceptor [exception] 136
   Execute and Wait Interceptor [execAndWait] 135
   File Upload Interceptor [fileUpload] 136
   Internationalization Interceptor [i18n] 136
   Logging Interceptor [logger] 136
   Message Store Interceptor [store] 136
   Model Driven Interceptor [modelDriven] 136
   Parameters Interceptor [params] 137
   Prepare Interceptor [prepare] 137
   Profiling Interceptor [profile] 137
   Roles Interceptor [roles] 137
   Scope Interceptor [scope] 137
   Scoped Model Driven Interceptor [scopedModelDriven] 136
   Servlet Configuration Interceptor [servletConfig] 137
   Static Parameters Interceptor [staticParams] 137
   Timer Interceptor [timer] 137
   Token Interceptor [token] 138
   Token Session Interceptor [tokenSession] 138
   Validation Interceptor [validation] 138
   Workflow Interceptor [workflow] 138

C

CascadeType.ALL 361
Class.forName() 192
Client Side Validations 182
com.opensymphony.xwork2.ActionInvocation 147
com.opensymphony.xwork2.ActionSupport 82
com.opensymphony.xwork2.interceptor.Interceptor 145, 147
com.opensymphony.xwork2.ModelDriven 217
Configuration Interface 201
    buildSessionFactory() 201
    configure() 201
    getProperties() 201
Configuration Manager 15
Connection 192
Controller 4, 18
Craig McClanahan 5, 8
createStatement() 193
Custom Struts 2 Dispatcher 357
Customer Database Application 339

D

DAO 211
defaultStack 133, 139
Design Patterns 9
Display Tag 395
Display Tag Library 350
Document Type Definition [DTD] 73
DOMAIN Model 196
Dot Notation 27, 157
DriverManager 192

E

Encapsulation 66
execute() 19, 65, 84
executeQuery() 193
executeUpdate() 193

F

FetchType.LAZY 363
Filter Configuration 203
Filter Dispatcher 11
Framework 2

G

Gavin King..197
getConnection()..192
GETTER / SETTER Method...68

H

Handler..4
Helper Class..354
Helper Interface..67
   Action Interface..70
      CONSTANTS..70
         ERROR...71
         INPUT..71
         LOGIN...71
         NONE...70
         SUCCESS..70
   ActionSupport Class..71
Hibernate...196
hibernate.cfg.xml..204
   mapping...210
hibernate.connection.driver_class...208
hibernate.connection.password...208
hibernate.connection.url..208
hibernate.connection.username...208
hibernate.dialect..208
hibernate.show_sql..208
HTTP Requests..4
HttpServletRequest..15
HttpServletResponse..356

I

i18n..99
Interceptor Interface
   destroy()..145
   init()..145
   intercept()..146
Interceptor Stack..24
Interceptors..12, 16, 22, 133
Interface...212
Internationalization...99
IteratorStatus Object...102

J

Jakarta Struts..5
Java Development Kit...35

Java SE Development Kit [JDK] 35
java.io.Serializable 210
java.persistence 209
java.servlet.FilterConfig 202
java.servlet.ServletException 202
java.sql 191
java.text.DateFormat 83
java.text.SimpleDateFormat 83
java.util.ArrayList 83
java.util.Date 83
java.util.List 213
JavaBean Paradigm 68
JavaBeans 4
JavaBeans Properties 68
Java's static modifier 83
JBoss Inc. 197
JPA Entities 209
jQuery 391

L

LIFO [Last In First Out] 154
LocaleProvide Interface 71

M

Mappings 69
Model 4
Model View Controller [MVC] 3, 9
    Controller 11
    Model 10
    View 10
ModelDriven 217
    getModel() 217
MVC Design Pattern 3
MySQL Connector/J 189

N

NAME-VALUE Pair 68
NetBeans 34
NetBeans Development Platform 34
NetBeans IDE 34
newInstance() 192

O

Object Relational Mapping Library 196
OBJECTS 196
OGNL [Object Graph Navigational Language] 27, 154

OpenSymphony WebWork Framework...5
org.apache.struts2.dispatcher.ng.filter.StrutsPrepareAndExecuteFilter.....................202
org.hibernate.cfg.Configuration 200
org.hibernate.HibernateException 200, 203
org.hibernate.service.ServiceRegistry..200
org.hibernate.service.ServiceRegistryBuilder..200
org.hibernate.Session 200, 213
org.hibernate.SessionFactory 200
org.hibernate.Transaction 213

P

Persistence 195
POJO [Plain Old Java Object] 66
Preconfigured Stacks 139
   basicStack 139
   chainStack 139
   defaultStack 140
   executeAndWaitStack..141
   fileUploadStack 139
   i18nStack 140
   modelDrivenStack..139
   paramPrepareParamsStack..140
   validationWorkflowStack 139
Primary Key 279
PrintWriter 356

R

RELATIONAL Paradigm...196
Request Workflow 91
required=true...125
ResourceBundles 99
Result Interface 85
Result Type 86
   dispatcher..86
      location..87
      parse 87
   redirect 88
      location..89
      parse 89
   redirectAction 89
      actionName 90
      namespace 90
Result Types 31
Results..11, 30
ResultSet 192

Index 409

S

Secure Login Mechanism ... 223
Serializable Interface ... 71
ServiceRegistryBuilder Interface ... 201
    applySettings() ... 201
    buildServiceRegistry() ... 201
Session
    beginTransaction() ... 214
    createQuery() ... 214
    delete() ... 373
    merge() ... 372
    save() ... 214
Session Management ... 223
SessionFactory ... 199, 354
    openSession() ... 201
Short Circuiting Validations ... 165
Simple Logging Facade for Java [SLF4J] ... 350
Statement ... 192
String constants ... 67
Struts ... 3
Struts 2 ... 5
Struts 2 Filter ... 72
struts.xml ... 4, 19, 73
    <include> ... 76
    <package> ... 73
        <action> ... 75
            <interceptor-ref> ... 143
            <result> ... 76
                <param> ... 90
        <default-interceptor-ref> ... 143
        <interceptors> ... 143
            <interceptor> ... 143
            <interceptor-stack> ... 143
                <interceptor-ref> ... 143
    <struts> ... 73
Struts2Dispatcher ... 357
struts-default Package ... 75
StrutsPrepareAndExecuteFilter ... 15, 18

T

Tag Libraries ... 4, 91
    Generic Tags ... 92
        Control Tags ... 101
            The if, elseIf And else Tags ... 103
            The iterator Tag ... 101

Data Tags 92
    The action Tag 92
    The bean Tag 94
    The i18n Tag 99
    The include Tag 97
    The param Tag 100
    The property Tag 93
    The set Tag 96
    The text Tag 99
    The url Tag 98
UI Tags 104
    Form UI Tags 105
        The checkbox Tag 112
        The checkboxlist Tag 114
        The file Tag 112
        The form Tag 107
        The head Tag 106
        The hidden Tag 108
        The label Tag 109
        The password Tag 111
        The radio Tag 115
        The reset Tag 117
        The select Tag 113
        The submit Tag 116
        The textarea Tag 110
        The textfield Tag 110
    Non Form UI Tags 117
        The div Tag 117
        The tabbedPanel Tag 119
        The tree Tag 120
TagLib 91
Template 104
TextProvider Interface 71
The cascade Attribute 361
The fetch Attribute 363
the interface Keyword 212
The key Attribute 125, 164
The mappedBy Attribute 363
The name Attribute 125
The short-circuit Attribute 164
The status Attribute 103
Themes 104
    ajax 104
    css_xhtml 104
    simple 104
    xhtml 104

Types Of validators 165
    conversion 173
        fieldName 173
    date 170
        fieldName 170
        max 170
        min 170
    double 169
        fieldName 169
        maxExclusive 169
        maxInclusive 169
        minExclusive 169
        minInclusive 169
    email 172
        fieldName 172
    expression 171
        expression 171
    fieldExpression 171
        expression 172
        fieldName 171
    int 168
        fieldName 168
        max 168
        min 168
    regex 173
        caseSensitive 174
        expression 174
        fieldName 174
        trim 174
    required 166
        fieldName 166
    requiredstring 166
        fieldName 166
        trim 166
    stringlength 167
        fieldName 167
        maxLength 167
        minLength 167
        trim 167
    url 173
        fieldName 173
    visitor 174
        appendPrefix 175
        context 175
        fieldName 175

V

validate=true 182
Validateable Interface 71, 163
   validate() 163
Validation 162
Validation Interceptor 162
ValidationAware Interface 71, 163
Validator Scopes 164
ValidatorFactory 164
Value Stack 25, 153
   Action Object 26, 153
   Model Object 26, 153
   Named Objects 26, 153
   Temporary Objects 26, 153
View 86

W

WebWork 2 .... 5, 8

X

XML Validation Configuration File 163
   <validators>
      <field> 164
         <field-validator> 164
            <param> 164

ABOUT THE AUTHORS

The author Sharanam Shah [www.sharanamshah.com] has 9+ years of IT experience and is currently a technical writer for Saba Software Inc. He also consults with several software houses in Mumbai, India, to help them design and manage database application.

Vaishali Shah [www.vaishalishahonline.com], his wife, co-author, a technical writer and a freelance Web developer, has a rich experience of designing, developing and managing database systems. She specializes in the use of Java to design and build web based applications.

Struts 2 for Beginners
3rd Edition

Accompanying CD of this Book can be downloaded from
http://www.shroffpublishers.com/support/9781619030046cd.zip

CPSIA information can be obtained at www.ICGtesting.com
Printed in the USA
LVOW09s0321311215

468564LV00009B/84/P